I0819858

RELIGIOUS DIVERSITY AND EARLY MODERN ENGLISH TEXTS

RELIGIOUS DIVERSITY AND EARLY MODERN ENGLISH TEXTS

Catholic, Judaic, Feminist, and Secular Dimensions

Edited by Arthur F. Marotti and Chanita Goodblatt

Wayne State University Press   *Detroit*

17 16 15 14 13 5 4 3 2 1

Library of Congress Cataloging-in-Publication Data
Religious diversity and early modern English texts : Catholic, Judaic, feminist, and secular dimensions / edited by Arthur F. Marotti and Chanita Goodblatt.
pages cm
Includes bibliographical references and index.
ISBN 978-0-8143-3955-8 (cloth : alk. paper) —
ISBN 978-0-8143-3956-5 (ebook)
1. English literature—Early modern, 1500–1700—History and criticism. 2. Religion and literature—Great Britain. 3. Christianity and other religions in literature—Great Britain. 4. Great Britain—Intellectual life.
I. Marotti, Arthur F., 1940– editor of compilation.
PR428.R46R47 2013
820.9'382—dc23

2013006166

♾

Typeset by Westchester
Composed in Warnock Pro and Meta

Plates in Lowell Gallagher's "Remembering Lot's Wife: The Structure of Testimony in the *Painted Life* of Mary Ward" published by permission of Congregatio Jesu Augsburg (Germany). Photos: Studio Tanner, Nesselwang.

Photographs in Chanita Goodblatt's "Performance and *Parshanut*: *The Historie of Jacob and Esau*" are by Adva Abergel Salomon and are printed with her permission.

The Israel Science Foundation and the Goldstein-Goren International Center for Jewish Thought at Ben-Gurion University of the Negev funded the international symposium "Religious Culture in the Early Modern Period: Tradition, Authority, Heterodoxy" (2005), in which many of the contributors to the present volume participated. We would like to thank Professor David Newman, Dean of the Faculty of Humanities and Social Sciences at Ben-Gurion University of the Negev, for providing a grant to support publication of this book.

Contents

Arthur F. Marotti and Chanita Goodblatt

Introduction

In recent work on the religious culture and literature of early modern England, one finds specialized treatments of Catholic culture and texts, of the representation of Jews, of the Hebraic influence on Christian writers, and of women and religion. This collection of essays addresses these topics but also attends to a fifth topic: the relationship of religion to processes of secularization under way in this era. The boundaries between religious confessions, the hybridization of religion, the inflection of religious conflicts and identities by gender, the representation in polemical and nonpolemical texts of religious "others," and the secular and/or agnostic and atheistic territory outside religion are all part of the complex and evolving culture of early modern England. Using a variety of critical methods, ranging from historical analysis, deconstruction, feminist inquiry, and intertextual interpretation to pedagogical experimentation, the contributors to this collection deal with this wide range of subjects, but all assume that what is often dismissed as marginal is in a real sense central to the religious and cultural life of what was being defined as the Protestant English nation. Catholics persisted as an important and politically dissident minority, and the residual elements of the "old religion" survived long after the break with Rome; the Hebrew Bible and Jewish biblical scholarship were formative intellectual influences as well as a cultural presence to which Catholics and Protestants responded both positively and negatively; early modern women had a culturally vital role in the religious changes taking place; religious conflicts and de facto pluralism could lead to skepticism, agnosticism, atheism, and the demand for the separation of the religious and secular orders.

In the chapters that follow the contributors deal with topics and writers from the mid-sixteenth to the late seventeenth century. They discuss not only major and minor canonical authors, such as William Shakespeare, Christopher Marlowe, John Donne, Aemelia Lanyer, and John Milton, but also lesser known or little known figures whose culturally symptomatic work reflects the religious and cultural changes taking place in this period. The scholars contributing to this collection are North American and Israeli. Many of them originally participated in the conference "Religious Cultures in the Early Modern Period: Tradition, Authority, Heterodoxy," which was held in Israel in 2005 at Ben-Gurion University of the Negev (the conference was supported by the Israel Science Foundation). Although papers from that conference were published in a 2006 volume,[1] many of these scholars have continued their dialogue, and the American and Israeli editors of this new collection have shaped this project to retain some of the emphases of the original international meeting. Three particular interests have persisted in the discussion: (1) the relationship of Judaism and Jewish texts to early modern Christianity and its internal conflicts; (2) the relationship of tradition and the hegemonic religious order to heterodoxy in its various forms; and (3) the phenomenon of religious hybridization in an era of sharpened confessional conflicts.

To group the individual contributions to this present collection in sections that highlight their shared concerns and focus, we have divided the thirteen essays into five topically focused parts: Minority Catholic Culture; Figuring the Jew; Hebraism and the Bible; Women and Religion; and Religion and Secularization. There is an undeniable emphasis on figures who were on the margins of the dominant religious culture—Catholics, Jews, women, and incipient secularists—but the assumption of all the contributors is that we cannot understand the culture as a whole without attending to the repressed, the marginalized, and the unacknowledged.

Minority Catholic Culture

Over the past two decades studies of early modern English Catholic culture have burgeoned in the fields of both history and literary studies. A previously marginalized or ignored Catholic minority community and its writers have received serious attention from scholars who have redefined the cultural functioning of English Catholics within the larger society, complicating our notions of religious change and diversity.[2] Whereas earlier studies of recusants emphasized Catholic suffering and martyrdom, current early modern Catholic studies include work on serial converts, church papists, religiously amphibious or ambiguous individuals, and former Catholics who retained a cultural attachment to the old religion but who were observant Protestants. Historians such as Eamon Duffy and Christopher Haigh emphasize the slow pace of England's change from being a Catholic country to a Protestant one, as well as the cultural hybridity of religious practice and belief, as England underwent, in Haigh's formulation, a series of reformations.[3] The three essays in this part of this collection deal with different aspects of English Catholic history and writing in the period, running from the time of the brief reign of the Catholic Queen Mary (r. 1553–1558) through that of King Charles I (r. 1625–1649).

The first of these pieces, by Arthur Marotti, concentrates on the political valences of poetry written to or about the Virgin Mary in Elizabethan England (Chapter 1). Marotti argues that, because of the Queen's adherence to a Protestant policy of displacing Mary from the center of devotion she had occupied in traditional Catholicism and the Queen's wish to make herself an object of respect and reverence, Catholic (and non-Catholic) poets who offered the usual forms of praise of Mary and asserted belief in her Assumption, Immaculate Conception, and heavenly queenship were, in effect, composing politically oppositional verse—not only protesting the large cultural program of replacing Catholicism with Protestantism but also objecting to Queen Elizabeth's assumption of a status to which she had no rightful claim. Marotti discusses, first, the large body of Marian verse composed by William Forrest in the Marian and Elizabethan periods, highlighting both its implicit and explicit religiopolitical criticisms. Because this little known work exists mainly in manuscript and because most of the pieces were never printed, Marotti includes a generous selection of them to introduce this writing to modern readers.

Marotti also examines a variety of Elizabethan Marian poems by lay and clerical Catholics, Catholic converts, anonymous writers, and even a non-Catholic aristocrat—all of which had a politically oppositional tenor. He concentrates on poems dealing with the destruction of the shrine of Our Lady of Walsingham and with the martyred Edmund Campion and on Marian verses by Henry Constable, Richard Verstegan, Robert Southwell, and the Earls of Arundel (Philip Howard) and Essex (Robert Devereux). In their specific historical context, these pieces asserted the beliefs of a repressed religious minority, rejected the tenets of the established English church, served as a bonding agent for a dispersed Catholic community, and/or criticized the female monarch who was in cultural rivalry with the Virgin Mary.

Phebe Jensen, in her essay on the manuscript writings of William Blundell (Chapter 2), demonstrates how one persecuted Catholic gentleman coped with religious oppression by creating a Catholic refuge within the larger Protestant polity, just as other Catholic families in their local neighborhoods created "islands of true Englishness." Blundell turned his antiquarian research and the happenstance discovery of a cache of medieval coins on his estate into an argument for the Anglo-Saxon and Catholic identity for England that could contest the mythology of pre-Roman British origins constructed by antiquarians who wished to construct a different lineage for England as a Protestant nation. What was at stake for Blundell was the character of English topography and sacred spaces; whereas the dissolution of the monasteries and the despoiling of most religious shrines and pilgrimage destinations by the Protestant government had the effect of desacralizing English geography, Blundell evoked an era in which English saints (some of them monarchs), holy places, and the more widespread ecclesiastical presence in the country gave religious meaning to his country and its topography. As Jensen observes, for Blundell and for many other Catholics "the idea that the land was composed of a matrix of holy places that commemorated the miracles of English saints, the good deeds of virtuous Anglo-Saxon kings, and the steadfastness of early modern Catholics was central to the definition of England." Late in the essay, however, Jensen points to a kind of compromise position or hybridization of traditional religious sites in the Protestant conversion of them into historically important national locations—an anticipation of what happened in modern times with the treatment of special places associated either with national triumphs or tragedies, such as the Gettysburg battlefield and the World Trade Center site, which have become virtually sacred spaces for the exercise of historical memory and hybridized civic and religious piety. In the large movement of English cultural history, the Catholic conception of a religiously marked public space finally yielded to the forces of desacralization and secularization, but it is important to understand how a countercultural position such as Blundell's functioned within the changing religiopolitical environment.

Lowell Gallagher, in his theoretically sophisticated essay on Mary Ward, the "female Jesuitress" (Chapter 3), concentrates specifically on the visual portrayal of Ward's history in the so-called *Painted Life*, the visual narrative commissioned by her order. Gallagher uses the biblical figure of Lot's wife to define the religious and cultural place of this innovative female reformer, who, as an uncloistered proselytizer and educator, was in many senses culturally out of place. Like Lot's wife, Ward was a cultural and religious boundary figure. Adopting Erich Auerbach's formulation, Gallagher sees her as poised between *veritas* and *historia*. Ward led an alternately approved and disapproved religious teaching order, which was banned by papal bull in 1631. First, Gallagher uses church father Irenaeus's reinterpretation of Lot's wife as a biblical type of *ecclesia*, "a paradigmatic martyr-witness" whose "arrested gesture of her looking back is the anamorphic rendering . . . of her steady gaze on the providential design of history." This interpretation contrasts with Luther's and the Protestant polemical interpretation of Lot's wife as an emblem of papalists' unhealthy attachment to past practices. But Gallagher also draws on mid-twentieth-century *ressourcement* theology and on Jacques Derrida's analysis of testimony to connect the figure of Lot's wife with Mary Ward as "a virtual anti-type . . . the errant woman and impossible witness." Gallagher argues that Lot's wife's "arrested gesture of looking back . . . yields a revisionist typology that envisions disaster and survival together, as converging terms of an ethics of action for the sake of what may be grasped from the wreckage of the past as well as from a posture of vigilance toward a categorically unknown future." For Gallagher this figure illuminates "Ward's anomalous and precarious place in both Counter-Reformation and Stuart theopolitical worlds." Just as the pre–Vatican Council Catholic Church found it difficult to accept the openness to modernity of *ressourcement* theology, so too Counter-Reformation Catholicism ultimately found its mission unassimilable (though it was an obvious model for later Catholic teaching institutions).

After recounting the troubled history of Mary Ward's teaching order and its finally failed attempts to secure papal approval, Gallagher analyzes the meanings for the banned religious order of the illustrations in the *Painted Life*, which he sees as "reclaim[ing] Irenaeus's counterreading of Lot's wife," commemorating "the at-once radiant and abjected figure of Ward's idea of ecclesial community together with its doubled orientation, looking backward and forward at the same time." He sees the *Painted Life* of Mary Ward as portraying the "testimonial condition" defined by Derrida, highlighting the "visionary component of Ward's apostolate." Within Counter-Reformation Roman Catholicism, then, Ward and her followers both functioned and were marginalized, barely surviving to receive somewhat reluctant validation by the modern Catholic Church and its popes.

Figuring the Jew

One distinctive feature of this collection is the series of essays examining the diverse ways in which the Jew and Hebraism are embedded in early modern English dramatic, sermonic, and poetic texts. This presence evokes a complex response, one that at once envisions the Jew as an image of the Other while at the same time acclaiming *Hebraica veritas* (Hebrew truth) as underlying the production of Christian biblical commentaries and translations. The image of the Jew comes into focus, for example, in the assassination plot against Elizabeth I (1592–1594) in the figure of Roderigo Lopez, Marrano physician to the Queen, who was tried and executed for his alleged part in the conspiracy.[4] Barabas in Marlowe's *Jew of Malta* (1589) and Shylock in Shakespeare's *Merchant of Venice* (1596–1597) may not be fictional transformations of Lopez himself, but the attention of these plays to the Jew as a figure of religious conflict, intrigue, and revenge has clear topical resonance.[5]

Such a figuring of the Jew plays out within a wider historical context: the establishment of a community of Marrano Jews in Tudor and Elizabethan England (including a secret synagogue), the struggle for formal readmission of the Jews into England, and the subsequent expansion of this community during the Restoration.[6] Inevitably wider cultural issues affected the role and image of this community. Thus (as with Lopez) we see the involvement of Marrano Jews in the religiopolitical conflict between Protestant England and Catholic Spain and the appeal to English apocalyptic thought (particularly by the Portuguese rabbi Menasseh ben Israel) to enable Jewish readmission into England.[7] In this latter context the Jew is reconstructed as a "glorious apocalyptic agent"[8] whose dispersion throughout the world is a prerequisite of messianic fulfillment.

The dual image of the Jew invokes therefore both hatred and awe, comprising ultimately "something one has to come to terms with before one can come to terms with oneself."[9] This complex interest in Jews is apparent in a great variety of texts (such as plays, poems, sermons, and parliamentary debates) and, accordingly, as James Shapiro observes, "provides unusual insight into the cultural anxieties felt by English men and women at a time when their nation was experiencing extraordinary social, religious, and political turbulence."[10] These anxieties relate to the constitution of English Protestants as a newer version of God's chosen people—one that rejects the anti-Semitic charges of usury and ritual murder, replaces physical circumcision of the "old law" by Christian faith, and ultimately defines English racial and national identity.[11]

In Chapter 4 Avraham Oz highlights the contribution of the dramatized figure of the Jew as Shakespeare's Shylock to this discourse of English nationhood. Oz adopts Homi Bhabha's discussion of mimicry as "the desire for a reformed, recognizable Other, as a subject of difference that is almost the same, but not quite," in order to study how the issue of alien infiltrators into early modern England was inseparable from the commodification of nationhood. Oz contends that a discussion of *The Merchant of Venice* must take into account both economic and political discourses. Thus, although the Christian society of Venice urges the Jew to adopt the immeasurable spiritual doctrine of mercy, the Jew on his part attempts to teach that same community the market value not only of human flesh but also of any concept, value, or moral tenet. In this reading of the play, Oz argues, "Jew" is a synonym for "usurer"; in other words, the Jews constitute a guild of economic significance. It is in this way that their existence as a nation—an ethnic and cultural group—was (in Oz's words) commodified.

Oz subsequently defines Shylock's mimic challenge to the Venetian (ergo English) national community regarding his status by demonstrating how this challenge incorporates the pragmatic concept of nationhood offered by Niccolo Machiavelli. Drawing on modern political thinkers, Oz reexamines Machiavelli's assertion that the need for nation derives from the economic imperative to create material and social market zones. Consequently, Oz proposes a distinctive reading of Shakespeare's concern with rewriting one thread of the national narrative, in which the ambiguous nationality in *The Merchant of Venice* of the Other as Jew presents a test for emerging nationhood. In this light Oz asserts that Shylock seeks to join the Venetian community to gain legal and occupational rights, thereby offering the Duke of Venice an opportunity to rewrite a national narrative in Machiavellian terms. Yet ultimately, as Oz argues, Shylock is unsuccessful, for his subversiveness and the tensions between alien and nation, Jew and Christian, landlessness and habitation leave the reader with a "multiplicity of discourses and identities, subject and other, desire and bonds."

Achsah Guibbory's essay (Chapter 5) moves the reader forward to the decades of the English Civil War, the Interregnum, and the Restoration. Complementing her comprehensive literary and cultural study, *Christian Identity, Jews, and Israel in Seventeenth-Century England*, in which she discusses how early modern England framed its concept of nationhood in relation to Jews, Judaism, and biblical Israel, Guibbory focuses here on John Milton's poetry and prose.[12] She traces his criticism of the established church and monarchy through changing political and historical conditions, maintaining that there is a connection between the Jewish idea of a chosen people and the Christian (New Testament, Protestant) revision of this in the notion of election. Guibbory demonstrates that in the period proximate to and including the Civil War, Milton assumes the prophetic voices of Ezekiel (*Lycidas*) and Moses (*Reason of Church-Government*) to attack the corrupt English clergy. What is more, Guibbory demonstrates that Milton subsequently uses language that evokes Isaiah to identify England as biblical Israel (*Areopagitica*), continuing as well to emphasize biblical regicide and to counter the royalist glorification of the executed Charles I (*The Tenure of Kings and Magistrates, Eikonoklastes*).

Guibbory highlights the change in Milton's prophetic voice, which accompanies the establishment of the Commonwealth and Protectorate. Milton first updates the warnings of the Hebrew prophets to reiterate for the English the biblical notion of their election (*Second Defense of the English People*), subsequently incorporating the words and visions of Jeremiah and Ezekiel to warn against their possible loss of being God's chosen (*The Readie and Easie Way*). With the Restoration Guibbory perceives that Milton's use of the prophetic voice is fraught with tension. His repudiation of the possibility of national redemption (*Paradise Regained, Samson Agonistes*) is subsequently countered by his use of Ezekiel (*Of True Religion*) to reimagine Protestant England as the redeemed Israel. Whether Milton was able to resolve this tension is unclear; perhaps, as Guibbory suggests, he "had too powerful a sense of evil, and of the threat to liberty, to sustain it in the world he lived in."

Hebraism and the Bible

These discussions of Shakespeare and Milton provide the opportunity to turn to the topic of Hebraism in two primary aspects: applying the Hebrew Bible to contemporary religious and political issues; and using Jewish exegetical texts to interpret and translate the Hebrew biblical text. These are relevant to Milton's reconceptualization of the Creation narrative and characters in *Paradise Lost* and of the story of Samson (and Delilah) in *Samson Agonistes.* They are important also for interpreting the decisive trial scene in *The Merchant of Venice,* with its insistence on the literal reading of the bond that reflects William Tyndale's emphasis on the "literall sence" of Hebrew and the resultant attention to Jewish exegetical sources for clarification.[13] The study of Christian Hebraism demarcates various issues: the use of transmitted knowledge of Hebrew and Aramaic sources through the citing of intermediate Christian texts;[14] the highly intertextual nature of Christian Hebraism, exhibiting the early modern predilection for "an emphasis on textual indeterminacy as opposed to textual closure and stability";[15] and the "double vision" of Christian Hebraism, which "appropriates the Hebrew Bible and its language, while it lays claim to the racial, national, and religious privileges befitting the true Children of Israel."[16] From the search during King Henry VIII's "Great Matter" (1527–1533) for the literal meaning of the opaque Hebrew biblical term *yevam* (brother-in-law or kinsman)[17] to Milton's close attention to the Jewish tradition of biblical commentary that informed the Geneva and King James Bibles,[18] Hebraism was a significant factor in English Reformation intellectual life.

Chanita Goodblatt and Anne Lake Prescott each address specific ways in which the Hebrew Bible was read as a paradigm for English religious beliefs about predestination and for such political issues as the nature of the monarchy. Goodblatt's essay on *The Historie of Jacob and Esau* (Chapter 6) examines sixteenth-century Reformation biblical drama, most specifically in its dramatic recreation in a university graduate seminar. This twenty-first-century encounter with a play written for early modern schoolboys involves, Goodblatt explains, two main issues: performance, that is, the pragmatics of script and stage; and *parshanut* (the Hebrew term used in its specific sense for biblical commentary or exegesis), that is, the reader's clarification of exegetical cruxes in the biblical text. The various decisions about performance, Goodblatt argues, reflect the students' response to the intensity of the familial drama and to the subversive humor of the play's performative aspect, which raises issues of gender and authority.

Goodblatt discusses the concept of a textual system to explain the play's reading of the biblical story and the subsequent rereading of both biblical and dramatic texts by the students. At the heart of the play, and of the dramatic recreation, is its predestinarian theology. Demonstrating this, Goodblatt particularly focuses on how aligning the text with the varied commentaries reveals how textual themes of parental authority, fraternal struggle, and divine mercy are written into the Reformation drama (primarily for didactic purposes), subsequently to be re-rewritten by a contemporary cast that translates these original concerns into a universal message about individual choice and identity. This grappling with *The Historie of Jacob and Esau* underlines its distinctly Protestant, even Calvinist character, and, as Goodblatt proposes, invites a study of Reformation exegetical texts: Martin Luther's lectures, John Calvin's commentaries, and the Geneva Bible. Furthermore, the Jewish background of Christian Hebraism, and of the Israeli graduate students, invites a study of the biblical commentaries of Rashi and Abraham Ibn Ezra, medieval Jewish exegetes regularly consulted by early modern Christian Hebraists. Ultimately, then, Goodblatt maintains, the modern performance of *The Historie of Jacob and Esau* reveals "a more extensive range of cultural associations than was possible with the original performance." She uses pedagogical experimentation and twenty-first-century reenactment of an early modern religious drama as a way to take a fresh look at historically distant religious and cultural material and to rediscover the emotional underpinning of intellectual abstractions of religious discourse and controversy.

Anne Lake Prescott's essay (Chapter 7) conveys the reader through two centuries of English texts that exploit the marginalized figure of the biblical

King Saul. Prescott's focus on the sixteenth and seventeenth centuries begins with the reign of Elizabeth I and continues through the Restoration. The use of Saul in the England of these periods, she argues, carries varied meanings; it is a tale "valuable for its ambiguities and contradictions." Prescott negotiates her way through a wide variety of texts, including sermons, homilies, and biblical translations, tracing a continuous intertextuality between them and the biblical narrative that highlights different interpretations of Saul. Thus she cites Sir Richard Baker's retrospective account (1643) of Elizabeth I's dilemma concerning Mary Stuart's execution, in which Baker cites Elizabeth's adviser's example of "Gods Judgements" for disobeying a direct divine order in his punishment of "Saul, for the sparing of Agag." Prescott then cites Donne, as well as Royalist comparisons of the Stuart monarchs with Saul, to highlight the issue of self-sacrifice and nobility inherent in the biblical figure.

Prescott sets out the issue of replacement as central to the use and representation in early modern England of the conflict between Saul and David. As she writes, the "second figure, covenant, or identity need not wipe out the first . . . but does supersede it"; in this light, Elizabeth I becomes David to Mary Tudor's Saul. Although Saul is often an image of tyranny, a truly Machiavellian figure, Prescott argues that the important lesson to be learned from the biblical text is of constraining "violence against an anointed monarch"; emulating David's loyalty to Saul restrains "murmuring, rebellions, resistance . . . or insurrection against their most deer and most dread sovereign Lord and king" (citing a 1594 homily). The political implications are evident, yet, Prescott maintains, so are the varied opportunities for reflection on "religious, social, and even medical and musical questions" (Saul's madness and David's music).

In their essays Elliott M. Simon and Noam Flinker highlight the highly significant intertextuality of the English religious lyric. Simon shows how the Sidneian Psalms reflect the thought of two medieval religious and philosophical thinkers: the Catholic Joachim de Fiore's theory of the Bible and the Jewish Moses Maimonides' concepts of prophetic inspiration and interpretations of equivocal biblical language. Flinker approaches George Herbert's poems in "The Temple" from the perspective of the Hebrew biblical text and Jewish exegetical traditions preserved in the Babylonian Talmud and Midrash Rabbah.

Simon's essay (Chapter 8) focuses on Philip Sidney's identification of "poetic creativity with the prophetic tradition of David's Psalms, in which preexisting texts considered sacred are translated into edifying ethical and spiritual precepts for the present or are interpreted as prescripted consequences for the future." Simon first demonstrates how Joachim's theory of the Bible as "sacred spiritual history" had a profound influence on Christian reform movements. For Sidney, what is crucial in Joachim's thinking is that the Old and New Testaments, from Genesis to the book of Revelation, constitute a united prophetic and spiritual narrative in which historical figures and events have their prescribed places. The poet-prophet is an interpreter of historical events, and his purpose must be to illuminate the different stages of the spiritual development of the devout Christian and thereby reveal a higher order of divine Truth. Simon examines Philip Sidney's translation of Psalm 2 and Mary Herbert's translation of Psalm 76, showing how their use of Joachim's model of *spiritualis intellectus* allows them, as English Protestants, to use their poetic voices to "continue the biblical narrative of progressive spiritual development."

Simon then asks, "How can a person translate (and perhaps transform) those [prior sacred] texts into his own idiom, time, and place?" An answer is to be found in Maimonides' conceptions of prophetic inspiration and transmission as well as of scriptural exegesis in the *Guide of the Perplexed,* which had an influence on Christian Hebraists. Maimonides uses the Aristotelian paradigm of the Active Intellect flowing into the Rational and Imaginative faculties of the mind as a mental creative process to show how the prophet is inspired to deliver in his own terms the sacred truth imaged in his prophecy. Maimonides is principally concerned with showing how the equivocal nature of biblical language, its figurative expressions and parables, must be understood and how it should be reinterpreted in each generation. Simon demonstrates how Maimonides' concepts of imagination, prophecy, and the equivocal language of the biblical texts were used by Sidney and Mary Herbert in their own experiments with language, as they translated and reinterpreted David's Psalms into their own "Protestant prophetic voices."

In Chapter 9 Noam Flinker discusses George Herbert's poems "The Collar" and "The Pearl" in terms of Julia Kristeva's conception of intertextuality. His twofold goal is to "add to a theoretical view of the relative stability of Herbert's texts" and to "include associations and motifs in the Hebrew Bible and in the New Testament that are not explicitly connected to a doctrine or text that the poet mentions." Flinker first turns to Kristeva to establish that (in her words) a text is "always plural, shattered, capable of being tabulated," thereby reflecting the various tensions implicit in the nature of signification. He then argues that this notion is relevant to discussing the speaker in Herbert's poems, who evokes biblical events to impart meaning on an intertextual level.

Flinker's readings of "The Collar" and "The Pearl" reveal a system of biblical echoes in the poems. Flinker argues that in "The Collar" Herbert's insertion of the words *wine* and *corn* introduces association to concepts of prosperity and material well-being found throughout the Bible. Whether it is Isaac's (misintended) blessing of Jacob (Genesis 27) or Moses's warning to the Israelites that God's blessing is linked to obedience (Deuteronomy 16 and 28), Flinker shows that the biblical passages shed light on the way in which the dramatic action of "The Collar" moves the poetic speaker away from the simple pursuit of material delight and back to God. In a similar manner, Flinker's reading of "The Pearl" links it not only to the Gospel according to Matthew (13) but also to the Jewish oral rabbinic tradition (already contemporaneous with Jesus) that includes references to pearls as an image of spiritual value. Flinker maintains that these intertextual echoes to the Hebrew biblical text, the Babylonian Talmud, and Midrash Rabbah act to destabilize the poetic texts, ultimately conveying their dramatic intensity and power.

Women and Religion

In recent years the scholars of early modern religion have highlighted women's religious activities and the gender codes of religious discourse.[19] Studies of particular women—for example, the Protestant martyr Anne Askew or the Catholic martyr Margaret Clitherow, devotional writers such as Catherine Parr and Gertrude More, female religious leaders such as Mary Ward, and female prophets and preachers such as Anna Trapnel—have highlighted the religious and social agency of these women and the importance of women as domestic religious educators and as independent religious thinkers whose impact was not limited to the home or the cloister but rather felt in the larger society.[20] Lowell Gallagher's intellectually complex and rewarding essay on Mary Ward deals with male ecclesiastical inability to accept her religious leadership and the mission of her teaching order. The two essays on women and religion contained in Part IV of this collection discuss, in turn, cases of gynocentric poetic production and the involvement in and representation of women in sermons.

Over the past two decades, partly in response to the edition of her poetry in the "Women Writers in English, 1350–1850" series,[21] Aemelia Lanyer has received much scholarly attention, particularly for her long religious poem *Salve Deus Rex Judaeorum*.[22] In his analysis of this text (Chapter 10), Yaakov Mascetti discusses the ways that Lanyer's gendered conceptions of sight and religious truth were founded on a boldly feminine renarration of biblical accounts characterized by an emphasis on male sinfulness and incapacity to acknowledge that which was not visible to the eye. He argues that Lanyer offers a "feminine response to the male-centeredness of contemporary Protestant lexica of belief and sight." Concentrating on feminine perception, Lanyer responded to Calvinist iconophobia as she moved "the iconic manifestation of Christ's self-sacrifice," the crucifix, "from the visual sphere to the textual one" and "merge[d] the act of reading with a visual perception of the Passion," making poetry "the locus of eucharistic presence, to be consumed and assimilated."[23] Thus, in the public sphere of print, Lanyer put herself in the midst of some of the theological arguments about "the nature and role of human artifacts in the religious sphere," including disputes about the Eucharist, the sacraments, and the nature of religious signs. Maintaining the Protestant emphasis on the primacy of the word, particularly the word of scripture, Lanyer invited her readers "to gaze upon the text . . . presenting its hermeneutical act as the veritable consumption of a ritual meal," making "her poetry . . . the living image of Christ." One of her desired readers, Queen Elizabeth, would see in the poem "the mirror image of her own monarchic glory" in the figure of Christ and would make a kind of eucharistic encounter with him. In the poem's narrative, then, women, not men, have and exercise the capacity for visual and cognitive communion with the Divine. There is, finally, in Lanyer's courageously feminist poem, a "paradoxical combination of iconodulia and iconophobia."

In early modern English social life and in print culture, the sermon loomed large as a literary genre. Not only were (sometimes quite lengthy) sermons preached regularly in English churches, but also they were delivered at court before the monarch and in the liminal ecclesiastical and civic space of Paul's Cross, where usually hundreds of citizens were in attendance.[24] In recent years editions of sermons have appeared or have been undertaken as large projects—for example, the sermons of Henry King and John Donne.[25] Jeanne Shami, who here contributes an essay on women and sermons (Chapter 11), has produced a number of valuable studies of sermon literature of the period.[26] In her chapter in this collection, she examines women's significance "first, as subjects, but then as patrons, consumers, and preachers of sermons." She uses manuscript miscellanies, inventories of women's libraries, wills, and other historical sources as evidence of women's importance as objects of attention in and avid readers, patrons, and reproducers of sermons (particularly in relation to their roles as domestic religious instructors for family members and servants). To discuss women as preachers, Shami broadens the definition of preaching to include "any voicing of religious opinion—in print, in the church or congregation, in the company of others anywhere, and even in the home." To shed light on the topic, she uses women's sermon notes and their written scriptural interpretations, including the sermonic text written by Anne of Denmark's courtly associate, Anna Walker.

In her essay, however, Shami focuses on the representation of women in sermons, particularly funeral sermons. As subjects of funeral sermons (which had to be paid for and which were therefore limited to the upper classes), women were praised for their domestic virtues rather than, as in the case of men, for their service in the public world. But Shami offers several case studies to demonstrate the biographical value of these sermons and the ways in which the lines between the domestic and the public were blurred. Among them are Edward Rainbowe's sermon for Lady Anne Clifford, John Donne's sermon for Lady Magdalen (Herbert) Danvers, John Carter's sermon for Lady Frances Stanley Egerton, Thomas Hassall's sermon for Martha Moulsworth, and Edmund Calamy's sermon for Elizabeth Moore. Calamy, for example, wrote that Lady Anne Waller had kept a "commonplace book crammed with observations out of scriptures and fed by her habit of hearing sermons twice a day." Some of these texts were published and thus presented to a wide readership the exemplary character of the women being praised. Whether or not their stories escaped the confines of the household and the family through print, these women often functioned "as exegetes, preachers, and patterns for imitation" within the spheres in which they functioned. Shami calls attention to the importance of their religious agency in a world in which the most noise was made in public by men engaged in harsh debate and polemic.

Religion and Secularization

Although the secularization thesis has been criticized recently by those who have observed the still powerful force of religion in public life and in world affairs, for many years the dominant historical narrative of the period from the Reformation, through the sixteenth- and seventeenth-century religious wars, the Enlightenment era, and the modern scientific revolution to the present assumed a progressive secularization of Western culture—moving from the struggles for religious hegemony in nations and territories that had official state religions, through various degrees of official or de facto toleration of religious diversity (such as that in seventeenth-century Netherlands), to a belief in the salutary benefits of the separation of church and state in more modern times.[27]

This process of secularization was aided, in a Protestant country such as England, by a desacralization of the landscape—enacted through the dissolution of the monasteries and the destruction (or, in some cases, the repurposing) of shrines, wayside crosses, and pilgrimage sites. Topographically church territory was circumscribed, as civic life took place in what could be perceived as a new secular space.[28] Religious conflicts in the form of vicious polemical attacks or in bloody warfare did not just destroy the kind of religious and social consensus necessary to a unitary polity in which church and state occupied the same territory of allegiance. The visible existence of dissident, recusant, nonjuring groups allowed citizens to distinguish the secular and religious orders. In toleration debates, antitolerationists (like their counterparts today) were unable to imagine a state that did not have an official religion, but those who argued for at least limited forms of toleration began to conceive of a state in which a plurality of religious denominations could coexist within the political order—the ideal finally embodied in the U.S. Constitution. Even when there was not official religious toleration, contradictions and ambiguities could abound in the polity—for example, in the mixed theology and ceremonial practices of the Elizabethan religious settlement and in the uneven and inconsistent enforcement of laws governing religious conformity. Official policy could contrast with the realities of local social arrangements, where, for example, English Catholics could function with more freedom than was theoretically possible.

In literary studies of the 1980s and 1990s new historicist and cultural-materialist approaches, which habitually translated religious beliefs and phenomena into economic, social, and political language, found the notion of progressive secularization congenial. For example, critics such as Stephen Greenblatt and Louis Montrose conceived of the drama of Shakespeare's time as drawing on the "charisma" of religion for secular purposes, turning it into theatrical "magic."[29] One of the effects of the recent scholarly studies of early modern English drama, which have highlighted the religious content that could resonate in the responses of religiously diverse theater audiences, is that the plays we were disposed to perceive as fundamentally secular now seem laden with religious meaning. Nonetheless, theatrical space differed from ecclesiastical space, and it was possible in plays to put religious ideology and struggles under critical, skeptical scrutiny, thus adopting a secular vantage point outside religion. This is the territory feared by, for example, the authorities in the Catholic Church who compiled the Index of Forbidden Books or by any other system of religious censorship, including the English one that was presided over by Anglican bishops.

Noam Reisner's discussion of Christopher Marlowe's approach to religion (Chapter 12) puts the dramatist at a vantage point outside religion, skeptically, if not cynically, dismantling both Catholic and Protestant positions—in fact, all forms of religious ideology and practices. Reisner points to the creation of a secular sphere outside religious culture(s), the inevitable consequence perhaps of the (sometimes bloody) struggles between different Christian sects, each with its own distinctive truth claims. Once a dominant religion was challenged, producing conflicting groups within a social order that was once religiously unified, it was possible to take a position above the fray in a space not bound by the confines of any single religious ideology. In its time such a critical vantage point was sometimes labeled atheistic, but from our point of view it might simply be classified as secular. Reisner sees the "gratuitous blasphemy that runs throughout [Marlowe's plays] as a dark thread of sinister relativism and skepticism" as "framed by profound reflections on contemporary religious habits of thought and the temporal violence . . . attached to them." He portrays Marlowe not just as an equal opportunity cynic but as a cultural dissident in an era of deadly religious conflict. In the "heightened metatheatricality of Marlovian drama" Reisner sees a connection between "the implied ethics of the playwright's craft in theory and Marlowe's distinctly religious subversiveness *as* a playwright in practice." The dazzling rhetorical performance of Marlovian protagonists "allows them to create a meta-Euclidean space in which to act out their gargantuan defiance to a received social order" and to "compete for the cultural spaces inhabited by the tyranny of religious dogma." Reisner's conclusion is that "Marlovian poetic craft emerges as a new kind of pluralist mock religion, and the theatrical stage on which such poetry competes with reality emerges as the secular spatial alternative to the churches and courts of Europe where absolute metaphysical or temporal power corrupts absolutely." This is the world of modernity anticipated in the work of an early modern dramatist.

Looking ahead to Kant's analysis of moral feeling, in Chapter 13 Sanford Budick discusses Shakespeare's *King Lear* in the framework of general ethical principles rather than of traditional religious morality. He argues that, although "structures of representation . . . are inherited from religious narrative . . . in *King Lear* these structures are secular." Budick makes Shakespeare a kind of Enlightenment thinker *avant la lettre.* He discusses the play's serial humiliations and the language of blessing not in the familiar religious vocabulary often associated with them but rather in terms of a secular moral philosophy articulated by Kant. What he calls in *King Lear* the zero narrative of seemingly endless humiliation "produces the conditions for freedom and moral feeling," and "the collective, transformative language of the 'nothing' . . . enable[s] the emergence of the human . . . of freedom and moral feeling, in benediction," with the play emphasizing "the possibility of this individual rebirth in concert with others . . . within the tragic community." Although Budick looks forward to Kant for a full articulation of these ideas, he also evokes the biblical and literary models to be found in the book of Job and in Sophoclean tragedy. The end result of the multiple humiliations dramatized in Shakespeare's play is the "recognition of something exalted, or sublime, in human nature," a phenomenon Kant, in his *Critique of Practical Reason*, clarified "by explaining the aesthetic-moral nexus within the tragic pattern that produces the sublime." In discussing Kant, however, Budick resorts to a religious vocabulary when he calls attention to the philosopher's identification of holiness as "the internal goal toward which the experience of the 'endless progress' of humiliation leads us." Cordelia thus seems "part of a Christ-like mysterium," and she is "from the beginning both holy woman and prophet." But such a reversion to the religious terminology by way of the later philosophical and ethical explanation has the effect of converting religious moral philosophy into its secular successor. Set within the ethical framework he has established, Budick's analysis of "nothing" and its cognates in the play points to new and rich meanings. His conclusion is one that makes sense in terms of modern secular humanism: "For Shakespeare in *King Lear* . . . the relations of the experience of the nothing, freedom, and the achievement of moral personality—the emergence of the human—are much the same as they are for Kant." We have moved beyond the boundaries of the ordinary religious imagination of the early modern period into a broader secular realm.

Religious struggles and crises in early modern England (and in Europe), which were intensified in the new medium of print, brought with them the large-scale cultural changes that produced, finally, the modern world. The blurred boundaries between Catholicism and Protestantism, the sectarian and theological fault lines in the established church, and the development of national and international religious diversity and the debates about the possibility and limits of religious toleration, the renewed examination of the Judaic roots of Christianity and of the importance of the Hebrew scriptures and commentary traditions, the conflict between religious authority and the spiritual autonomy of the individual (male or female) believer, the growing awareness of a space outside religion from which one could critically examine religious belief systems and truth claims—all these factors were part of a complex and evolving culture. The essays in this collection address such issues, paying special attention to the importance of what was characterized at the time as marginal or peripheral (English

Catholics, Jews and Hebraism, religiously active women, secularists or atheists). A master narrative of English religious and cultural history that does not highlight their importance distorts our sense of the past.

Notes

1. Chanita Goodblatt and Howard Kreisel, eds., *Tradition, Heterodoxy, and Religious Culture: Judaism and Christianity in the Early Modern Period* (Beer-Sheva, Israel: Ben-Gurion University of the Negev Press, 2006).

2. See, especially, Alison Shell, *Catholicism, Controversy, and the English Literary Imagination* (Cambridge, UK: Cambridge University Press, 1999); Alison Shell, *Oral Culture and Catholicism in Early Modern England* (Cambridge, UK: Cambridge University Press, 2007); Arthur F. Marotti, ed., *Catholicism and Anti-Catholicism in Early Modern English Texts* (Basingstoke, UK: Macmillan, 1999); Arthur F. Marotti, *Religious Ideology and Cultural Fantasy: Catholic and Anti-Catholic Discourses in Early Modern England* (Notre Dame, IN: University of Notre Dame Press, 2005); Susannah Brietz Monta, *Martyrdom and Literature in Early Modern England* (Cambridge, UK: Cambridge University Press, 2005); Anne Dillon, *The Construction of Martyrdom in the English Catholic Community, 1535–1603* (Aldershot, UK: Ashgate, 2002); Robert S. Miola, ed., *Early Modern Catholicism: An Anthology of Primary Sources* (Oxford, UK: Oxford University Press, 2007); and Christopher Highley, *Catholics Writing the Nation in Early Modern Britain and Ireland* (Oxford, UK: Oxford University Press, 2008).

3. See, especially, Eamon Duffy, *The Stripping of the Altars: Traditional Religion in England, c. 1400–c. 1580* (New Haven, CT: Yale University Press, 1992); and Christopher Haigh, *English Reformations: Religion, Politics, and Society Under the Tudors* (Oxford, UK: Clarendon Press, 1993).

4. The term *Marrano* was applied to Spanish and Portuguese Jews who formally converted to Christianity.

5. David S. Katz, "The Jewish Conspirators of Elizabethan England," in his *Jews in the History of England, 1485–1850* (Oxford, UK: Clarendon Press, 1994), 102. For an examination of the relationship between these two plays and the Lopez affair, see John Russell Brown, Introduction to William Shakespeare, *The Merchant of Venice*, Arden edition, ed. John Russell Brown (London: Methuen, 1964 [1955]), xxi–xxiv, xxxi.

6. See the early works by Lucian Wolf: "The Jewry of the Restoration: 1660–1664," *Jewish Historical Society of England: Transactions* 5 (1908): 4–33; "Jews in Elizabethan England," *Jewish Historical Society of England: Transactions* 11 (1928): 1–91; and "Jews in Tudor England," in *Essays in Jewish History*, ed. Cecil Roth (London: Jewish Historical Society of England, 1934), 71–90.

7. See David Katz, "From Admission to Revolution," in his *Jews in the History of England, 1485–1850* (Oxford: Clarendon Press, 1994), 107–44. Although

not concluding with a formal readmission of the Jews to England, the notable 1655 Whitehall Conference did assert that on the legal front "there is no Law that forbids the Jews return into *England*" (144).

8. Avihu Zakai, "The Poetics of History and the Destiny of Israel: The Role of the Jews in English Apocalyptic Thought During the Sixteenth and Seventeenth Centuries," *Journal of Jewish Thought and Philosophy* 5 (1996): 349.

9. Harold Fisch, *The Dual Image: The Figure of the Jew in English and American Literature* (New York: Ktav, 1971), 13.

10. James Shapiro, *Shakespeare and the Jews* (New York: Columbia University Press, 1996), 1.

11. For complementary studies, see Martin D. Yaffe, *Shylock and the Jewish Question* (Baltimore: Johns Hopkins University Press, 1997). See also Peter Berek, "The Jew as Renaissance Man," *Renaissance Quarterly* 51 (1998): 128–62; and Sharon Achinstein, "John Foxe and the Jews," *Renaissance Quarterly* 54 (2001): 86–120.

12. Achsah Guibbory, *Christian Identity, Jews, and Israel in Seventeenth-Century England* (Oxford, UK: Oxford University Press, 2010).

13. William Tyndale, *The Obedience of a Christen Man* (1528), ed. David Daniell (London: Penguin, 2000), 156–80.

14. For further discussion of these issues, see Chanita Goodblatt, *The Christian Hebraism of John Donne: Written with the Fingers of Man's Hand* (Pittsburgh, PA: Duquesne University Press, 2010).

15. Leah S. Marcus, "Renaissance/Early Modern Studies," in *Redrawing the Boundaries: The Transformation of English and American Literary Studies*, ed. Stephen Greenblatt and Giles Gunn (New York: Modern Language Association of America, 1992), 43.

16. Jason P. Rosenblatt, *Renaissance England's Chief Rabbi: John Selden* (Oxford, UK: Oxford University Press, 2006), 32.

17. For a detailed discussion of the "Great Matter," see J. J. Scarisbrick, "The Canon Law of the Divorce" and "The Struggle for the Divorce," both in his *Henry VII* (Berkeley: University of California Press, 1968), 163–97 and 198–240; David Katz, "The Jewish Advocates of Henry VIII's Divorce," in his *Jews in the History of England, 1485–1850* (Oxford: Clarendon Press, 1994), 16–48; and Rosenblatt, *Renaissance England's Chief Rabbi*, 32–45.

18. For studies of Milton's Hebraism, see Golda Werman, *Milton and Midrash* (Washington, DC: Catholic University of America Press, 1995); Jason P. Rosenblatt, *Torah and Law in Paradise Lost* (Princeton, NJ: Princeton University Press, 1994); and Jeffrey Shoulson, *Milton and the Rabbis: Hebraism, Hellenism, and Christianity* (New York: Columbia University Press, 2001).

19. See, for example, Patricia Crawford, *Women and Religion in England, 1500–1720* (London: Routledge, 1993); Frances Dolan, *Whores of Babylon: Catholicism, Gender, and Seventeenth-Century Print Culture* (Ithaca, NY: Cornell University Press, 1999); Erica Longfellow, *Women and Religious Writing in Early Modern England* (Cambridge, UK: Cambridge University Press, 2004);

Kimberly Anne Coles, *Religion, Reform, and Women's Writing in Early Modern England* (Cambridge, UK: Cambridge University Press, 2008); and Claire Walker, *Gender and Politics in Early Modern Europe: English Convents in France and the Low Countries* (New York: Palgrave, 2005).

20. See, for example, Peter Lake and Michael Questier, *The Trials of Margaret Clitherow: Persecution, Martyrdom, and the Politics of Sanctity in Elizabethan England* (London: Continuum, 2011); Janel Mueller, "Devotion as Difference: Intertextuality in Queen Katherine Parr's *Prayers or Meditations*," *Huntington Library Quarterly* 53.3 (1990): 171–97; Janel Mueller, "A Tudor Queen Finds Voice: Katherine Parr's *Lamentations of a Sinner*," in *The Historical Renaissance: New Essays on Tudor and Stuart Literature and Culture*, ed. Heather Dubrow and Richard Strier (Chicago: University of Chicago Press, 1988), 14–47; Janel Mueller, "Complications of Intertextuality: John Fisher, Katherine Parr, and 'The Book of the Crucifix,'" in *Representing Women in Renaissance England*, ed. Claude J. Summers and Ted Larry Pebworth (Columbia: University of Missouri Press, 1997), 24–41; Lowell Gallagher, "Mary Ward's 'Jesuitresses' and the Construction of a Typological Community," in *Maids and Mistresses, Cousins and Queens: Women's Alliances in Early Modern England*, ed. Susan Frye and Karen Robertson (Oxford, UK: Oxford University Press, 1999), 199–217; Maria Magro, "Spiritual Autobiography and Radical Sectarian Women's Discourse: Anna Trapnel and the Bad Girls of the English Revolution," *Journal of Medieval and Early Modern Studies* 34.2 (spring 2004): 405–37; and Arthur F. Marotti, ed., *Gertrude More, the Early Modern Englishwoman: A Facsimile Library of Essential Works*, ser. 2, *Printed Writings, 1641–1700*, pt. 4, v. 3 (Aldershot, UK: Ashgate, 2009), ix–xxiv.

21. Aemelia Lanyer, *The Poems of Aemelia Lanyer*, ed. Susanne Woods (Oxford, UK: Oxford University Press, 1993).

22. See, for example, the collection of essays in Marshall Grossman, ed., *Aemilia Lanyer: Gender, Genre, and the Canon* (Lexington: University Press of Kentucky, 1998).

23. For an illuminating discussion of the transfer in Protestant England of visual material into the imaginative sphere of written texts, see James Knapp, *Illustrating the Past in Early Modern England: The Representation of History in Printed Books* (Aldershot, UK: Ashgate, 2003).

24. The classic study of the Paul's Cross sermons is Millar MacLure, *The Paul's Cross Sermons, 1534–1642* (Toronto: University of Toronto Press, 1958). See also the recent book by Mary Morrissey, *Politics and the Paul's Cross Sermons, 1558–1642* (Oxford, UK: Oxford University Press, 2011).

25. See Mary Hobbs, ed., *The Sermons of Henry King (1592–1669), Bishop of Chichester* (Madison, NJ: Fairleigh Dickinson University Press; and Menston, UK: Scolar Press, 1992); and the forthcoming Oxford University Press edition of Donne's sermons under the general editorship of Peter McCullough.

26. See, in particular, Jeanne Shami, *John Donne's 1622 Gunpowder Plot Sermon: A Parallel-Text Edition* (Pittsburgh, PA: Duquesne University Press,

1996); and Jeanne Shami, *John Donne and Conformity in Crisis in the Late Jacobean Pulpit* (Cambridge, UK: D. S. Brewer, 2003).

27. See, for example, C. John Sommerville, *The Secularization of Early Modern England: From Religious Culture to Religious Faith* (New York: Oxford University Press, 1992).

28. See Alexandra Walsham, *The Reformation of the Landscape: Religion, Identity, and Memory in Early Modern Britain and Ireland* (Oxford, UK: Oxford University Press, 2011).

29. See, for example, Louis Montrose, *The Purpose of Playing: Shakespeare and the Cultural Politics of the Elizabethan Theatre* (Chicago: University of Chicago Press, 1996); and Stephen Greenblatt, *Hamlet in Purgatory* (Princeton, NJ: Princeton University Press, 2001).

I

Minority Catholic Culture

1

Arthur F. Marotti

Marian Verse as Politically Oppositional Poetry in Elizabethan England

Queen Elizabeth I had problems with three Marys: first, her monarchical predecessor; second, her cousin from Scotland; and, third, the Virgin Mary, who was venerated by devotees of what English Protestants called "the old religion."[1] Before she became queen, Elizabeth was imprisoned in the Tower by Queen Mary. In the middle of her reign she was politically menaced by the presence in her kingdom of the exiled Queen of Scots, in line to inherit the English throne in the event of her death (by natural causes or by assassination). Throughout her reign, as she projected her power and authority symbolically, she in effect competed as "Supreme Governor" of the English church and as idealized monarch with the Virgin Mary as an object of reverence. She survived to be crowned monarch in 1558. She kept a tight rein on Mary, Queen of Scots, and finally, in the face of real and fabricated plots, consented to her execution for treason in 1587. Elizabeth replaced church images of the Virgin Mary (especially on rood screens)[2] with her own royal symbols and countenanced the creation of a personal cult constructed of materials from Catholic Marian devotion and Petrarchan erotic idealism.[3]

As Miri Rubin explains in her comprehensive study, *Mother of God: A History of the Virgin Mary*, over the many centuries in which Mary developed as a focus of devotional attention, she served several functions for Christians: She was conceived as a mediator for the prayers and petitions of the faithful; she was portrayed as a protector of individuals, groups, and even whole countries (the last in the case of Spain of the Reconquista era);[4] she was a model for personal religious behavior for both men and women; and she was an exemplary figure of loving maternity and affective responsiveness. In the early Byzantine era Mary was celebrated as *Theotokos*, or "God-bearer," and later as "Mother of God," the second identity portrayed, for example, in carved statues of Mary that open up to reveal the figures of the Trinity within her body, making her the "Great Mother," a virtual goddess. Mary also had a function as the enemy of heretics and non-Christians (especially Jews)—a role that allowed her use as a sponsor of religious persecution, anti-Semitic violence, and colonial brutality. Ubiquitous throughout the Christian world in the many churches named in her honor, in the religious feasts dedicated to her (particularly that of the Assumption), in the Marian shrines or pilgrimage destinations associated with ongoing miracles, in the reported visions and dreams of famous saints, and in such scattered supposed relics as the pieces of her garments and samples of her (dried) milk, Mary was a feminine presence at the heart of Christian (and, in the post-Reformation era, Roman Catholic) belief and practice.

Regarding Marian devotion as idolatrous, for some good and some bad reasons, Reformation (especially non-Lutheran) Protestantism sought to displace Mary in the devotional economy of Christianity to strengthen the individual believer's unmediated relationship with God.[5] In 1538 the shrine of Our Lady of Walsingham, a visit to which Erasmus described in one of his colloquies,[6] was destroyed by royal command, part of a program of cultural eradication of Catholic practices.[7] Queen Elizabeth's later effacement of Mary as an object of reverent devotion, then, was in line with the reformist agenda of the English Protestant church,[8] although her assumption of aspects of the religiocultural status of the Virgin could look suspiciously like the cultivation of a new form of idolatry.[9] In any event, Mary and Elizabeth were cultural rivals. One of the effects of this situation is that expressions of Marian devotion could be intended and/or understood as politically oppositionist acts.

Although the production of poetry addressed to or about the Virgin Mary generally (and drastically) declined in early modern England,[10] Marian verse was written during the reign of Queen Mary and later on the Continent by Catholic exiles and at home by embattled recusants during the reigns of Queen Elizabeth, King James I, and King Charles I. Most of the poems written during the reign of Protestant monarchs were either circulated in manuscript in Catholic social networks or printed on the Continent for importation into England. Setting these poems against the background of what preceded them, I concentrate here on Elizabethan Marian verse.[11]

Following the more radically Protestant regency rule under Edward VI (1547–53), during which religious iconoclasm peaked, in the reign of Queen Mary (1553–58) Marian devotion was once more officially sanctioned in the (briefly) restored Catholicism of the period.[12] In his most famous poem, "A New Ballade of the Marigolde," William Forrest, who was a relative of the Henrician martyr John Forrest and became one of Mary's royal chaplains,[13] welcomed the Queen's accession in Marian terms.

> To Marie, our Queene, that Floure so sweete,
> This Marigolde I doo apply,
> For that the Name doth serve so meete
> And properlee, in eache partie;
> For her enduryng paciently
> The stormes of such as list to scolde
> At her dooynges, with cause why,
> Loth to see spring this Marigolde.
>
> Shee may be calde Marigolde well
> Of Marie (chiefe), Christes mother deere,
> That as in heaven shee doth excell,
> And Golde in earth, to have no peere:
> So (certainly) shee shineth cleere,
> In Grace and honour double folde,
> The like was never earst seene heere,
> Suche is this floure, the Marigolde.
> (stanzas 7 and 8)[14]

Although Forrest had earlier been a client of the royal protector, the Duke of Somerset, dedicating to him a poetic translation of fifty psalms, and although he later seemed to have thrived under Queen Elizabeth, this religiously amphibious but persistently Catholic poet wrote the most extensive body of Marian verse of the century.[15] As Gary Waller has noted, during Elizabeth's reign, Forrest composed the longest Marian poem of the period, a 4,000-line Lydgatean piece bemoaning England's loss of Mary as protector.[16]

Forrest's (unpublished) shorter poems devotionally addressed to the Virgin Mary survive in the large collection found in British Library MS Harley 1703.[17] Some of the dates attached to individual pieces in this collection place them in the first half of the reign of Queen Elizabeth, indicating that Forrest's Marian verse was composed under both the Catholic and the Protestant queens. In this verse Forrest laments what he saw as England's fall into heresy in the Henrician era and criticizes the Protestant assault on traditional Catholic devotion, particularly devotion to Mary. In one of his poems he expresses his hope that God will reconvert Protestant leaders, including Queen Elizabeth, so that the English church can be restored to spiritual health.

> Wheare Subjectes in this: can doo lyttle ease,
> but All in their handes, that beare the Swaye:
> Thorowe your prayers; God he maye so please:
> to bringe heades A wrye: into the readye way.
> Without Bloode sheadinge: as he can: and maye,
> Suche Reformation weare moste joyfull game:
> God (of his mercye) Assigne onse the Deye:
> And thorowe your prayer to helpe in the same,
>
> Right well is it knowne: & sayde (lorde) of thee,
> the heartes of pryncences, in earthe, over All:
> In thy Dysposytion fullye to bee:
> Owre noble Quene heere, & kynges unyversall:
> their hartes then into the right waye thowe call,
> to thy wyll Accordinglye, their willes to frame:
> so to rayse uppe, that Sathan made to fall:
> Lorde, of thy mercye, thowe doo in the same.
> (fol. 75v)

In another poem Forrest defends the status of "lady" for the Virgin Mary, which he perceived as under attack in Protestant England.

> by yeares, hundreths, and mo:
> the name of ladye, borne hath shee:
> and nowe (of late) taken her fro,
> of sett purpose.
> (fol. 67v)

Forrest elevates Mary's status finally to queen and empress, defending her traditional appellation, "Mother of God":

> Mother of God, none maye Denye:
> this woorde Theotycos doo scan:
> Whiche provethe her: passinge ladye,
>
> So ladye, Queene: and Emperesse bothe,
> withe Mother of God taken is she.
> (fol. 68)

Such Marian poetry would have been protected during the reign of Queen Mary, but it clearly functioned as oppositionist verse during Elizabeth's reign—for example, the poem "Uppon the Anteme: Salve Regina" (fols. 64v–66r) laments the absence in Christian devotion of the traditional Marian hymn. In Harley 1703 this piece is subscribed at the end "Quod W. fforrest, 1571." The last (narrative) poem in the Harley manuscript, fols. 127v–53r, is about Theophilus (and has a repentant prayer by him asking for help from Mary—fols. 140–42); it ends with the subscription "ffinis,—27 Octobris 1572 per me: [W.] Guilmm forrestum" and the note:

> To confirmation of this historye
> the catholike church of Antiquyte
> sonnge in prayse of the glorious Ladye
> tu, Theophilum: reformans gratiae
> God (her Sonn) wolde her: magnifyed to be
> whose freindes to David, honorable weare
> Then, who so specyall: as Christys mother
> (fol. 153)

At a date some fourteen years into the reign of Elizabeth, and after the 1570 papal bull excommunicating her, Forrest's poem in praise of Mary is politically subversive.[18]

Harley 1703, which was apparently transcribed in the 1570s,[19] collects an astonishingly large body of Marian verse at a time when it would have been both anachronistic and religiopolitically oppositional. The England it defines is one that has strayed into heresy and widespread sinfulness. One of the poems begins:

> Abowte the yeare of our lorde Jesue Christe,
> A thousand, fyve hundred, fortye & fyve,
> Englande overshadowed with the fowle myste:
> luthers errours: that heere dyd then Aryve:
> wheare thorowe: England dyd neaver syns thryve:
> (fol. 33)

The speaker of the poem recounts an experience of being invited during King Henry's reign to an aristocratic house, where there

> was great Recreation,
> with lorde of mysrule in much brave fashion.
> Of Mysrule, right well yt myght be so sayde:

for mysrule, theare: by all the yeare longe stayde,
In hereasye, whoredome, swearing, & suche,
with other Abhomynations, that myght bee:
which unto mysrule, of properte dyd tuche.
(fol. 33)[20]

The poem recounts an episode in which a knight and a ruffian disrupt a Christmas service by mocking a hymn to Mary and dishonoring Mary herself, behavior for which, Forrest claims, God punished them with ignominious deaths.

This is not, however, the only case in which Forrest's poems illustrate the bad consequences of disrespecting Mary. One poem tells the story of a priest who kept a concubine: He talked loosely in an alehouse about Mary, insulting her by treating her as an ordinary woman. The poem's heading states: "Theis fortye yeares togeather (excepte A fewe betweene) / hath theis Blaspheamyes bene used Againste the glorye of / vyrgyn marye: some requyted for the same (Indifferentlye) / As Appearethe by their Doinges heere after followinge" (fol. 27). In the margin is the date corresponding to Henry VIII's break with Rome ("Ab anno / 1532"). The poem includes the following lines, referring to the disrespectful words about Mary:

This knave, who had whoore in steade of nagge:
lykened owre ladye: to A safforne Bagge,
which, for the season, safforne was thearin:
was sweete and saverye: so she from hym.
But, Christe departed owte of her wombe, than:
she was no better: then other woman,
his tawlke, so open odyous yt was:
that certayne honest (that tyme) in the plase:
bydde hym mend his Communycation:
or to Avoyde the Congregation,
This varlet, he wolde not his tawlke desyste:
tyll hee (throughe drynkinge) had neeare hym beepyste,
Then, owte he went to A Gardeyne thearbye,
and at the Doore, moste myserablelye:
he fell done Dead, and theare grovelynge he laye:
his Sowle Departed.
(fol. 27v)

This Chaucerian tale of clerical corruption takes aim at those who would demote Mary from her traditional elevated status in Christian devotion.

Another poem tells the story of a common woman who tries to reduce Mary to her own level.

> In Manchester Towne: A woman theare Dwelte,
> who: with our ladye: dyd syckle, and pelte,
> In Althinges, that made to her Dyshonour:
> . . . .
> This woman, emonge her Gossypps wolde saye
> owre ladye, she was no better to waye,
> then she: or suche other, of the Meane sorte:
> howeaver Idyotes: of her dyd reporte,
> In her Comparinges, no better was shee:
> then Bagge, in the whiche sweete Safforne had bee,
> The safforne, owte shake, she was but A Bagge:
> no better to her: then olde woaren Ragge,
> To Safforne Bagge, her lykenyng so longe:
> that the yolowe Jawnders: to her dyd clonge,
> which made her so faynte, not hable to goe:
> medycyns taken: to rydde her thearfore.
> But remeadye none: on her myght prevayle:
> so sore the dysease: dyd her stylle Assayle,
> Laboringe thearin, the tyme God pleased:
> her greif encreasinge: she nowhyt eased.
> No remeadye was, but thearon to Dye:
> neaver relentynge: to Aske God mercye,
> for her evyll tawlke Againste his Mother:
> Offendinge the one: lyke so the other,
> Certayne, I thinke: God doth obsecat [*sic*],
> such, as his Mother doth calumnyat,
> they to be sufferers of his vengeaunce:
> witheout powre: to fall to repentaunce
> . . . .
> So this partye, Againste our ladye bent:
> was kept from grace: her doinges to Repent,
> Offendinge the leaste: to God belonge,
> better, withe Myll stone: to suffer Drownynge,
> What, to his lyttle ons, Any shall doe:
> he yt repenteth: as doone hym untoo,
> Desprycinge Anye of his ffamylye:
> he hym Dyspleasethe, by vearye playne preeif,
> On this sayde woman, the Jawnders so spred:

that they encumbred: both boadye and hedde.
In such kynde: after Saffaron lykenes.
scurfye, clammysche, and yelowische thycknes:
withe fylthye savour, odyous to smell:
more, then at full: Anye hable to tell,
Departinge this lief, so heere I leave herr:
but hyther: to God I that dooe Referre.
Of well sayinge, theare neaver cummethe harme:
then, Tunge to vse well: is speciall goode Charme.
ffinis.
(fols. 29r–v)

Calumniating the Virgin Mary brings on divine vengeance in a particularly ugly form.

Finally, another poem recounts how a heretical man of some accomplishments likened Mary's receiving the Eucharist to a sow's eating her own farrow.

Off yeat, one other: we have for to tell;
in love of owre ladye: that dyd rebell,
And, as other of hereatycal kynde:
shewed hym, towardes her: he had but small mynde,
This partye I knewe, as Anye on lyve:
whearfore, the better: I can hym Descryve,
he was A Man: muche properlye made:
and had qualyteis: of specyall trade,
To singe, to shute, to wrestle, to Roonne:
most singular praise: of All men: he woonn,
To hawke, to hunte, he cowlde doo with the beste:
suche syngular gracys: in hym dyd rest,
Also, he was of Complexion: pure,
as myght be Judged; by gyfte of nature,
But, as hathe bene saide, longe before our Age:
one yll herbe marrethe A pott of potage,
he was, to hym selfe: singularlye bent:
what styche he eaver tooke: he wolde not relent,
All that he helde, was moste certaynelye true:
I meane not Religyon: so to Construe
But, what other thinge, he sayde or dyd holde:
of woman thearin: he wolde bee controlde,
As in thinges, besydes Relygyon:

so, in the same: his lyke condytion,
Who, in hearesye to the Chyn dyd swym;
As ferder we shall reporte heere of hym,
This man, on A tyme: to A Barbar he came,
for to bee trymmed: as some dothe yt name,
Emonge other tawlkes, this came in his hedde,
when Christe, his Dyscyples, with his Boadye fedde:
whyther his mother: Receaved lykewise?
The Barbar sayde yea: as he dyd surmyse,
hee sayde then Agayne, withe countynaunce bigge:
A Sowe cowlde nomore: but eate her owne pigge,
withe other contumelyous sayinges:
Againste that gloryous vyrgins praysinges,
In hearesye wallowinge: deye, by deye,
his tyme he passed: none myght hym saye naye,
But, ere long while he loste one of his iyes:
& became Man: after much farre straunge guyse,
his strenght, yt faylde hym, his shootinge also:
unsemelye, in his Appayrayle dyd go,
In face, and fashyon, Altered much:
that, as we have saide: he had neaver bene suche,
Scourfye also, and lothesome to beholde:
his tyme to reacon: not fyftye yeares olde,
Wheare hee (before tyme) taken with the best:
nowe with the meane sorte: contented to rest,
Nothing regarded, as in tyme before:
fewe, of his servyce dyd passe Anye more,
But, for he had bene of olde Acquayntaunce:
hee myght els have gone: and ledde the pigges Daunce,
So thinke I, God plaged hym after suche sorte:
for, by his mother: so evyll to reporte,
Neaver knewe I Anye playne that so dyd:
but, some mysfortune (by them): at lenght ryd.
Whea[r]fore (As my selfe) I all men Advyse:
but, as becummethe: so to enterpryse,
ffinis
(fols. 30r–v)

Reproducing an early example of barbershop bullshitting, Forrest suggests that God will punish whoever mocks or dishonors Mary, whether they be high-born or low-born.

Forrest deals with aspects of Marian devotion that are clear markers between Catholic and Protestant practice: Mary's Assumption into heaven, her Immaculate Conception, her special function as the best mediator or intercessor with God, her title as Mother of God. With regard to the first, however, one of Forrest's poems acknowledges the theological debates over the question of Mary's Assumption into heaven, body and soul. Not yet official church doctrine, the Assumption was disputed by theologians of the time.[21] With regard to Mary's appellation "Mother of God," Forrest has a poem that defends calling her "Our Lady" and "Mother of God" in the face of Protestant objections ("To say Christes mother: A ladye" [fols. 87–88r]). There are times, however, when Forrest seems to let his desire for religious unity move him toward a kind of compromise position. In one long poem, "To the Gloryous vyrgin Marye / to shewe her helpe: to Peters Navye," he calls on Mary in her role as enemy of heretics (such as "cursed Luther" [fol. 74v]) to help cleanse the English church, but, because the strong assertion of papal governance was one of the most objectionable features of Roman Catholicism to Protestants, he suggests the establishment of a kind of English Gallicanism that would give greater authority to an English archbishop.

> ffor one man, the Busshoppe of Rome (I dooe meane)
> let not Chystes Churche: suche myserye systeyne,
> As to conculcat, and overthrowe cleane:
> sith yt their partyes: rather to mayntayne,
> In eaverye Royalme: as thus to ordayne,
> As James, and the Rest had placys by name:
> So, in eache Countrye A Busshoppe soveraigne,
> to have, and to Doo: in chardge of the same.
> (fol. 76)

Forrest concludes his poem, however, with a strong plea to Mary to "purge" the English church of "Errours festure" (fol. 76).

After Elizabeth's accession, especially after the acceleration of the persecution of Catholics following the 1570 papal bull excommunicating the queen and, from 1574 onward, the steady flow of Catholic missionary priests from abroad, the situation for English Catholics was perilous. Catholic poets who composed verse to or about the Virgin could address their work, especially in manuscript, to sympathetic coreligionists, but such work in the larger sociopolitical context would have been seen as protest literature. Such texts were not only associated primarily with militant Catholic recusancy, religious conversion to Catholicism, and martyrdom, but also with some religiously ambiguous or non-Catholic politically alienated writers' use of the cultural code of Marian devotion to question or attack the cult of Elizabeth.

One of the clearest examples of Marian verse as protest literature was the ballad lamenting the destruction of the shrine of Our Lady of Walsingham. Looking back to the 1538 desecration of the shrine and the burning of the statue of Mary,[22] this piece expresses recusant loss and alienation.

In the wrackes of walsingam
  Whom should I chuse,
But the Queene of walsingam
  to be guide to my muse
Then thou Prince of walsingam
  graunt me to frame,
Bitter plaintes to rewe thy wrong,
  bitter wo for thy name.
Bitter was it oh to see,
  The seely sheepe
Murdred by the raveninge wolves
  While the sheephardes did sleep,
Bitter was it oh to vewe
  the sacred vyne,
While the gardiners plaied all close,
  rooted up by the swine
Bitter bitter oh to behould,
  the grasse to growe
Where the walles of walsingam
  so statly did sheue,
Such were the workes of walsingam
  while shee did stand
Such are the wrackes as now do shewe
  of that holy land,
Levell Levell with the ground
  the towres doe lye
Which with their golden glitteringe tops
  Pearsed once to the skye,
Wher weare gates no gates ar nowe,
  the waies unknowen
Wher the presse of peares did passe
  While her fame far was blowen

Oules do scrike wher the sweetest himnes
  lately weer songe
Toades and serpentes hold ther dennes,
  Wher the Palmers did thronge
Weepe weepe to walsingam
  Whose dayes are nightes
Blessings turned to blasphemies
  Holy deedes to dispites,
Sinner is wher our Ladie sate
  Heaven turned is to Hell.
Sathan sittes wher our Lord did swaye
  Walsingam oh farewell.[23]

The destruction of Mary's shrine, the prime destination for English pilgrims, is presented here as a cultural and religious disaster, a sign of the country's betrayal of its protector and of its diabolical turning away from true religion. The physical violence against the feminized shrine ("shee") is portrayed as an assault on both Mary and Christ. The pained outcry of English Catholics captured in this poem is reflected in the Catholic Elizabethan composer William Byrd's "Walsingham Variations," which alludes musically to the plight of his culturally repressed fellow Catholics.[24]

There is a Marian poem in the Arundel Harington Manuscript in Sir John Harington's hand, possibly by the Jesuit Edmund Campion, who was tried and executed (for treason) in 1581.[25]

fflower of Roses Angells joy
Tower of David Arke of Noy
first of sayntes whose trew protecting
Of the younge and weake in spryte
Makes my soule thease lynes endyte
to thy throne her playnte dyrectinge

Orphan chylde alone I lye
childlyke to thee I crye
Queene of Heaven usde to cherishe
Eys of grace behold I fall
ears of pitty heare my call
least in swadling clowts I perishe

Hyde the greatnes of each fawlte
my Desert yf thear be awghte

by thie meryts be enlarged
that the debts whearin I fall
paying nought but owing all
by thie prayer be discharged

Pray to him whose shape I beare
by thie love thie care thy feare
by thy gloryous byrthe and breeding
that thoughe ower synnes towche the skye
yet his mercyes (may not dye)[26]
all his other woorks exceeding

Tell him that in strengthning me
with his grace he graceth thee
every litle one defending
Tell him that I cloy thine ears
with the cry of chyldishe tears
from his footstoole still assending
Hear my cryes and grant me ayd
perfect mother parfect mayd
hear my cryes to thee addressed
ffrom my payntes turne not thie face
humble and yet full of grace
pure, untowcht for ever blessed.
ffinis[27]

Ruth Hughey says of this piece: "I have found no other copy of this hymn to the Virgin. I suggest that it was found in the books of Edmund Campion, which the elder John Harington had special permission to carry about with him."[28] The Campion execution was one of those cultural moments in which English Catholics were shocked by the brutality of the Elizabethan regime and the English government had to defend its actions in an international arena.[29] A Marian poem, emphasizing the Virgin's "trew protecting" of the anguished believer could console suffering Catholics and, at the same time, protest official oppression. Thus this poem, in conjunction with the poem on Campion's martyrdom signaled Catholic resistance.

In *The Societie of the Rosary* (2nd ed., 1597), the Jesuit Superior for the English Mission, Henry Garnet, introduced his book by using the metaphor of a "deluge of heresie" overwhelming England, characterizing "the glorious Virgin" (sig. A2r–v) as the equivalent of the rainbow shown to Noah after the biblical flood. Marian devotion represented a hope for the future emergence of the country from a disastrous period of Protestant hegemony. She is called "a rainbow against Heretickes" because "she hath destroied all heresies in the whole world, and therfore is a perticuler signe and aboade of the ceassing thereof" (sig. A3v). In the context of the Jesuit order's promotion of Marian devotion, especially through its "sodalities," Garnet encourages the use of the rosary because of what he sees as a Protestant assault on Mary.

> Even as with all manner of deceitful subtleties and blasphemous untruthes, heresie doth ever go about to derogate unto the glory of the most soveraigne Queene of heaven and earth: so is it the part of every zealous Catholicke with as much care and diligence, to procure to set forth, amplifie, and increase, her wonderfull praises, and most deseruved honour. (sig. B1)[30]

Catholic verse could circulate in manuscript through networks of Catholic literary transmission or in print in Catholic publications produced on the Continent or, by secret presses, in England. A work domestically printed at a secret press but bearing a foreign imprint ("Printed at Antwerp. 1598"), *A Methode, to meditate on the Psalter, or great Rosarie of our blessed Ladie*, begins each section (on one of the "mysteries" or meditative focuses of the rosary) with an illustrated two-quatrain poem. For example, the first poem dealing with the Annunciation reads:

> Here Gabriel the Archangel doth,
> Our blessed Ladie greete:
> Who with content conceived Christ,
> Our soveraigne Saviour sweete.
>
> God graunt the power and strength of God,
> My soule may dayle haile:
> That it conceiving Christ may bring
> Forth teares of good availe.
> (sig. C5v)

Although most of the "mysteries" do not directly involve Mary, those that do emphasize Catholic beliefs in her special status. The fourth "glorious" mystery celebrates her Assumption into heaven, body and soul.

> Our Ladie who on earth had livde
> From earthly sinne so free,

Deservde with heavenly glory great,
  Assumpted thus to bee.
Sweet virgin pray unto thy sonne,
  In life to grant me grace,
To serve you so in earth as I
  In heaven may have a place.
   (sig. F6v)

Mary's function as mediator and as object of special devotional attention marks this poem as exclusively Catholic, as does the poem that follows on her being crowned Queen of Heaven.

Our Ladie here is crownde with blisse,
  In pay of all her paines,
Where for each crosse of earthly cares,
  An heavenly crowne she gaines.
O Queene of heaven which worldly cares
  Escaped hast so free,
Pray that our bale may be our blisse,
  Rightly to follow thee.
   (sig. F8v)

This devotional attitude would have had a particular urgency for persecuted Elizabethan Catholics.

In 1601 the Catholic writer and communications agent Richard Verstegan published in Antwerp his *Odes in Imitation of the Seaven Penitential Psalmes, with Sundry other Poemes and dittie tending to devotion and pietie,* a significant portion of which is given over to Marian verse. A sequence of poems on the fifteen mysteries of the rosary concludes with poems on the Assumption and coronation of Mary (pp. 39–40), followed by a versification of the Ave Maria (p. 41), "Epithetes of Our Blessed Lady" (pp. 42–49), "Our Blessed Ladies Lullaby" (pp. 50–54), and, finally, a poem that defends Catholic Marian devotion against Protestant critics, "A Reprehension of the Reprehending of our ladies praise" (pp. 55–56). This last poem highlights the polemical context of Marian poetry.

Fy foule contempt of self-defyling breath,
That dar'st disgorge, gainst so great puritie,
The poisson issued from defect of faith,
To serve to witnes thy impietie.

Whence can it come but from infernal hate
That earth-bred wretches are become to brag,
As Gods owne mothers glorie to abate,
To call and compt her but a saffron bag.

Or that a Jil[31] the subiect unto sin
Dare equalize her self as good as shee,
In whome no thought impure hath ever bin,
Or least of purenesse-want might ever bee.

No Saint or Angel ever taught them thus,
For heaven did her entytle ful of grace,
And her conception of the king of blis
Her high regard comends to ev'ry race.

Her self of her own praise was prophetesse,
And of the races that should it conserve,
Needes must they then her ever-praise professe
That love and law envyteth to observe.

The honor to a mother such as shee
To such a forme must argue greater love,
Which may not unto him offensive bee,
In whome kynde love can it no lesse approve.

But hatred of her laud may never grow
Of zeale that love unto her sonne may raise,
Nor can the chyld his love on such bestow,
As kindle hatred at the mothers praise.

He which is mighty her hath magnifyde,
Let faithful then her ever magnify,
Whyle the unfaithful in conceit abyde,
Of doing wel her praises to deny.

And let performance of her woorthy praise,
Of her praise-yeilding race remaine the signe,
That so the blame that for it others raise,
Become the marck of their dissenting lyne.

And let contempt of her with such abyde,
As pay in hel the tribute of their pryde.

The reference to the slander against Mary for being merely like a "saffron bag," found also in two of the poems by Forrest quoted earlier, goes back to a charge made against Bishop Latimer that would associate him with the most radical reformers. Latimer discusses it in his "Sermon on the Plowers," sounding defensive about Protestant treatments of Mary.

> I have been slandered of some persons. . . . It hath been said of me, "Oh, Latimer! nay, as for him I will never believe him while I live nor never trust him, for he likened Our Blessed Lady to a saffron bag." Where indeed I never used that similitude. But it was, as I have said unto you before now, according to that which Peter saw before in the spirit of prophecy and said that there should come afterward men *per quos via veritatis meledictis afficeretur.* There should come fellows "by whom the way of truth should be ill spoken of and slandered" (II Peter 2:2). But in case I had used this similitude, it had not been to be reproved but might have been without reproach. For I might have said thus: as the saffron bag that hath been full of saffron or hath had saffron in it doth ever after savor and smell of the sweet saffron that it contained, so Our Blessed Lady, which conceived and bare Christ in her womb, did ever after resemble the manners and virtues of the precious babe which she bare. And what had Our Blessed Lady been the worse for this or what dishonor was this to Our Blessed Lady?[32]

Verstegan's poem, written abroad at the end of Elizabeth's reign, portrays the English denigration of the Virgin Mary as a sign of impiety, faithlessness, and infernal hatred. Although he does not specifically accuse Queen Elizabeth of being an enemy of the Virgin, that criticism is implicit in such a poem.

Some Catholic verse was domestically printed in approved publications, but often it appeared in expurgated or censored forms.[33] Manuscript collections of Robert Southwell's verse usually begin with a sequence of Marian poems, invoking Mary in her role as protector of the English mission. The printed collections of Southwell's verse marketed to a largely Protestant readership eliminate some of these lyrics.[34] Two of the Marian sonnets were not printed in the main editions of Southwell's verse appearing in 1595, *Saint Peter's Complaint* and *Moeoniae*: "The death of Our Lady" and "The Assumption of our Lady." The latter poem concentrates on a (not yet doctrinal) belief in the translation of the Virgin to heaven in both body and soul, a notion decidedly unacceptable to Protestants.[35] This poem emphasizes Mary's queenship.

Gemm to her worth, spouse to her love ascendes,
Prince to her throne, Queene to her heavenly kinge,
Whose court with solemne pompe on her attends,
And Quire of Saintes with greeting notes do singe.
(ll. 13–16)[36]

The contrast with earthly queens, including Elizabeth, is implicit in this passage.

Converts to Catholicism could refer to their change of religion with Marian writing. For example, Thomas Lodge seems to have signaled his conversion in 1596 by publishing *Prosopopeia Containing the Teares of the holy, blessed, and sanctified marie, the Mother of GOD.* Henry Constable, who worked on the Earl of Essex's behalf for a number of years, composed after his conversion to Catholicism a number of religious sonnets, including four poems addressed to the Virgin Mary.[37] One poem to the Virgin contrasts ambitious suitorship to earthly monarchs with prayerful petitioning addressed to the Queen of Heaven.

Sovereigne of Queenes: If vayne Ambition move
my hart to seeke an earthly prynces grace:
shewe me thy sonne in his imperiall place,
whose servants reigne, our kynges & queenes above.
. . . .
And love, my hart to chaste desyres shall brynge,
when fayrest Queene lookes on me from her throne
and jealous byddes me love but her alone.
("To our blessed Lady," ll. 1–4, 12–14)[38]

Constable portrays Mary as jealous of any special attention directed at an earthly queen, such as that expressed by poets and courtiers toward Elizabeth.[39] In another poem, also titled "To our blessed Lady," Constable refers to other women as, by comparison with Mary, "baser beutyes" (l. 2).[40] The most politically oppositionist of Constable's Marian sonnets, however, might be the following poem, which foregrounds the Catholic belief in the Immaculate Conception and makes an invidious comparison of Mary with ordinary queens:

In that (O Queene of queenes) thy byrth was free
from guylt, which others doth of grace bereave
when in theyr mothers wombe they lyfe receave:
God as his sole-borne daughter loved thee.

To matche thee lyke thy byrthes nobillitye,
he thee hys spyryt for thy spouse dyd leave:
of whom thou dydd'st his onely sonne conceave,
and so was lynk'd to all the trinitye.
Cease then, O Queenes who earthly crownes do weare
to glory in the pompe of worldly thynges:
if men such hyghe respect unto yow beare
Which daughters, wyves, & mothers ar of kynges;
What honour should unto that Queene be donne
Who had your God, for father, spowse, & sonne.
("To our blessed Lady")[41]

In the manuscript poetical miscellany in which the best collection of Constable's poetry is found, Victoria and Albert Museum, Dyce MS 44, there is a poem to the exiled poet written by a friend who urges him to return to England and to the church he had left when he converted to Catholicism.

To H C upon occasion of Leaving his
countrye and sweetnesse of his verse.

Englands sweete nightingale what frights thee so
As over sea to make thee take thy flight?
And there to live with native countryes foe
And there him with thy heavenly songs delight.

What did thy sister swallowe thee encite
with her for winters dread to flye away?
Who is it they hath wrought his other spite
That when as she returneth thow shouldst stay?

As soone as spring begins she cometh ay,
Returne with her and thow like tidings bring,
when once men see thee come what will they say?
Loe now of English poesie comes the spring.
Come feare thow not the cage but loyall be
And ten to one thy soveraigne pardons thee.
(fol. 44r)

The writer hopes that Constable will return, profess loyalty to the Queen, and thereby avoid prison.

Catholic verse was composed in prison as well as in exile. The Catholic convert Philip Howard, Earl of Arundel, wrote his "Fourfold Meditation" from prison. This poem was published in 1606, eleven years after his death, but in a version that omits four stanzas on the angels and their (and "Men'"s) adoration of the Virgin Mary.

> The Angels then are next in their degree,
> Whose orders rise in number to be nine;
> No hart can thinke what joy it is to see
> How al these troupes like lampes in glorie shine:
> The joy is more then writing can expresse,
> O happie eies that may this joy possesse.
>
> Above them al the Virgin hath a place,
> Which made the world with comfort to abound;
> The beames do shine in her unspotted face,
> And with the starres her head is richely crown'd:
> In glorie she al creatures passeth farre,
> The Mone her showes, the Sunne her garments are.
>
> O Quene of heven! o pure and glorious sight!
> Most blessed thou above al women art;
> This Cittie drunke thou makest with delite,
> And with thy beames revivest ev'ry hart:
> Our blisse was lost, and thou did'st it restoare,
> The Angels al and Men do thee adore.
>
> Loe here the looke which Angels do admire;
> Loe here the Spring from whom al goodnes flowes;
> Loe here the sight which men and Sainctes desire;
> Loe here that Stalke on which our comfort growes;
> Loe this is she whom heven and earth imbrace,
> Whom God did chose, and filled ful of grace.[42]

A major aristocrat and courtier, Howard had converted to Catholicism and, even before his attempted escape to the Continent, had acted out his religiopolitical oppositionism on several courtly occasions. From his cell in the Tower, where he died in 1595—the same year as the execution of Robert Southwell, who had lived in the Countess of Arundel's house and set up a secret press there—Howard composed this poem and other works proclaiming his Catholic identity. Validating the adoration of the Virgin would have been unacceptable in an authorized publication in either the Elizabethan or Jacobean era. In one of the many manuscripts in which the text of the "Fourfold Meditation" is found (Bodleian MS Rawlinson Poetical 219), the poem is followed by a 27-quatrain poem on the Eucharist (fols. 14v–15r) and by the only surviving manuscript copy of the Catholic lament for the loss of the Walsingham shrine ("In the wrackes of Walsingam").[43]

The Earl of Essex, in the prison poem he composed before his execution for treason, included the following stanza imploring the Queen of Heaven rather than the Queen of England:

> And thou faire Queene of mercy and of pittye,
> Whose wombe did once the World's Creator carry,
> Bee thou attentive to my painefull dittye,
> Further my Sutes deare gracious blessed Mary;
> If thou begin the Quire of holy Saints
> Will all be helping to preferre my plaints.
> (ll. 25–30)[44]

Using the language of courtly suitorship, Essex replaces his punitive royal patroness with a benevolent celestial queen. When the poem was printed in 1601, this stanza was omitted.[45] Although some of the politically disaffected members of Essex's faction were Roman Catholics, Essex, of course, was not their coreligionist, but, like them, he could use the figure of Mary as a cultural antagonist to Elizabeth. It is interesting that, in his epitaph for Queen Elizabeth, Hugh Holland managed both to praise her as an earthly monarch and to subordinate her in death to the Virgin Mary. The concluding couplet to his poem, sometimes reproduced as a separate piece, asserts, "She was and is, what can there more be said? / On earth the chiefe, in heaven the second Maide."[46]

When Protestant poets used the figure of Mary in their verse, they often went out of the way to avoid certain roles and qualities attributed to her in traditional Catholic poetry. For example, *The Song of Mary the Mother of Christ* (1601) does not make Mary a privileged mediator, carefully depicts her subordination to the Trinity, refuses to call her "Mother of God," and, in portraying her as a spokesperson for sinful humanity who has her own "sinne" (p. 20, l. 4), does not accept the notion of her Immaculate Conception and its corollaries.[47] It finesses the question of her maternal authority over Christ by, first, portraying the young Jesus's obedience to her as a lesson for others and, then, having it counteracted by the moral of the episode of the presentation in the Temple, which teaches that duty to God is superior to duty to one's parents. This Protestant Mary is not a

Queen of Heaven to whom humanity appeals for help, and she is certainly not a virtual goddess or religious idol. She is, instead, a narrator and expositor of the biblical story of Christ and his Passion. She even seems to steer clear of emphasizing transubstantiation when she describes the Last Supper, playing down the eucharistic moment by embedding it in a description of Judas's treachery.

> *Judas* doth cast within his wicked head,
> His Soveraigne Lord and Master to betray:
> *Jesus* in the meane while, doth blesse the bread,
> And gives himselfe a lasting foode for aye,
> O heaven and earth! cry out, exclaime and say,
> O monstrous malice, matcht with wondrous love!
> O poysoned toad, and patient simple Dove!
> (p. 15, ll. 5–11)

The blessed (not "consecrated") bread is not identified with the body and blood of Christ, although there is a reference to "the table furnished that night, / With heavenly *Manna*, holy Angels foode" as well as "The Paschall Lambe" and "honny" (p. 15, ll. 20–21).

In the cultural changes wrought by the Reformation in England, then, the Virgin Mary was either scaled down to the status of a virtuous Christian believer and servant of God or, in effect, eliminated from the devotional economy of Protestant Englishmen. Even with Queen Elizabeth gone from the scene, the Virgin Mary and her cult continued to be viewed by Protestant Englishmen as religiously and therefore politically threatening to the state and its official church. In the Caroline era a foreign Catholic princess with "Maria" as part of her name exacerbated Protestant anti-Marianism.[48] Catholic writers both at home and abroad, such as Tobie Mathew and Richard Crashaw, who wished to rewrite English national identity in a way that was different from that of the now-dominant Protestant model, could still turn to Marian devotion as a politically oppositionist code. There is a poem by "T[homas] freeman" in British Library MS Harley 6917 on the birth of a new child named Mary to Charles I.

> of the Suddaine Christning, and name:
> Borne and baptized? blest Trinity bestow
> All heavenly blessing in this holy Deaw;
> And with the sacred Virgin name of Mary?
> yes princesse, and thine owne hereditary;

Thy great Grand-mother, grandmother, thy mother
all Marys calld, how could they call thee other?
(fols. 81v–82r)

The poem traces a lineage of Marys, including Marie de Medici, Mary, Queen of Scots, and Henrietta Maria—enough Marys to make Queen Elizabeth spin in her grave.

Through the Elizabethan period and beyond, during England's slow religious transition from Catholicism to Protestantism, the figure of Mary could be invoked by Catholic recusants and religious conservatives to proclaim religious resistance to what was officially being imposed on the country and what was anthropologically changing on a grassroots level. It was a losing battle for them, but their voices are still audible in what they wrote.

Notes

1. See Peter McClure and Robin Wells, "Elizabeth I as a Second Mary," *Renaissance Studies* 4 (1990): 38–70; and Helen Hackett, *Virgin Mother, Maiden Queen: Elizabeth I and the Cult of the Virgin Mary* (Houndmills, UK: Macmillan, 1995). Hackett criticizes scholars such as E. C. Wilson, Frances Yates, and Roy Strong who see a simple transfer of idealization from the Virgin Mary to Elizabeth in Protestant England. Although she is right to point to sources of the idealization of Elizabeth other than the cult of Mary—for example, an ancient veneration of virginity, the figure of the biblical Deborah, and the "scriptural texts [such as the Song of Songs] which for Protestants too used the figure of the virginal bride of Christ for the Church" (*Virgin Mother,* 55)—I think she underestimates the influence of Catholic Marian devotion and the cultural challenge it posed to Elizabeth's rule. I find problematic her reading of the statement in Sir Henry Lee's retirement poem that he planned to substitute "*Vivat Eliza,* for an *ave mari*": "The point is not that he should pray to Elizabeth as if she were a new Virgin Mary, but that he should pray for her rather than fighting for her" (*Virgin Mother,* 148). I also find it hard to accept Hackett's general argument that the appropriation of features of the Marian cult by Elizabeth and her courtiers was not very strong.

2. See John Philips, *The Reformation of Images: Destruction of Art in England, 1535–1660* (Berkeley: University of California Press, 1973); and Margaret Aston, *England's Iconoclasts* (Oxford, UK: Clarendon Press, 1988).

3. For a discussion of the connection between Petrarchan idealism, Marian devotion, and the cult of Elizabeth, see Stephen Hamrick, *The Catholic Imaginary and the Cults of Elizabeth, 1558–1582* (Farnham, UK: Ashgate, 2009).

4. The Spanish used Mary as a patroness of their military campaigns during the Reconquista. At the time of the Armada, the English prominently displayed in London the Marian banner captured from the Spanish, and during their 1597 attack on Cadiz they vandalized a statue of the Madonna and Child. The damaged statue became the emblematic and revered Madonna Vulnerata representing the Catholic resistance to Protestant attacks on traditional religious practices. See Alison Shell, *Catholicism, Controversy, and the English Literary Imagination* (Cambridge, UK: Cambridge University Press, 1999), 200–7.

5. Patricia Crawford, *Women and Religion in England, 1500–1720* (London: Routledge, 1993), 47, cites William Perkins's attack (in *A Reformed Catholike*) on the idolization of Mary, in particular, regarding her as "a Ladie, a Goddesse, a queene, whom Christ her sonne obeyeth in heaven, a mediatresse".

6. See Erasmus, "A Pilgrimage for Religion's Sake," in *Ten Colloquies of Erasmus*, ed. and trans. Craig R. Thompson (New York: Liberal Arts Press, 1957). Although Erasmus was impressed by the shrine at Walsingham, he mocked the alleged relics of Mary's milk and the piece of the Holy Cross (68), inserting a fictional letter from Mary herself complaining about the excesses of her devotees: "I was all but exhausted by the shameless entreaties of mortals. They demanded everything from me alone, as if my Son were always a baby . . . still needing his mother's consent and not daring to deny a person's prayer: fearful, that is, that if he did deny the petitioner something, I for my part would refuse him the breast when he was thirsty" (60). Despite this, Erasmus himself composed several deeply devout Marian works in poetry and prose, including a Greek lyric to Our Lady of Walsingham; see Erasmus, *Collected Works of Erasmus*, v. 85, *Poems*, trans. Clarence H. Miller, ed. Harry Vredeveld (Toronto: University of Toronto Press, 1993), 120–23.

7. See the discussion of cultural eradication of Catholic practices and of other acts of iconoclasm particularly directed at Marian objects in Gary Waller, *The Virgin Mary in Late Medieval and Early Modern English Literature and Popular Culture* (Cambridge, UK: Cambridge University Press, 2011), 80–105 and *passim*; see also Dominic Janes and Gary Waller, eds., *Walsingham in Literature and Culture from the Middle Ages to Modernity* (Farnham, UK: Ashgate, 2010).

8. Eamon Duffy, *The Stripping of the Altars: Traditional Religion in England, 1400–1580* (New Haven, CT: Yale University Press, 1992), emphasizes the popular resistance to the top-down imposition of religious changes in the period and the delayed effects of the program, which took until the late 1570s to have a full impact. He discusses, among other topics, the popular and elite attachment to primers or books of hours, which incorporated "The Little Office of Hours of the Blessed Virgin Mary" (210–32), the removal of Mary plays from the traditional cycles of religious drama and the suppression of this drama as religiously heterodox in the new Protestant state (580–81), and the

successive waves of iconoclasm and reform directed against the material traces and social practices of the "old religion." On the first of these subjects, see also Eamon Duffy, *Marking the Hours: English People and Their Prayers, 1240–1570* (New Haven, CT: Yale University Press, 2006).

9. Christopher Highley, *Shakespeare, Spenser, and the Crisis in Ireland* (Cambridge, UK: Cambridge University Press, 1997), 110–11, discusses the case of an Irishman who was arrested for destroying an image of the Queen and who defended himself by charging that this was a blasphemous appropriation of religious imagery proper to Mary and the saints, not to a secular ruler.

10. There was, however, a large body of late medieval Marian carols with a continuing life in both popular and elite culture of the time. See the sections "Carols to the Virgin," "Carols of the Five Joys," and "Carols of the Annunciation" in Richard Leighton Greene, ed., *The Early English Carols* (Oxford, UK: Clarendon Press, 1977), 115–62.

11. I do not discuss the drama of the period, where Marian elements were transformed in various ways. See, for example, Regina Buccola and Lisa Hopkins, eds., *Marian Moments in Early Modern British Drama* (Aldershot, UK: Ashgate, 2007); and Ruben Espinosa, *Masculinity and Marian Efficacy in Shakespeare's England* (Aldershot, UK: Ashgate, 2011). Espinosa examines nine of Shakespeare's plays to demonstrate how the dramatist responded in complex ways to the post-Reformation religious diminishment of the Virgin Mary.

12. Shell notes that writers of the period, including Myles Hogarde, "exploited the coincidence of Mary's name with the Virgin's, sent to re-evangelise England" (*Catholicism*, 10).

13. See the biography of Forrest by Peter Holmes in the *Oxford Dictionary of National Biography* (http://www.oxforddnb.com/view/article/9892?doc Pos=1, accessed August 10, 2011). See also the additional biographical material on Forrest in John Milson, "William Mundy's 'Vox Patris Caelestis' and the Accession of Mary Tudor," *Music and Letters* 91.1 (2010): 1–38, esp. 2–9.

14. The text of this poem, which was published originally as a broadside ballad, is found in Hyder E. Rollins, ed., *Old English Ballads, 1553–1625* (Cambridge, UK: Cambridge University Press, 1920), 8–12. See also the ballad by Leonard Stopes (13–24), which celebrates Queen Mary in a series of stanzas whose initial words reproduce the first half of *Ave Maria*. A printed version of this appeared in *An Ave Maria in Commendation of our most Vertuous Quene* (1553?), sig. Ai. As Holmes notes, Forrest also composed for Mary a long poem titled "The History of Griseld the Second," celebrating her mother, Queen Katherine of Aragon (*Oxford Dictionary of National Biography*). Milson argues that Forrest composed the Marian "Vox Patris" as an allegorical political piece to be sung to Queen Mary on the way to her coronation ("Mundy's 'Vox Patris Caelestis,'" 1–38). In citing poetry and prose from the period, I modernize i/j and u/v forms and expand contractions. I retain original punctuation and capitalization.

15. Steven May and William Ringler, comps., *Elizabethan Poetry: A Bibliography and First-Line Index of English Verse, 1559–1603*, 3 vols. (London: Thoemmes Continuum, 2004), index some twenty Marian poems by William Forrest: EV 10455, 10642, 12295, 16878, 17607, 17975, 18219, 19639, 19719, 20136, 21922, 22774, 24795, 25621, 25682, 25724, 27804, 30324, 30779, 30784. Holmes calls attention to Forrest's ability to survive the change of regimes and England's reversion to an official Protestant church: "The accession of Elizabeth did not adversely affect Forrest who seems to have adapted yet again to a change in religious emphasis. He had been appointed parson of Bledlow in Buckinghamshire on 1 July 1556, and continued to hold this post for the next twenty years, despite the change of religion" (*Oxford Dictionary of National Biography*).

16. Waller, *Virgin Mary*, 116. Since the fourteenth century, England had been called "the dowry of Mary" or "Our Lady's Dowry." In the dedication to his poem *Palestina* ("Florence" [London], 1600), the Catholic author Robert Chambers ambiguously addresses both Queen Elizabeth and the Virgin Mary: "To our most Gracious, and Soveraigne Ladie and Princes, whose dowrie is little England, and the largest heavens her fayrest inheritance, all happinesse and heavenly blisse" (para. 3). I am grateful to Lucy Underwood for this reference. For a discussion of the use of the idea of the "dowry of our Lady" as a means of resistance for persecuted English Catholics, see Christopher Highley, *Catholics Writing the Nation in Early Modern Britain and Ireland* (Oxford, UK: Oxford University Press, 2008), 20–22.

17. This manuscript was edited as a doctoral dissertation by Joseph Patrick Kenna, "An Edition of the Marian Poems of the Recusant Writer, William Forrest, from MS. Harleian 1703" (Ph.D. diss., University of Notre Dame, 1960). I have used the British Library manuscript for the poems I cite, checking my text against Kenna's edition. I retain Forrest's strange habit of using strong punctuation to mark caesuras.

18. A poem not by Forrest included in Harley 1703, Lord Vaux's "I Loathe that i dyd love," is headed "A dyttye or sonet made by the lorde Vaus / in time of the noble queene Marye / representing the Image of deathe" (fol. 100). This poem assumes an Elizabethan vantage point. Another poem in the manuscript, John Heywood's "A discription of A most noble Ladye / advewed by John Heywoode; presently / who advertisinge her graces, as face / Saith of her thus, in much eloquent phrase' (fol. 108), has two concluding stanzas, probably by Forrest, explaining the identity of the woman praised, the Princess Mary (before she became queen):

This worthye ladye too beewraye
    a kinges doughter was shee,
Of whom John Heywood lyste to saye,
    in such worthye degree,

And Marye was her name weete yee,
    with these graces Indude,

At eightene yeares, so flourisht shee,
so doth his meane conclude.
(fol. 109)

Again, the past tense ("Mary was her name") indicates a date beyond Queen Mary's reign. Greg Walker, *Writing Under Tyranny: English Literature and the Henrician Reformation* (Oxford, UK: Oxford University Press, 2005), notes that this poem was composed at a key moment: "To produce such a text at the time when Mary was being deprived of her royal title and the Henrician court was re-forming around the new queen, Anne Boleyn, gave the claims for Mary's timeless beauty and virtue a powerful political charge" (103). The poem was printed in every edition of Tottel's *Miscellany*, but in a text differing considerably from that in Harley 1703. See Richard Tottel, *Tottel's Miscellany, 1557–1587*, rev. ed., 2 vols., ed. Hyder Edward Rollins (Cambridge, MA: Harvard University Press, 1966), 2: 274–76.

19. Milson states that this collection, "was compiled over an unspecified number of years but including the period 1572–1581" ("Mundy's 'Vox Patris Caelestis,'" 3).

20. The full text of this poem is reproduced in Milson, "Mundy's 'Vox Patris Caelestis,'" 37–38.

21. Forrest writes, "Though some dothe holde: the contrarye, / she, in the earth: to putryfye," he has Protestants in mind, not reluctant Catholics. The belief in the Assumption becomes a hard-line Catholic marker. And Forrest refers to the Catholic Church when he writes, "In thinges, that Reason cannot preeve: / we ought Christes Churche for to beleeve, / whiche holdeth, she sowle and boadye: / to bee Assumpte."

22. Hackett, *Virgin Mother*, 159, argues that the poem was written shortly after the destruction of the shrine, but stylistically this seems unlikely, although the poem may precede the composition by Sir Walter Ralegh of his "Walsingham" poem ("As You Came from the Holy Land," in *The Poems of Sir Walter Ralegh: A Historical Edition*, ed. Michael Rudick [Tempe, AZ: Renaissance English Text Society and Arizona Center for Medieval and Renaissance Studies, 1999], 16–17). Waller, *Virgin Mary*, 123, notes that the piece is ascribed to Philip Howard in Bodleian MS Rawlinson Poetical 219.

23. I quote the text of this poem as found in H. R. Woudhuysen and David Norbrook, eds., *The Penguin Book of Renaissance Verse* (London: Penguin, 1992), 531–32.

24. See Waller, *Virgin Mary*, 125; and Bradley Brookshire, "'Bare ruin'd quiers, where late the sweet birds sang': Covert Speech in William Byrd's 'Walsingham Variations,'" in *Walsingham in Literature and Culture*, ed. Janes and Waller, 199–216.

25. It precedes the famous piece by Thomas Alfield about Campion's death, "Why doe I use my paper ynke and pen."

26. Ruth Hughey, ed., *The Arundel Harington Manuscript of Tudor Poetry*, 2 vols. (Columbus: Ohio State University Press, 1960), 2: 56, points out that "mownt more hye" is written in pencil in the right margin here in the same hand as the rest of the text. The parentheses signal the scribe's emendation.

27. Hughey, *Arundel Harington Manuscript*, 1: 105–6.

28. Hughey, *Arundel Harington Manuscript*, 2: 56.

29. For this purpose, William Cecil, Lord Burghley, wrote *The Execution of Justice in England* (1583), provoking the response by William, Cardinal Allen, *A True, Sincere, and Modest Defense of English Catholics* (1584).

30. For a study of the use of the rosary by Catholics in early modern England, see Anne Dillon, "Praying by Number: The Confraternity of the Rosary and the English Catholic Community, c. 1580–1700," *History* 88 (2003): 451–71.

31. "Jil" is "Gill" or "Jill" (*Oxford English Dictionary*, definition 1a, "A familiar or contemptuous term applied to a woman; a lass, wench").

32. "Sermon on the Plowers, January 18, 1548," in *Selected Sermons of Hugh Latimer*, ed. Allan G. Chester (Charlottesville: University Press of Virginia, 1968), 30. Chester notes the charge of error leveled in 1536 at those radical reformers who claimed "that our lady was no better than another woman, and like a bag of pepper or saffron when the spice is out; and that she can do no more with Christ than another sinful woman." Robert Miola cites a Catholic poem from British Library MS Additional 15225 that complains that "The mother of our living God / . . . compared is by many a Jack / Unto a saffron bag" ("Catholic Writings," in *A New Companion to English Renaissance Literature and Culture*, 2 vols., ed. Michael Hattaway [Oxford: Wiley-Blackwell, 2010], 1: 451).

33. Shell, *Catholicism*, 200, mentions the censoring in print of the twenty-third stanza of "Jerusalem, my happy home": "Our Ladie singes *magnificat*, / with tune surpassinge sweete, / And all the virginns beare their partes, / siting aboue her feete" (Rollins, *Old English Ballads*, 169, from text of the poem in British Library MS Additional 15225, fols. 36v–37v). A poem on the Magnificat is found in Robert Chambers's *Palestina*, sig. G3.

34. *Moeoniae* (1595) has five of the Marian poems on sigs. B1–3, but the poems on "The death of our Ladie" and "The Assumption of our Lady" are omitted. For a discussion of Southwell's attachment to Mary as the protector of the English Mission through his membership in the Jesuit Sodality of the Blessed Virgin Mary and his apologetic and apostolic strategies in his Marian poetry, see Scott R. Pilarz, *Robert Southwell and the Mission of Literature, 1561–1595* (Aldershot, UK: Ashgate, 2004), 219–28. For a discussion of Marian devotion and poetry, see also Louis L. Martz, *The Poetry of Meditation*, rev. ed. (New Haven, CT: Yale University Press, 1962), 96–112. For a discussion of the place of Marian poetry in Southwell's work and its publication, I am also indebted to a paper by Robert Miola presented at a CUNY Graduate Center Renaissance Seminar "Publishing the Word: Robert Southwell's Poetry" (February 2011).

35. See Waller, *Virgin Mary*, 118–19, for a discussion of this poem in relation to Southwell's Marian piety and to English Protestant sensibilities.

36. I cite the text from Robert Southwell, *The Poems of Robert Southwell, S.J.*, ed. James H. McDonald and Nancy Pollard Brown (Oxford, UK: Clarendon Press, 1967), 12.

37. See the discussion of Constable in Hackett, *Virgin Mother*, 137–39; and Shell, *Catholicism*, 107–8, 122–27.

38. I cite the text of Constable's poetry from Henry Constable, *The Poems of Henry Constable*, ed. Joan Grundy (Liverpool, UK: University of Liverpool Press, 1960). This poem appears on p. 189.

39. Helen Hackett remarks, "The erotic/religious/political devotion of the Elizabethan courtier to his Queen provides Constable with a language for reconversion to service of the heavenly Queen" (*Virgin Mother*, 139).

40. Constable, *Poems*, 190.

41. Constable, *Poems*, 185. In his online *Catalogue of English Literary Manuscripts*, Peter Beal points out that this poem was first published in the second edition of Donne's *Poems* (1635) and that it is found in ten surviving manuscripts, some of which have large collections of Donne's writings (British Library MS Stowe 962, Harvard MS Eng. 966.5, Huntington MS EL 6893, and Yale Osborn MS b 114). It is found in Berkeley Castle, Select Books 85, p. 5, as part of a quire of poems titled "Certen Spirituall Sonnetts to the honner of God and his Sainctes: Withe Nyne other directed by particuler devotion to :3: blessed Maryes: by Hen. Conestable Esquire." In British Library MS Harley 7553 it is part of what Beal describes as a "quarto composite volume of papers relating to religious matters, in various hands . . . incorporating . . . a series of seventeen 'Spirituall Sonnettes To the honour of God: and hys Sayntes. by H: C:." It shows up, surprisingly, in the parliamentarian Robert Overton's verse and prose miscellany, Princeton MS CO199, no. 812.

42. I quote from the text found in Steven W. May, *The Elizabethan Courtier Poets: The Poems and Their Contexts* (Columbia: University of Missouri Press, 1991), 354–55. May points out that these four stanzas "were omitted from the 1606 print, no doubt because their exaltation of the Virgin Mary was considered too 'Romish' for publication even in Jacobean England" (219). See May's discussion of the printed edition's deleted stanzas on pp. 349–50. His text of these is taken from manuscript pages bound with a Folger Shakespeare Library's copy of Robert Southwell's *Saint Peters Complaynt* (STC 22957).

43. The text of this poem is reproduced in *The Penguin Book of Renaissance Verse*, ed. Woudhuysen and Norbrook, 531–32. The four poems that constitute the collection of Catholic verse in this manuscript are in the same hand. Another hand adds a moralizing six-line poem about a miser. Most of the remaining (and some of the preceding) folios of this bound manuscript are blank.

44. May, *Elizabethan Courtier Poets*, 255.

45. May, *Elizabethan Courtier Poets*, 104. May points out that the stanza survives only in the version of the poem found in Folger Shakespeare Library MS V.a.164, fols. 134ff.

46. I reproduce the text from William Camden, *Remains Concerning Britain*, ed. R. D. Dunn (Toronto: University of Toronto Press, 1984), 352. The "first" maid in heaven was, of course, the Virgin Mary.

47. Similarly in Aemilia Lanyer's *Salve Deus Rex Judaeorum*, for example, the section of the poem addressed to Mary depicts her not as a Mother of God but, more restrictedly, as a humble "Mother of Our Lord" (l. 1031) who has a "submissive heart" (l. 1073), "Servant, Mother, Wife, and Nurse / To heaven's bright King (ll. 1087–88). Text cited from Aemilia Lanyer, *The Poems of Aemilia Lanyer*, ed. Susanne Woods (Oxford, UK: Oxford University Press, 1993), 95, 97–98. Having "Servant" precede "Mother" and keeping "King" at some grammatical distance blurs the traditional identity of Mary as "Mother of God." Following "Mother" with "Wife," the second term referring to the soul of the believing Christian as spouse of Christ, pushes the term in a metaphoric direction. For a good discussion of *The Song of Mary* as a Catholic work carefully designed to be acceptable to a Protestant audience, see Alison Shell, "What Is a Catholic Poem? Explicitness and Censorship in Tudor and Stuart Religious Verse," in *Literature and Censorship in Renaissance England*, ed. Andrew Hadfield (London: Palgrave, 2001), 99–102.

48. See the discussion of the connection between anti-Mariolatry and misogyny in Stuart England by Frances E. Dolan, *Whores of Babylon: Catholicism, Gender, and Seventeenth-Century Print Culture* (Ithaca, NY: Cornell University Press, 1999), 95–156.

2

Phebe Jensen

Religious Identity and the English Landscape

William Blundell and the Harkirk Coins

As recent scholarship has shown, the dissolution of the monasteries during the reign of Henry VIII radically changed both the English countryside and the representation of that landscape in polemical, chorographical, and imaginative texts. Margaret Aston has argued that the physical devastation of churches, abbeys, and monasteries created a "spectacle of physical loss" that affected even "those whose Protestant convictions made them wholly endorse the process at large," spurring "nostalgia and poetry" as well as increased antiquarian interest in the medieval period.[1] These physical destructions provoked textual reimaginings of the English landscape that provided new interpretations of England's past and contributed to discourses of England as an emerging Protestant nation.[2] For example, as Jennifer Summit has recently shown, whereas for late medieval chorographers such as William of Worcester the lives of the medieval English saints provided the primary geographic coordinates by which England's topography was defined and navigated, the sixteenth-century chorographies of John Leland, John Speed, and William Camden "translated" or erased those saints, progressively also obscuring the monastic and abbey ruins that disturbingly recalled the violence of the Reformation. In such ways early modern Protestant writers participated in a larger project through which the English landscape was "forcibly remade, its formerly sacred spaces actively converted, like its inhabitants, to support new structures of belief and government."[3]

In this context the antiquarian activities of William Blundell, a Catholic recusant landowner who lived in Little Crosby, Chester, from 1560 to 1638, can provide a way of exploring alternative, Catholic ideas about landscape and nationhood that resisted (and perhaps informed) mainstream Protestant discourse. Blundell's manuscript writings, preserved in a family miscellany known as the Great Hodge Podge and in other papers, include translations of the work of Luis de Granada, original songs and ballads, and detailed narratives of the persecutions suffered by Blundell's family, his servants, and his tenants at the hands of both local and national authorities.[4] Blundell wrote one antiquarian tract: an account of the cache of primarily Anglo-Saxon coins discovered on his estate in 1611. The coins were found in a makeshift graveyard that Blundell had created for Catholics after the sexton in nearby Sefton had barred Catholic corpses from the parish churchyard. Modern scholarship has determined that the treasure was deposited by Danes in the early tenth century. It includes coins from the reigns of the Anglo-Saxon kings Alfred the Great and Edward the Elder; the Dane, Cnut of Northumbria; the ninth- and early-tenth-century Italian kings Berengarius and Hludovicus; and the ninth-century French king Charles-le-Simple. The cache also holds ecclesiastical coins of Northumberland and East Anglia, and one coin was apparently minted by Plegmund, archbishop of Canterbury from 891 to 923. Blundell recorded this spectacular find with pen and ink sketches of the coins; he turned the sketches into copperplate impressions, which circulated among his neighbors in the north of England. Blundell also described the events surrounding the discovery of the coins, and he used his extensive learning and library to write a historical narrative that describes their medieval origins.[5]

D. R. Woolf's invaluable account of this event shows that the circumstances surrounding the find, coupled with Blundell's narrative effort to assess it, reveal the lineaments of a broader "historical culture" of seventeenth-century England, a culture Blundell shared with amateur and professional antiquarians across the confessional divide. As Woolf demonstrates, Blundell's explication of the coins is in most ways unpolemical.[6] But although Blundell's narrative illuminates broad habits of historical thinking that transcend religious controversy, it also expresses an understanding of the relationship between sacred land and English nation that reflects the writer's personal experience as an early modern recusant property owner. It reflects a Catholic, Anglocentric vision of English nationhood then being constructed, as Christopher Highley has recently shown, in the expatriate writings of Elizabethan and Jacobean Catholic exiles.[7] In addition, the incidental representation of Anglo-Saxon saints in this tract reveals an identifiably Counter-Reformation sense of the English landscape as a matrix of sacred sites associated with divine and saintly miracles.

Recent scholarship has demonstrated that the priests of the continental Counter-Reformation, in Alexandra Walsham's words, "sought to harness and revitalise the late medieval geography of the sacred" and that "there is much to suggest that . . . Welsh and English priests employed similar strategies, suitably modified to obviate the considerable problems posed by persecution and proscription."[8] Blundell's narrative, especially compared to his personal experience as a recusant landowner, reveals an identifiably Catholic belief in the importance of traditional holy sites through which God and the saints spoke to the Anglo-Saxon monarchs and to the beleaguered Catholic faithful of early modern England.

William Blundell's life was defined by his refusal to renounce Catholicism and the risks he incurred as a result. Born in 1560, Blundell was educated at Douay with his brother Richard, who later became a priest. As he reveals in an account of his "troubles" included in the Great Hodge Podge, in June 1590 pursuivants searching Little Crosby manor discovered "one Mr. Woodroffe, a seminarie priest" (21).[9] For this offense Blundell and his father, also named Richard, were imprisoned at Chester Castle, where the father died in 1591 or 1592, leaving William Blundell the lord of Little Crosby. From this time until the civil war, parts of Blundell's estates were intermittently searched, seized, and leased out on account of the family's recusancy, and Blundell himself spent most of the 1590s in prison or exile. In 1593, for example, Blundell was "apprehended" and imprisoned locally before being transported to London and then Canterbury for interrogation by Whitgift, then archbishop of Canterbury, and imprisonment at "the Gatehouse of Westminster" until July 1595 (22–23); in 1598, after local authorities searched his house, Blundell's wife and other local Catholics (including his sister-in-law, Elin Blundell) were seized and imprisoned in Chester Castle. In this case Blundell himself escaped, "tarried secretly att Countrie houses some 3 quarters of a yeare," fled with his newly released wife into Wales, where they lived for several years, and returned to England to live under an alias in Staffordshire, where he remained "untill the Queene's death, where, comminge home, I soone after obtained from K. James a free and large pardon" (23–24).

As this narrative suggests, like many English recusants, William Blundell's hold on his family's ancestral estate was tenuous. Because of recusancy, his land, livestock, and property were subject to searches, attacks, and seizures, and at times Blundell chose to abandon his property altogether and retreat (to Wales and Staffordshire) instead of risking further imprisonment. Blundell wrote about his experiences in both prose and verse in the Great Hodge Podge, including the poem "A Doleful Ditty," a response to the "persecution made in Sefton Parish, especially by . . . Vaughan, Bishop of Chester, and Nutter, parson of Sefton and Deane of Chester" in the early 1590s. In this poem Blundell laments that "Howses with our growndes we must sett to others, / And in other coasts seeke our dwellinge place" (25). Blundell's concern about the risk of losing his "growndes" is suggested by the scrupulous list of how his lands were "begged . . . for Recusancie" from 1592 until 1624 (31).[10] To Blundell the fact that he was able to retain possession of his estate was proof of God's protection. In the 1590s "Charles Grimston had gott a new grant of 2 parts of my lands, and laboured to gett a Composition, but through god's goodnesse hee had nothing" (31). In 1601 "Gervise Travise . . . laboured verie busilie to gett possession or Composition, but (blessed bee god) gott neither." The failure of Ambrose Astell to get any more property than a single head of cattle when "hee came to sease uppon my goods" in a 1613 incident elicits a prayer of thankfulness from Blundell: "Blessed bee god for all his mercies and goodnesse for evermore, Amen" (33).

Like other early modern recusant landowners, Blundell was conscious that he valued his religious convictions over his property and was confident that his ability to hold onto his "growndes" was proof of God's approval of his continued commitment to Roman Catholicism. The experience of being a recusant brought with it the risk of exile, which he suffered intermittently, as well as what Highley has termed the sense of "internal exile" experienced by "stay-at-home Catholics."[11] That sense of internal exile is vividly suggested in the Star Chamber testimony of the bailiff Robert Becconsall concerning the 1624 effort by the sheriff of Lancaster to seize the property of Edward Rice, a Little Crosby recusant who had missed an Assize Court appearance in 1622.[12] After seizing "two oxen and a nag" belonging to Rice, the sheriff's party allegedly were set on by "haulf a Hundred persons or thereabouts out of litle Crosby, beinge able people and well weaponed with pykeforks, longstaves and muckroukes, one speare or pyke for warre and other weapons," who forcibly took back Rice's livestock. Passing by the manor house at Little Crosby, the bailiffs witnessed the household and tenants locked inside.

> And [as the bailiffs] passed by the said house the gates and doores were presently shutt, locked or barred and divers gentlefolkes, men and women, both yonge and olde, looked forth at the casements to the said house upon [the bailiffs], and William Blundell and Emilia his wife looked out from the casements and Mr. Blundell and his wife incourraged the persons who made the rescue to do the same.[13]

Even given that this testimony is by a hostile witness, the image here suggests that the household felt itself in a state of actual as well as metaphorical siege. As a poem in a seventeenth-century Catholic commonplace book from Warwickshire suggests, recusants at times saw themselves as islands of true Englishness, reduced to the tiny territories of their households. The first lines of the poem, "Att my house at home," introduces the idea that will be the poem's central allegory.

> This house is England's ile
> Of late renowned by fame
> But now by errours guile
> Is fallen out of frame
> And I the church the goodwife Am
> Which makes this wofull mone
> And Jesus christ is my good man
> Which now is gone from home.[14]

The constant threat of seizures and attacks, the sense of siege, the need to create a literal (and probably psychological) barricade and to defend turf with "pykeforks, longstaves . . . muckroukes," and spears, and the providential rescue "through god's goodnesse" all suggest that the recusant manor could feel like a metaphorical country that had to be defended in the name of the Catholic covenant with God. As glimpsed in "Att my house at home," this experience created a vision of nationhood that identified England as a household "out of frame," awaiting the return of the householder (Christ) to restore the true church. For the Blundells the true English nation had shrunk to the grounds of their manor house.

This Catholic alienation is also powerfully expressed in the events leading up to the creation of the Harkirk burial ground. The graveyard was established after a gruesome incident, later described by Margerie Coppalla, a witness for the defense in the Star Chamber case brought against Blundell for the 1624 fracas. Coppalla told how her mother

> dyeinge att Inceblundell was brought to the parish Churche of Sefton to have beene buried, and the then Minister of Sefton refused to burie the said deade person, after which refusall the said Jane Harvie was buried in the highway neare unto a Cross standinge in a lane called Crosse lane, after whic buriall the swyne rooted the earth upon the grave of the said Jane, and [she, Margerie] after carried sand and stones to fill upp the said grave withall.[15]

The rejection of the physical body of a dead Catholic from English ecclesiastical ground, the violation of the body (by unclean animals no less), and the resulting sense of desecration make this incident a visceral symbol of the English Catholic's internal exile and alienation. In response, as he wrote in his account of the creation of the graveyard, Blundell "caused a litle peece of grownde to bee enclosed within myne owne demaine land in a place called of ould tyme (as it is nowe also) the Harkirke."[16] To create the graveyard, Blundell had the site "dytched and enclosed it on twoe sydes (for theothere twoe sydes were fenced before)" (45). This alternative burial site was particularly resonant with the medieval church, for Harkirk means "old, hoary church" in Anglo-Saxon; oral tradition established the land's pre-Reformation sacredness.[17] By providing a resting place for Catholic corpses exiled from the territory of the parish church, Blundell develops an alternative site for the observance of the Catholic faith, a site that recalls the Catholicism of England's past through an etymological trace that associates it with medieval religion.

Blundell's creation of the Harkirk graveyard reflects what Lisa McClain, Anne Dillon, and Alexandra Walsham have noted about early modern recusant culture more broadly: its ability to improvise sacred sites, objects, and rituals in the absence of an official church and the traditional material elements of Catholic worship and piety.[18] It is clear that Blundell was, in McClain's words, "using what's at hand" in partitioning off a piece of land that was both spiritually appropriate (because of its possible associations with an old church) and practical (it was already fenced on two sides).[19] In creating sacred space out of an ordinary plot of land, Blundell was, to adapt Summit's argument about Leland, "translating" late medieval conceptions of sacred sites and places in a way that reflected the practical needs of early modern recusants and the imperatives of Counter-Reformation spirituality.[20] This translation is articulated, as McClain has noted, in the creation of new ideas about sacred sites in Robert Southwell's *Short Rule of Good Life*. Southwell urges recusants to make their houses and land serve the same function that in the Middle Ages was performed by pilgrimage sites, describing how he himself uses his imagination to create virtual shrines.

> If I will keepe my minde continually attentive in goodnes, and goe in continual awe of offending, I may take this course. I must in every roome of the house where I dwell, imagine in some decent place thereof, a throne or chaire of estate, & dedicate the same and the whole roome to some Saint, that whensoever I enter into it, I enter as it were into a chappell or church that is devoted to such a

Saint, and therefore in minde doe that reverence that is due to them.[21]

Here, in the standard spiritual move of the Counter-Reformation, what had been external and usually distant sites of pilgrimage have moved into an interior domestic space and then even further inward, into the mind of the individual Christian. Southwell is recommending imaginary, not actual, shrines and indeed devotes several pages to designing strategies that will "helpe [one's] memory, and . . . avoid confusion" when recalling memorials that are not physically present. The imagination changes the ordinary into the sacred, a phenomenon McClain demonstrates to have occurred frequently with recusants who used ordinary rooms or clearings as chapels and domestic objects as altars, chalices, and rosaries.[22]

Even more important for understanding Blundell's transformation of Harkirk and his later antiquarian tract, Southwell extends these recommendations to include the grounds and lands, for "not only in the house, but also in the wallkes, gardens, and orchards about the house may I doe the same: and so make my walkes as it were short pilgrimages, to visit such Saints as are patrones of the place I goe unto."[23] As in the Catholic ballad "At our house at home," it seems that the larger ground of England shrinks to the confines of the recusant estate, which is now a microcosm of the land once traversed by pilgrimage routes. Southwell's directive may also reflect a larger Counter-Reformation effort to confirm the special sanctity of specific places.[24] Given the threat of exile, imprisonment, and martyrdom always present to the recusant householder, the early modern Catholic estate could itself be seen as a newly sacred site that had replaced the desecrated saint's shrines, monasteries, and abbeys.

The creation of the Harkirk burial ground can be seen, then, as part of a larger recusant pattern through which sacred sites were improvised in the face of present necessity but with an eye toward the traditions of the past. As a symbol of Blundell's willingness to use his land for the local Catholic community, the ground there was particularly well prepared for the powerful symbolism of the coins' sudden appearance, the day after the first burial in April 1611. According to Blundell's written account, after "an old tenant" of Blundell's was refused burial at the Sefton churchyard,

> the Neighbours . . . whoe caried and attended or accompanied the corse, came to the foresaid place in my grownd, which they or some of the cheefeste of them had hearde was by mee enclosed from the reste of my grownde there for such a purpose: And there buried the Corpes about twelve a Clocke. (46)

The next day, "a servant boye of myne of fowerteene yeares old" took a shortcut through the graveyard, coming into the site by hopping over a stone wall, where "hee sawe uppon the sandie coppe caste within the sayde place certayne peeces of Coyne scattered (as it seemed) with the throwinge of them with the sand owte of the dytch" (46).

As Woolf notes, the insistence that the coins were found on, not in, the ground, probably reflects Blundell's precise understanding of the Tudor-Stuart laws of treasure trove, which dictated different rules for the dispensation of artifacts found on or beneath the surface.[25] But Blundell also interprets the find as a small miracle, "a sign of divine pleasure at Blundell's charity and the people's adherence to Catholic burial rites."[26] Blundell's initial response to the discovery suggests his understanding of his role in God's sacred economy. God is recompensing him for his religious steadfastness, and the first thing Blundell does with the coins is to return some of them to the church by having them melted down and made into a pyx and a chalice, items that remained at Little Crosby's Catholic church in the nineteenth century.[27] The significance of this act is clear. As Woolf writes:

> In . . . returning the coins into historical time, and giving them back to the church, Blundell was . . . reversing a painful episode of more recent history, the spoliation of church plate and property that had begun during the reign of Henry VIII, when, as Blundell put it, new religions had been "coined" each day, out of monastic and chantry property.[28]

Blundell's gesture symbolically reversed the Reformation, revealing his awareness of his role in a sacred economy that connected him to God through the conduit of the English land.

If Blundell's first offering to God in response to the coins was the pyx and chalice, the second was a copperplate engraving of the coins—arranged in a cross to further underscore the divine message they conveyed—that was published and distributed "in the country."[29] The third offering was the antiquarian account of the coins, which Blundell wrote with the aid of a wide range of chronicles and chorographies, including the late medieval chronicles of William of Malmesbury and Roger of Hoveden, the *Polychronicon* of Ranulf Higden, Polydore Vergil's *Anglica Historia*, John Foxe's *Acts and Monuments*, Thomas Stapleton's translation of Bede, John Stow's *Annales*, William Camden's *Britannia*, Robert Parsons's *Treatise of Three Conversions*, and Richard Verstegen's *Restitution of Decayed Intelligence*.[30] The purpose of the narrative is to describe the coins' origins and especially to explain the pairings of names on the obverse and reverse sides.

As a result, the text is primarily structured around ink drawings of the coins, and Blundell's paragraphs jump from the reign of one Anglo-Saxon monarch to the next, as they move from "This coine" to "These twooe coins" to "These 6 precdent Coines" (53, 55, 59). The narrative becomes a series "of biographical mininarratives" of the Anglo-Saxon monarchs, primarily Alfred the Great but also Alfred's heir, Edward the Elder; Alfred's grandson, Aethelstan; and Edelstan, Edered, and Edmund, King and Martyr.[31] The text is digressive, wandering off into details that are not relevant to the parsing of the coins, and this may well be because, as Woolf suggests, Blundell lacks a sense of "the broader picture of Anglo-Danish history."[32] But it is within these digressions that Blundell's particularly Catholic understanding of the relationship between landscape, nation, and the English medieval past emerges.

In the broadest sense Blundell's work seizes on the discovery of Anglo-Saxon coins to interpret the past through the standard Anglocentrism of English Catholic history. As much recent work has shown, Tudor Reformers located the origins of the English church in the time of the ancient pre-Roman Britons (and often their mythical Trojan forefathers). This Protestant narrative of nationhood involved, in Donna Hamilton's words, "the privileging of British origins, a castigation of the Saxons as the brutal pagan intruders, and an emphasis on the British King Arthur as a descendant of Constantine and the source of the Tudor line."[33] As Philip Schywzer has recently shown, the "nationalism of the English" in the sixteenth century was in fact "British nationalism," although it was "a version of Britishness that served English interests."[34] Reformist historians did praise the virtue of particular Anglo-Saxon kings, especially Alfred the Great, who was (as John Foxe wrote) "worthy of high renowne and commendation."[35] But the dominant Tudor assessment of the Anglo-Saxon migration, thought at the time to be an invasion, was that through it (again in Foxe's words) "the miserable Britaines . . . were berived of their land, by the cruel subtilty of the Saxons," resulting in "the declining tyme of the Church and of true Religion, preparing the way to Antichrist, which not long after followed."[36]

In contrast, sixteenth- and early-seventeenth-century Catholic writers insisted that the English church and nation originated in the conversion of England by Rome and the close relationship of the Anglo-Saxon kings to the medieval Catholic church.[37] As Highley has shown, these arguments were expressed in writings by English Catholic exiles on the continent, especially during the polemical feud with Bishop Jewell in the 1560s, the decade that produced Thomas Stapleton's notorious translation of Bede, which became "the standard Catholic authority on the British past."[38]

Richard Verstegan's *Restitution of Decayed Intelligence*, with its startling (in 1605) claim that the English, like their language, descended from the German Saxons, continued in a different vein the argument made by both Stapleton and Robert Parsons's 1603–1604 *Treatise of Three Conversions*.[39]

In Robert S. Miola's words, Blundell took the opportunity presented to him by the revealed Anglo-Saxon coins to "advance . . . the Saxon argument" of Stapleton, Parsons, and Verstegan "through numismatics."[40] Blundell's narrative supports this argument not just by virtue of its subject, which was provided fortuitously (or providentially) by the coins themselves; the text also emphasizes the connections between the nation, the land, and the Roman church by stressing the centrality of Anglo-Saxon sainthood to the early English monarchy. The saints in Blundell's narrative are either kings themselves (Oswald; Edward the Confessor; Edmund, King and Martyr),[41] the relatives of kings (Elfegia, perhaps Aelfgifu, the widow of Edmund the Magnificent), or saints and ecclesiastical authorities who closely advised monarchs (Swithin, Cuthbert, Wilfred, Odo, Dunstan, and John of Beverley). The text describes King Alfred's devotion to Saint Cuthbert, King Aethelstan's love of St. John of Beverley, and the relationship between St. Dunstan and three different kings, Edmund the Magnificent, Edered, and Eadwerde the Elder: The first was "altogether counseled and led by St. Dunstan," the second "devoted his lyfe to God and St. Dunstan," and the third "preferred the Councell of St. Dunstan before all treasure" (58–59). In two cases the mention of the saints is necessary to Blundell's numismatic wonderings, as the names WFRED (which Blundell thinks might be Wilfred) and CUTHBERT appear on the coins, but the rest of the saints mentioned are irrelevant to the main topic of the text. What the digressions on Saints Cuthbert, John of Beverley, and Oswald do reveal is Blundell's characteristically Catholic understanding of the English sacred landscape as a topography defined by sacred sites that "offered access to a higher cosmic order, implying a proximity, even presence, of the Divine."[42] In Blundell's narrative the holy wells, churches, monasteries, and abbeys of Anglo-Saxon England commemorate the miraculous intervention of God through (and for) the English saints. In this way the anecdotes of the saints in Blundell's narrative reiterate the message of the Harkirk coins, in which God spoke directly to Blundell on the hallowed ground of the newly created graveyard.

The section of Blundell's narrative that most elaborately suggests the text's overall representation of a sacred landscape is the story of how, at the nadir of his fortunes, Alfred the Great received a vision of Cuthbert. This portion of the text—the longest of all its digressions—is actually a direct transcription from Parsons's *Treatise of Three Conversions*. Blundell includes the story ostensibly to explain why Alfred established a monastery at "Ethelinge, where St. Cudberht, appearinge unto him, encoraged and Comforted him, beinge in great distresse and heavines" (49–50). In this way the immediate rhetorical purpose of the Cuthbert anecdote is to define the sacredness of a particular site: the monastery established in commemoration of a divine visitation. Blundell may well have seen himself in Parsons's account of Alfred, for there are parallels between the representation of the land in the Cuthbert anecdote and in Blundell's own life. Alfred was so beset by Danes that "hee had onelie three shyres to hyde himself in upon the south Sea," so that he fled "into a little Iland in Somersetshyre called the Adelinge (wholye beset with waters and myre in the middest of Marishe grounde and a lttle wood joyned thereunto)." Having sent some of his men "to seeke some fishe by nighte (for that they durst not shewe themselves by daye)," Alfred and his mother went to sleep in a "sweinheardes howse," where,

> beinge entred into a little slumber, behoulde . . . there appeared to the K. St. Cudberht, tellinge him both his name and that he was sente by God to comforte him, and to tell him that albeit his justice had hitherto chastened Englishe for there sinnes by the swoorde of the Danes, yet that hee woulde not extinguishe them in respecte of so manie saints that had bine of that nation; and from this daye forward woulde set them upp againe. Nowe at length God for the meritte of English saints doth looke upon England with the eye of mercie. (50)[43]

As Woolf notes, here, as in other points in the text, Blundell is "obliquely commenting on the present"; just as Cuthbert came from England's past to comfort Alfred, so this story comes from the Anglo-Saxon era to assure early modern English Catholics that for the sake of the holy saints who "had bine of that nation," God would "looke upon England with the eye of mercie" (50).[44] The anecdote also reflects Blundell's own struggles with his property as an English recusant. For Alfred the territory of the true English "nation" had shrunk in the face of Danish incursions, first to three shires and then to the island of Aetheling, described to suggest a sense of siege ("wholye beset with waters and myre" [50]). The message of the visitation is verbally articulated by Cuthbert, but Cuthbert also sends a material "signe or token" to Alfred, one that recalls the coins that miraculously emerged from the graveyard at Harkirk. In this case the sign emerges from the river, where Alfred's men had been sent off on their unpromising expedition. Cuthbert promises that they will return "loaden with incredible abundance of fish," and so they do: Even though "that night was a verie contrarie tyme for fishes," the men return with "so greate store of fishe as it might seeme to be sufficient to satisfye the hunger of never so greate an armie" (51), a miracle that replicates Jesus's transformation of five loaves and two fishes in the Gospels.[45] As a direct result of the dream, Alfred is "encouraged" to "adventure . . . a strange attempt": infiltrating the Danish camp disguised as a minstrel, a gambit that provides him with the intelligence he needs to rout the Danes the next day and to begin a series of military successes "untill hee had recovered all his whole kingdome againe" (52). Cuthbert's visitation, then, is a sacred intervention that not only marks off the island at Atheling as a holy site but also sets in motion a series of events that lead to the creation of a unified English nation. For Parsons, as for Blundell, God defines the England he will save through the history of the saints "that had bine of that nation," and he articulates that message both through Saint Cuthbert and through the topography of England, in the form of a river suddenly abundant with fish.[46]

In the story of Alfred's dream, like the story of the Harkirk coins, the English past speaks to the English present through the territory of the English land. Blundell draws other parallels between the difficulties faced by Alfred and other Anglo-Saxon kings and the situation of early modern English Catholics. The narrative equates the destruction of the marauding Danes with the dissolution of the monasteries when it describes how King Edered, who "erected a newe the Abbey of Crowland (belyke destroyed afore by Danes)," was "sorry that by destruction of the monastery prayers for the soules of kings his predecessors have bine intermitted, with charter subscribed by twooe Archbishoppes, fower Bishopps, manie Abbots and Earles, the kinge, sealed with seales of goulde" (59). The same sense of timeless traditions lost is invoked when Blundell elsewhere describes how the payment of "Peter pence" that began with "Inas K. of the west Saxons" was "continuallie paide by all our kings till K. Henrie the 8 whoe paide it also for above twentie yeares of his raigne, untill hee brake offe from the Pope and Sea of Rome for causes whiche all men knowe" (48). Whereas the invasion of the Danes is seen as historical precedent for the dissolution of the monasteries—and as Highley has shown, "from a Catholic perspective, the new religion was itself a foreign innovation"—Blundell's record of the establishment of monasteries, abbeys, and churches by Alfred, Aethelstan, Offa, Edelstan, Ingulphe, and Edered can be seen to imaginatively reverse the dissolution, as the text reestablishes monastic foundations that had been destroyed by 1611.

In several ways, then, the story of Cuthbert can be seen to recertify the importance of sacred sites. This subtext of Blundell's treatise is also evident in the text's shorter digressions on St. John of Beverley and St. Oswald. Blundell describes how King Aethelstan, who was particularly devoted to St. John, was on his way to the Battle of Brunnaburh when he detoured to visit the church in Beverley that held Saint John's relics. As a result of this visit,

> God so blessed his devotion as in the battell hee slewe . . . the Kinge of Scotts and fyve kings more, 12 Earles, innumerable multitude of his enemies, and gott one of the the greatest victories that ever englishe wonne, and in his returne gave greate gifts and privileges to St. John of Beverley, and made it a sanctuarie for all debtors and malefactors. (57)

As in the Cuthbert anecdote, it was the power of the sacred site associated with an earlier Anglo-Saxon saint that created a military victory for the "englishe," and, as recompense for this success, the site was further acknowledged as an important holy spot and given the special status of "sanctuarie."

Similarly, the digression on Saint Oswald is as much about the presence of two sacred sites commemorating him in early modern England as it is about the medieval doings of the saint himself. Blundell's purpose in discussing Saint Oswald is not to parse a particular coin but rather to intervene in an apparently long-running dispute about whether Saint Oswald died near "winwicke" (in Lancashire) or "Osestree" (Oswestry, in Shropshire): "And thus I have thought good to take or rather seeke occasion here to write of the place of this blessed K. and martir his death, because the same is by wronge information saide in a late pious booke to have bine at Osestree" (56). Identifying the correct site of Oswald's martyrdom is vital because it is a place of special, potentially efficacious holiness, like St. Oswald's well appropriate for "greate pilgremage" (56). The narrative almost adopts the language of travelogue as Blundell provides precise information about the site of the battle where Oswald was killed and the location of a nearby holy well also dedicated to the saint, describing, for example, the "little well walled with stone within, which the people call St. Oswald's well," that lies "on that syde of Newton parke wch is towards Winwick not eight roods . . . from the pale" (55).[47]

The precision of the directions underscores the importance to Blundell of preserving correct information about the holy spot, perhaps for reinsertion into the oral and manuscript networks so crucial to the recusant community. Those channels of communication are indeed foregrounded in the

Oswald passage. Although Blundell cites a verse tribute to Oswald engraved at Winwick Church from the Latin edition of Camden's *Britannia*, he supplements that printed authority with personal correspondence from "a Catholique gentleman, a friend of mine, whoe had dwelte heretofore nere to the saide place" (55). That "gentleman" tells Blundell the specific information about St. Oswald's well and that "the people thereaboute have yet in there mouthes" another story about Oswald founding Winwick Church. Blundell's reliance on letters and anecdotes is characteristic, as Woolf shows, of early-seventeenth-century "historical culture," but oral and manuscript transmission of information was also crucial, for different reasons, to the early modern recusant community.[48] Like the stories "yet in there mouthes," the letter from the Catholic gentleman, and the name of the Harkirk site, Blundell's own writings, some of which (as Margaret Sena has shown) circulated within recusant manuscript networks, may have functioned as a way of preserving information about sacred Catholic sites on the English landscape.[49]

The attitude toward holy sites in Blundell's narrative reflects a particularly Catholic idea of the relationship between the saints, the land, and the nation, but that is not to say that antiquarian interest in saints and monasteries necessarily indicates Catholic sympathies. Michael Drayton directly refutes that claim in the twenty-fourth book of his chorographical poem, *Poly-Olbion*, published with the second part of the work in 1622. This section of the poem provides a chronicle of British and English saints, organized chronologically as well as geographically. At the start of the eclogue, Drayton's narrator, the River Welland, anticipates that she will be accused of "vaine worship" because of her subject. But, she assures her readers, she is herself "as free / As is the most precise" from such charges; she records the "venerable names" of the saints because it is "Antiquitie I love."[50]

William Camden was provoked into a similar self-defense in the "Preface to the Reader" included in later editions of his *Britannia*, in which he noted that "there are certain, as I heare who take it impatiently that I have mentioned some of the most famous Monasteries and their founders."[51] Camden's work indeed provides a clear example of what Aston has shown to be characteristic Protestant regret at the devastations of the Reformation.[52] Camden records the haunting presence of ruined abbeys and monasteries on the land and describes the events of the dissolution as "a sudden floud" that "breaking thorow the banks with a maine streme, fell upon the Ecclesiasticall State of England; which whiles the world stood amazed, and England groned thereat, bare downe and utterly overthrew the greatest part of the Clergie, together with their most goodly and beautiful houses."[53] Both the eradication of the saints from cultural memory—what Drayton's narrator laments as the "blot[ting]" of the "venerable names" of the saints "from memory"—and the destruction of the monasteries could be lamented on aesthetic and historical grounds, not religious ones.[54]

As the examples of Camden and Drayton suggest, neither an antiquarian interest in saints nor an investment in the ancient holy sites of England always suggested Catholic sympathies. In fact, Protestants retained an attachment to religiously charged places and times, and on the other side Counter-Reformation authorities sought to reform the excesses of medieval ritual devotion, including pilgrimage.[55] In England not all holy sites were demolished at the Reformation; some, like St. Winifred's Well, were adapted to Protestant uses, their healing powers confirmed but reascribed to God's providentialism, not the intervention of an Anglo-Saxon saint.[56] Even though wholesale destruction was the most visible and notorious aspect of the English reform of medieval holy sites, English Protestants, as they reinterpreted the relationship between the Divine and specific places within a post-Reformation framework, adapted rather than rejected wholesale Catholic beliefs in the enhanced sacredness of specific times and places.[57]

But although Catholic and Protestant ideas about holy sites had some similarities and even overlapped, Blundell's emphasis on saints and monasteries as demarcating sacred sites is definitively Catholic. It is significant that even though the Harkirk graveyard was not identified with a particular saint, Blundell's tract connected it to Saint Cuthbert through the parallel story carefully chosen from Parsons. The way in which the English land was reconceptualized to erase the traces of medieval sacred sites can be seen in the different representations of Athelney Abbey—the monastery that Blundell imagines to have been founded by Alfred to commemorate Cuthbert's dream—in Leland's *Itinerary*, Foxe's *Acts and Monuments*, the chorographies of Camden and John Speed, and the *Life of Alfred*, a history by the Protestant biographer Robert Powell.[58] When Leland conducted his perambulation of Somerset in the 1530s, there was still "a bridge of wood to entre to thabbay," but the abbot of Athelney surrendered to royal commissioners in February 1539, at which time the building was presumably dismantled.[59] Foxe does not mention the establishment of the abbey at all in *Acts and Monuments*, although he does briefly refer to the story of Alfred's dream of Cuthbert, which he dismisses as a "dreaming fable." As in the Protestant reinterpretation of St. Winifred's Well, Foxe insists that Alfred's victory after the retreat at Athelney was the result not of the intervention of the saint but rather of Alfred being "strengthened and comforted more, through the providence of God."[60] By the time Camden arrived at the site in the course of compiling his *Britannia*, there was "in manner no accesse into" the island, although Camden notes that at one point there had been "a bridge . . . built by Aelfred." He describes the site as "a pretty Island betweene two rivers . . . now commonly knowen by the name of Athelney . . . a place . . . famous among us for King Alfreds shrowding himselfe therein." Camden notes from "William of Malmesbury (whose words these are and not mine)" the information that Alfred "founded a little Monasterie" on the island, "the whole frame whereof, hanged upon foure maine posts pitched fast in the ground, with foure round isles of Sphaerick work contrived and brought round about the same." Despite the apparent complaints about Camden's unseemly interest in monasteries and abbeys, *Britannia*'s representation of Athelney makes a characteristically Protestant antiquarian gesture by denuding this once holy spot of special sacred status. Camden does not mention either Cuthbert or the legendary purpose for the founding of the monastery (to thank God for Cuthbert's vision) but records only the physical facts of its curious architecture; as Summit notes more generally about Camden, in his work "the Reformation is entirely about property."[61] Instead of linking Alfred to the Anglo-Saxon saints, Camden connects him to the classical world by comparing his behavior on Athelney to that of Gaius Marius, the Roman general who "lurked" in the "Marishes of Minturney."[62]

Camden's description of Athelney has much in common with that provided by Robert Powell, who leaves out all mention of Cuthbert from his account of Alfred, noting only that Alfred "out of a locall gratitude erected . . . [a] religious house." With this phrase Powell purges the Anglo-Saxon saint whose presence gave the site sacred meaning in the original story, imagining the object of Alfred's thankfulness in generalized, secularized, and depersonified terms.[63] Finally, perhaps the most extreme example of the reorientation of Athelney occurs in John Speed's *Theatre of the Empire of Great Britaine* (1612). Speed does not mention either Cuthbert or Athelney Abbey; instead he recounts a fabliau of Alfred, in which the king goes into the swineherd's house "in very poore attire disguised," "trimming of his bow and shafts" while a "cake of dow" burns in the hearth. He is, as a result, chastised by the cowherd's wife, who "check[s] him as her Groom," saying, "Thou fellow, doest thou see the bread burne before thy face, and wilt not turne it?" Speed, like Foxe, sees Alfred as "the very mirrour of Princes," but his account denudes the king of his characteristically Anglo-Saxon piety, commitment to the Roman church, and dedication to the saints. At the same time, Speed's chorography drains the land of the sacred hot spots so central to Blundell's representation of the English land, both in the past and in the present.[64]

English Catholics fought to preserve the sacred places of England, even though they had been destroyed physically at the dissolution and were, by the time of William Blundell, being textually erased by the early modern chronicles, histories, and chorographies in Blundell's library. The idea that the land was composed of a matrix of holy places that commemorated the miracles of English saints, the good deeds of virtuous Anglo-Saxon kings, and the steadfastness of early modern Catholics was central to the definition of England for Blundell, Robert Parsons, and unnamed men and women, such as Blundell's "gentleman" correspondent. The landscape of early modern England was a material text on which the country's past was written, but how that text was read depended on the observer's religious identity. Although the Protestant narrative of English land and nationhood ultimately won the day, it was forged in competition with an alternative, Catholic narrative that continued to see the English landscape through the dual lenses of the English medieval past and the Counter-Reformation present.

Notes

1. Margaret Aston, "English Ruins and English History: The Dissolution and the Sense of the Past," *Journal of the Warburg and Courtauld Institutes* 36 (1973): 232.

2. For an overview of the expanding field of early modern cartographic studies, see the introduction to Andrew Gordon and Bernhard Klein's *Literature, Mapping, and the Politics of Space in Early Modern Britain* (Cambridge, UK: Cambridge University Press, 2001), 1–12. Major works within this field that deal specifically with the relationship between landscape and nationhood include Richard Helgerson's pioneering *Forms of Nationhood: The Elizabethan Writing of England* (Chicago: University of Chicago Press, 1992); Claire McEachern, *The Poetics of English Nationhood, 1590–1612* (Cambridge, UK: Cambridge University Press, 1996), esp. ch. 4 ("Putting the 'Poly' Back into *Poly-Olbion*"); and Philip Schwyzer, *Literature, Nationalism, and Memory in Early Modern England and Wales* (Cambridge, UK: Cambridge University Press, 2004).

3. Jennifer Summit, "Leland's *Itinerary* and the Remains of the Medieval Past," in *Reading the Medieval in Early Modern England*, ed. David Matthews and Gordon McMullan (Cambridge, UK: Cambridge University Press, 2007), 161.

4. On Blundell, see D. R. Woolf, "Little Crosby and the Horizons of Early Modern Historical Culture," in *The Historical Imagination in Early Modern Britain*, ed. Donald R. Kelley and David Harris Sacks (Washington, DC: Woodrow Wilson Center Press; and Cambridge, UK: Cambridge University Press, 1997), 93–132; and Daniel Woolf, *The Social Circulation of the Past: English*

Historical Culture, 1500–1730 (Oxford, UK: Oxford University Press, 2003), 247–55 and *passim*. See also Alexander Goss's introduction and Thomas Ellison Gibson's preface to his edited volume *Crosby Records: A Chapter of Lancashire Recusancy* (London: Chetham Society, 1887). On Blundell's original writings and their circulation through recusant manuscript networks, see Margaret Sena, "William Blundell and the Networks of Catholic Dissent in Post-Reformation England," in *Communities in Early Modern England: Networks, Place, Rhetoric*, ed. Alexandra Shepard and Phil Withington (Manchester, UK: Manchester University Press, 2000), 54–75. On William Blundell's grandson and heir, also named William Blundell, see Geoff Baker, *Reading and Politics in Early Modern England: The Mental World of a Seventeenth-Century Catholic Gentleman* (Manchester, UK: Manchester University Press, 2010).

5. One copy of the text of this narrative survives among the Blundell papers; see Woolf, "Little Crosby," 103. The manuscript is published in Gibson, *Crosby Records*, 45–62; all citations to Blundell's writings are from this edition. On the coins themselves, see the nineteenth-century description of them by D. H. Haigh in Gibson, *Crosby Records*, 63–65; and Woolf, "Little Crosby," 102–3 and 123.

6. On "historical culture," see Woolf, "Little Crosby," 94, and the more extended discussion in Woolf, *Social Circulation of the Past*, 8–14, and 7–8 on polemical uses of the past.

7. Christopher Highley, *Catholics Writing the Nation in Early Modern Britain and Ireland* (Oxford, UK: Oxford University Press, 2008).

8. Alexandra Walsham, "Holywell: Contesting Sacred Space in Post-Reformation Wales," in *Sacred Space in Early Modern Europe*, ed. Will Coster and Andrew Spicer (Cambridge, UK: Cambridge University Press, 2005), 220–21. See also Walsham's more recent, magisterial study, *The Reformation of the Landscape: Religion, Identity, and Memory in Early Modern Britain and Ireland* (Oxford, UK: Oxford University Press, 2012), a book that promises to become the definitive work in the field.

9. The Great Hodge Podge is Lancashire RO DBB1 Acc 6121; page numbers, given parenthetically, are from Gibson, *Crosby Records*, checked for accuracy against the manuscript.

10. In 1592 and 1593 several men were given the right to lease Blundell's land, and in 1599, as Blundell writes, "all my lands and goods were forfaited becase I did not come in and appeare uppon proclamation," although these lands were restored with Blundell's later pardon by King James (Gibson, *Crosby Records*, 32). Despite this pardon, local authorities continued to try to seize the land and property of Blundell and his tenants in 1607, 1613, and 1624.

11. Highley, *Catholics*, 7.

12. The case is analyzed by Frank Tyrer in "A Star Chamber Case: Assheton v. Blundell, 1624–31," *Transactions of the Historic Society of Lancashire and Cheshire* 118 (1966): 19–37; quotations from the record, PRO STAC 9/1/2, are taken from Tyrer's transcriptions.

13. Quoted in Tyrer, "Star Chamber Case," 19–20.

14. Bodleian MS Eng. Poet. b. 5, f. 102. On this manuscript, see Cedric Brown, "Recusant Community and Jesuit Mission in Parliament Days: Bodleian MS Eng. Poet. b. 5," *Yearbook of English Studies* 33 (2003): 290–315; Frank M. McKay, "A Seventeenth-Century Collection of Religious Poetry: Bodleian Manuscript Eng. poet. b. 5," *Bodleian Library Record* 8 (1970): 185–91; and Gerard Kilroy, *Edmund Campion: Memory and Transcription* (Aldershot, UK: Ashgate, 2005), 77–80.

15. Quoted in Tyrer, "Star Chamber Case," 32–33.

16. Walsham discusses this incident in the context of larger recusant efforts to find new spaces for religious rites in *Reformation*, 175–81.

17. Gibson, *Crosby Records*, xv; Woolf, "Little Crosby," 109.

18. Alexandra Walsham, "Translating Trent? English Catholicism and the Counter Reformation," *Historical Research* 78 (2005): 288–310; Lisa McClain, *Lest We Be Damned: Practical Innovation and Lived Experience Among Catholics in Protestant England, 1559–1642* (London: Routledge, 2004); Anne Dillon, "Praying by Number: The Confraternity of the Rosary and the English Catholic Community, c. 1580–1700," *History* 88 (2003): 451–71.

19. Lisa McClain, "Using What's at Hand: English Catholic Reinterpretations of the Rosary, 1559–1642," *Journal of Religious History* 27 (2003): 161–76.

20. Summit, "Leland's *Itinerary*," 168; Walsham, *Reformation*, 156–66 and 194–96.

21. Robert Southwell, *A Short Rule of Good Life* (St. Omers, 1622), 162.

22. Southwell, *Short Rule*, 163; McClain, *Lest We Be Damned*, 58–59, 82, and *passim*. For a more detailed discussion of the process by which "church papists and recusants evidently sacralized the spaces surrounding their houses," see Walsham, *Reformation*, 183–89.

23. Southwell, *Short Rule*, 165.

24. Walsham, "Holywell," 235; see also Walsham, *Reformation*, ch. 3 ("*Britannia sancta*: Catholicism, Counter-Reformation, and the Landscape," 153–232, *passim*).

25. Woolf, "Little Crosby," 103–6.

26. Woolf, "Little Crosby," 104.

27. Woolf, "Little Crosby," 106.

28. Woolf, "Little Crosby," 106.

29. This account of the copperplate engraving was given in a letter by Blundell's grandson and heir, also William Blundell (known as "the Cavalier"), in a letter to James Scarisbrick in 1655; Gibson, *Crosby Records*, 42. See also Daniel Woolf, *Crosby Records: A Cavalier's Note Book, Being Notes, Anecdotes, and Observations of William Blundell*, ed. T. E. Gibson (London, 1880).

30. For a full list of Blundell's sources, including the specific editions used, see Woolf, "Little Crosby," 122–32.

31. Woolf, "Little Crosby," 123. Other kings mentioned more briefly include Egbert; Alfred, King of Northumberland; and Edmund the Magnificent.

32. Woolf, "Little Crosby," 123.

33. Donna Hamilton, "Richard Verstegan's *A Restitution of Decayed Intelligence* (1605): A Catholic Antiquarian Replies to John Foxe, Thomas Cooper, and Jean Bodin," *Prose Studies* 22 (1999): 5. For recent work on the Tudor myth of British origins, see Schwyzer, *Literature, Nationalism, and Memory*; and David J. Baker and Willy Maley, eds., *British Identities and English Renaissance Literature* (Cambridge, UK: Cambridge University Press, 2002), a book that gathers together essays by leading scholars in the field. For work on the related issue of the proposed union of Scotland and England, see Andrew Hadfield, *Shakespeare, Spenser, and the Matter of Britain* (Basingstoke, UK: Palgrave, 2003); and Brendan Brashaw and Peter Roberts, eds., *British Consciousness and Identity: The Making of Britain, 1533–1707* (Cambridge, UK: Cambridge University Press, 2003).

34. Schwyzer, *Literature, Nationalism, and Memory*, 6.

35. On Archbishop Matthew Parker and Protestant interpretations of Anglo-Saxon history, see F. J. Levy, *Tudor Historical Thought* (Toronto: University of Toronto Press, 2004), 114–22; and Donna Hamilton, "Catholic Use of Anglo-Saxon Precedents," *Recusant History* 26 (2002): 537–55, esp. 537–38; and Hamilton, "Richard Verstegan's *A Restitution*," 4–8.

36. John Foxe, *Actes and Monuments . . . Volume 1* (London, 1583), 134. Foxe represents Alfred as a proto-Protestant hero by downplaying his relationship to Rome and dedication to the English saints, emphasizing the king's textual scholarship (according to Foxe, Alfred translated the Psalms into the vernacular), and including an apocryphal account of Alfred's support for Johannes Scotus, the Irish monk and theologian denounced as a heretic by the pope. On late medieval and early modern ideas about the Anglo-Saxon invasion, see Philip Schwyzer, *Archaeologies of English Renaissance Literature* (Oxford, UK: Oxford University Press, 2007), 40–41.

37. Highley, *Catholics*, 84–91; Hamilton, "Catholic Use," *passim*; Colin Kidd, *British Identities Before Nationalism: Ethnicity and Nationhood in the Atlantic World, 1600–1800* (Cambridge, UK: Cambridge University Press, 1999).

38. Highley, *Catholics*, 85; on Stapleton, see also Hamilton, "Catholic Use," 537–41.

39. Hamilton, "Richard Verstegan's *A Restitution*," 15–17 and *passim*; Walsham, "Holywell," 225.

40. Robert S. Miola, ed., *Early Modern Catholicism: An Anthology of Primary Sources* (Oxford, UK: Oxford University Press, 2007), 423.

41. Blundell, following Petrus de Natalibus, describes "an other St. Eadmund, kinge and Martir" (not to be confused with the East Anglian saint) "whoe was sonne to K. Eadweard," known as Edmund the Elder or Edmund I, who was assassinated by a thief in 946.

42. Bernhard Klein, "*Tamburlaine* and the Heritage of Medieval Cartography," in *Reading the Medieval in Early Modern England*, ed. Gordon McMullan and David Matthews (Cambridge, UK: Cambridge University Press, 2007), 146.

43. This passage is, with spelling variations, taken verbatim from Robert Parsons, *A Treatise of Three Conversions* (St. Omer, 1603–1604), 418–22. See also the Latin version of this episode in the *Chronicon* of Henrici de Silgrave, published as *A Chronicle of English History, from the Earliest Period to A.D. 1274, by Henry of Silegrave*, ed. Charles Hook (London: Caxton Society, 1849), 44–47.

44. Woolf, "Little Crosby," 121.

45. I am grateful to the anonymous reader for Wayne State University Press for this point.

46. Highley, *Catholics*, 14.

47. Oswald, Blundell claims, "was slaine by the Pagan Kinge Penda, in a place called in their language Maserfelthe, which seemeth to have bine at or neere Winwicke Chrch, in the Countie of Lancaster, which is within a certaine precinct or libertie called even to this daye Macarfeldt or Macarfeldffee." This idea is taken from Bede and contradicts the (probably correct) information in Camden that the actual site of the battle was near Ossetree. The etymological orientation of this information may reflect Blundell's reading of Verstegan. See Walsham's discussion of this reference in the context of a larger Catholic project: "staking a claim to obliterated spaces and structures and the stories of their origin on paper" (*Reformation*, 211–12).

48. Woolf, "Little Crosby," 94.

49. Sena, "William Blundell," 55 and *passim*; on Catholicism and orality, see Alison Shell, *Oral Culture and Catholicism in Early Modern England* (Cambridge, UK: Cambridge University Press, 2007).

50. Michael Drayton, *The Second Part, or a Continuance of Poly-Olbion* (1622), 75.

51. William Camden, *Britain, or A Chorographicall Description of the Most Flourishing Kingdomes, England, Scotland, and Ireland*, trans. Philemon Holland (1610), sig. 4*. All citations from Camden's *Brittannia*, which Blundell consulted from the 1584 Latin edition (Woolf, "Little Crosby," 127), are taken from Holland's translation.

52. On nostalgia, see Aston, "English Ruins," 243–54; on Camden, see Summit, "Leland's *Itinerary*," 168–70. See also Walsham's account of the "religious and cultural backlash against the iconoclastic outrages perpetrated by the early reformers" in *Reformation*, 273–96.

53. Camden, *Britain*, 163; Summit, "Leland's *Itinerary*," 169–70.

54. Drayton, *Poly-Olbion*, 75. See also Schwyzer's comparison of Robert Aske's and John Bale's views of the loss of the abbeys, in *Literature, Nationalism, and Memory*, ch. 2 ("Bale's Books and Aske's Abbeys: Nostalgia and the Aesthetics of Nationhood," 49–75).

55. As Bob Scribner has demonstrated, characterizing Catholicism as "a religion of cultic observance set in a sacralized world" and Protestantism as "a religion of non- or even anti-ritual forms . . . set in a desacralized world in which there were not specially sacred times, spaces, places, persons or things"

(315) is an oversimplification that does not do justice to the complexities of the Reformation or to devotional behavior on either end of the confessional spectrum. See Robert Scribner, "The Impact of the Reformation on Daily Life," in *Mensch und Objekt im Mittelalter und in der Fruhen Neuzeit*, ed. Gerhard Jaritz (Vienna: Osterreichischen Akademie der Wissenschaften, 1990), 316–43; and Robert Scribner, "Reformation and Desacralisation: From Sacramental World to Moralised Universe," in *Problems in the Historical Anthropology of Early Modern Europe*, ed. R. Scribner and H. Po-chia Hsia (Wiesbaden: Harrassowitz, 1997), 75–92. See also Walsham, who urges scholars "to resist the temptation to speak of secularisation" when speaking of Protestant attitudes toward holy wells ("Holywell," 235).

56. Walsham, "Holywell"; and Alexandra Walsham, "Reforming the Waters: Holy Wells and Healing Springs in Protestant England," in *Life and Thought in the Northern Church, c. 1100–c. 1700: Essays in Honour of Claire Cross*, ed. Diana Wood (Woodbridge, UK: Boydell, 1999), 227–55.

57. On the way in which Protestant seventeenth-century almanacs continued to register what looks very much like a Catholic sense of the particular holiness of specific sites and times, see Alison Chapman, "Marking Time: Astrology, Almanacs, and English Protestantism," *Renaissance Quarterly* 60 (2007): 1257–90.

58. Summit provides a blueprint for this comparative analysis in her discussion of William of Worcester, Leland, Camden, and Speed, in "Leland's *Itinerary*," 161–75.

59. Lucy Toumin Smith, ed., *The Itinerary of John Leland In or About the Years 1535–1543, Parts I to III* (London: Bell, 1907), II: 161. On the surrender of the abbey, at which time "the materials of the buildings were valued at 80 pounds," see William Page, "Houses of Benedictine monks: The Abbey of Athelaney," in *A History of the County of Somerset, Volume 2*, ed. William Page (London: Constable, 1911), 99–103.

60. Foxe, *Actes and Monuments*, 142.

61. Summit, "Leland's *Itinerary*," 171.

62. Camden, *Britain*, 224.

63. Robert Powell, *The Life of Alfred, or Alvred* (London, 1634), 49. This process is parallel to what Alison Chapman has described as Milton's Protestant effort in *A Masque Presented at Ludlow Castle* to replace St. Winifred as the local spirit of Wales with the classicized genius loci, Sabrina; see Alison Chapman, *Patrons and Patron Saints in Early Modern English Literature* (London: Routledge, 2012).

64. John Speed, *Theatre of the Empire of Great Britaine* (1612), 357.

Lowell Gallagher

Remembering Lot's Wife

The Structure of Testimony in the Painted Life *of Mary Ward*

"But Lot's wife, behind him, looked back, and she became a pillar of salt."

Genesis 19:26

I am looking at a capital letter "L" (Figure 1). It belongs to a series of ornamented letters, the so-called "talking letters" (*iniziali parlante*), produced in the studio of the sixteenth-century Florentine typographer Bartolomeo Sermartelli.[1] Sermartelli's "L" stands for Lot. You can see Sodom in flames on the horizon, to the left of the letter's spine. Filling the space bounded by the spine and foot is the cave near Zoar, where Lot's two daughters, believing themselves and their father to be the sole survivors of the catastrophe, have hit upon the solution that will ensure the family's survival. Given the visual prominence and ethical provocation of the incest scene, it is easy to forget that Sermartelli's letter also depicts the most startling instance of divine retribution in the story: the sudden cancellation of Lot's wife from salvation history.[2] Where is Lot's wife in Sermartelli's design? The mutating figure, near the left margin, is barely visible, lost in the background.

The discreet position of the figure makes it easy to miss, but this feature also issues a provocation by indicating an event that falls outside the operative scope of the normative relation between testimonial sign and historical event in received protocols of biblical literacy. The figure is literally *avant la lettre* and symbolically beyond exegetical capture. Through this single gesture Sermartelli's "L" gives silent witness to a tectonic shift in the understanding of the negative exemplarity of Lot's wife—the figure's identity as type of impenitent error and improvident curiosity—in

Figure 1. Bartolomeo Sermartelli, "L[ot]." Courtesy of Special Collections, Honnold/Mudd Library of The Claremont Colleges.

Reformation and Counter-Reformation biblical cultures. By siting the prospect of illegible elements in the story of the flight from Sodom, Sermartelli's "L" marks an important juncture in what I want to call the figural history of Lot's wife. The letter imagines Lot's wife as the figure of the *unthought* in the Abrahamic cycle: an impossible yet lived intimacy between the chosen and the cast out.[3] In this essay I argue that the essential paradox of such intimacy, as imagined in Sermartelli's letter, takes material shape in the career of Mary Ward (1585–1645), the early modern "Jesuitress" missionary whose progressive, and controversial, pastoral program ran afoul of the judgment of ecclesiastical authorities on both sides of the Romanist-reformist confessional divide. The record of Ward's pastoral ambitions and misadventures constitutes a powerfully suggestive witness to the figural range and provocation of Lot's wife in ecclesial history. But that is not all. The witnessing gesture, I propose, is also reciprocal, in the sense that the Sodomitical undertow to Ward's career effectively enlarges and reorients understanding of the transhistorical scope and critical legacy of Ward's community-building ethos.

Before pursuing the story I want to tell, I need first to narrow the parameters of what I intend by figural history. The semantic field of the expression is conspicuously marked by the normative procedures of biblical typology, memorably described in Erich Auerbach's account of the exegetical practice underpinning the Western tradition of literary *figura*, to say nothing of the Hegelian reading of that tradition, whereby the proleptic orientation of *figura* constitutes a premonitory symptom of the supersessionist drive of history: from mythos to logos.[4] Although the continued cultural force of these controversial legacies remains in play in what follows, the sense most relevant to the guiding animus of the events described in this essay can be found in the revisionist typology, both anti-Hegelian and antidogmatic, that briefly flourished in European Catholic theology between World War II and the Second Vatican Council, and I begin there.

The so-called *nouvelle théologie*, associated with the work of Marie-Dominique Chenu, Jean Daniélou, Henri de Lubac, and Hans Urs von Balthasar, among others, mounted a strenuous critique of the prevailing neo-Thomist rubric of orthodox Catholicism. That rubric, codified in Leo XIII's encyclical *Aeterni Patris* (1879), responded to the perceived secularism of modernity by effectively declaring that the essential meaning and purpose of salvation history had been authoritatively parsed in the scholastic principles inherited from Counter-Reformation era recensions of Thomist theology.[5] Confronting the apparent refusal of the ecclesiastical hierarchy to face up to unprecedented pastoral and ethical challenges posed to the church in the postwar era, proponents of the *nouvelle théologie* contested the privilege given by neo-Thomist habits of thought to an ossified system of dogmatic rationality and to an intransigently legalistic approach to moral questions, neither of which bore more than a superficial resemblance to the deeply assimilative and dialectical character of the Angelic Doctor's intellectualism. *Ressourcement* theologians (the name preferred by the movement's leading voices) sought to reengage the spiritual passion and wide-ranging intellectual curiosity that had informed Thomas's effort to bring the wealth of contemporary human knowledge, as received from Hellenistic, Arab, patristic, and mystical traditions, into contact with the biblical and Pauline proof-texts of orthodox Christianity. The guiding intuition of *ressourcement* theologians was that the essential vitality of the church resided in its capacity to respect and to deepen the transhistorical mutuality of pastoral and theological expressions of Christic revelation.[6]

Henri de Lubac's contributions to the *ressourcement* movement provided unflinching descriptions of the at times bruising yet also generative intimacy between Incarnational, Trinitarian, and Eucharistic paradoxes in theological history and the analogous *complexio oppositorum* through which diverse historical embodiments of the church could be said to remain in communion with each other, without being reducible to dogmatic expression.[7] In essence, de Lubac's enterprise, like many of his peers', inhabited a figural understanding of the paradox and mystery informing the varied manifestations of the body of Christ. Although wholly conversant with the wide range of figural invention found in the canon (scriptural patterns, patristic and medieval elaborations), de Lubac's sense of figure was not primarily exegetical.[8] It did not advance a new theory of reading guided by the assumption of the unitary legibility of providential history as mapped in the scriptural canon. Neither did it prescribe a devotional regimen of imitative models designed to gauge the progress of the soul (e.g., through type scenes from biblical narrative and saints' lives). Rather, it gave witness to the profoundly *sacramental* character of the figural. Figure, in this sense, was not so much a conveyance of meaning or a mnemonic aid as an intuitive flashpoint generating intimacy of contact and communication between natural and supernatural orders and between pastoral and theological orders of truth.[9] For de Lubac and *ressourcement* theologians in general, advocacy of the figural life of the church was not meant to jettison the rationality of the neo-Thomist language favored by the Vatican but rather to restore it to a condition of genuine and productive dialogue—intimate contact—with the mystical symbolism of biblical language on the one hand and the exigencies of the contemporary world on the other. In short, figure stood for the risk of exposure to forgotten, suppressed, or unthought dimensions of the sacramentality of the church.[10]

Ressourcement theology had a significant influence on the ecumenically progressive agenda of the Second Vatican Council (1963–1965), but it would have been hard to predict such an outcome in the preceding decade. Pius XII's encyclical *Humani Generis* (1950) issued an emphatic castigation of the movement, reasserting the neo-Thomist ethos of the papal magisterium and stigmatizing the *nouvelle théologie* with the twin charges of "false irenicism" and "dogmatic relativity."[11] To return to the place where we began, *ressourcement* theologians found themselves cast into the figural space Sermartelli assigns to Lot's wife, a space suspended between excommunication from the ecclesial community (rendered narratively as the sudden extinction of the Sodomites in the Genesis text) and full membership (the survival of Lot and his daughters).[12]

Humani Generis does not mention the Sodom narrative. This is no surprise, given the entrenched association of Sodom with a perceived moral disorder (stigmatized sexual practices) not directly at issue in the present circumstance. The encyclical nonetheless enters into the figural orbit of the Sodom text by invoking the fundamental aberration of the Sodomites in the Genesis narrative: rooted inhospitality, of which the scenes of anticipated sexual violence are but a symptom. To borrow Robert Alter's words, the Ur-sin of Sodom, inhospitality, includes a "nexus" of associations designating an ethos of "anti-covenant," the spectral manifestation of all that threatens the Israelite community's place in the covenantal economy.[13] The encyclical remembers that threat through a strategic volley of images designed to raise precisely the kind of free-floating contamination anxiety conjured up in scriptural tradition and in the long cultural history of Sodom. Thus the "dogmatic relativity" of the *nouvelle théologie* is called both a "disease" and a "deadly fruit," language generic enough to convey the perceived enormity of the threat and specific enough, through its invocation of the biblical proof-texts linking disease, sin, and death, to define the *nouvelle théologie* as modernity's latest iteration of the catastrophic anticovenantal gesture: the reversion to Sodom.[14]

What was most irksome about the *ressourcement* ethos in the magisterium's view was the fact that the movement's prospective decoupling of the covenantal economy and the timeless authority of dogmatic utterance was being disseminated from theological and educational strongholds within the *ecclesia*. *Ressourcement* theology spoke to a border crisis, the erosion of the magisterium's declared distinction between Catholic teaching and modernity—that is, between *veritas* and *historia*, the framing categories of the covenantal drama to which, in Auerbach's reading, the typological imagination, *figura*, served as middle term. The paradigm of that crisis, and of its mutating character, is Lot's wife.

Let's take a second look at Sermartelli's letter. Consider again the suggested element of visual encryption in the design. Similarly gauged depictions of Lot's wife abound in early modern visual media, giving testimony to the era's fluency in using the resources of perspectival composition and recessional space to indicate Lot's wife's condition of radical homelessness in pictorial terms. The catastrophic consequence of the backward turn, given indisputable prominence in exegetical tradition, is here italicized by the visual calculus of negative magnitude. The enormity of Lot's wife's errancy finds its proper gauge in the sheer difficulty of locating the distant figure in the blasted landscape.

This oblique element retrieves the etymological suggestiveness of the Hebrew word for the thing into which Lot's wife is transformed in Genesis 19:26—a pillar (*netziv*), referring to a lookout, garrison, or boundary marker.[15] I take Sermartelli's "L"—more precisely, the graphic trace positioned outside and before the "L"—as sentinel to a network of kinships, dispersed across different cultural locations, between the Sodom story and variously documented experiences of early modern Christian subjects who find themselves not simply cast in the role of erring soul or prodigal daughter but also called to the place of witness to events suspended between *historia* and *veritas*. This place is the vanishing point where *figura*—Auerbach's middle term between *historia* and *veritas*—discovers its proximity to disaster.

Christology has always recognized the peculiar radiance of this place. It is the crux of the Passion narrative, the cry of the abandoned Son on the Cross ("*Eli, Eli, lema sabachthani*" / "My God, my God, why did you abandon me?" [Matthew 27:46]). One of the signal ambitions of *ressourcement* theologians was to reemphasize the centrality of this moment of abjection in the incarnational mystery and, by extension, in the historical being of the church. In *ressourcement* thought, for example, the "valid meaning" of Christic time does not issue, in the manner of the neo-Thomist tradition, from "some timeless philosophical or mystical 'eternity'" but rather sustains itself in a condition of vigilance, of readiness "to say yes to everything, to be available for everything, always open to the infinite."[16] From the vantage point just described, the position espoused by *Humani Generis* ran counter to a genuine theology of time, to the degree that it tried to inoculate the very possibility of revelation from exposure to the historical horizons of the contemporary *ecclesia*. In contrast, *ressourcement* theology sought to reopen communication between the decisive figure of dispossession in Christian thought (the cry of abandonment on the Cross) and the particular challenges of modernity, without insisting on a preestablished doctrinal standard of recuperative truth.

To the extent that it sought to remain open, in von Balthasar's words, to "every *possible* revelation from God," *ressourcement* theology entered into a relation of what could be called patient proximity to one of the most trenchant postwar atheologies of time, Maurice Blanchot's *Writing of the Disaster*.

Plate 1. *Painted Life*, panel 1.

Plate 2. *Painted Life*, panel 2.

Plate 3. *Painted Life*, panel 22.

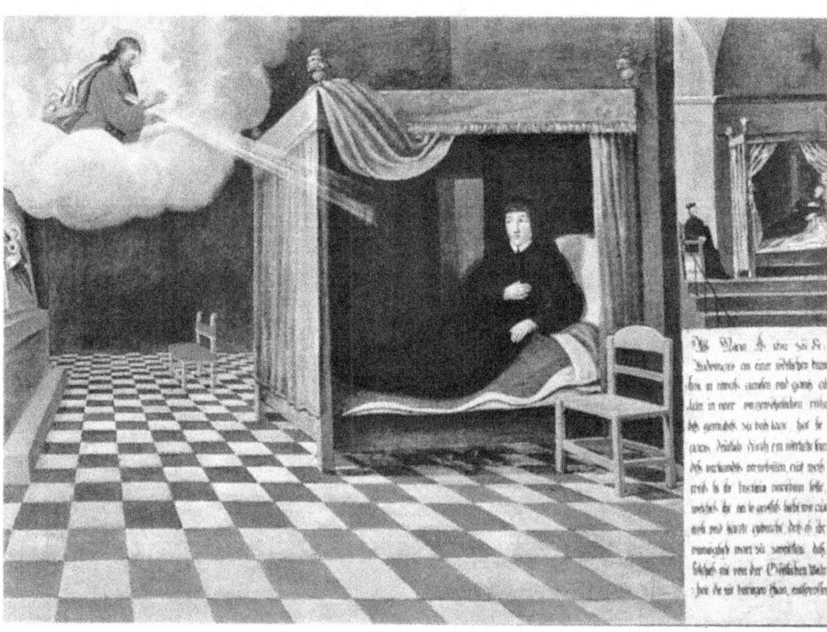

Plate 4. *Painted Life*, panel 24.

> The disaster: break with the star, break with every form of totality, never denying, however, the dialectical necessity of a fulfillment; the disaster: prophecy which announces nothing but the refusal of the prophetic as simply an event to come, but which nonetheless opens, nonetheless discovers the patience of vigilant language. The disaster, touch of the powerless infinite: it does not come to pass under a sidereal sky, but here—a here in excess of all presence. Here: where, then?[17]

Blanchot's language throughout *The Writing of the Disaster* carries resonances from several tributaries of biblical and ethical thought, not least Emmanuel Levinas's provocative associations of passivity, responsibility, and vigilance.[18] I am not concerned here with that particular history, and still less do I propose to conflate Blanchot's project with that of the *nouvelle théologie*.[19] What interests me is the point of friction between the two contemporaneous projects, the mutual, though not identical, access each gives to the rupture and consummation of meaning brought about by disaster. That encounter illumines a way into the corridor between *veritas* and *historia*, the domain that belongs not to *chronos*, with the consolation it affords of manageable time, but to *figura*, understood not as the finished image of experience or thought but as the passion (or "infinite passivity," as Blanchot would say) of the image unmoored from either knowing subject or timeless model.[20] Lot's wife stands here, at the crisis point, the *punctum*, where disaster lodges, where home and homelessness collapse into each other and where Sermartelli's design and Blanchot's question—"Here: where, then?"—converge.

It is no accident that in the twentieth century Lot's wife should be reclaimed in art and literature of the Shoah as a sign of the paralysis of memory and the limits of historical comprehension in the wake of catastrophe, or that the figure should surface in the burgeoning critical literature on childhood sexual abuse as an emblem of the "contemporary drama over recovered memory."[21] In such instances, to take up the position of Lot's wife is to be caught in the vortex of Blanchot's "break with the star," made witness to the "excess of all presence" that marks the peculiar consistency of traumatic history, outside the economic circulation of collective memory and prudential disbursement of cultural patrimony. There are ways to parse the question, however, that open up otherwise undetected tributaries in the figural history of Lot's wife. In these zones of contact with the legacy of the Sodom narrative, the paradoxes of witnessing become the means through which the arrested gesture of looking back—the Genesis text's figure for stalled mourning—yields a revisionist typology that envisions disaster and survival together, as converging terms of an ethics of action for the sake of what may be grasped from the wreckage of the past and from a posture of vigilance toward a categorically unknown future.

The career of the English Catholic "Jesuitress" Mary Ward illustrates the gesture just described, and the principal index to that gesture can be discerned in the series of paintings commissioned by the religious community that Ward founded in the first decade of the seventeenth century. Composed somewhere between the 1630s and 1670s, the so-called *Gemaltes Leben* (Painted Life) both commemorates and, against all odds, argues for the legitimacy of Ward's religious community under the proselytizing mandate of the Counter-Reformation. Nowhere, however, in the documentation of Ward's career is the figure of Lot's wife explicitly mentioned. Traversing different grounds—different crises, different losses—from those precipitating the figure's resurgence in late modernity, Ward's career parses the subtextual domain of the Sodom narrative in a manner exquisitely tuned to Ward's anomalous and precarious place in both Counter-Reformation and Stuart theopolitical worlds. Translating the career, the *Painted Life* solicits a hermeneutic attuned to the figural afterlife of the estranged woman in the Sodom story. We are not looking for pillars.[22]

The task, then, is to follow the curve traced by the dispersal of the figure. The movement has a double origin, beginning with two foundational voices in ecclesial history, each representing a decisive turn in the developing history of orthodoxy, from the patristic and Reformation eras: Irenaeus of Lyon and Martin Luther. Together, their respective readings of Lot's wife identify the contradictory terms of the domain inhabited by Mary Ward. In the *Adversus haereses* Irenaeus decides, against the preponderance of biblical tradition, that Lot's wife does not signify abjection, sin, or depravity. Instead, she is the biblical type of the *ecclesia*, the sanctified community: suffering, patient, stranded in history, and holding onto the promise of the bridegroom's return.[23] She is the paradigmatic martyr-witness; the arrested gesture of her looking back is the anamorphic rendering in the biblical narrative of her steady gaze on the providential design of history, in particular, its deepest recesses: the pillar figuring the empathic witness to all that was annihilated in the destruction of Sodom. Irenaeus's reasons for this astonishing (it is tempting to call it proto-Benjaminian) counterreading of the Sodom text can be ascribed to the typological features of his thought for which he is remembered in church history: his insistence, contra Marcionite and Gnosticizing views, that the integrity of the bond between "old" and "new" testaments is profound and inviolable (even Lot's wife can be recuperated) and his intuition that the eschatological promise of Christ's resurrection is premised on an essentially ecological and recursive experience of time.[24]

In 1526 Erasmus established the *editio princeps* of the *Adversus haereses*. But Irenaeus's revisionist reading of the Sodom text was largely lost on the humanist-reformist exegetical cultures of the sixteenth century. Luther's commentary on the Sodom text, in the 1539 lectures on Genesis, offered a judgment that spoke more powerfully to the reformists' controversialist sensibility. Lot's wife, he argued, is the typological emblem of the papists' refusal to let go of the bankrupt authority of the past—that is, the Catholic past. Like Lot's wife, they "are looking back and thus disregard the word they have before them."[25] Their gaze is faulty precisely because it is not historical enough: It fails to recognize the continued unfolding of God's providential design through the reformists' enterprise.

The Romanist response appears to have been that of silence. Irenaeus's idiosyncratic insight did not make its way, to my knowledge, into Counter-Reformation assertions of apostolic fidelity. Not until *ressourcement* theologians undertook a careful rereading of the patristic antecedents of Thomist thought did the ecclesial significance of Lot's wife resurface, notably in de Lubac's survey of female figures of the church in biblical narrative and patristic exegesis.[26] Luther's reading, on the other hand, catalyzed a subgenre of controversialist and homiletic literature in England in which Lot's wife encapsulated the perils of papist survivalism in the reformist world. No surprise that the figure of Lot's wife should surface in both juridical and pastoral responses to the Gunpowder Plot.[27] The mythography of the narrowly averted disaster seemed to corroborate reformists' suspicions of the alternately intransigent and volatile character of the papist enclave. The Gunpowder Plot also indicated the alarming relevance of the specific problem foregrounded in the Genesis story: how to measure Sodom.[28] After the onset of the Jesuit mission to England in the 1580s, the papist remnant in England, the new Sodomitical diaspora, had become a diversified community constituted by known or suspected recusants, church papists (of uncertain allegiance), and, most troublingly, multiple apostates, all of whom could be thought of—and were so conjured in homilies on the subject—as monstrous recurrences of the recidivist gesture exemplified by Lot's wife.[29]

I take the Gunpowder Plot as my point of entry into the career of Mary Ward. Biographically, she was separated by only one degree from the scandal. Her father, Marmaduke Ward, was among the suspects rounded up in the early stages of the inquiries into the plot.[30] Ideologically, Ward's career was separated from the scandal by degrees difficult to measure. Unlike the Gunpowder Plot conspirators, Ward was no terrorist, but the fact that her principal ambition—to establish a worldwide teaching and missionary religious order for women based on the Jesuit protocol—observed the Counter-Reformation mandate to reclaim lands lost to reformist heresy was no consolation to the Protestant church-state. Moreover, in the Romanist enclave Ward's career also reactivated the Sodomitical problem of counting, in the sense that Ward's personal sense of mission, by taking up the apostle Paul's call to be "all things to all men" (1 Corinthians 9:22), repeatedly challenged the Romanist hierarchy's sense of how far a woman should go in embodying the apostolic and militant ethos of the *ecclesia*.[31] In effect, Ward's movements across Europe and in England placed her at the intersection of two orthodox vantage points, reformist and Romanist, and the target she represented was a virtual antitype—a repetition with difference—of Lot's wife, the errant woman and witness to a community found to be irregular and in some respects scandalous.

As already noted, Lot's wife is not explicitly mentioned in the archive on Ward. The figure functions rather as the narrative infrastructure and embedded testimony of Ward's unorthodox social practice and combustible relations with ecclesiastical authorities on both sides of the confessional divide. Consider, in this light, the arc of her career. In recent decades Ward has been celebrated as a pioneering figure in the advancement of female ministry within the Catholic Church and in the promotion of public education for girls. Superficially, Ward's career is legible as an instance of the post-Tridentine mandate of educational expansion and reform directed toward global propagation (and reterritorialization) of the faith.[32] Despite Ward's declared good intentions, however, the church hierarchy possessed neither the language nor the pastoral incentive to make sense of, and still less to endorse, Ward's radical program for a female apostolate governed neither by traditional rules of claustration or conventual garb nor submission to episcopal authority. Full recognition would not come until after the progressive mission of *ressourcement* theology (its so-called deadly fruit) had found expression in the widespread pastoral reforms of Vatican II.

The one thing Ward most wanted and needed was the intervention of the papal magisterium on behalf of her enterprise. But Ward's repeated petitions to three successive pontiffs failed to win unmitigated support. In 1631 contretemps turned into catastrophe, with the publication of Urban VIII's papal bull (*Pastoralis Romani Pontificis*) extinguishing Ward's institute (known as the School of the Blessed Mary). Less than a month after Urban VIII signed the bull, Ward, then residing in Munich, was arrested and imprisoned on charges of heresy. One year later the charges were dropped. But the central terms of the bull remained in force.

> Certain women or virgins, having taken the title of Jesuitresses . . . [and] on the pretext of living a customary religious life . . . wander about at will and . . . employ themselves at many . . . works which are most unsuited to maidenly reserve. . . . [These] poisonous growths in the Church must be torn up from the roots lest they spread themselves further. And, therefore . . . we totally and completely suppress and extinguish them, subject them to perpetual abolition . . . and we wish and command all the Christian faithful to regard and repute them as suppressed, extinct, rooted out, destroyed and abolished.[33]

Without naming the extinguished city, the text implicitly places Ward's community in the shadow of Sodom, and its language (like that of *Humani Generis* in 1950) is rigorously faithful to the dominant rhetorical function of Sodomitical allusion within the intertextual fabric of biblical prototypes. Sodom is the intimate enemy, the image of broken covenant, and the hallucinatory reminder of the fine edge separating the chosen community from disaster.

As it turned out, the impact of the bull was not total, and the lapses are telling, in the sense that the document's uneven reach over time and space shaped what may be called the intermittent history of Mary Ward's enterprise. After 1631 scattered remnants of the community survived, notably in Bavaria, under the quiet ad hoc protection of sympathetic bishops. In 1703 partial approbation of the diaspora community was allowed, but it was not until 1877 that the Congregation of Propaganda granted full confirmation of Ward's institute. In the event, formal recognition of Mary Ward as founder of the institute was the act of a twentieth-century pope, Pius X, in 1909, and, as suggested, the full measure of Ward's intentions for the institute (the incorporation of the Ignatian Constitutions into the protocol of the order) was not realized until 1978, not until the revitalized ecumenical ethos of Vatican II had left its imprint—*tupos, figura*—on the church.[34]

Ward's place in the annals of Counter-Reformation history is assured, in part because of the archival labors of Jesuit historians going back as far as Tobias Lohner in the late seventeenth century. The contributions of historians belonging to Ward's institute have been no less significant, and the list is long. All have been keen to minimize the gap between hagiography and critical biography, although it must be said that none is entirely successful in this regard. Only recently (2008) has a critical edition in English of Ward's several writings appeared in print.[35]

The *Painted Life* has not received comparable attention. Despite the clear cultural and art historical interest of the ensemble, to date no critical edition of the visual narrative exists, and most accounts of the paintings in recent scholarship tend to treat the works as ancillary proofs of Ward's aspirations and achievements.[36] The basic facts regarding provenance can be told in a few words. The paintings are housed in the convent of the congregation in Augsburg. The range of dates of execution is uncertain, although it has been conjectured that the paintings were installed there by the founder of the Augsburg house in 1662.[37] Lohner's biography (1689) seems to have been the first to use the paintings to corroborate incidents described in written archives, but it is by no means the last to do so. The words written by Mary Chambers in her 1882 biography of Ward have evidently acquired the status of a mantra. The paintings, she wrote, constitute a "rather singular kind of testimony to numerous facts in Mary Ward's life."[38] Virtually all modern biographies replicate Chambers's assessment, tacitly ascribing a numinous (quasi-photographic) authority to the representational medium of painted, visual narrative.

Although it is surely high time for a more critically aware, historicized account of the *Painted Life*, my approach does not entail treating Chambers's remark as a precritical artifact. I think Chambers's words are absolutely right. The *Painted Life* indeed constitutes "a singular kind of testimony to numerous facts" relating to Ward's legacy. To see how this is so, however, it is necessary to recognize the semantic volatility of such words as "singular" and "testimony" as they bear on "facts." To put the matter in terms of Ward's complicated excursions into the figural afterlife of Sodom, I suggest that the testimonial power of the *Painted Life* reclaims Irenaeus's counterreading of Lot's wife. In both cases—and this is the decisive factor—the pillar does not stand for paralysis. It stands for survival and, more, for unanticipated means of survival. That single change of orientation invites us to consider how the paintings' mimetic apparatus may not be entirely governed by established or dogmatic iconographic conventions of pictorial argument. Again, we are not looking for literal pillars. In other words, in the *Painted Life* mimetic craft discovers, inhabits, and is marked by the testimonial provocation of the mutating figure in the Sodom narrative. By entertaining the fictive consanguinity of Irenaeus's intuition and the visual grammar of the *Painted Life*, we can better grasp the scope of the paintings' commemoration of the at-once radiant and abjected figure of Ward's idea of ecclesial community together with its doubled orientation, looking backward and forward at the same time.

Neither art historical connoisseurship nor the early modern florilegia of ecclesiastical commentary will be of much help in decoding the Irenaean subtext to the *Painted Life*'s visual argument. Instead, I turn to what could be called a late modern footnote to Irenaeus's habit of mind, one of Jacques Derrida's last and most beautiful ruminations on the "structure of testimony."[39] The essay, *Demeure*, takes the form of a commentary on Maurice Blanchot's postwar testimonial fiction titled "The Instant of My Death." Both texts, Derrida's and Blanchot's, emphasize the profound equivocality of testimony. This trait turns on two seeming contradictions, which constitute what Derrida calls the "testimonial condition."[40] Testimony would not be testimony were it not singular, "unique and irreplaceable."[41] But its singularity must also be exemplary—that is, replaceable by substitutes or cognates. Otherwise, testimony would be mere idiosyncrasy. The first condition of testimony, then, is that in the instant of its articulation, the singular becomes universalizable.[42] The second condition turns on the relation of this at-once singular and universal event to time. The one who gives testimony—the witness—is necessarily a survivor. Whether the event in question is banal or extraordinary, "one testifies only when one has lived longer than what has come to pass."[43] Yet a kind of temporal vertigo disrupts the "commonsense ordering of time" that would otherwise guarantee the belated status, as well as juridical value, of testimony. Because of the first condition of testimony (as point of articulation between the singular and the universal), the matter of testimony—the event to which testimony gives witness—is, at the same time, interred and reactivated in discourse. As Blanchot insists, what is caught in the sights of testimony is "the imminence of what has always already taken place."[44] And, as Derrida points out, "this is an *unbelievable* tense."[45] "This is why," he adds, "reflection on testimony has always historically privileged the example of miracles." This is also why "testimoniality belongs *a priori* to the order of the miraculous"—because when one testifies, "even on the subject of the most ordinary and the most 'normal' event, one asks the other to believe one at one's word as if it were a matter of a miracle."[46]

It is perhaps not surprising that Derrida's meditation repeatedly gestures toward the paradigmatic place of Christian martyrs in church history and thereby aligns itself with Irenaeus's counterreading of Lot's wife. The testimonial acts of the martyrs are apt figures of a discourse that closes the distance between singularity and universality, while also defining the

Figure 2. *Painted Life*, panel 38. Published by permission of Congregatio Jesu Augsburg (Germany). Photo: Studio Tanner, Nesselwang.

flash point at which historical, chronological time bursts into an eschatological time zone punctuated by a messianic urgency. The instance of martyrological testimony also marks the juncture at which Derrida's meditation broaches concerns registered in the Augsburg paintings. The case I want to make here is that the *Painted Life* of Mary Ward sustains the "testimonial condition" of which Derrida writes and that it does so with a figural discretion that captures the peculiar historicity of the surviving remnant of Ward's community for whom the series was presumably composed in the last decades of the seventeenth century.

We need to recall that the first viewers of the *Painted Life* were very much aware that Ward's aspirations had been deleted from the rubrics of ecclesiastical history and that the community's prospects for rehabilitation were slim. The *Painted Life* responds to these facts by mobilizing the visionary component to Ward's apostolate. Although no tableau directly depicts the events of 1631, the historical reality and binding political force of the papal bull are neither disowned nor ignored. Instead, they are recalibrated according to the testimonial force and scope of Ward's visionary experience.

Panel 38 in the series is especially suggestive (Figure 2). The devotional scene, depicting Ward's orthodox commitment to Marian devotion to-

Figure 3. *Painted Life*, panel 38, detail. Published by permission of Congregatio Jesu Augsburg (Germany). Photo: Studio Tanner, Nesselwang.

gether with the practice of the rosary, provides the setting for a polemical divine communication and consolation. "God," the text reads, makes "known to her that [the] prosperity, progress and security [of her institute] did not depend upon wealth . . . and the favour of princes, but [only] . . . on 'Him from whom proceed all strength . . . and protection.'" Anyone acquainted with the course of Ward's career would have known that princes (at least Continental ones) were not her problem. In sum, the painting should be taken as a tactful reminiscence of where the real problem lay. The text indicates that the vision occurred on the "feast of Saint-Peter-in-Chains 1625."[47] This is not the date of Urban's bull, of course, but it does mark the beginning of the apparent end of Ward's project. The schools that Ward founded in Rome were shut down in 1625. The notation of the feast day is a pretty clear marker of the papal authority that would ultimately suppress the institute globally. So too is the object that figures prominently in the pile that signifies "junk" in the foreground (Figure 3). The florid headgear looks like a papal tiara to me. With such a visual cue virtually italicized, it would not be surprising to discover a papal bull in the vicinity as well.

If testimony conveys the "imminence of what has always already taken place," panel 38 in the *Painted Life* corroborates the point. The stark black bar dividing Ward's devotional scene from the pile of discarded emblems of ecclesial and political authority discloses the hidden burden and promise of this condition, which is to recollect a past that "has never been present."[48] This single compositional detail discloses the central testimonial act in the *Painted Life* at large, which is to present the historical erasure of the community as phantasmatic symptom of its imminent justification.

A further element from the visual grammar of the argument underscores the point. I am looking at red chairs. Red chairs in the *Painted Life* testify to the vexing asymmetry between two competing claims of discursive authority in the matter of the institute: Ward's word and the papacy's. I say "asymmetry" because Ward's ambition was clearly more problematic than that of the pontiffs she dealt with. Ultimately, Urban VIII had simply to say yes or no. There was no fundamental discrepancy between spiritual and apostolic or political domains in the pope's judgment. Ward, on the other hand, had to say both yes and no, at the same time, positioned as she was between her visionary convictions and her steadfast allegiance to the Apostolic See. After 1631 her community had no option but to take up residence in the discrepancy between yes and no and between historical and eschatological time: the time of *figura*.

Part of this story is conveyed in the first painting in the series, which depicts the first word Ward was said to have uttered as a child, the messianic name of "Jesus" (Plate 1). The toddler stands next to a red chair, with the word "Jesus" filling the space in between. It's a charming domestic miracle: baby's first word—in this case the transition from *infans* to Jesuitress-to-be. The presence of the chair reinforces the ordinariness of the event. The child is gaining entrance into the symbolic domain of language but still needs the support of a chair to move about. Considered in context, however, as the inaugural event in the *Painted Life*, the visual nexus of speaking child, numinous divine name, chair, and the chair's vivid red color—the color of cardinals and the blood of martyr-witnesses—carries a more pointed argument. We are invited to dwell on a virtual nonevent and on the complicated stakes to be considered in giving testimony to the *eventfulness* of a nonevent.

What is not happening in the painting can be thought of as the reverberation of a visual pun: Ward is not speaking "from the chair," ex cathedra. The phrase, of course, had not yet assumed its place in the dogmatic description of the pontiff's discretionary power to speak with supreme and infallible apostolic authority. This would not be formalized until the First Vatican Council, in 1870. But the phrase was already being used instrumentally in Counter-Reformation discussions of the scope of papal prerogatives.[49] In any event, neither Ward nor her community needed the dogmatic formulation to appreciate the binding force of the pontiff's apostolic authority as expressed through the actions of the *Propaganda Fide* or the promulgation of papal bulls. The argument in the painting, however, is not unilateral. The visual nexus represents both Ward's prescient deference to ecclesiastical authority and the charisma of her voice as unmediated channel of messianic truth. More precisely, the tableau represents the noncoincidence of ecclesial and messianic truth, and the divergence is no more than a filament between chair and hand.[50]

Other paintings address more squarely the practical effects and visionary prompting of Ward's discursive agency. The second panel depicts Ward's refusal of a marriage proposal, one of several arranged by her parents. Seated decorously in a red chair, she is *in cathedra*, so to speak, just saying no (Plate 2). Panel 22 depicts the informal constitution of Ward's first community in 1609. Several young English "ladies of noble birth," all seated in red chairs, are "won over," the marginal text reads, by "Mary's edifying life and persuasive words" and cross over "with her to Saint-Omer, to serve God in the religious state under Mary's direction." The depicted society of red chairs testifies to the foundational impact of Ward's "persuasive words" (Plate 3). Panel 34, on the other hand, presents the conspicuous absence of the red chair. Commemorating one of Ward's several mystical experiences, the painting shows the usual furniture of Ward's intimate space: private devotional altar, four-poster bed, walls cast in shadow, geometrically patterned floor. Instead of the chair, typically situated between altar and bed, we see Ward's luminous vision of Christ (Figure 4). We also see the effect of the substitution. In a sacred autopsy Ward's heart is exposed, revealing the incised figure—*tupos*—of Christ in miniature.

Other panels confirm the code promoted by these samples. When Ward is seated in the red chair, she is making things happen, moving proactively toward the fulfillment of her apostolic vision. Conversely, when the chair is empty (or occupied by someone else), Mary's submissive or passive position is emphasized. When the chair is displaced, as in panel 34, we witness the theoretical and theological ground of Ward's apostolic program, its investment in the Christic paradoxes of the Incarnation and the Passion, to the point of dissolving logical distinctions between passive and active. The radiant focal point of the tableau—the replica of Christ's image incised in Ward's heart—envisions a space for legitimate ecclesial enterprise unseen by the papal magisterium.[51]

The most provocative instance of the red chair occurs in panel 24 (Plate 4). The painting depicts the second of three mystical visions that Ward's writings define as decisive stages in her understanding of the course her apostolic mission should take. The second vision (in 1611) arguably posed the greatest testimonial challenge, for it touched on the pivotal question of which exemplar Ward would follow in devising the rule for her institute.

Figure 4. *Painted Life*, panel 34. Published by permission of Congregatio Jesu Augsburg (Germany). Photo: Studio Tanner, Nesselwang.

In two letters written nearly a decade after the vision, Ward recalled the terms of the divine instruction "without adding or altering one syllable": A voice not heard "but intellectually understood" said, "'Take the same of the Society [of Jesus].'"[52] The challenge Ward's descendants faced was to hold in mind several equally compelling truths about the instruction: that the terms were divinely inspired, unambiguous, preposterous, and also principally responsible for Ward's eventual collision course with the Apostolic See.

Panel 24 renders the required negotiation. The caption makes no mention of the Jesuit order, noting simply that Ward "received quite plainly by an interior voice in what way she was to organize her Institute." But the red chairs are eloquent. On the right-hand side we see Ward recovering from an illness and taking instruction from a confessor or spiritual adviser, who is seated in a red chair.[53] The caption says nothing about this conversation, but from what is known about the dismay with which Ward's "Jesuitical" intentions were met generally by her Jesuit advisers, it is safe to say that the priest here is not saying, "Follow your interior voice."[54] More likely, the authority of the red chair is invoked to recall the opposition of the ecclesiastical hierarchy to Ward's Jesuitical program. In any case the most arresting detail in the tableau is not the occupied chair but the empty one. This chair takes up the space typically occupied by a window in the *Painted*

Life. Like many of the windows in the series, the chair lies on a devotional axis between Ward and sacred image, and it italicizes the visionary component to Ward's devotional practice. It also adds something that a window, in this painting, could not.

The empty red chair is the figure of the double truth that would remain in force for centuries. Empty, the chair figures the absence of the papal seal of approval, which kept the community in an irregular condition, outside the canonical history of religious orders—stranded between Sodom and Zoar, in Lot's wife's place. Empty, the chair figures the lingering presence of another body of knowledge, the memory of Ward's visionary conviction and the "divine Truth" that authorized it. Here, again, is Lot's wife's place, as remembered by Irenaeus but largely forgotten by the orthodoxy he helped found. In sum, the red chair is not so much an iconographic surrogate for the salt pillar as it is a witness to the intuition lodged in the recesses of the figure: the mutating character of the distinction between perceived and real borders of ecclesial community.

No wonder that by the end of the seventeenth century the legend of Ward's particular interest in this painting had taken its place in the collective memory of the community. One of the community's first archivists, Mary Cramlington, recorded word of Ward's having commissioned this very painting (date unknown), and shortly after the publication of the papal bull, she gave specific orders that the painting be placed in safekeeping, urging her companions to remember that current "times are different from what they have been and will be."[55] Even if apocryphal, the story is as true as the double truth of the red chair.

In view of the twentieth-century rehabilitation of the institute, Mary Ward seems to have had the last word. But perhaps not quite—no more so, all things considered, than the legislated reforms of Vatican II can be said to have had the last word in orienting the direction of global Catholicism in the late twentieth and early twenty-first centuries. Consider for starters the status of Ward's case for beatification. In 1983 John Paul II declared his intention to "beatify her in his pontificate," and given his documented efficiency in advancing candidates, interested parties would have had every reason to expect breaking news before the turn of the millennium.[56] With an irony that surely would not have been lost on Ward, the case is still pending in the Congregation of Rites.[57]

It cannot be said that the secular world should be waiting breathlessly for signs of progress on this score, especially when the more legibly consequential goal of securing Ward's place in the canon of English women's writings is now virtually assured. But the conjecture is not idle, because it holds in reserve another speculation that warrants attention. We need only pause to consider how the political impact of the pontiff's views of the marriage between theology and ecumenism, between *veritas* and *historia*, extends far beyond parochial or denominational demarcations of the contemporary *ecclesia* in the global community. Although Benedict XVI was known to have been a former advocate of *ressourcement* theology, in part because of its declared investment in mining patristic reservoirs of thought, it is far from clear whether the current magisterium will be susceptible to the radical intuition housed in Irenaeus's writings and reclaimed in Ward's apostolic career. Such a prospect, if realized, would impose recognition of the intimacy between the living face of the *ecclesia* and the turning, mutating figure of Lot's wife, the figure that both embodies and interrogates the limits of hospitality toward the outsider.

Mary Ward surely belongs in the canon of early modern women's writing. Just as surely, the testimonial condition advanced by the reversals and contretemps of her career opens a productive breach in the territorial instincts of canonicity and periodization—the engines of cultural tradition and apostolic authority alike. Through this breach the archived data of Ward's enterprise may be said to enter into the continuing ethical and theological provocation of what Irenaeus saw in the Sodom story, and this, I have been arguing, is a component of Ward's legacy that deserves critical recognition. The silent, patient witnesses to that legacy are the anonymous hands that invented a pictorial lexicon and grammar for expressing the strange but vital figural kinship between pillar of salt and red chair in the *Painted Life*.

Notes

1. Luigi Pulci, *Il Morgante* (Florence: Bartolomeo Sermartelli, 1574), 198. For an account of Sermartelli's typographical designs, together with bibliographical details of the letter "L," see Franca Petrucci Nardelli, *La lettera e l'immagine: le iniziali parlante nella tipografia italiana, secc. XVI–XVII* (Florence: Leo S. Olschki, 1991), 74–75. I thank Paul Gehl for pointing out this reference.

2. For a discussion of the relation between talking letters, rhetorical techniques of *copia*, and mnemonic arts in the sixteenth century, see Lina Bolzoni, *Gallery of Memory: Literary and Iconographic Models in the Age of Printing*, trans. Jeremy Parzen (Toronto: University of Toronto Press, 2001), 98–105.

3. The Abrahamic cycle famously includes two maternal figures that exemplify the positions of the chosen and the cast out in the covenantal economy: Sarah and Hagar. The third maternal figure in the cycle, Lot's wife, occu-

pies a unique symbolic position between Sarah and Hagar. On the one hand, Lot's wife is left behind and seemingly forgotten by the survivors of the destroyed cities; on the other hand, her abrupt deletion from the story also creates the condition for the subsequent incest, the offspring of which includes, many generations later, the Moabite Ruth, ancestor of the messianic line of David. For an examination of the metonymic association of Sarah, Hagar, and Lot's wife in the covenantal drama of hospitality, see Tracy McNulty, *The Hostess: Hospitality, Femininity, and the Expropriation of Identity* (Minneapolis: University of Minnesota Press, 2007), 15–20.

4. See Erich Auerbach, "Figura," in his *Scenes from the Drama of European Literature: Six Essays* (New York: Meridian, 1959), 11–76. For an account of the relation between typology and Hegelian dialectic, see Cyril O'Regan, *The Heterodox Hegel* (Albany: State University of New York Press, 1994).

5. See John A. Gallagher, *Time Past, Time Future: An Historical Study of Catholic Moral Theology* (New York: Paulist Press, 1990), 123–61. For a helpful account of the key figures and issues associated with the *nouvelle théologie*, see Jürgen Mettepenningen, *Nouvelle Théologie—New Theology: Inheritor of Modernism, Precursor of Vatican II* (London: T & T Clark International, 2010).

6. Gallagher, *Time Past*, 144–46.

7. For a lucid account of de Lubac's sense of the *complexio oppositorum*, or "complex of opposites held in tension," see Dennis M. Doyle, "Henri de Lubac and the Roots of Communion Ecclesiology," *Theological Studies* 60 (1999): 209–12. Such an orientation explains why the notion of catholicity for de Lubac could imply, as Doyle suggests, "not only an encompassing of various dimensions of truth held in tension, and not only a socially conscious embrace of all that is good and worthy, but also a radical inclusion of all human beings in all of their depth and mystery" (212). Catholicity, for de Lubac, entailed an appreciation, both reasoned and intuitive, of the intimate compact between transcendence and immanence and between theological and pastoral expressions of the Christ event in history.

8. I refer here to the engaged pastoralism of de Lubac's project generally, as distinct from his magisterial recuperation of biblical intertextuality and Christian exegetical practice in his three-volume survey, *Exégèse médiévale* (Paris: Aubier, 1959–1964).

9. For an account of the theological controversy prompted by de Lubac's revisionist arguments, see John Milbank, *The Suspended Middle: Henri de Lubac and the Debate Concerning the Supernatural* (Grand Rapids, MI: Eerdmans, 2005). For an authoritative reading of the ferment of *ressourcement* thought, which includes a nuanced appreciation of de Lubac's commitment to revitalizing a sense of sacramental ontology in the church, see Hans Boersma, *Nouvelle Théologie and Sacramental Ontology: A Return to Mystery* (Oxford, UK: Oxford University Press, 2009), 4–12, 88–99.

10. In the phenomenological and ethical sense developed by *ressourcement* theologians, *figura* stands for exposure to the trace or passage of the infinite

within the material embodiment of events. In a phrase fully cognizant of its figural resonance, de Lubac argues that knowledge of God is irreducible to propositional language, because it is already, primordially, the existential trace of "an 'image,' an 'imprint,' a 'seal' . . . the mark of God upon us," multiply disseminated throughout the envelope of creaturely existence (de Lubac, *Discovery of God*, trans. Alexander Dru [London: Darton, Longman & Todd, 1960], 7). The phrase recalls the etymological scope of *figura*'s Greek antecedent, *tupos*, which signifies a blow or wounding gesture as well as the impression left by invasive or intimate contact and, by extension, the material representation of an idea, concept, or absent thing. See Mark Taylor, *Erring: A Postmodern Theology* (Chicago: University of Chicago Press, 1984), 56–57. See also Gallagher, *Time Past*, 147. The act of exposure corresponds to what Auerbach identifies as the pivotal function of *figura* in patristic writing as a "middle term" between the literal sense of a described event (*historia* or *littera*) and the spiritual "fulfillment" of the event (*veritas*). See Auerbach, "Figura," 47. For a succinct account of de Lubac's nuanced sense of the sacramental character of the church, see Doyle, "Henri de Lubac."

11. Gallagher, *Time Past*, 149–50. See also Joseph O'Malley, *What Happened at Vatican II* (Cambridge, MA: Harvard University Press, 2008), 36–43, 75–76.

12. The incest scene involving Lot and his two surviving daughters provokes ambivalent responses from rabbinic and Christian commentators alike, but from the standpoint of providential history as construed in Christian exegesis, the fact that the house of David grew out of the incest could not be ignored. For a wide-ranging account of the afterlife of the story of Lot's daughters, see Robert M. Polhemus, *Lot's Daughters: Sex, Redemption, and Women's Quest for Authority* (Stanford, CA: Stanford University Press, 2005).

13. Robert Alter, "Sodom as Nexus: The Web of Design in Biblical Narrative," in *Reclaiming Sodom*, ed. Jonathan Goldberg (New York: Routledge, 1994), 28–42. For the text of the encyclical, see www.papalencyclicals.net/Pius12/P12HUMAN.HTM (accessed December 3, 2012).

14. For an excellent survey of the wide-ranging appropriation of the Sodom narrative in biblical and patristic texts, see J. A. Loader, *A Tale of Two Cities: Sodom and Gomorrah in the Old Testament, Early Jewish, and Early Christian Traditions* (Kampen, Netherlands; J. H. Kok, 1990). Although the encyclical's mention of deadly fruit bears Edenic associations, postbiblical Sodom lore also makes much of the so-called "apples of Sodom," first documented in Josephus, *Bellum Judaicum*, IV, viii, 4. Alluring in appearance, the fabled apples were believed to dissolve into smoke and ashes upon touch.

15. The Hebrew text of Genesis 19:26 reads: *vatabet ishto me'aharav vatehi netziv melah*. The semantic range of *netziv* is covered in Francis Brown, S. R. Driver, and Charles A. Briggs, eds., *A Hebrew and English Lexicon of the Old Testament* (1907; rpt. Oxford, UK: Oxford University Press, 1977), 662. The unstable exemplarity of Lot's wife is partly registered, if not caused, by a problem in translation that entered Christian biblical cultures quite early. The

Vulgate translates *netziv* (pillar) as *statuam* (standing figure or object, statue). In Continental and English vernacular bibles based on the Vulgate, Lot's wife becomes either a statue or an "ymage." Thus we read in a thirteenth-century French vernacular bible: "La fame Loth regarda arrieres soi, si fu muee en une ymage de sel" (see *La bible française du XIIIe siècle: edition critique de la Genèse*, ed. Michel Quereuil [Geneva: Droz, 1988], 200). William Tyndale's Pentateuch, which follows the Hebrew, introduces the figure of Lot's wife into early modern English as a pillar, and so she remains in virtually all the vernacular bibles printed in England, up to and including the King James Version. Visual representations of the episode in the early modern period continued the practice established in medieval illuminations and authorized by the Vulgate, figuring Lot's wife as a statue. Gradually, however, the object that the Hebrew text indicates came into view. For example, the woodcut from the celebrated *Nuremburg Chronicle* (1493), shows Lot's wife either in the process of becoming a pillar or, the transformation completed, as a hybrid figure, part pillar, part statue. See Heinrich Schedel, *Chronicle of the World, 1493: The Complete and Annotated Nuremburg Chronicle* (Cologne, Germany: Taschen, 2001).

16. Hans Urs von Balthasar, *A Theology of History* (New York: Sheed & Ward, 1963), 44. For von Balthasar, Christic time "assumes into itself the growing emptiness and desolation of the unreal time of sin"; and its "truth and validity" contain "the modality of untrue, non-valid time; not only in order to know it and having known it to overcome it, but in order to fill it with valid meaning" (42–43). In other words, Christic time does not disown the epochal fracture of the Cross, which is to say that it also respects what disaster entails: the mortification of meaning and of the *sense* of history. For a relevant account of the symbolic crisis provoked by the death of Jesus in Christian testament writings, see Roy A. Harrisville, *Fracture: The Cross as Irreconcilable in the Language and Thought of the Biblical Writers* (Grand Rapids, MI: William B. Eerdmans, 2006).

17. Maurice Blanchot, *The Writing of the Disaster*, trans. Ann Smock (Lincoln: University of Nebraska Press, 1995), 75. Published in 1980, Blanchot's text resumes a constellation of themes that germinated in the postwar years, during the time of his early contact and friendship with Emmanuel Levinas, whose impact on Blanchot's thought is readily discernible in *The Writing of the Disaster*. An unwritten page in the cultural history of *ressourcement* theology concerns its tacit conversation with the developing thought of Blanchot and Levinas in the postwar years and during the ecumenical period of Vatican II.

18. Blanchot's ruminations on passivity in *The Writing of the Disaster* (16–34) make the impact of Levinas's thought explicit.

19. For a suggestive opening into the relation between Blanchot and the theological culture animating the *ressourcement* movement, see Kevin Hart, *The Dark Gaze: Maurice Blanchot and the Sacred* (Chicago: University of Chicago Press, 2004), 22–49.

20. "This is what is strange: passivity is never passive enough. It is in this respect that one can speak of an infinite passivity: perhaps because passivity

evades all formulations—yet it seems that there is in passivity something like a demand that would require it to fall always short of itself. There is in passivity not passivity, but its demand, a movement of the past toward the insurpassable. Passivity, passion, past, *pas* (both negation and step—the trace or movement of an advance): this semantic play provides us with a slippage of meaning, but not with anything to which we could entrust ourselves, not with anything like an answer that would satisfy us" (Blanchot, *Writing of the Disaster*, 16–17).

21. See Janice Haaken, *Pillar of Salt: Gender, Memory, and the Perils of Looking Back* (New Brunswick, NJ: Rutgers University Press, 1998), 18. The most famous use of Lot's wife in art relating to the Shoah is perhaps Anselm Kiefer's 1989 multimedia work *Lots Fräu* (Cleveland Museum of Art). See www.clevelandart.org/exhibcef/consexhib/html/aboLots.html (accessed December 3, 2012). For an illuminating account of the negative exemplarity of Lot's wife in postmodern aesthetics, see Martin Harries, *Forgetting Lot's Wife: On Destructive Spectatorship* (New York: Fordham University Press, 2007).

22. For a methodologically congenial account of the surprising afterlife of Lot's wife in colonial America, see the penetrating analysis of Mary Rowlandson's crisis in Mitchell Robert Breitwieser, *American Puritanism and the Defense of Mourning: Religion, Grief, and Ethnology in Mary White Rowlandson's Captivity Narrative* (Madison: University of Wisconsin Press, 1990).

23. "And while these things were taking place, his wife remained in [the region of] Sodom, no longer corruptible flesh, but a pillar of salt [*statua salis*] which endures for ever; and by those natural processes which appertain to the human race, indicating that the Church also, which is the salt of the earth, has been left behind within the confines of the earth [*sal terrae*], and subject to human sufferings [*patiens quae sunt humana*]; and while entire members are often taken away from it, the pillar of salt still endures, thus typifying the foundation of the faith which fortifies and advances children toward their Father. . . . For the Church alone sustains with purity the reproach of those who suffer persecution for righteousness' sake, and endure all sorts of punishments, and are put to death because of the love which they bear to God, and their confession of His Son; often weakened indeed, yet immediately increasing her members, and becoming whole again, after the same manner as her type, Lot's wife, who became a pillar of salt. Thus, too, [she passes through an experience] similar to that of the ancient prophets, as the Lord declares, 'For so persecuted they the prophets who were before you,' inasmuch as she does indeed, in a new fashion, suffer persecution from those who do not receive the word of God, while the self-same spirit rests upon her [as upon these ancient prophets]." Irenaeus, *Adversus haereses*, ed. Adelin Rousseau and Louis Doutreleau (Paris: Editions du Cerf, 1982), 4.31.3, 4.33.9. My translation is from the preferred modern critical edition by Rousseau and Doutreleau.

24. For a pertinent discussion of the second-century debates about bodily resurrection in the emergent orthodoxy of the church, see Caroline Walker Bynum, *The Resurrection of the Body in Western Christianity, 200–1336* (New

York: Columbia University Press, 1995), 27–58. It is no coincidence that Irenaeus's treatise should have proved a central source of inspiration for *ressourcement* theologians. For an account of Balthasar's debt to Irenaeus, see Kevin Mongrain, *The Systematic Thought of Hans Urs von Balthasar: An Irenaean Retrieval* (Chestnut Ridge, NY: Crossroads, 2002), 27–50.

25. Martin Luther, *Lectures on Genesis*, v. 3, trans. George V. Schick, ed. Jaroslav Pelikan (St. Louis, MO: Concordia, 1961), 299. Like most of the polemical applications of Genesis 19:26 in the decades to follow, Luther takes his moorings from the note of eschatological urgency attributed to Jesus's conjuring of Lot's wife in the End Times segment of the Gospel according to Luke: "Remember Lot's wife" (Luke 17:32). Luther's commentary: "From this we readily understand what it means to look back, namely, to depart from God's command and to be occupied with other matters—matters outside one's calling. . . . For everyone should stick to his own calling and not concern himself with what others are doing. At the present time the papists beset us a great deal with the example of a former age during which everything lay in darkness. 'Your doctrine,' they say, 'is new and unknown to our ancestors; therefore if it is true, all our ancestors have been condemned.' They, too, are looking back and thus disregard the word they have before them. . . . Thus the church is never without a trial, for the world does not continue on the proper and steady course of its calling but looks back like Lot's wife. . . . To be drawn away from the Word by new and strange ideas is . . . no joke or slight trial. . . . Such were the beginnings of nearly all heresies."

26. "From one end of the Bible to the other there is scarcely a woman of prominence who is not in some way a figure of that Church. The ingenuity of the first commentators, encouraged by the speculations of the rabbis, saw her in Lot's wife; following Paul, they recognized her in Sara; she it was, too, that they found in Rachel and Rebbeca, in Deborah, and in Samuel's mother Anne, in the widow of Sarepta and in Esther" (Henri de Lubac, *Catholicism: Christ and the Common Destiny of Man*, trans. Lancelot C. Shepherd and Sister Elizabeth Englund [San Francisco: Ignatius Press, 1988], 187–88). De Lubac's catalog does not mention Irenaeus's text, however, nor does it pause to consider the impact of the "ingenuity" involved in recasting Lot's wife as a figure of the church.

27. To take one example, Robert Wilkinson's sermon *Remember Lot's Wife: A Sermon Preached at Paules Crosse* (1607) ruminates obsessively (in the wake of the Gunpowder Plot) over the several ways in which the pillar of salt signifies the mortal dangers posed by the papist community, not least the peril of apostasy: "Apostates and back-sliders, you that come out of Sodom, and then look back again. . . . No man that begins a good course, and then quailes in it . . . shall ever have part in God. . . . You perverse and crooked of heart . . . such a raging lust there is in nature to do forbidden things. . . . And there is a breed of such singular spirits that turne their backes upon us, and go to Sodom, only for that cause, because we go to Zoar, Fugitives & runagates of the Romish Church,

that have renounced not their country only, but their faith too, and there by barking like dogs in a den, to pronounce for heresie whatsoever we say . . . sworne enemies to Church and Common-wealth, to Prince, Priest, people, and to all men" (37).

28. The proof-text is Genesis 18:20–33, which describes Abraham's strenuous effort to ratchet up the prospects for Sodom's survival under the imminent threat of extinction in God's incendiary judgment.

29. On the mutable contours of the papist community, see, for example, Michael Questier, *Conversion, Politics, and Religion in England, 1580–1635* (Cambridge, UK: Cambridge University Press, 1996); and Alexandra Walsham, *Church Papists: Catholicism, Conformity, and Confessional Polemic in Early Modern England* (Woodbridge, UK: Boydell, 1993). Homiletic interest in Lot's wife is a subset of broader investment in the Sodom story for ecclesial boundary drawing in early modern sermon literature; see Mary Morrissey's brief discussion of this point in the context of puritan preaching at Paul's Cross in the early seventeenth century, in *Politics and the Paul's Cross Sermons* (Oxford, UK: Oxford University Press, 2011), 216–17.

30. See Henriette Peters, *Mary Ward: A World in Contemplation* (Leominster, UK: Gracewing, 1994), 55–67.

31. For a discussion of the several ways in which Ward's ambitions violated prevailing ecclesial norms for female religious orders, see Lowell Gallagher, "Mary Ward's 'Jesuitresses,' and the Construction of a Typological Community," in *Maids and Mistresses, Cousins and Queens: Women's Alliances in Early Modern England*, ed. Susan Frye and Karen Robertson (New York: Oxford University Press, 1999), 202. See also Laurence Lux-Sterritt, "Mary Ward's English Institute: The Apostolate as Self-Affirmation?" *Recusant History* 28 (2006): 192–208; as well as Lux-Sterritt's account of Ward's pedagogic and apostolic ambitions in *Redefining Female Religious Life: French Ursulines and English Ladies in Seventeenth-Century Catholicism* (Aldershot, UK: Ashgate, 2005).

32. The assessment is based on the phenomenal success of the educational programs Ward initiated and deployed across Europe, modeling her enterprise after the protocols for the Jesuit order. The most detailed modern account of Ward's career is Peters, *Mary Ward*. For an illuminating account of Ward's practice in Germany, see Ulrike Strasser, *State of Virginity: Gender, Religion, and Politics in an Early Modern State* (Ann Arbor: University of Michigan Press, 2004).

33. Cited in Margaret Mary Littlehales, *Mary Ward: Pilgrim and Mystic* (London: Burns & Oates, 2001), 253–57.

34. In 2004 the Vatican further acknowledged the institute's close ties to the Jesuit order by giving official approval to the institute's new name: The Institute of the Blessed Virgin Mary is now known as the Congregation of Jesus.

35. See Christina Kenworthy-Browne, ed., *Mary Ward (1585–1645): A Brief Relation . . . with Autobiographical Fragments and a Selection of Letters*, Cath-

olic Record Society, v. 81 (Woodbridge, UK: Boydell & Brewer, 2008). Although not exhaustive, Kenworthy-Browne's edition provides a well-balanced group of foundational documents, including the *English Vita*, attributed to Mary Poyntz, one of Ward's first companions. For a survey of trends in scholarship on Ward before Kenworthy-Browne's fine edition, see David Wallace, "Periodizing Women: Mary Ward (1585–1645) and the Premodern Canon," *Journal of Medieval and Early Modern Studies* 36.2 (spring 2006): 397–453.

36. For an overview of the visual narrative correlated with details from Ward's life, see M. Gregory Kirkus, *The Painted Life of Mary Ward* (York, UK: Bar Convent, n.d.). Lux-Sterritt (*Redefining Religious Life*, 186–89) offers sensitive readings of a few of the panels, using a hermeneutic guided by a logic of correspondence between scenographic details in the panels and Ward's devotional meditations on traditional ideals of martyrdom and sacrificial selflessness. Without discounting the paintings' evident commemorative and quasi-hagiographic elements, I am arguing that the paintings also harbor a polemical edge prompted by the community's memory of the radically ambivalent reception of Ward's project. The paintings are reproduced online at www.congregatiojesu.org/en/maryward_painted_life.asp (accessed December 3, 2012). I wish to thank Christina Kenworthy-Browne for her generous assistance in obtaining permissions for images of the *Painted Life*. Many thanks also to Andreas Zachrau and the members of the Congregation of Jesus for their assistance in the archives at the Geistliches Zentrum Maria Ward in Augsburg.

37. M. C. E. Chambers, *The Life of Mary Ward (1585–1645)*, 2 vols. (London: Burnes & Oates, 1882–1885), 1: xlvi, 2: 554.

38. Chambers, *Life of Mary Ward*, 1: xlvi.

39. Maurice Blanchot, *The Instant of My Death* / Jacques Derrida, *Demeure: Fiction and Testimony*, trans. Elizabeth Rottenberg (Palo Alto, CA: Stanford University Press, 2000), 45.

40. Derrida, *Demeure*, 41.

41. Derrida, *Demeure*, 40.

42. "The exemplarity of the 'instant,' that which makes it an 'instance,' is that it is singular, like any exemplarity, singular *and* universal, singular *and* universalizable. The singular must be universalizable; this is the testimonial condition" (Derrida, *Demeure*, 41).

43. Derrida, *Demeure*, 45.

44. Blanchot, *Writing of the Disaster*, cited in Derrida, *Demeure*, 49.

45. Derrida, *Demeure*, 49.

46. Derrida, *Demeure*, 75.

47. English translations of the German captions are in Kirkus, *Painted Life*.

48. Derrida, *Demeure*, 50.

49. The notion of papal infallibility was already implicit in Irenaeus's argument that all the churches participating in the Christian dispensation must conform to the teaching of the church of Rome, the bearer of the "certain gift of truth" (*Adversus haereses*, IV, 26, 2).

50. My point is not that the anonymous authors of *The Painted Life* were deliberately following iconographic precedent in the tactical use of red chairs to depict a discursive privilege associated with papal authority. Not enough is known about the authorship of the painted narrative to make such a claim. My point is that the pictorial grammar of the *Painted Life* is partly constructed as an ad hoc assemblage of available semantic associations attached to the color red and the hieratic significance of chairs. Coincidentally, one of the most famous papal portraits of the era, Diego Velázquez's portrait of Pope Innocent X (c. 1650), shows the pontiff seated in a red chair, as does Pietro da Cortona's 1627 portrait of Urban VIII, a pontiff with more immediate relevance to Ward's career. Neither of these works could possibly have been a reference point for the authors of the *Painted Life*, although each testifies to the contemporary legibility of the associative index presented in the painted narrative.

51. From this vantage point the tableau represents a provocative extension of Richard Crashaw's expression of the mystical experience of Teresa of Avila in "The Flaming Heart": "Love's passives are his activ'st part. / The wounded is the wounding heart" (ll. 73–74).

52. Ward reported the visionary instructions to follow the Jesuit protocol in a 1619 letter to John Gerard, her confessor, and again in a 1621 letter to Antonio Albergati, the papal nuncio in Cologne; see Kenworthy-Browne, *Mary Ward*, 141–48.

53. For an account of Ward's illness, see Littlehales, *Mary Ward*, 64.

54. For an account of Ward's variable success in gaining the support of Jesuit advisers and authorities, see Peters, *Mary Ward*, 211–95.

55. Cited in Littlehales, *Mary Ward*, 67. Mary Cramlington's compilation provided material for one of the earliest accounts of Ward's institute: Marcus Fridl, *Englische Tugend-Schul* (1732).

56. Littlehales, *Mary Ward*, 9.

57. The process on behalf of Ward was officially opened in 1929 and, after eight decades, resulted in Ward's recognition as "venerable" (and thus "heroic in virtue") by the church in December 2009. See www.congregatiojesu.org/en/maryward_canonization.asp (accessed December 3, 2012). In order for the process to proceed to the next stage, beatification, a reported miracle must be evaluated and authenticated by the Congregation of Rites.

II

Figuring the Jew

4

Avraham Oz

Early Mimics

Shylock, Machiavelli, and the Commodification of Nationhood

V. S. Naipaul opens his novel *The Mimic Men* by describing the first meeting of his protagonist, Ralph Singh (né Ranjit Kripalsingh), with his London landlord, ironically called Mr. Shylock.

> I thought Mr Shylock looked distinguished, like a lawyer or businessman or politician. He had the habit of stroking the lobe of his ear inclining his head to listen. I thought the gesture was attractive; I copied it. I knew of recent events in Europe; they tormented me; and although I was trying to live on seven pounds a week I offered Mr Shylock my fullest, silent compassion.[1]

The use of the charged name Shylock involves a complex gesture of mimicry in exercising his "fullest, silent compassion" toward his exploiter. The act of mimicry allows Singh to participate in the cultural agenda of hegemony, thus subverting the hegemonic ideology by rendering it ambivalent. Shakespeare, obviously, was not aware of the full implication of colonialism, only initially budding in his own age. Yet, as we shall see, his charged use of aliens, such as the original Shylock attempting to come to terms with the Christian community of Venice while treading simultaneously among his fellow members of the Jewish "nation," intuitively relies on a similar gesture of mimicry.

The concept of mimicry is a kind of camouflage that is often invoked in the discourse of nationhood. As Homi Bhabha explains, "Within that conflictual economy of colonial discourse which Edward Said describes as the tension between the synchronic panoptical vision of domination—the demand for identity, stasis—and the counter-pressure of the diachrony of history—change, difference—mimicry represents an ironic compromise."[2] Mimicry, Bhabha goes on to say, "is the desire for a reformed, recognizable Other, *as a subject of a difference that is almost the same, but not quite* . . . the discourse of mimicry is constructed around an *ambivalence*"; yet it is also the sign of the inappropriate, a difference that "intensifies surveillance, and poses an imminent threat to both 'normalized' knowledge and the disciplinary powers" (emphasis added).[3] Although much more notable in later colonialism, similar gestures of mimicry can be noticed already in the early days of European cultural expansionism, at least when the encounter with the other is presented from European perspectives and the tension is between barbarism and civility. Bhabha insists on the comic nature of mimicry, although, as I have shown elsewhere, the concept applies to Marlovian tragedy as well; but then, *Tamburlaine the Great* or *The Jew of Malta*, though nominally tragedies, often verge on the grotesque and do not hold such a polarized binary from the world of comedy as some Shakespearean tragedies do.[4] Indeed, both functions of mimicry are useful to Shakespeare's comic strategy, as exemplified in *The Merchant of Venice*: The double vision to which the audience is exposed—the powerful presence of barbarism within civility or grotesque within cordial serenity—involves both the horror of surveillance revealing the gaze of otherness and the absurd absence involved in what Bhabha terms "the metonymy of presence."[5]

Because xenophobia is strongly related to nationhood, the issue of aliens figures high on the dramatic agenda of Elizabethan and Jacobean dramatists. Whereas the Muscovites or Don Armado in *Love's Labour's Lost* are situational characters, other aliens (from Aaron to Shylock, Othello, or Caliban) become prominent representatives of the process of infiltration of others into the community, defining its contours and boundaries and arousing controversial issues. It is my contention that the issue of aliens as addressed in early modern England has to do with economic processes. In other words, the issue of alien infiltrators into the emerging national unity in sixteenth- and seventeenth-century England, as reflected in the theater of Shakespeare and his contemporaries, is inseparable from the issue of what I call the commodification of nationhood.

Can a nonquantified notion such as nationhood be commodified? Upon Shylock's entrance into the court of Venice, the Duke speculates on his intentions at "the last hour of act" (*MV* 4.1.19).[6] As I have pointed out elsewhere, we never know the ultimate answer: Portia's intervention leaves Shylock's final designs unknown to anybody but him.[7] Halfway through the trial scene, between speculation and resolution, in an ironic attempt conducted by Portia, Shylock is urged in the name of the Christian society of Venice to relinquish his claim to a pound of Antonio's flesh by adopting the immeasurable spiritual doctrine of mercy. It is an awkward appeal directed to the one who, scales in hand, is still toiling (as he was throughout the play) not only to teach that same community the market value of human flesh but also to impose commercial evaluations on many other immeasurable concepts, feelings, or moral tenets. A few minutes before Portia wields her lecture on Christian grace, Shylock is busy probing aloud the moral extension of service, reifying it into purchased slavery and exploring the measure of cruelty involved in using slaves as a commodity. Earlier, in the course of the play, Shylock measures the goodness of a person in terms of the person's financial sufficiency (*MV* 1.3.14–15), informs time with financial values, and equates both Rialto and synagogue as loci devoted to financial activity and trading information for commercial benefit. Shylock the father also commodifies parental love.

> I never heard a passion so confus'd,
> So strange, outrageous, and so variable
> As the dog Jew did utter in the streets,—
> "My daughter! O my ducats! O my daughter!
> Fled with a Christian! O my Christian ducats!
> Justice, the law, my ducats, and my daughter!
> A sealed bag, two sealed bags of ducats,
> Of double ducats, stol'n from me by my daughter!
> And Jewels, two stones, two rich and precious stones,
> Stol'n buy my daughter! Justice!—find the girl,
> She hath the stones upon her, and the ducats!"
> (*MV* 2.8.12–22)

Shylock the landlord calculates feasting or food providing by a measure of profit, whereas Shylock the Jew grasps his faith as a means to multiply the market value of his proverbial livestock, turning a biblical moral fable into a blueprint for a commercial transaction. In fact, the major trait of Shylock's character may be epitomized as the commodification of any concept, value, or moral tenet. Launcelot Gobbo's satirical notion regarding the making of new Christians as reflected by the rising price of hogs is hardly surprising in this context. It may have been forged during the time he served the Jew—an apprentice in the practice of trade capitalism, a merry devil in the hellish headquarters of the devil incarnate, the powerhouse of commodification that shuts its casements to any sound not fabricated (and therefore not controlled from) within. Shylock's primary rule of conduct is to remain in control of his calculated initiatives to the very end without failing, no matter the price. If so, can it be assumed, perhaps, that even his downfall by the end of the trial has not really thwarted his original intentions? Can it be read rather as a prediction fulfilled or at least as the outcome of a calculated risk, an implicit constituent of any commercial transaction? As we shall see, not just purely economic considerations are operating here. Yet this surplus interest does not necessarily belong (as many critics of the play would have it) to the realm of revenge, a psychological consideration of a betrayed ego. It is rather a political gesture in which a crude awareness of the market value of nationhood is practiced as a tool in the meeting point between politics and economy. My discussion of the play, therefore, will necessarily and simultaneously take into account both economic and political discourse.

In demanding that Shylock give up the liberties of his financial transactions—originated and established in the commercial practices of rising mercantile capitalism and allegedly protected by Venetian law—for a religious principle, Portia (if only for a moment) joins Antonio's anachronistic demand of Shylock to suspend his practice of usury. She thus ignores the fact that this requires Shylock to give up a fundamental constituent of his identity. Being a Jew, for that matter, is a synonym for being a usurer. Such a demand could have been a viable option when addressed to a tradesman within early mercantile practices, in which the itinerant trader of commodities served merely as an arbitrating link between closed local markets. But such a demand loses its viability in the financial context of fifteenth- and sixteenth-century Venice, where early outlines of a unified market began to emerge on both a national and an international scale of commercial reality. In a world where gold and silver indeed become the equivalents of the commodified value of ewes and rams, money is naturalized as a primary form of livelihood. Jewish moneylenders became inevitable in northern Italy particularly in answering the need to credit and finance "the smaller people." Official agreements regarding the financial activities of Jews as "public bankers" (*feneratores publici*), including controlled interest rates, were signed in Florence, Ferrara, Venice, and many other local authorities. The Duke of Ferrara even managed, in 1448, to secure the blessing of the pope himself for his agreement with Jewish moneylenders. Three years later the pope repeated his ratification of such privileges accorded to Jews, "not to weaken Christian faith, but for the need and commodity of the Christian residents."[8] In 1408 the Padua city council worried that the interest rates of 20–25 percent charged by Jewish moneylenders by agreement threatened "to transfer the entire financial assets of the Christians into the hands of the Jews." They therefore applied to the Venetian authorities (to whom Padua was subject) to lower the rates, and after seven years of concentrated efforts, they were able to obtain permission to dictate the rates of 15 percent for smaller loans and 12 percent for larger ones. The Jews, saying that they could not maintain the loan business at such rates, closed their shops. The subsequent protests of the lower classes, students, low-ranking officers, and peasants forced the Venetian senate to raise the rates back to the former 20–25 percent. Similar controversy erupted in 1431, when the renewal of the agreements was negotiated and concluded with the same solution. In 1453, when, under the influence of the bishops, the Venetian senate closed the Jewish banks in Padua, the Jewish moneylenders settled in nearby villages and charged up to 40 percent interest rates. The senate soon allowed the Jews back into Padua, first for three days a week and then for full-fledged activity, restoring the old interest rates.

In all these controversies "Jews" should be read primarily as "usurers"; namely, the Jews primarily constitute a guild of economic significance, whose religious otherness is only a secondary issue. The appeal to their community was similar to their collective status as referred to by Shylock as "my nation." It is this sense of the term that Rabbi Solomon Ashkenazi uses in his petition, written in Istanbul about two decades before *The Merchant of Venice.* This petition was written to abrogate the 1571 Venetian decree of expulsion of the Jews, brought before the Council of Ten following the peace with the Ottomans by Francesco Barbaro; here Ashkenazi writes about helping "his own nation."[9] Furthermore, Jewish businessman Hayyim Saruq is described in the documents of the Holy Office as "the Consul of the Levantine nation."[10] Even if a relatively small number of Jews were involved in foreign trade, Arbel comments, "their impact on the Mediterranean economy was sufficiently marked to create an association between Jews, as an ethnic and cultural group—or in sixteenth-century terminology, a 'nation'—with the world of international trade and finance."[11] Under these circumstances a "nation" was a term ready to be commodified. Within a discourse where the synagogue was but a communal branch of the Rialto, a place where business meetings were held and commercial information commodified, a substitute had to be found for religion as a constitutive ideology giving weight to the commercial bond of a given community. Such an ideology underlying the desire for a communal bond is not far-fetched when it also applies to the Christian society, although it is only seldom openly confessed. G. M. Trevelyan attempts to account for the consolidation of the English nation-state in terms of the social history of the English textile trade.[12] In Tudor England such an ideology, whether covert or explicit, was handed down from above, as an instrument enhancing unification among the subjects of the newly established nation-state; it thus hopefully secured collective loyalty to the monarch, whose public body in turn symbolized the nation and in practical terms conducted a centralized trade and production policies.

As Shakespeare reads the communal solidarity of the Jews, he makes no effort to differentiate between tribalism and nationalism; both terms (*tribe* and *nation*) are functional attributes equally serving Shylock to refer to his fellow Jews, evoked or summoned mainly to discuss and evaluate business transactions. Nation is indeed an early instance of what will later be dubbed an "imagined community," because the local significance of its members' presence as a commercial network is complemented by its relevance to international trade. When, in the following century, the Venetian authorities allowed Levantine Jews a temporary presence in the city, they had in mind the regaining of trade with the Turkish empire, which was controlled to a great extent by Jewish merchants of Spanish and Portuguese origins.[13] Indeed, Jonathan Israel argues that "no Italian ruler with an eye on the Levant traffic could afford to hold back from the scramble to attract Levantine Jews."[14] And John Brackett, writing on Jews in and around Florence who were seeking exemption from wearing the distinctive dress mandated for Jews to secure safe passage into and out of town, asserts, in a similar context: "The commercial activities of Jewish merchants were vital to the economic well-being of the entire Tuscan state."[15] Arguments of a similar nature were advanced in Shakespeare's lifetime by Sir Thomas Sherley, when he tried unsuccessfully to persuade King James I to allow a group of Levantine Jews, his clients, to settle in England and Ireland in return for paying an ample annual tribute per head for the privilege of religious freedom and establishing synagogues.[16] Subsequently and more successfully, Menashé Ben-Israel negotiated the return of the Jews to England in 1655. We shall later return to both these enterprises, the failed one and the almost successful other, in another context.

"Imagined communities," Benedict Anderson's telling attribute for a nation,[17] does not yet apply to the Venetians themselves surrounding Shylock. Antonio, Venice's prince of merchants, is deeply invested, however, in what is becoming the global trade of early modern Europe, in which the world becomes an integrated network of commerce reflecting an international trading system and where markets are increasingly governed by nation-states that correspond to national interests.

He hath an
argosy bound to Tripolis, another to the Indies, I
understand moreover upon the Rialto, he hath a

> third at Mexico, a fourth in England, and other
> ventures he hath squand'red abroad.
> (*MV* 1.3.15–19)

It has become a justifiably critical commonplace to assume that Shakespearean Venice is a fable for commercial London of his time. It is England where "landlords took their rents from tenants who increasingly behaved like capitalists, often employing wage labour, and producing cost-effectively in order to succeed in an increasingly competitive market, what was to become the first truly national market in Europe or indeed the world."[18] It is an England indeed where "national mercantilism was supported by, and in turn heightened, national patriotism."[19] In the hands of Tudor monarchs since Henry VIII nationhood became a convenient political commodity, serving, among other ends, to contain economic unrest, especially by the peasants, by distributing an ideology of communal equality. Shylock's otherness in this respect is related to the debate on usury in Elizabethan England (not entirely resolved by the famous Act of Parliament) rather than to his religion. Whereas references to his religion serve mainly as folkloric seasoning of the narrative, his claim to nationhood is commonly ignored throughout the play, establishing an ideology promising Shylock financial equality and protection under the commercial chapter of the law.

> The Duke cannot deny the course of law:
> For the commodity that strangers have
> With us in Venice, if it be denied,
> Will much impeach the justice of the state,
> Since that the trade and profit of the city
> Consisteth of all nations.
> (*MV* 3.3.26–31)

Up to the outset of the trial scene, it looks indeed as though Venice is determined to abide by this policy. In view of the fatal consequences, however, that the maintaining of equality may bear for the life of its prince of merchants, Venice (represented by Portia in her capacity as the judge appointed by the Duke) resorts to accepting Shylock's status of foreign nationality, differentiated from and indeed contrasted with his commercial standing in Venice. Shylock's defeat in the trial is brought about by Portia's denial—in the name of Venice, as an exclusive quasi-nation-state (whose status as such is bound less to historical accuracy than to its constituting a parable for Elizabethan England)—of Shylock's promised "commodity."

This she accomplishes by evoking a hitherto covert, expressly nationalist law, subjecting universal justice to a specific national code discriminating between brothers and others.

> Tarry, Jew,
> The law hath yet another hold on you.
> It is enacted in the laws of Venice,
> If it be proved against an alien,
> That by direct, or indirect attempts
> He seek the life of any citizen,
> The party 'gainst the which he doth contrive,
> Shall seize on half his goods, the other half
> Comes to the privy coffer of the state,
> And the offender's life lies in the mercy
> Of the Duke's only, 'gainst all other voice.
> (*MV* 4.1.342–52)

By the end of the play, then, Shylock is excluded from the community of Venice by means of an "extra-economic" mode of coercion and declared an alien, and the "commodity" he holds as a stranger is confiscated to the national coffers. This opens a wide critical discussion relating the presence of Shylock in Venice to the presence of various aliens in Tudor London, some of them Jews, and to its commercial and political implications.

One of the less discussed of these options is the one whereby the story of Shylock in Venice problematizes the desired harmony between commerce and nationhood in a society governed by an ideology asserting such harmony. According to such a reading, Shylock teaches the Venetians a complex lesson in the relations between individual and society, patriarchy and commodity, nationhood and commerce. And he is doing so, in his usual manner, by commodifying nationhood, labeling it with its market value even at the peril of losing all his other material commodities (which, as the Jewish experience in Europe testified, was subject to more powerful forces of coercion than the market laws). In other words, by making Venice treat him as an alien and confiscate his money, Shylock buys its recognition of his nationhood, which albeit foreign, accords him a better status than that of folkloristic devil. Such a reading challenges Anderson's insistence on nationalism as an exclusively modern phenomenon. Yet already in Shakespeare's virtual Venice (and probably in his real-life London), Shylock, who relates to his fellow Jews as members of his "nation," subjects this term to the commercial aspect. At the trial he forfeits his capital but gains a negative, yet valid assertion of his well-established, if foreign, nationality.

A major way to consider the buds of nationalism in sixteenth- and seventeenth-century Europe may be provided by Shylock's frequent use of the practice of mimicry, as part of his attempt to establish his proper standing in the Venetian economic community. The recurrence of the actual term *nation* is significantly lower in Shakespeare's comedies than in his historical plays or the tragedies. In Shakespeare's comic writing it is telling that the term is most frequently used by one of Shakespeare's most distinguished mimics: Shylock is practicing mimicry when he refers to his "imagined community"—members of his religious and ethnic group—as "our sacred nation." His mimicry, however, is given away by the fact that at one and the same time he refers to them as "my tribe." The term looks back to ancient times in ways that "nation," even in its sixteenth-century version, does not. None but Shylock in the play refers to the Jews as a nation. The attribute "tribe" is used mainly by him as well, except on one occasion, when one of his two Christian tormentors uses the term to introduce the approaching of Tubal: "Here comes another of the tribe: a third cannot be matched, unless the devil himself turn Jew" (*MV* 3.1.70–71). What Shylock refers to as nationhood equals for Salerio a dark mold of ancient tribalism; the Christian response to Shylock's mimicry is to relate his inferior tribe to the train of Lucifer.

For the Christians in the play, national differences boil down to stereotypical properties, which could serve for comic distinctions, such as in Portia's comic depiction of the list of her suitors. Nationhood derives here from its folkloristic aspects. It is an age where the nationalist grouping is a form of desire, the pragmatic nature of which has not yet been shaped by the required political advancement of the social position of the bourgeoisie and the economic progress of capitalist conditions of production. Thus the concept of nation must rely to a greater extent on folkloristic gestures, of the kind more readily open to the comic aspects of mimicry. In this respect Shylock's behavior in court can be read as corresponding to the gesture of mimicry on which his most frequently quoted speech in the play is founded, where nationality is dissected and privatized into its separate organs and components.

> Hath not a Jew eyes? hath not a Jew hands, organs, dimensions, senses, affections, passions? fed with the same food, hurt with the same weapons, subject to the same diseases, healed by the same means, warmed and cooled by the same winter and summer as a Christian is?—if you prick us do we not bleed? if you tickle us do we not laugh? if you poison us do we not die? and if you wrong us shall we not revenge?—if we are like you in the rest, we will

> resemble you in that. If a Jew wrong a Christian, what is his humility? revenge! If a Christian wrong a Jew, what should his sufferance be by Christian example?—why revenge! The villainy you teach me I will execute, and it shall go hard but I will better the instruction. (*MV* 3.1.52–66)

The major difference between the pledge of communality underlying this speech and the ideology of nationhood assimilated by the English subjects of the Tudor dynasty is the total lack of alleged morals (or similarly primary substantial principles) in Shylock's speech, as well as its dependence on a rationale of market values whereby gestures, cultural and social responses to natural stimuli, and adopted principles of civility are measured. In other words, in mimicking the market value of nationhood, preached to him indirectly by the Christian society, Shylock—a stranger in the community whose function in the financial order is an inevitable part of Venice's economy—is drawing attention to the worth of nationhood for those who will not count him as a member of the nation. What is suggested in this speech of mimicry matures into a moral dilemma at the end of the trial scene, in which Shylock coerces the Venetians to choose between the commercial code of justice (where all are equally subjected to the laws of commerce) and the national code (where exclusion from the national community contradicts the principles of commercial equality). Subversively, Shakespeare draws attention to a moral discrepancy informing the supposed reconciliation between commerce and nationhood suggested by the commercial law on which Shylock's legal suit is founded.

Here Shylock is also the equivalent of Brabantio, Lear, and Cymbeline, all of whom are involved in a complex narrative informing the clash between the private demand of the father-daughter relationship and the public demands of national tensions. In a period where the term *nation* appears with greater frequency, whether in texts of political significance (such as John Foxe's *Book of Martyrs*) or in texts of fiction (such as Shakespeare's histories or Marlowe's tragedies), it is curious to note that nationalities are usually regarded as playing a marginal comic role in the canon.

It is Shylock who provides Venetian society with the ideological tool that may bridge this gap. He has a prophetic solution—his "nation," surprisingly preceding Anderson's definition in constituting an early imagined community: "Tubal, a wealthy Hebrew of my tribe, / Will furnish me" (*MV* 1.3.52–53).

In *The Merchant of Venice* Shylock hardly ever refers to his material assets without relating them to his tribe or nation as a collective body. In *Cymbeline* Imogen, with her prophetic intuition, feels some covert empathy with her two brothers, but she also betrays their remoteness from reality, which is conducted far away from their isolated caves in the wilderness of Wales. It is the prophecy imprinted in her nature, which is the antidote to a thoroughly commodified world, and Shakespeare would stress it almost paradoxically when he evokes an ancient prophecy with which to address the final solution of his romance, as he does at the end of *Henry V* or *Henry VIII*. The pathos and bathos combined in prophecy are the counterparts of Shylock's mimicry, both comically and bitterly pointing out to the rising national community its ideological relation to a new commercial ethos.

But what is the contemporary political notion on which Shylock's mimicry is drawing? Although being carefully attentive to the market economy, Shylock's mimic challenge to the Venetian "national" community regarding his status draws surprisingly on the pragmatic view of nationalism offered by a fairly contemporary political thinker: Niccolo Machiavelli. If the famous Jewish character introduced on the Elizabethan stage by the figure of "Machevill" is Marlowe's Barabas (although it is indeed Fernese, the Christian governor of Malta),[20] in this essay I demonstrate that it is Shakespeare's Shylock who deserves such recommendation, even though on entirely different premises.

Imagine this: a tired, if relentless Machiavelli, sitting at his desk, confined to his country farm at St. Andrea, about 7 miles from the duomo daunting central Florence. He is detached from Florentine political life, to which he actively contributed for so many years, and from the ranks of Florentine administration, to which he still desires to return and yet of which he may only write his sharp observations, owing to his forced detachment. Yet he regards his present writings mainly as the means by which he might be granted readmission, which indeed he will never be granted. Thus, finally, only from afar may he present his beloved city with the caveat against the barbarians that concludes *The Prince*. This complex dynamics of belonging—inherent in Machiavelli's ambiguous position as a practitioner finding refuge in theory, who craves to be reinstated as a practitioner to help put his theory into practice—seems to be symbolic of the subject matter of his work. That is, how can he define the crisis and desire of belonging that epitomizes a community of citizens sharing a collective memory in terms of the power of one representative individual chosen to lead them, whose power of representation derives from their choosing him while losing their legal (and moral) power of choice once he has assimilated their will, expressed in their prerogative to elect him? Both structure and meaning are shaped in the form of a riddle, yet both shun a simple solution. Is this lack of solution inevitable, or is it politically or culturally premature?

Does not this ambiguous and confused appeal to political solidarity correspond to the diversified yet ever dialectical narrative of early European desire for nationhood, curbed by some ambitious princes, who in turn promoted that very ideology among their subjects when it appeared to sustain their will to power? Not fortuitously the crux of the matter is inherent in that charged term *chosen*. Its religious overtones prompted Hans Kohn (who distinguishes between voluntarist and organic concepts of nationalism)[21] and other influential theorists of nationalism to prevent the term *nation* as a form of desire from being pushed back to the Middle Ages; and yet others, such as Huizinga before him, would discern the desire for nationhood as already operating in the Middle Ages.[22] Only few nowadays would dispute the viability of the desire for nation for a Renaissance humanist such as Machiavelli; some would argue, with John Langton, that Machiavelli's nationalism, as reflected in *The Prince*, overcame his republicanism.[23] The Machiavellian notion of nationhood (while not overriding the tension between the voluntarist and organic elements) means, in one sense, severing the Gordian knot connecting the religious overtones of the concept of election to their sanctified source and leaving the vagaries of power to the jurisdiction of goddess Fortune, who feels more at home in the Machiavellian halls of political realism than in the Augustinian shrines of faith. Is Machiavelli's separation of religious tenets from political realism so different from, say, the positions taken by Raleigh or Bacon in Elizabethan England?[24] It is my contention that Shakespeare, their contemporary, is attempting to fashion a narrative based on such a vision of nationhood in his parable of Shylock the Jew. This figure presents the Venetian emergent notion of nationhood with a sharp riddle questioning the basic relation between the community and the individual, evoking a crisis of belonging crucial to its self-definition and prophetically coercing it to relate to an inevitable factor shaping its future existence.

To a modern political thinker such as Antonio Gramsci, Machiavelli (in his epilogue to *The Prince*) is prophetic in his notion of "a new order" that the Prince is required to constitute. For Gramsci it is not the individual but "the political Party" whose function it is to found the new order, namely, "a new type of State."[25] Accounting for Machiavelli's appeal to Gramsci, Louis Althusser spells out the exact nature of this new state: "The state that Machiavelli expects from the Prince, for the unification of Italy under an absolute monarch, is not the state in general (corresponding 'to its concept') but a historically determinate type of state, required by the conditions and exigencies of nascent capitalism: a *national* state."[26]

Machiavelli's concept of nation is obviously pragmatic: The need for nation derives from the economic need to create material and social market zones. In this respect it anticipates Habermas's distinction that "a people becomes a 'nation' in this historical sense only in the concrete form of a particular form of life."[27] Shylock, less of an individualist than Marlowe's Barabas, is well aware of this; and although far from founding a Gramscian political party, he intends to make use of nationhood in another, more Machiavellian sense. In Venice, as Shylock well knows, that particular form of life (to be invoked by Habermas) depends already on an economy regulated by markets, and in Shakespeare's *Merchant of Venice* (a text greatly attentive to Machiavelli's advice to his Prince) this affects the legal system, which is crucial to Machiavelli's political science as the core factor for regulating the welfare of the state. Following the gradual separation of the state from the economy differentiates between public and private law. And the individual subject is allowed to acquire "at least a core of private autonomy."[28]

For Machiavelli collective memory, which for modern writers is one of the essential foundations of national consciousness, is hardly an enshrined treasure. Machiavelli does not regard it as any more than a construct, of which the Prince is expected to take advantage as a vehicle for maintaining his power over his subjects. Less of an idealized narrative of republican solidarity, the nation is chiefly a social ploy, an ideology designed to serve the needs of its ultimate representative, the Prince, to maintain and enhance his power, the chief source and warranty of his subjects' well-being. It is an early capitalist form of utilitarianism that prompts Fabrizio (Machiavelli's alias in *The Art of War*) to provide his famous answer to the question of using a cannon from within the ranks of troops: "the artillery marches in one direction and fires in the other."[29] This dictum is what we might call today a Brechtian answer, involving both *gestus* and a moral; to wit, sometimes the obvious function of a strategic weapon, such as a cannon (or a nation, for that matter) should be dialectically suppressed for the better achievement of a goal. Nationhood, like the cannon, is to be handled with caution and care, according to advantage and the changing circumstances.

By the same token Machiavelli advises the Prince, who seizes a new province or city, to "create everything anew," namely, to construct the citizens' national memory as stemming from him. In other words, Machiavelli advises the Prince to appropriate collective memory and create a new national consciousness in his new subjects' minds.[30] The consolidation of the Prince's power runs parallel to the creation of a new national construct and narrative.[31] It is my contention that Shakespeare's concept of a nation is to a significant extent shaped by the influence of flexible Machiavellian use of national ideology, passed on to him either directly or indirectly. In an age where religion becomes less of a dominant faith and more of a social institution, nationhood—both for Machiavelli and Shakespeare—serves as a political surrogate for the paternal controls whereby ancient and medieval religion kept European culture in a tight grip of containment, repression, and servitude.

The ancient narrative of the birth of the nation is the story of negating the tribal bonds of blood, namely, the desire of humanity to escape the terror of its unprotected, unmediated gaze into the face of nature. This is the source of Machiavelli's attraction to antiquity, in which he seeks the protective power of cultural memory. One of the earliest dramatic statements affirming social bonds enunciated at the dawn of Western dramatic tradition is Aeschylus's acquittal of Orestes, charged for revenging the breach of the marriage bond by his mother, thus placing the bond of marriage above the bond of blood in the moral hierarchy of humanity. In a less stern mode, perhaps a parody on the same theme, Machiavelli the playwright (in the comedy *La Mandragola*) demonstrates his preference for the love of one's nation over the love of one's blood by presenting the ignoramus attorney Messer Nicia, his notoriously comic butt, as prepared to let a compatriot die for him to have an offspring. That, ironically, the child to be born is to be after all the offspring of the alleged victim of murder emphasizes the priority of a large-scale social order as a vessel containing collective memory over that of an inferior social structure in which a much narrower, hence less effective, body of memory is enshrined.

This idea, depicted in *La Mandragola* in a farcical form, is reiterated in Machiavelli's admiration for Brutus, who sacrificed his sons for the good of his country.[32] What seems to be stated by Machiavelli is a sense of the quantitative reading of collective morality; the larger the body of individuals bonded together in the interest of preservation and served by an act of aggression, the more justified the measure of violence inherent in it. In 1603 a Scottish monarch ascended to the English throne and embarked almost immediately on Machiavelli's advice to performatively reconstruct the national memory. James conferred knighthood on former compatriots (such as his favorite, Robert Carr, James Hay, or Robert Ker) and instructed his parliament four years later to consider that "Irish, Scottish, Welsh, and English, divers in Nation, [were] yet all walking as Subjects and servants within [his] Court, and all living under the allegiance of your King."[33]

The ease with which pure nationhood was thus slighted and transformed by the king aroused the indignation of some traditional English patriots and could readily be associated with practices preached by Machiavelli to his Prince. I would argue that these practices had already been represented in the former decade in Shakespeare's treatment of nationhood.

In this essay I have chosen to go beyond manifest treatments of issues of nationhood, such as in *Henry V* or the history plays as a whole, or in *Cymbeline*, where a redefinition of the nation realistically follows the controversial expansion of English nationhood into a nascent British empire. Rather, I suggest a tentative, experimental reading of Shakespeare's more abstract concern with rewriting one thread of the national narrative, influenced by the practice advocated by Machiavelli the thinker but apparently quite different from Machiavelli the Italian nationalist. In terms of content it may rather anticipate Montesquieu's observation that commerce should be fostered because it may ameliorate the manners of both individuals and nations and, in particular, "polishes and softens barbarous mores, as we see every day."[34] It is located in a commercial republic such as Venice, where, unlike London, a Moor may become a general and a Jew a major banker; and yet it is a plausible reading of the play to view Shakespeare himself as toying with the idea that a national narrative can be expanded to contain or absorb the other.

Central as is the issue of English or British nationhood, the tension between nationhood and capitalism is perhaps no less emphasized in early modern drama in terms of its representation of the ambiguous nationality of the Jew, presenting emerging nationhood with a test case questioning some of its crucial assumptions. It is, to be sure, a subversion of the practical advice given by Machiavelli to the Prince regarding the uses of rewriting collective memory; containing the barbarous within such forged narratives is hardly reconcilable with his political agenda. Yet Machiavelli himself, in a 1513 letter to Vettori, draws the line between his political understanding and his lack of an economic one.[35] Thus one does not expect to find in *The Prince* a thorough analysis of the way in which national politics is limited by economy. The issue here is an investment in the welfare of the community. To paraphrase Althusser's aforementioned dictum, at a certain point in the life of a nation, historically determinate moments may emerge, such as required by the conditions and exigencies of nascent capitalism, in which even the narrative of anti-Christ calls for becoming the subject of reconstruction. In regard to Machiavelli's *Prince*, Althusser draws the distinction between the place of political ideology and its effect: "As for the people who expect this impossible Prince to transform them into a nation, and from whose perspective Machiavelli defines the Prince's politic, nothing obliges or even prompts them to constitute themselves as a people, to transform themselves into a people, or—*a fortiori*—to become a political force."[36]

Indeed, using the example of Moses as a model of *virtù*, leading the enslaved Israelites toward liberation,[37] would hardly suit Shylock, let alone Barabas. Yet becoming a political force is one matter; joining an existing nation is another. Jews in the Renaissance often sought the latter form of recognition, not for matters of faith (they did not wish to convert or to convert others, Judaism not being a missionary faith) or for political benefits, but mainly for normalizing their citizenship and economic existence. This is the interest of "the people," to use Machiavelli's terms in *The Prince*, and Shylock and his fellows indeed answer the description of the enslaved community desiring a redeeming prince. What is there for the Prince himself? Acting generously for generosity's sake is critically censured by Machiavelli: "It would be good to be thought generous; nevertheless, if you act in the way that will get you a reputation for generosity, you will do yourself damage."[38] In a similar manner he opposes leniency, showing (in the notorious Chapter 17 of *The Prince*) how leniency almost cost the Roman general Scipio Africanus his glorious reputation. Nor does the requirement that the Prince keep his word (in our case, preserve the commitment of Venetian law to grant justice equally to everyone) count at any price. What counts in the case of Shylock and the Venetians is the practical difficulty that Shylock's moral riddle has managed to present to Venice. The moral predicament that the Venetian prince, the Duke of Venice, has incurred is the effect of a law system affected by the market economy, allowing Shylock a measure of private autonomy, as described by Antonio.

> The Duke cannot deny the course of law,
> For the commodity that strangers have
> With us in Venice, if it be denied,
> Will much impeach the justice of the state,
> Since that the trade and profit of the city
> Consisteth of all nations.
> (*MV* 3.3.26–31)

To preserve his *virtù*, the Prince is allowed by Machiavelli not to keep his word (ch. 18); this, indeed, is the kind of solution the Duke seeks and finally obtains from the disguised Portia.

Shylock may be regarded, however, as offering the Duke another strategy for the acquisition of power for his principality, one that may allow him to be "a founder of a new society" without going back on his word. It is a strategy that anticipates a more modern phase of "the inclusion of the other" within the nation-state, in which economic forces are allowed to undergo a sociopolitical transformation, one "first accomplished by the urban . . . middle classes before it found a resonance in the wider population."[39] Is Shakespeare's Venetian Prince (or for that matter, his English counterpart) ready to meet such a revolutionary challenge, which even if not approved by the historical Machiavelli is nevertheless legitimately derived from his own teaching and justifies what Maggie Günsberg defines as the "end-orientation" of the narrative of *The Prince*?[40]

On June 10, 1593, about three years before Shakespeare wrote *The Merchant of Venice*, the Grand Duke Ferdinand I dei Medici, the ruler of Tuscany, issued a patent letter inviting "all nations" to come and settle in the new town of Leghorn (Livorno), which was designed to replace the sand-blocked port of Pisa. In his letter, to which many Jewish conversos responded by coming to settle in Leghorn, the duke guarantees safe conduct, religious liberties, a Tuscan citizenship, civil and partly criminal jurisdiction among the Jews, the right to own property, and permission to return to Judaism. In 1550 Henri II of France issued an edict granting religious liberties and legal jurisdiction to the Jewish communities in the southwest, and this edict was ratified by Henri III in 1574. In Venice, back in 1475 and following a blood libel, the Doge Mocenigo issued a manifesto that strongly protected the Jews of the town.

What is more, at least one premature attempt to reach a similar understanding between the Jews and the English Crown was made during Shakespeare's lifetime. It is described in detail in a 1607 letter from Sir Thomas Sherley, a former employee of the Grand Duke of Tuscany, to King James I. In that letter, in which he unsuccessfully attempts to intercede on behalf of a group of Levantine Jews who wish to settle in England, Sir Thomas argues for the economic advantage of a positive answer from the king; they could be a monetary asset, profitable in many ways, a good source for a more or less forced loan, as they had served the Duke of Mantua (who, albeit one of the least prosperous of the Italian states, "one in three years . . . picks 300,000 or 400,000 crowns out of his Jews"). Sir Thomas warns that "at the first they must be tenderly used for there is great difference in alluring birds and handling them when they are caught; and your agent that treats with them must be a man of credit and acquaintance amongst them who must know how to manage them, because they are very subtile people."[41] This sounds very much in the spirit of Machiavelli; the alluring of birds has a different impact when coming from Sir Thomas Sherley regarding the Jews than from Juliet regarding Romeo and pertains more readily to reifying rather than affectionately taming. The capitalist resources of the Jews sustained the less prosperous Duke of Mantua as they did the financial capital of medieval Europe, Machiavelli's Florence, whose secular authorities, having "prohibited credit transactions altogether . . . then imported Jews to conduct a business forbidden to Christians."[42]

Jewish readmission to England was slow to materialize. James Harrington, whose utopian *Oceana* was published in late 1656, "permit[s] its merchants the practice of lending upon interest (though not, apparently, to readmit the Jews)."[43] The catalyst for readmission was the serious negotiations in 1655 between Cromwell and Menashé Ben-Israel, a leader of the Jewish community in Amsterdam. Ben-Israel's letter, addressed to "the Lord Protector of the Commonwealth of England, Scotland and Ireland," is written "on behalf of the Jewish nation." Cromwell was persuaded of the financial utility of letting the Jews officially back to England. In both cases the Jews, offering to settle in England, sought incorporation into the nation-state without relinquishing their religion, because this option had been open for them much earlier. All this led to the 1753 "Jew Bill," suggested by Joseph Salvador and endorsed by Prime Minister Henry Pelham. Has Shakespeare, through Shylock and under the influence of Machiavellian practices, prophetically anticipated such a historical moment in which ideas of that sort, existent if not yet materialized, hovered in the air? In other words, may one assume a reading of *The Merchant of Venice* in which Shylock offers to join the Venetian community rather than perpetuate his eternal otherness and thus offers the Duke of Venice an opportunity to rewrite (in Machiavellian terms) a national narrative that, unlike religion, is open to change? Unlike Marlowe's Machevill, Shylock does not "count religion but a childish toy," but he certainly never regards his faith as relevant to his aspired citizenship of Venice, through which he expects equality of legal and occupational rights. This is the distinction he makes between buying, selling, and talking with his fellow Venetians and eating, drinking, or praying with them as his enemies the Christians.

The question of a Jewish nation, as distinct from a religion, has troubled ancient and modern minds alike. Did Jewry pertain to race, nation, or religion? Andrew Willett paraphrased Paul in Romans in saying that "Jews have never been grafted onto the stock of other people," yet Paul himself already problematized his dictum.[44] In *The Merchant of Venice* Shylock refers to his native community three times as "my tribe" and three times as "my nation." To these Jessica adds another, somewhat awkward third category, when she accounts for Tubal and Chus as her father's "countrymen." I would argue that this third category provided by Jessica is a main key to Shakespeare's transformation of the ancient parable of the pound of flesh into a narrative charged by a desire for nationhood.

Machiavelli's advice to the Prince to reconstruct the national collective memory of his newly acquired community of subjects assumes that such a collective memory (or its biography) is accepted by the given imagined community as a material cornerstone of its nationhood. Therefore tampering with its past narrative will affect a future desired by the Prince. Shylock, representing an elusive community with a memory but without a master narrative connecting it to any of the accepted material constituents of nationhood separated from religion (namely, ethnicity, language, or territory), is significantly devoid of a biography, either collective or personal. Shylock's conspicuous lack of personal biographical details, in which he stands out among the characters of *The Merchant of Venice*, suggests that he partakes in the general fairy-tale biography offered by the popular imagination for the cultural construct of the Jew.[45] Such an exemplary biography is provided by Marlowe for his own Jew, Barabas, presented from the outset as an ardent follower of none else but Machevill, resurrected at the prologue to stamp the protagonist with his own features. Whereas (in the prologue of *The Jew of Malta*) Machevill's soul "but flown beyond the Alps, / And now, the Guise is dead, is come from France, / To view this land, and frolic with his friends,"[46] Barabas's colorful biography involves all the clichéd activities and occupations traditionally associated with the Jew, from well poisoning and killing sick Christians, through practicing "physic" to the detriment of his Christian patients, and finally to usury (*JM* 2.3.176–202).

In terms of that nonbiography the Jew is indeed close to Marx's definition, cited by Greenblatt: "a universal *antisocial* element of the *present time*."[47] Shylock's wish to see his daughter "dead at [his] foot, and the jewels in her ear . . . and the ducats in her coffin" (*MV* 3.1.80–82) belongs to the same order of transgressive acts as Barabas's murdering of Abigail; both are simultaneously deeds and nondeeds, devoid of the necessity of representation. In the case of that cultural construct turned dramatic character, one cannot easily separate the positive limits, the finitude of the subject—which in Foucault's hostile description "is marked by the spatiality of the body, the yawning of desire, and the time of language"[48]—from the transgression of the subject that suggests an absence of knowledge, or a knowledge of absence. Barabas has accomplished considerable mischief, as he himself admits and is seen in the play. Regardless of what he has actually done, however, there is a permanent stock of evil, inherent in the cultural construct of the Jew, and ever ready to be assigned to him in people's minds with no need for factual evidence.

> Barnardine: . . . go with me and help me to exclaim against the Jew.
> Jacomo: Why, what has he done?
> Barnardine: A thing that makes me tremble to unfold.
> Jacomo: What, has he crucified a child?
> (*JM* 3.6.45–49)

Marlowe even provides his reader with a lively illustration of the common process in which such a fictional identity, or "biography," is forged. This is when the drunken Ithamore gratuitously constructs the clichéd image of the mean Jew before the courtesan and her bully while Barabas in disguise provides the truth for us, as he always does in his asides.

> Ithamore: 'Tis a strange thing of that jew: he lives upon pickled grasshoppers and sauc'd mushrooms.
> Barabas: [*aside*] What a slave's this! The governor feeds not as I do.
> Ithamore: He never put on a clean shirt since he was circumcis'd.
> Barabas: [*aside*] O rascal! I change myself twice a day.
> Ithamore: The hat he wears, Judas left under the elder when he hang's himself.
> Barabas: [*aside*] 'Twas sent me for a present from the great Cham.
> (*JM* 4.4.65–74)

Such an imaginary biography potentially awaits Shylock as well, but, unlike in the case of Barabas, which Marlowe took pains to draw carefully to the last detail, it is not furnished in Shakespeare's play with actual, reliable details, as Shylock lives in the public domain of common fictionality. Technically, of course, Shylock is a dramatic subject like any other character in the play. But even in his asides, even when citing his dreams, he seems to be nothing more than an abstract measure, qualifying and defining the immanent constitution of the others. Shylock is the zero point of all the other identities in the play: signifying all, representing none. Unlike an individual case of transgression, such as an evil eye cast by a local witch, the Jew is not counted as a particular threat on a personal level. His effect is of a different, universal order. He is the archetypal other whose desire structures the subject. On the one hand, he is the great menace, penetrating the dream of love and humanity offered by the play with his blunt discourse of vulgar rationality, his seemingly soluble riddles, to reduce a mystery of enchanting volume into an impoverished pageant of disenchantment. Yet paradoxically he also represents the secret, unconscious desire of all the rest for a momentary (or maybe eternal?) liberation from the fetters of "legitimate" discourse and official ideology. Shylock may not be the only one in Venice to dream of moneybags (*MV* 2.5.18), but he is certainly the only one to admit it freely in public. Moneybags investing a dream, Jacob's staff informing a fable or a swear (*MV* 2.5.36), and even a vision of jewels in the ear of one's dead daughter (*MV* 3.1.81) acquire a different symbolic resonance than "some more ducats" (*MV* 2.6.50) gilding a romantic elopement in plain reality. The plain monetary transaction that threatens to reduce the narrative of the play to the level of a fortuitous, if curious, court proceeding suddenly acquires an aura of poetic acuteness and necessity. Shylock, an archetypal representative of an elusive nation, may invest more than financial wealth, but he invigorates the communal unconscious with fresh perspectives on the symbolic order of rising capitalism. This is a poetic Shakespearian vision of what Montesquieu will dryly phrase: "Commerce cures destructive prejudices, and it is an almost general rule everywhere there are gentle mores, there is commerce and that everywhere there is commerce, there are gentle mores."[49]

How does Shylock offer to infiltrate the national narrative of a community for whom he is the constant other? First, by holding the Venetians to the requirement to abide by their republican law of commercial tolerance, which he pushes to its limit. Unlike his daughter, he is not invited to blur the boundaries between nations and to assimilate easily into Venetian society. On the face of it, it is chiefly his religion that bars his way to being incorporated as a member of the Venetian nation. More complex in this context, however, are the implications of Jessica's aforementioned obscure reference to Tubal and Chus as Shylock's "countrymen" (*MV* 3.2.284). Country, as a territorial signifier of nationhood, was a recent semantic development in the sixteenth century. Although an elusive attachment between nation and territory often occurred in the Middle Ages, the chief motivations of a medieval English monarch to start a war against France or join a crusade pertained more to his status as a feudal landlord than as a leader of a nation. With the emergence of English nationalism under the Tudors, what had been the exclusive signifier of territory began to submerge into the discourse of nationhood. As Liah Greenfeld demonstrates, "while 'country' was defined as 'nation,' 'nation' was defined as 'country.'"[50] Where does this development place the landless Jew? As opposed to Marx's reference to the "*chimerical* nationality" of Judaism as "the nationality of the merchant, of man of money in general," which may be read as sociological or theological, the reference to a Jew as a countryman is purely symbolic, implying absence rather than identity. Rather than plain local habitation, Shylock's country suggests a Deleuzian "de-territorialization," a dislocated assemblage defying its traditional "aura" but retaining its privileges.[51]

Because Jews reached Europe through expulsion and a process of gradual dispersion rather than conquest, colonization, or mass migration, they could possess no economic positions that depended on hegemonic power or expropriation of lands.

I must confess we come not to be kings:
That's not our fault: alas, our number's few,
And crowns come either by succession,
Or urg'd by force.
(*JM* 1.1.127–30)

Even where the Jews could be in possession of lands, such as in Barabas's island ("a house / As great and fair as is the Governor's" [*JM* 2.3.13–14]), they often preferred to deal in landed property not so much as "a form of family investment, as it was for the Christians in Malta as elsewhere, so much as a method of making money," because the tricky mortgage system served "to avoid the odium which the taint of usury brought with it."[52] With the continuing practice of expulsion of Jews, which became widespread in Western Europe throughout the fifteenth century, such a prospect became a considerable factor in the Jews' own investment policy.[53] The lack of lasting property in feudal and early modern Europe meant a temporary status of citizenship and a perpetual state of alienation.

In *The Merchant of Venice* all the characters are identified by local habitation: Portia's suitors are classified by their countries; there is a clear division at the outset between the Venetians and the residents of Belmont; Launcelot Gobbo defines himself as an Italian (*MV* 2.2.150); and his father, who owns a horse and brings a dish of doves as a present, must own a plot of land in the country. Even "a poor Turk of tenpence" such as Ithamore seasons his fantasy of marrying the courtesan with the vision of settling in "a country."

Content: but we will leave this paltry land,
And sail from hence to Greece, to lovely Greece.
I'll be thy Jason, thou my golden fleece.
(*JM* 4.2.92–94)

Whereas all the others may be referred to by their local habitation or country of origin, the Jew cites a list of places where he has visited for a purpose (Shylock's Frankfurt, Barabas's Italy, France, etc.) or at best related to his latest country of temporary residence where he was residing in "hell" (*MV* 2.3.2). Not even the ancient, spiritual locus of Jewish desire will do. For "creep[ing] to Jerusalem" (*JM* 4.1.62) is brought up by Barabas as a mode of penance only when he shams a wish to become a Christian. Calling their fellow Jews countrymen—as do both Jessica (who, whether she reports faithfully or lies about Shylock's particular talk with Tubal or

Chus, probably quotes her father's habitual terminology) and Barabas—betrays the aliens' conspiracy rather than the citizens' local pride or patriotism: Barabas says, "Let 'em combat, conquer, and kill all, / So they spare me, my daughter, and my wealth" (*JM* 1.1.152–53).

Shylock takes it from there, but the master stroke in his subversive transformation of the national narrative is fully revealed only in the subtle and creative manner in which he conducts his lawsuit in the Venetian court. Shylock's covert claim for Venetian nationhood has solid roots in Venice's practice of political economy. "Perhaps the most characteristic practice of the Venetian and Florentine communes' 'state' activity," argues Janet Coleman, "was their reliance on loans, voluntary or forced: a funded state debt paid by citizens." Basing her analysis on Janet L. Abu-Lughod, Coleman relates this to the eagerness of merchants to participate in and control the state's decision making, "especially if government was run as a corporation of merchant proto-capitalists."[54] Abu-Lughod herself adopts Jacques Le Goff's distinction between urban merchant-artisans, not yet capitalist, and the merchant-bankers who were the vanguard for the new world system.[55] When *The Merchant of Venice* was written, capitalist political economy was making its first official move. As a countermeasure to the decree issued in 1597 banishing the English Merchant Adventurers from the markets of the empire, Elizabeth reciprocated by throwing out the merchants of the Hansa and thereby protecting the interests of her own merchants.[56] National and commercial interests are thus interwoven, creating a new club that the Shylocks of London, if such would have been, would have liked to join. In a similar vein Shylock may prophetically regard his loan to Venice's prince of merchants as a further step from his status as a tolerated alien to one that may silently reconcile his major participation in Venetian economy with his elusive nationhood. Despite Antonio's admonition against Shylock's practice of usury, he regards Shylock's loan to him as an act of kindness, namely, as an act practiced between people belonging to the same kind—an act, as it were, of political kinship or solidarity. Thus Shylock's demand for justice may not be regarded as an act of revenge but rather as pertaining to the new social order dictated by political economy, a Machiavellian agenda designed to claim his political belonging to the protocapitalist Venetian nationhood.

Having pushed his demand for equal justice beyond any moral limit, Shylock is defeated by Portia in court. But on what grounds, in what terms is he defeated? The only way the republic of Venice may overtake the disastrous implications of Shylock's moral riddle is to forgo its liberality, namely, its much advertised identity as a commercial republic. In this it may practice an obvious Machiavellianism, by adopting Machiavelli's advice to the Prince not to keep his word while at the same time abandoning his more implicit teaching that (as Isaiah Berlin explains) reveals pluralist values out of the tension between his pagan *virtù* and the doctrines of Christianity, which opens the way "to empiricism, pluralism, toleration, compromise."[57]

It is not clear to what extent his daughter's flight induces Shylock to exact his bond upon Antonio; at least when talking about it with the Christians, he stresses the personal aspect of her "rebellion" (*MV* 3.1.31) rather than proclaiming it to be a cause for religious revenge, as Barabas's sharp irony (lost on the gullible Friar Jacomo) makes clear in similar circumstances: "Why, brother, you converted Abigail; / And I am bound in charity to requite it" (*JM* 4.1.106–7).

And yet some tokens of ideological motivation are still betrayed in Shylock's behavior. To cite but one example, let us return to Shylock's "country" matters. Whether or not one believes Jessica's evidence concerning her father's initial intentions to harm Antonio, her reference to Tubal and Chus as Shylock's countrymen is significant in this respect. As in the case of Barabas, who addresses his fellow Jews in a similar way ("Why, how now countrymen?" [*JM* 1.1.141]), we do not know which is their common country of origin. This expression, however, together with Shylock's repeated references to his nation and tribe, casts an ideological shade on his attitude throughout the play.

Aside from the particular case of his Jewishness, then, Shylock represents a more subversive element within the dominant Christian, capitalist order in Venice. Together with Othello he belongs in the company of "aliens," whose danger to the ideological integrity of the Venetian ruling class is so menacing that special legislation had to be issued to curb their rights and activities within the liberal state of Venice. Shylock is no self-styled Machiavellian like Barabas, who (cunningly, but decisively) defies the law entirely (unless he can turn it cynically into a vehicle of his anti-Christian vengeance, as in the case of Friar Jacomo), and all he cares about is himself: "If anything shall there concern our state, / Assure yourselves I'll look unto [*aside*] myself" (*JM* 1.1.170–71).

Barabas's selfish attitude ("Ego mihimet sum semper proximus" [*JM* 71.1.188]) is shown not only as subversive toward the state but also indifferent to his "tribal" or "national" solidarity. His careless use of the term may refer to members of his own imagined community ("They say we are a scatter'd Nation" [*JM* 1.1.227]) as well as to Christendom in general ("these swine-eating Christians, / (Unchosen Nation, never circumciz'd)" [*JM* 2.3.7–8]). Shylock's case is made in terms of his "tribe" while insisting on its legal resolution. Thus his complaint cannot find any institutional outlet until his specific function within the trade-capitalist process, which moves Venetian economy, is directly addressed. Significantly enough, this opportunity occurs when emotion is mixed with business: The financial implications of courting Portia belong to the subversive parts of "pure" love in the same way that Shylock the alien is an inevitable constituent of the Venetian economic system. It is here that we see Power at work, as Foucault has described it, namely, as "force relations . . . forming a chain or a system, or on the contrary, the disjunctions and contradictions which isolate them from one another; and . . . the strategies in which they take effect, whose general design or institutional crystallization is embodied in the state apparatus, in the formulation of the law, in the various social hegemonies."[58] Once Shylock is allowed to interfere with the financial operations of Venice's prince of merchants, the subversive process of rebellion is set in motion.

Throughout the play Shylock is consistently urged to adopt a "gentle" attitude ("We all expect a gentle answer Jew" [*MV* 4.1.34]). This is but another way of demanding of him to embrace a "gentile" ideology, a demand that is finally imposed on him legally with the verdict of the trial that suddenly turns out to be his own. Shylock's perception of the law of Venice is indeed alien, because the use he makes of the Venetian constitution rests on the word of the law but contradicts its spirit. It is, however, the essence of Shylock's proto-"terrorism." In an ironic move anticipating a Brechtian gesture, an act of mimicry, Shylock consciously subverts the soul of Venetian order, namely, its book of laws, and turns it on itself. The only countermeasure Venice can take against Shylock's act of legal terrorism, without subverting its own premises as a national community, is to subvert the spirit of language on which the law rests in order to reinstate the normal procedure of justice and social order by which Venice's mainstream national ideology abides.

Not, however, that this peculiar countermeasure does not leave much room for ambiguity. Official order is reinstated, but Shylock's moral riddle is far from being solved. As I suggest, his riddle turns on Machiavelli's vision of nationhood, which is totally separated from the realm of faith. There is in store another solution to his moral riddle, which lies perhaps even beyond the flexibility of the vision of Machiavelli, who would probably advise the Duke of Venice to resort to force in his dealing with the Jew: "Moses, Cyrus, Theseus, and Romulus would not have been able to make their people obey their new structures of authority for long if they had been unarmed."[59] According to this radical version, however, the nation-state of

Venice could offer Shylock national rights without coercing him to convert his faith. Would Machiavelli himself accept this solution?

Shakespeare did not yet allow it. The official adoption of Shylock's bond of *jouissance* by hegemonic Venice's court of law leaves a world in which culture is arranged by a multiplicity of discourses and identities, subject and other, desire and bonds. It is significant, as it is curious, that this reinstatement through subversion is brought about by an alien of a different order: a woman disguised as a man, a country feudal who comes from afar in order and in time. An alienating riddle is cracked by a strategy of alienation.

Notes

1. V. S. Naipaul, *The Mimic Men* (London: Andre Deutsch, 1967), 7.

2. Homi K. Bhabha, *The Location of Culture* (London: Routledge, 1994), 85–86.

3. Bhabha, *Location of Culture*, 86.

4. Avraham Oz, "Prophecy as a Cultural Model and a Gaze: The Face of Barbarism in the Politics of *Tamburlaine the Great*," in *Marlowe: A New Casebook*, ed. Avraham Oz (Houndmills, UK: Palgrave, 2003).

5. Bhabha, *Location of Culture*, 89.

6. William Shakespeare, *The Merchant of Venice*, new Arden edition, ed. John Russell Brown (London: Methuen, 1964). All quotations in the text refer to this edition, notated hereafter as *MV.*

7. Avraham Oz, *The Yoke of Love: Prophetic Riddles in "The Merchant of Venice"* (Newark: University of Delaware Press, 1995).

8. For "non tamen in con temptum fidei catolicae sed pro necessitate et comonoditate," see Isaac Schiffer, *History of Jewish Economy* [Hebrew] (Tel Aviv: Stiebel, 1935), 431. The discussion of the facts and numbers are taken from Schiffer and from Benjamin Arbel, *Trading Nations: Jews and Venetians in the Early Modern Eastern Mediterranean* (Leiden: E. J. Brill, 1995).

9. "Non l'havea potuto far resistenza all'obligo della sua natione." See Arbel, *Trading Nations*, 90.

10. Arbel, *Trading Nations*, 159.

11. Arbel, *Trading Nations*, ix.

12. G. M. Trevelyan, *History of England*, 3rd ed. (London: Longmans, 1952).

13. John Edwards, *The Jews in Christian Europe, 1400–1700* (London: Routledge, 1988), 89.

14. Jonathan Israel, *European Jewry in the Age of Mercantilism, 1550–1750* (Oxford, UK: Clarendon Press, 1985), 45.

15. John K. Brackett, *Criminal Justice and Crime in Late Renaissance Florence, 1537–1609* (Cambridge, UK: Cambridge University Press, 1992), 40–41.

16. David William Davies, *Elizabethans Errant: The Strange Fortunes of Sir Thomas Sherley and His Three Sons* (Ithaca, NY: Cornell University Press, 1967), 181.

17. Benedict Anderson, *Imagined Communities: Reflections on the Origin and Spread of Nationalism*, rev. ed. (London: Verso, 1991).

18. Ellen Meiksins Wood and Neal Wood, *A Trumpet of Sedition: Political Theory and the Rise of Capitalism, 1509–1688* (New York: New York University Press, 1997), 6.

19. Carlton J. H. Hayes, *Nationalism: A Religion* (New York: Macmillan, 1960), 35.

20. See Bob Hodge's reading of Marlowe's play: "Fernese is the closest to an exemplary prince, since he survives at the end in a more powerful position than he was at the beginning."

Bob Hodge, "Marlowe, Marx, and Machiavelli: Reading into the Past," in *Literature, Language, and Society in England, 1580–1680*, ed. David Aers, Bob Hodge, and Gunther Kress (Dublin: Gill & Macmillan, 1981), 8.

21. Hans Kohn, *The Idea of Nationalism: A Study in Its Origins and Background* (New York: Macmillan, 1945).

22. "The framework within which national consciousness and a sense of fatherland were to evolve in Europe . . . was established by around 1100." Johan Huizinga, *Men and Ideas: History, the Middle Ages, the Renaissance*, trans. James B. Holden and Hans van Marle (New York: Harper & Row, 1959), 105.

23. John Langton and Mary G. Dietz, "Machiavelli's Paradox: Trapping or Teaching the Prince," *American Political Science Review* 81 (1987): 1277–88.

24. At least Felix Raab thinks it is not. See Felix Raab, *The English Face of Machiavelli: A Changing Interpretation, 1500–1700* (London: Routledge & Kegan Paul, 1965), 70–76.

25. Antonio Gramsci, *The Modern Prince, and Other Writings*, trans. Louis Marks (New York: International, 1968), 146.

26. Louis Althusser, *Machiavelli and Us*, trans. Gregory Elliot (London: Verso, 1999), 11.

27. Jürgen Habermas, *The Inclusion of the Other: Studies in Political Theory*, ed. Ciaran Cronin and Pablo De Greiff (Cambridge, MA: MIT Press, 1999), 107.

28. Habermas, *Inclusion of the Other*, 109.

29. Niccolo Machiavelli, *Art of War*, trans. and ed. Christopher Lynch (Chicago: University of Chicago Press, 2003), bk. 3, 76.

30. Niccolo Machiavelli, *Discourses on Livy*, trans. Julia Conaway Bondanella and Peter Bondanella (Oxford, UK: Oxford University Press, 1997), 1: 26.

31. Niccolo Machiavelli, *The Prince*, ed. and trans. David Wootton (Indianapolis: Hackett, 1995), ch. 3.

32. Machiavelli, *Discourses on Livy*, 1: 16. See also Bruce James Smith, *Politics and Remembrance: Republican Themes in Machiavelli, Burke, and Tocqueville* (Princeton, NJ: Princeton University Press, 1985), 88–89.

33. David J. Baker, *Between Nations: Shakespeare, Spenser, Marvell, and the Question of Britain* (Stanford, CA: Stanford University Press, 1997), 45.

34. Montesquieu, *The Spirit of the Laws*, trans. and ed. Anne M. Cohler, Basia Carolyn Miller, and Harold Samuel Stone (Cambridge, UK: Cambridge University Press, 1989), bk. 20, ch. 1, 338.

35. Albert O. Hirschman, *The Passions and the Interests: Political Arguments for Capitalism Before Its Triumph* (Princeton, NJ: Princeton University Press, 1977), 41.

36. Althusser, *Machiavelli and Us*, 26–27.

37. Machiavelli, *The Prince*, ch. 6, 19.

38. Machiavelli, *The Prince*, ch. 16, 49.

39. Habermas, *Inclusion of the Other*, 110.

40. Maggie Günsberg, "The End Justifies the Means: End-Orientation and the Discourse of Power," in *Niccolò Machiavelli's "The Prince": New Interdisciplinary Essays* (Manchester, UK: Manchester University Press, 1995), 121–24.

41. Davies, *Elizabethans Errant*, 182.

42. Richard Henry Tawney, *Religion and the Rise of Capitalism* (Harmondsworth, UK: Penguin, 1969 [1926]), 49.

43. John G. A. Pocock, *The Machiavellian Moment: Florentine Political Thought and the Atlantic Republican Tradition* (Princeton, NJ: Princeton University Press, 1975), 391.

44. James Shapiro, *Shakespeare and the Jews* (New York: Columbia University Press, 1996), 168.

45. Oz, *Yoke of Love*, 100.

46. Christopher Marlowe, *The Jew of Malta*, ed. N. W. Bawcutt (Manchester, UK: Manchester University Press; and Baltimore: Johns Hopkins University Press, 1978), 1–4. All quotations in the text come from this edition, notated hereafter as *JM*.

47. Stephen Greenblatt, *Renaissance Self-Fashioning from More to Shakespeare* (Chicago: University of Chicago Press, 1980), 204.

48. Michel Foucault, *The Order of Things: An Archaeology of the Human Sciences* (London: Tavistock, 1970), 315.

49. Montesquieu, *Spirit of the Laws*, bk. 20, ch. 1, 338.

50. Liah Greenfeld, *Nationalism: Five Roads to Modernity* (Cambridge, MA: Harvard University Press, 1992), 32.

51. Gilles Deleuze and Felix Guattari, *A Thousand Plateaus*, trans. Brian Massumi (Minneapolis: University of Minnesota Press, 1987), 334.

52. Godfrey Wettinger, *The Jews of Malta in the Late Middle Ages* (Valletta, Malta: Midsea, 1985), 40.

53. Jacob Katz, *Tradition and Crisis: Jewish Society at the End of the Middle Ages* (New York: Free Press of Glencoe, 1961), 47.

54. Janet Coleman, *Renaissance* (Oxford: Blackwell, 2000), 214–15.

55. Janet L. Abu–Lughod, *Before European Hegemony: The World System, AD 1250–1350* (Oxford, UK: Oxford University Press, 1989), 117–18.

56. Liah Greenfeld, *The Spirit of Capitalism: Nationalism and Economic Growth* (Cambridge, MA: Harvard University Press, 2001), 36.

57. Isaiah Berlin, *Against the Current: Essays in the History of Ideas* (New York: Viking, 1980), 78.

58. Michel Foucault, *The History of Sexuality: An Introduction*, trans. Robert Hurley (London: Allen Lane, 1979), 92–93.

59. Machiavelli, *The Prince*, ch. 6, 20.

5

Achsah Guibbory

Milton, Prophet of Israel

New Canaan, Goshen, Bethel. These are the names of towns in New England, in Connecticut, traces of the fact that the people who founded the colonies thought they were the new biblical Israel and that the land they had come to was Canaan. As John Winthrop said in his famous sermon ("A Model of Christian Charity") preached in 1630 (perhaps on the ship *Arbella*), it was "the city on the hill," Jerusalem, an image famously recalled by President Ronald Reagan three and a half centuries later, as he expressed his vision of America. Winthrop invoked the Hebrew Bible, calling his Puritan audience God's special people, and advised them to follow the prophet Micah's counsel "to do justly, to love mercy, and to walk humbly." Then they would find that "the God of Israel is among us." Winthrop closed with Moses's words of farewell and warning in Deuteronomy 30, as the Israelites were about to enter Canaan: If they followed God's ways, they would flourish; if they didn't, they would perish. "The eyes of all people are upon us," said Winthrop. "So that if we shall deal falsely with our God in this work we have undertaken, . . . we shall be made a story and a by-word through the world."[1]

It is well known that the Puritans who settled New England thought of themselves as like the Israelites. It is less well recognized that these settlers brought their sense of connection with Israel from England. Since at least the 1570s, English people had been describing themselves and England in terms of analogies with biblical Israel.[2] The Bible was the intimate possession of most men and women, not just the university educated, and English Protestants knew the Old Testament better than most of us do today. They turned to it to understand their lives and their nation, finding that the history of the ancient Israelites (as the "first" people of God) spoke to contemporary English experience. In this essay I briefly examine Milton's career-long preoccupation with England as Israel within this context and his evolving sense of himself as England's prophet. I focus on certain moments when Milton uses the Hebrew Bible to talk about England and himself.

More than forty years ago, William Haller argued that England, influenced by John Foxe, saw itself as an elect nation, like biblical Israel—a claim reinforced by Christopher Hill's position that "the idea that England was a chosen nation came easily to Englishmen."[3] But for years revisionist scholars have been busy refuting Haller, and Patrick Collinson has chided Christopher Hill, insisting that England might have thought of itself as *an* elect nation but almost never as *the* elect nation, like the Jews.[4] The notion of a chosen nation is uncomfortable to many people for its sense of exclusivity. Moreover, because Christianity understands itself as universal, a religion enlarged beyond particular peoples and nations, it would seem to oppose the idea of a chosen people—an idea that tends to be thought of as Jewish. I would argue, however, that the idea of a chosen people with a special bond with God, the notion of election in the New Testament, and the Protestant emphasis on election are connected; the last two ideas revise but do not dismiss the idea of chosenness. We cannot simply oppose so-called Jewish particularism to Christian universalism, certainly not in early modern England, when religion and the nation were intertwined in ways that complicate the internationalist aspect of Protestantism. National, communal, and personal identities were described in terms of biblical Israel and narratives from the Hebrew Bible.

Christianity has always defined itself in relation to Jews and the Judaism from which it emerged. That relationship has been complex, difficult, ambivalent, and shifting. We might think of Jesus's pronouncements and the Gospels but also of Paul, the converted Jew, who interpreted the Old Testament to Christian advantage. Although Paul in Romans expresses hope that the Jews, though now "broken off," would eventually be redeemed (Romans 11:17–27), in Galatians he opposes Christian Israel to Jews and Judaism. Augustine more fully appropriated the idea of Israel, God's chosen, when he defined the Christian church as the "true" spiritual Israel, in contrast to "carnal" (Jewish) Israel.[5]

The Reformation had to renegotiate the relation between Christianity and Judaism, and along with that came new uses of the Old Testament. Because the Protestant imagination identified Catholic worship with Jewish ceremony, the potential for anti-Judaism intensified. But reformers also identified with Zion. According to Luther's narrative (later embraced by

John Foxe), the true church was like biblical Israel in its struggle with idolatry, its suffering, its deliverance from "Babylonian captivity" (now identified with Rome and the pope), and its assurance of redemption.[6]

Biblical narratives of Israel were useful in constructing national and religious identity. To authorize the English nation and its institutions after the break with Rome, people turned to the Old Testament. Elizabeth was England's Deborah or David; James I was "the British Solomon," who (like his counterpart) united the northern and southern kingdoms, in this case Scotland and England.[7] Richard Hooker and subsequent defenders of the ceremonial, episcopal church invoked the precedent and practices of the Jewish temple. Identification with ancient Israel gave the reformed nation and its institutions legitimacy, although that legitimacy would be challenged in the seventeenth century by others who saw *themselves* as representing the true Israel and who understood Christian Israel differently.

⁂

Milton came of age in an England that was constructing an Israelite identity for itself. But he was one of those who challenged the spiritual legitimacy of, first, the established church and, then, the Stuart monarchs.

In 1637 Milton announced his anger at the state of the church but also his claim to be a prophet like those in the Old Testament, indicting corruption among those in power. At the center of "Lycidas" lies the famous attack on the corrupt clergy: the "pilot of the Galilean lake" exposes the greedy priests and bishops who "creep and . . . climb into the fold," shoving away the "worthy bidden guest" from the "feast."[8] Reclaiming Peter from the Church of Rome, which asserted that the bishop of Rome inherited his authority, Milton echoes Jesus's comments about bad shepherds in John 10 and Matthew 23:8, but even more precisely and fully the prophet Ezekiel, whom Jesus himself had been echoing. Ezekiel was brought by God to "the Lord's house," where he saw abominations of idolatry (Ezekiel 8:16–17). In chapter 34 comes the long prophetic passage that lies behind Milton's attack on the clergy.

> And the word of the Lord came unto me, saying, Son of man, prophesy against the shepherds of Israel, prophesy, and say unto them, Thus saith the Lord God unto the shepherds; Woe be to the shepherds of Israel that do feed themselves! Ye eat the fat, . . . ye kill them that are fed: but ye feed not the flock. . . . with force and with cruelty have ye ruled them. And they were scattered, because there is no shepherd: . . . Behold, I am against the shepherds; and I

will require my flock at their hand, and cause them to cease from feeding the flock; neither shall the shepherds feed themselves any more: for I will deliver my flock from their mouth. . . . so will I seek out my sheep, and will deliver them out of the places where they have been scattered. (Ezekiel 34:1–5, 8, 10, 12)

As in Ezekiel, so in "Lycidas," the attack on bad shepherds yields to the promise of retribution and the deliverance and feeding of the faithful. Adapting Ezekiel's prophecy to England's circumstances in 1637, Milton assumes the voice of God's prophet in an Israel rampant with corruption. The last lines of Milton's poem describe the poet rising up, taking his "Mantle," which is not just the generic shepherd's cloak but the mantle associated with the prophets Elijah and Samuel.[9] The headnote added in 1645 would explicitly proclaim that Milton had prophesied the fall of the bishops, but the 1637 poem had already announced his prophetic vocation to those in his audience well versed enough in the Hebrew prophets to know.

In the early 1640s Milton joined the Presbyterian ministers who were criticizing the discipline and worship of the church. Here in his antiprelatical tracts Milton stresses the discontinuities between Christianity and Judaism: The English church was insufficiently reformed, having maintained supposedly Jewish practices and precedents that Christ had abolished but had been perpetuated by the Church of Rome. Where the defenders of bishops pointed to Aaron and the Levitical priesthood, Milton's *Reason of Church-Government* paraphrased Paul: "The imperfect and obscure institution of the Law . . . cannot give rules to the compleat and glorious ministration of the Gospell" (*Complete Prose Works* [*CPW*] 1: 762).[10] Yet Milton began his tract by invoking Moses (*CPW* 1: 747); he claimed his poetic abilities were such as to be found in "those frequent songs throughout the law and prophets" (*CPW* 1: 816). He recalled the "burden" of "the sad Prophet *Jeremiah*" (*CPW* 1: 802–3), who also could not resist God's "command to take the trumpet and blow a dolorous or jarring blast" (*CPW* 1: 803). So, if Milton opposed himself to the authority of the Old Testament, he also legitimized himself by invoking it. In his divorce tracts, rather than opposing the New Testament to the Old, Milton rescued a law of Moses allowing for divorce. He saw Christ's words as consistent with Moses's; Jesus's words should be interpreted in light of the Christian virtue of charity, which was actually already there in Mosaic law.

In the early 1640s Milton thus identified with Moses and the Hebrew prophets as well as with Christ. But in *Areopagitica* (1644) he proclaimed England to be the Israel spoken of in the prophets.

Presbyterian ministers had been preaching to Parliament for several years at monthly fasts, asserting that the English nation—engaged in reforming religion—was Judah, returned from Babylon and rebuilding its temple. Most fast sermons were structured on analogies drawn between contemporary England and Israel.[11] England was God's chosen nation, repeating the history of biblical Israel, but this time with the possibility of getting it "right."

It is this idea of England that Milton himself invokes toward the end of *Areopagitica,* even as he announces his break from the Presbyterians. Having acknowledged England's debt to "the strong assistance of God" and the "guidance" of Parliament (*CPW* 2: 487) and having made his argument for why books must be allowed freely to be born into the world, Milton praises England in language that evokes Isaiah. He asks the "Lords and Commons of England" to "consider what Nation it is wherof ye are, and whereof ye are the governours" (*CPW* 2: 551): "The favour and the love of heave'n, we have great argument to think in a peculiar manner propitious and propending towards us. Why else was this Nation chos'n before any other, that out of her as out of *Sion*, should be proclam'd and sounded forth the first tidings and trumpet of Reformation to all Europ?" (*CPW* 2: 552). England here is the redeemed Zion or Jerusalem described by Isaiah. "Out of Zion shall go forth the Law" (Isaiah 2:3). Isaiah had spoken God's promise that in the future a redeemed Israel (God's servant) will be "a light to the Gentiles," spreading "salvation unto the end of the earth" (Isaiah 49:6). Israel will be the center to which the rest of the nations will come to worship God but also the center from which God's truth and light emanate. In Milton this redemptive function belongs to England, the first place to proclaim reformation "to all Europe." Now, in this "new great period in his Church," if the press is liberated, England will spread more light. "What does he [God] then but reveal himself to his servants, and, as his manner is, first to his Englishmen?" (*CPW* 2: 553) What is important to note is not just Milton's patriotism but his identification of England with the Israel of the prophets. England will receive the blessings God promised to Israel, for England is the true Israel, the Christian Israel, special and particular, even as Milton imagines truth as universal, spreading throughout the world.

"Jerusalem" and "Zion" are interchangeable names in the Hebrew prophets, signifying the people of Israel, the land, the nation, and the city, which is its symbol. Milton knew this, which is why, in emphasizing the connection between city and nation, he looks to London, "this vast City; a City of refuge" (*CPW* 2: 553). London is England's Jerusalem. Years before, William Laud had preached in London before the king and the House of Lords on Psalm 122:3–5 ("*Jerusalem* is builded as a *Citie* that is at *unity* in it selfe"). Laud had compared the situation in Stuart England, where puritans objected to the ceremonies of the church, with that of the Jews in the first century, when dissention within the Temple led to its downfall.[12] He thought that an imposed uniformity of worship was the solution. But Milton envisions his city purged of Laudian, popish error. Milton's London represents a redeemed England, which Milton aptly compares to Samson. Samson's renewed strength symbolizes a spiritually powerful nation: "Methinks I see in my mind a noble and puissant Nation rousing herself like a strong man after sleep, and shaking her invincible locks" (*CPW* 2: 557–58). Milton addresses England as Isaiah addressed the rising Zion at the beginning of chapter 52: "Awake, awake; put on thy *strength*, O Zion; put on thy beautiful garments, O Jerusalem, the holy city." Jesus, in his sermon on the mount, reinterpreted and decentered Zion, addressing the "multitudes" as Zion. Paul put his hopes in the heavenly Jerusalem above, not the earthly city in bondage to Rome (Galatians 4:25–26). Milton, however, more like Isaiah, emphasizes the city, the land, and the people of his nation. London—center of England—will be the holy mountain of the Lord.

We know the major historical developments after the mid-1640s, although we may not think enough about the language in which they were described. Charles was tried and executed and made into a kingly martyr by his supporters, a figure who wore both David's crown and the crown of thorns. Royalists and regicides, Presbyterian ministers and Fifth Monarchists, all invoked analogies with biblical Israel. At stake was the claim to be the true Israel, but also the question of who or what Israel was. People on various sides appropriated different narratives and figures from biblical Israel's history. When Charles I's son was crowned in Scotland in 1649, he was exalted as David, legitimate ruler over all Israel, though in exile. Meanwhile, political reformers such as James Harrington resurrected republican alternatives to the monarchy, going back not only to classical models but also to the period when Jewish Israel was a commonwealth.[13] Fifth Monarchists proposed that England reinstitute the Mosaic judicial and legal system. In 1655 William Aspinwall published *An Abstract of Laws and Government*, a compendium of Old Testament judicial and civil laws that had been "collected and digested" by his friend John Cotton in America. Cotton, before his death, had presented the compendium to the "Generall Court" of Massachusetts, hoping that each town of the colony would "ratifie" these laws.[14] Massachusetts turned down Cotton's proposal, but Aspinwall hoped England would embrace it.

Israelite analogies proliferated in the 1650s. Cromwell, ascending to power, was extolled as England's Gideon, the military leader of the Israelites when they entered Canaan. But when Cromwell became Lord Protector in 1653, religious radicals, disappointed by his betrayal of their hopes for toleration, thought Cromwell not the deliverer of Israel but its worst enemy. The Fifth Monarchist John Rogers, who gave all his pamphlets Hebrew titles, addressed Cromwell as Nebuchadnezzar. Languishing in prison in 1657, Rogers in his pamphlets, using the prophet Daniel's words, prophesied against Cromwell from his captivity.[15] The English nation turned out to be Babylon; the saints, rather than ruling, were imprisoned. For many sectaries during the Protectorate, the true Israel was to be found not in a "nation" but among individual believers, persecuted by the powerful who claimed to be the godly but were really the enemies of Israel.

During these years, Milton continued to speak about England as biblical Israel. *The Tenure of Kings and Magistrates* looked to the Hebrew Bible to show the venerable "custom of tyrant-killing among the Jews" (*CPW* 3: 213).[16] *Eikonoklastes* countered the royalist glorification of the executed king as Davidic martyr by relentlessly referring to Charles as Pharaoh. The English saints were God's beloved; the royalists, the enemies of Israel depicted in the Bible. But a change appears in Milton's *Second Defense of the English People* in 1654, after Cromwell had become Lord Protector. Milton was still writing for Cromwell's government as its spokesman and defender, and the pamphlet opens with Milton announcing the extraordinary favors that England and he himself have received, as if his election mirrors that of the nation.[17] But ominous warnings are sounded toward the end. No longer the propagandist, Milton turns to admonish the nation.

First, he warns Cromwell not to "invade" the "liberty" (*Complete Poems* [*CP*] 835) that has been obtained (as if liberty could be invaded and devastated, like Scotland). Like the Hebrew prophets before him and like England's other self-proclaimed prophets in the 1650s, such as Rogers in his pamphlets or Anna Trapnel in visions that were recorded and published by others, Milton warns the powerful, the "great ones."[18] But he also addresses England's "citizens." Fearing that, newly liberated, they will become degenerate like the "royalists" or that they will choose "the vilest miscreants" from taverns and brothels to be their "senators," Milton updates the warnings of the Hebrew prophets to the conditions of England in 1654, bringing together biblical notions of election with Roman values of wisdom, temperance, and frugality. Should the people "fall into . . . an abyss of corruption," they will, like the Romans, lose their liberty, and God will become "weary of protecting you" (*CP* 835–36). The English nation will then be, not the redeemed Israel of Isaiah, a light to the world, but idolatrous Israel, object of God's wrath. When Milton suggests that her glorious potential may be transferred to other nations, much as the promises to Jewish Israel were transferred to the Christians, we see Milton still thinking of redemption in particular national terms.

In 1660, with *The Readie and Easie Way,* Milton turned again to the example of biblical Israel, not out of any sense of a shared elect identity but out of anger that the English were about to become unchosen like the Jews. The desire to return to "regal dominion" (*CPW* 7: 429) is a shameful repetition of Israelite history.[19] The English seem like the idolatrous Israelites, who in the wilderness wanted to return to Egypt, who once in Canaan rejected the rule of God and his judges in favor of having a king like the gentiles (*CPW* 7: 449) and who later in Babylon longed for Egypt. God's "chosen" are "chusing them a captain back for *Egypt*" (*CPW* 7: 463). Milton exhorts his countrymen *not* to be like ancient Israel but seems on the verge of despair. At the end, speaking to England as Jeremiah spoke at the Lord's command, Milton incorporates a few of the prophet's words to Judah (22:29). "Thus much I should perhaps have said though I were sure I should have spoken only to trees and stones; and had none to cry to, but with the Prophet, *O earth, earth, earth*! to tell the very soil itself what her perverse inhabitants are deaf to" (*CPW* 7: 462–63). Milton's invocation of the earth, together with his sense that he is addressing an unresponsive audience, produces the image of stony ground—an image that miraculously sprouts hope. In Ezekiel 37:1–7 the "dry bones" came to life: God caused "breath" to "enter them" even as Ezekiel prophesied to them. This famous vision in Ezekiel, which suggests that there is hope even when things seem most desolate, seems to have comforted Milton. Appearances to the contrary, maybe his words have persuaded "some . . . , whom God may raise of these stones to become children of reviving libertie" (*CPW* 7: 463).

Milton is still Israel's prophet, but gone is his dream of an elect nation. At most there will be the "remnant" spoken of in the prophets. By the 1660s the true Israel could no longer be identified with the nation for Milton—in part because of his disappointment with the English but also because the idea of England as the redeemed Israel had been taken over by the royalists restored to power. When Charles II returned to England in May 1660, he was greeted in poems and sermons as England's David, having (like the biblical king) survived rebellion, hiding, and exile. Milton went into seclusion, writing an epic that presented an antitriumphalist view of history and distanced itself from the court, the reestablished church, and any celebration of nation. Meanwhile, John Dryden rose to the position of England's poet laureate. The very year that *Paradise Lost* appeared, Dryden published *Annus Mirabilis,* his "heroick" poem celebrating England's defeat of Holland.[20] Now it was Dryden, not Milton, who presented England as God's beloved. In the war with Holland, God and

"Heav'n" have been on "Britain's side" (st. 19–20), Dryden declared. His patriotic fervor contrasts with yet echoes Milton. The devastation of the plague and the London fire are God's punishments. But Dryden concludes with a prophetic description of newly risen London that recalls the Hebrew prophets' vision of Jerusalem, which he updates and commercializes, imagining the expansion of trade.

> Me-thinks already; from this Chymick flame,
> I see a City of more precious mold:
> Rich as the Town which gives the Indies name,
> With silver pav'd, and all divine with Gold.
> (*Annus Mirabilis*, st. 293, ll. 1169–72)

London, "the Royal city," is (once again) Jerusalem, and Dryden compares the Londoners returning to rebuild the city after the fire to the Jews returning from Babylon.

For Dryden an emergent British Empire, with London its metropolis, is about to enjoy the blessings God had promised the Jews in Isaiah and the other prophets. But not for Milton. Far more explicitly than *Paradise Lost*, Milton's last two poems detach the poet from England and from any national ideal of Israel.

In *Paradise Regained* Satan tempts the Son to interpret the prophecies in the Hebrew Bible as concerning the Jews and an earthly material deliverance. Jesus, progressively throughout the course of temptations, turns away from Jewish Israel, and Milton (through the Son) distances himself from an England that had been identified by so many people as Israel. First, the Son ignores Satan's urging to liberate Judaea, which is under Roman rule; then he rejects Satan's challenge to deliver the ten tribes, dissociating himself from "My brethren, as thou call'st them," he tells Satan. As the Son discards these Israelites as not his people, he echoes Milton's attacks on idolatrous nations and on an England unworthy of liberty. We hear Milton's disgust as the Son denounces the "unrepentant, unreform'd" Israelites who "serve Idols with God" (*Paradise Regained*, ll. 403, 429, 432). National redemption is not a possibility in this poem, and the idea of an earthly kingdom of God is, at worst, Satanic delusion; at best, infinitely deferred.

We see a parallel detachment from Israel as a people or nation in *Samson Agonistes*. Samson, in captivity to the Philistines, is a symbol of biblical Israel and of England—once God's chosen, now fallen into bondage through its own bad choices. Milton's retelling of the narrative from Judges implies a dangerous parallel between Israel in bondage to the Philistines and England in the Restoration. The biblical analogies in Milton's poem identify Stuart monarchy with Philistine rule and the reestablished Church of England with the worship of Dagon.[21] Moreover, Milton describes Samson in the very terms in which the Hebrew prophets had described Jerusalem, conquered by the Babylonians. Samson's opening speech echoes both Jeremiah's Lamentations and Milton's predictions about England in *Ready and Easie Way*. Samson laments his fall from grace; "debas't / Lower than bondslave," "made of my Enemies the scorn and gaze" (*Samson Agonistes*, ll. 37–38, 43). Compare this with the opening of Lamentations, describing Jerusalem: "How doth the city sit solitary, that was full of people! How is she become as a widow, / That was great among the nations" (1:1). Samson symbolizes captive Israel and Restoration England. His spiritual labor in the poem is to reconnect with God, but to do so, he must not only acknowledge his errors but divorce himself from a corrupt Israel.

There has been intense debate recently about Samson. Some critics have argued that Samson is, for Milton, a negative example, even that Samson's "carnal" understanding of liberation marks him as irredeemably "Jewish."[22] But I would argue that Milton's Samson is a double figure: He represents both faithless Israel and the Israel that trusts in God. In Milton as in the Hebrew Bible, bondage is the punishment for apostasy. Yet Samson's bondage is itself equivocal, not just signifying idolatry. We might remember Milton's contemporary Quakers who complained about "servitude and bondages, being sold as slaves out of their native Countrey."[23] As Milton well knew, for radical nonconformists in the Restoration, suffering and imprisonment were the sign that one belonged to the true Israel. In the unfolding of the poem Samson is gradually transformed from symbol of faithless Israel to symbol of faithful Israel—flawed but nevertheless exemplary. As different as Samson might seem from the Son, he shares something important with the Son that is overlooked by those who condemn Samson as un-Christian in using violence: Both protagonists detach themselves from Jewish Israel.

Samson's "reviving [spiritual] liberty" entails a rejection of apostate Israel that both echoes the Son's rejection and voices Milton's rejection of England. As he talks with the Chorus, Samson casts off the Israelites as unworthy of deliverance, much as the Son did in *Paradise Regained*. The "men of Judah" (*Samson Agonistes*, l. 256) have proved treacherous, and the Israelites "despise, or envy, or suspect / Whom God hath of his special favor rais'd / As thir Deliverer" (*Samson Agonistes*, ll. 272–74). Samson's progressive detachment from the Jewish Israelites—including his rejection of his father Manoa's offer of ransom—is a necessary step, but so is his renunciation of Dalila, who mirrors aspects of Samson that he must conquer, and not only sensuality. Dalila is a patriot, loyal to her nation, just as Israel's heroes are, and anxious for fame "in my country" (*Samson Agonistes*, l. 980).[24] Samson's separation from Dalila marks his rejection of an eroticized idolatry that includes idolizing one's nation.

Only as he detaches himself from an idolatrous Israel and Dalila (sounding very much like Milton) can Samson feel reconnected with God and become a model for the godly in Restoration England, whether or not we as readers approve of his violent iconoclasm at the end. No longer hoping to deliver an unworthy people or to liberate his "nation," he now defines himself as the "Champion" (*Samson Agonistes*, l. 1152) of "*Israel*'s God" (l. 1150), willing to die in service. As Samson experiences "rousing motions" (l. 1382), Milton echoes Isaiah 60:1, where Isaiah addresses Zion restored to God's favor: "Arise, shine; for thy light has come and the glory of the Lord is risen upon thee!" We might set the Semichorus's description of Samson's "fiery virtue rous'd / From under ashes into sudden flame" (*Samson Agonistes*, ll. 1690–91) against Dryden's rival image of the city of London, risen from the "Chymick flame" (*Annus Mirabilis*, l. 1169). Dryden and Milton offer two competing versions of the restored Jerusalem and of what "Israel" is. Devastated like conquered Jerusalem at the beginning and now renewed in his faith that he is God's beloved servant, Samson figures the resurrected Israel of the prophets, much as he did in *Areopagitica* almost thirty years before. But redeemed Israel can now be described only in terms, not of the nation, but of the imperfect, flawed individual in whom God's spirit dwells.

As I read them, Milton's 1671 poems suggest that he had permanently given up on the notion of a redeemed nation. Or did he?

Of True Religion, written on the occasion of Charles's Declaration of Indulgence in 1672, should make us reconsider the matter. Here, a year and a half before his death, Milton once again turns to Ezekiel to address the nation. The pamphlet begins with the convoluted announcement that "all good men" are "rejoicing" that "the increase of Popery is at this day no small trouble and offence to the greatest part of the nation" (*CPW* 8: 417). Milton finds this renewed antipopery, supposedly widespread and prompted by Charles's desire to extend toleration to Catholics, encouraging evidence that "God hath giv'n a heart to the people to remember still their great and happy deliverance from Popish Thraldom" (*CPW* 8: 417). As Paul Stevens has pointed out (to support his argument that Milton never gives up on the category of the "nation"), Milton is alluding to Ezekiel 36:26: "A new heart also will I give you, and a new spirit will I put within you: and I will take away the stony heart out of your flesh, and I will give you an heart of flesh."[25]

Early modern Christians believed that this verse describes regeneration, the birth of the new man, and the death of the old, sinful Adam. The verse was used by proselytizing Quakers like Margaret Fell who hoped to convert the Jews. But this passage also has nationalist potential. It occurs in Ezekiel 36, where God tells the prophet how he will redeem Israel. In the next chapter comes Ezekiel's vision of the dry bones. The "heart of flesh" is thus part of Ezekiel's prophecy about the redemption and restoration of the Jewish nation.

The *Readie and Easie Way* laments that England is the idolatrous, Jewish Israel. Still, Milton hopes that a few English men might yet take life and become "children of reviving liberty." In 1673 he senses that "the greatest part of the English nation" is being renewed. In *Samson Agonistes* Samson suddenly feels the spirit rising within. Here it is not one person but the nation. I wonder if Milton felt that his dramatic poem had some effect in producing the change. As in *Samson Agonistes*, that new life requires the godly to wage war on idolatry. Perhaps Milton has given up on violence as a means to produce change, yet his language remains militant as ever. In *Of True Religion* Milton's battle strategy is to draw together nonconformists and Anglicans, encouraging toleration among all those who "search all things according to the rule of Scripture" (*CPW* 8: 426). Toleration is a value supported by the Gospels, Milton insists; but it is also a defensive weapon. Toleration is the means to "save ourselves" and "resist the common enemy" (*CPW* 8: 436). We must "remove" the "Idolatry" of "our Natives." Even private Catholic worship in the home cannot be tolerated. Milton quotes Ezekiel 8:7–8, where God tells Ezekiel to peer into a hole in the wall of "a Door of the Court" and "behold the wicked Abominations that they do here." And verse 12: "Then said he unto me, Son of Man, hast thou seen what the Antients of the house of Israel do in the dark" (*CPW* 8: 431). Just as God was "offended" by "secret Idolatries" in Jerusalem, so God will be "provokt" if England countenances private Catholic worship (say, in the court of Charles II) and he will "hasten his Judgements upon the Land" (*CPW* 8: 431).

Even as Milton imagines Protestant England to be the redeemed Israel, converted from its idolatry, he has English Catholics assume the place of idolatrous Israel. Biblical Israel is reconfigured, split between the idolatrous and the redeemable. If the English do not weed out popery, popery will overtake them. Rigid as the categories of redeemed and reprobate might seem, they turn out to be permeable, which is why Milton is so intent on shoring up the boundaries. We see the complexity of his use of the Hebrew Bible and his attitude toward Jewish Israel. On the one hand, Milton perpetuates traditional Christian anti-Judaism and extends it to anti-Catholicism; he identifies a reprobate England with Jewish Israel, discarded by God; but, on the other hand, he looks to the Hebrew Bible and the history of the biblical Jews, seeing England in his most hopeful moments as the redeemable and restored Israel. Either way, Milton cannot get away from thinking about Israel. He is still, at the end of his life, an Ezekiel spying out secret idolatrous abominations and making them public. But whether England is the Israel that will be redeemed—or indeed, whether Israel can be a nation—remains an open question.

The phenomenon I have been tracing is part of an emergent nationalism. But the idea of Israel in seventeenth-century England was not necessarily or always tied to the nation. The belief that one is specially chosen or beloved by God has strong psychological appeal. The idea of Israel, like the Bible, was something at once shared and contested: It could unite people or divide them. It could be used to legitimize authority, or to intensify divisions, but also to provide consolation to the powerless. It could even become a vision of inclusiveness, as in the prophets, who imagined a future Jerusalem where all people would come and worship, where all would be chosen. One could say that Jesus, with his "Zion" of multitudes, built on the Hebrew prophets' vision. Milton glimpsed this inclusive ideal when in *Areopagitica* he described God's temple as built out of "many moderate varieties and brotherly dissimilitudes" (*CPW* 2: 555).[26] It is this ideal that drove Quakers and millenarians to dream of "one fold." It is what John Rogers had in mind when he described a restored Zion, whose temple will be made up of "*precious stones* . . . consisting of excellent *gems* and *jewels*, which shall be gather'd up in these *latter dayes* from all parts of the world: *East, West, North,* and *South*; *Jewes* and *Gentiles, Indians, Arabians, Medes, Persians, Scythians, Sardians,* as well as *English, French, Spaniards, Italians,* &c."[27] This, alas, was not Milton's vision. Even if it was his deepest desire, maybe he had too powerful a sense of evil, and of the threat to liberty, to sustain it in the world he lived in.

Notes

1. John Winthrop, *A Modell of Christian Charity (1630),* in *Collections of the Massachusetts Historical Society,* ser. 3, 7 (1838): 31–48.

2. For a full discussion of this subject, see Achsah Guibbory, *Christian Identity, Jews, and Israel in Seventeenth-Century England* (Oxford, UK: Oxford University Press, 2010). In the present essay I draw on the argument and some material from that book.

3. William Haller, *Foxe's Book of Martyrs and the Elect Nation* (London: Jonathan Cape, 1963); Christopher Hill, *The English Bible and the Seventeenth-Century Revolution* (London: Penguin, 1993).

4. Patrick Collinson, "Biblical Rhetoric: The English Nation and National Sentiment in the Prophetic Mode," in *Religion and Culture in Renaissance England*, ed. Claire McEachern and Debora Shuger (Cambridge, UK: Cambridge University Press, 1997), 24.

5. See St. Augustine, *Expositions on the Book of Psalms*, 6 vols. (Oxford, UK: John Henry Parker, 1849); here Sion and Judah now refer to God's Church of the Gentiles, which has replaced Jewish Israel. On carnal versus spiritual Israel, see Daniel Boyarin, *Carnal Israel: Reading Sex in Talmudic Culture* (Berkeley: University of California Press, 1993), 1–30.

6. See "The Babylonian Captivity of the Church," in *Luther's Works*, v. 36, *Word and Sacrament II*, ed. Abdel Ross Wentz (Philadelphia: Muhlenberg, 1959), 11–126.

7. See Bishop John Williams, *Great Britains Salomon: A Sermon Preached at the Magnificent Funerall of . . . James* (1625).

8. For Milton's poems I have used John Milton, *Complete Poems and Major Prose*, ed. Merritt Y. Hughes (New York: Odyssey, 1957).

9. Elijah used his mantle to smite the waters of the Jordan to make dry land (1 Kings 19:13, 19). Samuel also has a mantle, which is associated with prophecy—when Saul rends it, Samuel says thus will the kingdom be rent from Saul (1 Samuel 15:26–28).

10. John Milton, *Reason of Church-Government*, in *Complete Prose Works of John Milton*, 8 vols., gen. ed. Don M. Wolfe (New Haven, CT: Yale University Press, 1953–1982), 1: 736–861.

11. See, for example, Stephen Marshall, *Meroz Cursed, or A Sermon Preached to the Honourable House of Comons . . . Feb. 23, 1641* (1642).

12. William Laud, Sermon preached on February 6, 1626, in *Seven Sermons Preached upon Several Occasions* (1651), quotation on p. 103.

13. James Harrington, *The Comon-Wealth of Oceana* (1656).

14. William Aspinwall, *An Abstract of Laws and Government wherein as in a Mirrour may be seen the wisdom & perfection of the government of Christs Kingdom . . . Collected and digested . . . by Mr. John Cotton* (1655), "To the Reader," sigs. A2–3.

15. See John Rogers, *Mene, Tekel, Perez* (1654); and John Rogers, *Jegar-Sahadutha, An Oyled Pillar* (1657).

16. John Milton, *Tenure of Kings and Magistrates*, in *Complete Prose Works of John Milton*, 8 vols., gen. ed. Don M. Wolfe (New Haven, CT: Yale University Press, 1953–1982), 3: 190–258.

17. For the *Second Defence*, I have used the text in Milton, *Complete Poems and Major Prose*, 817.

18. Cf. Anna Trapnel's *The Cry of a Stone* (1654), *A Legacy for Saints* (1654), and *Strange and Wonderful Newes from White-Hall* (1654).

19. John Milton, *Readie and Easie Way*, in *Complete Prose Works of John Milton*, 8 vols., gen. ed. Don M. Wolfe (New Haven, CT: Yale University Press, 1953–1982), 7: 396–463.

20. For the text of Dryden's poem, I have used *The Works of John Dryden*, v. 1, ed. Edward Niles Hooker and H. T. Swedenberg Jr. (Berkeley: University of California Press, 1956).

21. Christopher Hill, *Milton and the English Revolution* (New York: Viking, 1978), 428–48, identifies Samson with England and as symbol for the revolutionary cause. Nicholas Jose, *Ideas of the Restoration in English Literature, 1660–1671* (Cambridge, MA: Harvard University Press, 1984), shows that Milton's allusions link the Philistines with "the Restoration state." Laura Lunger Knoppers, "'Revell Like Belshazzar': Censorship, Biblical Allusion, and Milton's 1671 Poems," in *Milton Studies*, ed. Albert C. Labriola (Pittsburgh, PA: University of Pittsburgh Press, 2008), 48: 113–34, explains how the text of Daniel, with its warning of the downfall of Belshazzar, was important for dissenters and religious radicals in the 1660s and 1670s and figures in Milton's 1671 poems. See also Blair Worden, *Literature and Politics in Cromwellian England: John Milton, Andrew Marvell, Marchamont Nedham* (Oxford, UK: Oxford University Press, 2007), 358–83.

22. Joseph Wittreich sees Samson as Milton's example of "what not to do" (*Interpreting Samson Agonistes* [Princeton, NJ: Princeton University Press, 1986], 12); see also Joseph Wittreich, *Shifting Contexts: Reinterpreting Samson Agonistes* (Pittsburgh, PA: Duquesne University Press, 2002). The most vehement recent attack on Samson and Samson's God is Michael Bryson, "A Poem to the Unknown God: Samson Agonistes and Negative Theology," *Milton Quarterly* 42 (2008): 22–43, which describes "The Satanic Samson." My position is closer to David Loewenstein's (*Representing Revolution in Milton and His Contemporaries: Religion, Politics, and Polemics in Radical Puritanism* [Cambridge, UK: Cambridge University Press, 2001], 269–91); Loewenstein sees Samson as Milton's hero of conscience, his "militant" "radical saint" following the "motions of the Spirit" (286, 291).

23. William Brend, *Oh ye Magistrates in and about this City of London* (1664), 1.

24. As Victoria Kahn well observes, "Dalila represents Milton's understanding that there is no rational basis for preferring England to any other nation" ("Disappointed Nationalism: Milton in the Context of Seventeenth-Century Debates About the Nation-State," in *Early Modern Nationalism and Milton's England*, ed. David Loewenstein and Paul Stevens [Toronto: University of Toronto Press, 2008], 266).

25. On Milton's allusion to Ezekiel, see Paul Stevens, "Bunyan, the Great War, and the Political Ways of Grace," *Review of English Studies* 59 (2008): 701–21, esp. 706–11.

26. John Milton, *Areopagitica*, in *Complete Prose Works of John Milton*, 8 vols., gen. ed. Don M. Wolfe (New Haven, CT: Yale University Press, 1953–1982), 2: 486–570.

27. John Rogers, *Ohel, or Beth-shemesh: A Tabernacle for the Sun* (1653), 521.

III

Hebraism and the Bible

6

Chanita Goodblatt

Performance and *Parshanut*

The Historie of Jacob and Esau

The mid-sixteenth-century play *The Historie of Jacob and Esau* was originally performed at Westminster Court by the boy choristers of the Chapel Royal.[1] Focusing on the biblical narrative in Genesis (chapters 25 and 27) that relates the struggle of Jacob and Esau over the birthright and blessing, the play belongs to the tradition of Reformation biblical drama. Yet it is specifically "a school play composed for a large cast of amateur actors";[2] indeed, these boys and their adult audience would have been enthralled by the familial drama (fraught with parental favoritism, jealousy, and stolen birthright) and captivated by the humor of this "mery and wittie comedie"[3] with its "saucy, quick-witted servants and their gullible masters"[4] and by the opportunity for young actors (in stern adult roles) to appropriate the authority of their own schoolmasters.[5]

Ruth Blackburn notes that among the "biblical drama of this period . . . *Jacob and Esau* achieves the greatest technical success. . . . [Readers] may still admire the neat handling of the intrigue and the excellent use of suspense."[6] This dramatic skill and its subversive humor are integral parts of the play's performative aspect, which ultimately highlights the concern with the concept of predestination. What is more, it is arguably the play's pedagogical aspect that informs and directs its theatrical production, for certainly its goal of offering (in Paul Whitfield White's words) "some message to wayward youths or their negligent parents"[7] is effected through the way in which printed text is transformed into dramatic performance.

A most effective way, therefore, to experience the play is to once again transform pedagogy into performance—as it was re-created dramatically in July 2009 as *The History of Jacob and Esau: An Amateur Production of a*

Figure 1. The cast of *The History of Jacob and Esau*. From left to right: Rebecca, Jacob, the Poetess, Isaac, and Esau.

Tudor Biblical Play by the students of the graduate seminar "English Reformation Biblical Drama" (Ben-Gurion University of the Negev, Israel). This production certainly reflects the interest of an academic enterprise, such as the production of the York Mystery Plays at the University of Toronto (1977–1978, 1998).[8] Yet one might well ask how do twenty-first-century Israeli-Jewish students deal with staging a play once performed with a large cast and supported by court resources? Furthermore, how do these students respond to "the play's staunchly Protestant (specifically predestinarian) theology [of Edward VI's reign]"?[9] Finally, how does such a reenactment of this play make available early modern cultural and religious concerns for the modern audience? Answering these questions involves discussing two overarching issues: performance, that is, the pragmatics of script and stage; and *parshanut* (the Hebrew term used in its specific sense for biblical commentary or exegesis), that is, the reader's clarification of exegetical cruxes within the biblical text.

Performance

My first task in this essay is to highlight the decisions made in producing *The History of Jacob and Esau*. Following the discussions of modern re-creations of the York Mystery Plays, I consider three aspects of performance: staging, costumes, and script. The original sixteenth-century production required an estimated performance time of two to three hours,[10] eleven dramatis personae, a blind character who creates a "scenario difficult to achieve" (e.g., he must be led on and off stage),[11] elaborate singing roles, three live hunting greyhounds, and a script that attempts to offer "a sense of historical reality," particularly with its innovative use of biblical period costumes[12]—as is written on the title page, "The Parts and Names of the Players who are to be considered to be Hebrews, and so should be apparelled with attire" (*JE* 2).

The modern production necessarily streamlined these elements, mainly for pragmatic reasons (limitations of time, space, and number of participants in the graduate seminar). Yet although the resources of chapel and court were unavailable, they were replaced by the enthusiasm and critical training of graduate literature students; as one faculty member said after the play was performed: "I should like to say I did not know what to expect. And I was really pleasantly . . . I won't even say surprised. You did a lovely job, you did it with all your heart, you did it with a great deal of enthusiasm. The fact that you could reproduce sixteenth-century English is amazing."[13]

Staging

The play was presented in a medium-size university lecture hall with a raised podium, in front of an audience composed of the actors' peers and their teachers (the students and faculty of the English Department; approximately thirty people). Each scene change was indicated by a musical interlude, chosen from the CD *Voices of the Renaissance* (Tel Aviv: Helicon, 2005), thus echoing musical interludes sung in the original play. The students who were not on stage at a given moment stood at the back and off to one side, behind wooden partitions. At the end of the play the actors all came forward to the front of the stage, sat down, and talked with their audience about the experiences of dramatizing a sixteenth-century biblical drama.

Six graduate students were involved in the production. One student was the director and was also in charge of props, costumes, music, and digital photography. The original eleven roles (which included various supporting actors such as neighbors and servants) were trimmed down to include the following: the parents Isaac and Rebecca; the sons Esau and Jacob; and a dual role as both the Poetess and the attendant Deborah. The student who performed this dual role commented:

> Why do I want to dramatize the play? Because plays are written to be acted, not read. For my B.A., I took a Contemporary Drama class, taught by an actor. He had the students perform short plays,

Figure 2. Rebecca observing Jacob and Isaac.

> which we enjoyed tremendously. I found that the play I performed made more sense to me when I acted in it than when I read it. Acting in a play gives one, I think, a better understanding of the character one portrays and of the action going on in the play.

What is more, the staging of this play raises a significant issue of performance, as illustrated by the photo of Rebecca observing Jacob and Isaac. The fact that the wooden partitions could not completely hide the characters offstage distinctly underlines the tenuousness of the distinction between reality and dramatic fantasy, whereby the cast alternates between the roles of actors and audience. Such tenuousness is further emphasized by the students—including the "blind" Isaac—reading their lines from printed scripts, rather than committing them to memory. What is more, in this particular instance it can be understood that Rebecca is watching over Jacob's meeting with his father Isaac, in order to ensure that the blessing is indeed bestowed. One can propose that for the audience there is therefore a questioning of mimesis as well as a suggestion of the interrelationship among biblical scenes—together providing a more complex literary and dramatic context for the performance.

Costumes

The costumes created for this performance reflected a variety of attitudes toward the biblical characters. Those of the Poetess/Deborah, Rebecca,

Figure 3. Esau and Isaac.

and Isaac were figured as re-creations of conventional pastoral characters (flowing skirts and robes; a crown of flowers for the Poetess), thereby reflecting the use of biblical period costumes in the early modern performance of the play.

The costumes for the two sons, Jacob and Esau, however, were much more unconventional, receiving their cues from the way in which the biblical text takes great care to distinguish between the physical and psychological characteristics of these siblings, particularly as explained in Genesis 25:27 (in the contemporaneous Geneva Bible [GB]): "Esáu was a cunning hunter, & lived in the fields: but Jaakób was a plaine man, and dwelt in tentes."[14] A heavyset male student played the role of Esau. He was dressed in modern clothes (shirt, pants, coat) and carried a sword and a game bird. He deliberately acted in a swaggering, blustery manner that both drew out the characteristics of being "a cunning hunter" and displayed the humorous side of this character (reflected in the use of the plastic props).

Finally, a female student played the role of Jacob. She was also dressed in modern clothes (shirt, jeans, cap). This deliberate decision to place a woman in this male role emphasizes the character's androgynous, even feminine side; the real necessity of providing roles for all the students participating in the graduate seminar became a starting point for asking questions about gender identification, which is a central issue in the discussion of early modern English drama.[15]

Figure 4. Rebecca and Jacob.

Script

The parameter of time set out for the modern presentation of the play necessitated a reconsideration of the script. Ninety minutes (the usual class time) was allotted for both presentation and discussion: fifty minutes for the play, and forty minutes for discussion with the audience.[16] The script was in consequence condensed to include the original prologue and a new epilogue and eight scenes, which place the main characters (Rebecca, Jacob, Isaac, and Esau) in direct confrontation. These chosen scenes had the effect of swiftly moving forward the play's dramatic action:[17] 1.3, Rebecca relates to Jacob the prophecy of his birthright; 1.4, Isaac and Rebecca discuss the birthright, focusing on Esau's misbehavior; 4.1, Rebecca instructs Jacob to obtain Isaac's blessing; 4.8, Rebecca and Deborah dress Jacob as Esau; 4.9, the disguised Jacob brings food to Isaac; 4.11, Isaac blesses Jacob with the birthright; 5.4, Esau and Isaac discover Jacob's deceit; 5.10, Rebecca appeases Esau to put aside his malice for Jacob.

As a consequence of the rapid dramatic development, the student who played the Poetess composed original rhymed verse to provide two transitions.[18] The structure of these verses follows that of the original play in the consistent use of rhyming couplets. Although rhyming couplets were indeed used by the early modern playwright with little distinction of character or dramatic situation,[19] for the modern students this structure was a clear poetic convention that they combined with the use of early modern English terms. Thus the Poetess declaims:

Figure 5. The Poetess.

Transition 1 (Conclusion of 4.11)
Jacob leaveth with such a blessing for good;
Then cometh Esau with the prepared food,
Thinking he would soon be blesséd well,
Unaware of all that hath befell.

Transition 2 (Conclusion of 5.4)
Rebecca adviseth her son Jacob so
That to his uncle Laban he would quickly go.
Thus Jacob wisely fleeth his angry brother
Who speaketh anon of Jacob with his mother.

Furthermore, this use of the Poetess—played by a mature student—to provide a dramatic framework for the play is something that is suggested by the text of the play itself. The original prologue and epilogue are spoken by "A Poet" (and are spoken in the present production by the Poetess).[20] The Poet's authority reflects that of the school headmaster (probably William Hunnis, musician and gentleman of the Chapel Royal),[21] who had written the play for performance by his pupils and who therefore originally played the Poet.[22]

The relationship between the prologue and the epilogue is at once structural and theological. On the one hand, they are set apart from the rhyming couplets used throughout the play by being composed in "rhyme royal"[23] (abab bcc); this distinction marks out the gravity of the passages through the use of a complex rhyme scheme that was at that time the "chief English stanza for serious verse."[24] On the other hand, they set out the various aspects of predestination, thereby providing the conceptual framework that is materialized through the dramatic aspects of plot and characterization. This is evident in the following stanzas, the first from the prologue and the second from the epilogue:

But before Jacob and Esau yet born were,
  Or had either done good, or ill perpetrate:
As the prophet Malachi and Paul witness bear,
  Jacob was chosen, and Esau reprobate:
  Jacob I love (saith God) and Esau I hate.
For it is not (saith Paul) in man's renewing or will,
But in God's mercy, who chooseth whom he will.
   (*JE* 3)

Yet not all flesh did he then predestinate,
But only the adopted children of promise:
For he foreknew that many would degenerate,
And willfully give cause to be put from that bliss,
So on God's behalf no manner default there is;
But where he chooseth, he showeth his great mercy:
And where he refuseth, he doth none injury.
   (*JE* 89)

The first passage espouses a concept of predestination in which "Jacob was chosen and Esau reprobated before they were born or had the opportunity to do good or ill."[25] To this end, the playwright weaves into this passage a direct citation from 1 Romans (9:11–13): "For yet *the children* were borne, & when they had nether done good, nor evil (that the purpose of God might remaine according to election not by workes, but by him that calleth). It was said unto her, The elder shal serve the yonger. As it is written [*Malachi* 1:1–2] I have loved Jacob, & have hated Esau" (GB, Newe Testament, fol. 73v). What is more, Helen Thomas argues that the epilogue not only strengthens the centrality of predestination necessary for understanding the play but also introduces the Catholic doctrine (suggesting an editing of the epilogue during the Marian reign) that "God's foreknowledge of man's future actions is given as the cause of His choice of the elect and the reprobated."[26] Together, the prologue and the epilogue clearly provide a didactic, homiletic argument for the play, intending it to be a dramatization of theological doctrines.

Such varying doctrinal positions demonstrate the complex controversial aspect of predestination and certainly point to the difficulties for modern Israeli-Jewish students in coping with concepts that are both historically and religiously distant. As the student playing Jacob commented, the "play is definitely entertaining; however, we should not forget about its didactic content, which in my opinion is subversive. On the one hand Jacob commits an immoral deed in buying the eldership of his brother and deceiving his blind father. On the other hand, he fulfills God's will." This (somewhat problematic) identification of predestination with the subversion of a moral stance generates a new epilogue, composed by this same student. It reads as follows:[27]

> We thank you all for lending us your ears
> And we hope our modest show has allayed your fears
> Of a play from a distant age and a distant land
> That speaks of the Bible but whose setting is really England,
> Its struggles, its monarchs, especially its queen,
> Elizabeth, who here is represented by the younger son,
> Jacob, who, according to the doctrine of predestination,
> Was worthier than Esau to receive the blessing from their father, blind
> Isaac, to whom Jacob was reluctant to be unkind.
> Gentle audience, you have seen tonight
> How Jacob can be played on the stage to your heart's delight
> By a young woman whose presence perhaps made you wonder
> And perhaps led you, we hope, to ponder
> Questions of male and female roles, of gender
> And, in our presentation, we pray, we did not offend your
> Sensibilities but instead made you see
> This play's meaning for Israel in the twenty-first century.
> For we have shown, or so we have tried,
> That, just as the waves along the shore can ebb and rise with the tide,
> So can people's fortunes, though seemingly low,
> Rise, and grow in a powerful crescendo.
> In short, the humble and meek
> Need only divine or human compassion to seek.

These lines stress several central issues with which the students engaged while reading and staging the play: the historical relevance of *The Historie of Jacob and Esau*, transposing the principle of election onto the reign of

Elizabeth I;[28] the issue of gender roles; and the reconstituting of the play's meaning for modern-day readers in terms of "compassion" (resolutely human as well as divine) rather than predestination. These issues provide the modern reader—whose performative and candid responses are presented in this essay—with an interpretive opportunity that participates in the multitextual dialogue about *The Historie of Jacob and Esau.*

Parshanut

My second task in this essay is to attend to the *textual system* (as Julia Kristeva has termed it)[29] composed of homiletic and exegetical texts, which reveal the traditional Jewish and Christian interpretive concerns focused on the biblical story of Jacob and Esau. The largely Protestant character of *The Historie of Jacob and Esau* evokes three Reformation texts: Martin Luther's *Lectures on Genesis* (delivered in 1541–1542);[30] *A Commentarie of John Calvine, upon the First Book of Moses called Genesis* (delivered in 1550–1552);[31] and the 1560 Geneva Bible, with its copious marginal notes, those "brief annotations upon all the hard places as wel for the understanding of suche wordes as are obscure" (GB, fol. iiii[v]). It is also important to return to the Hebrew Bible—as the student director of the play comments, "as a Jew, first I read the Jewish story of Jacob and Esau in the Hebrew Bible, then the story at it appears in the Geneva Bible and only then did I approach the play." Finally, it is advantageous to look at two medieval Jewish exegetes, in consequence of their importance to the Reformation project of Bible commentary and translation[32] and of the familiarity of some of the Israeli-Jewish students with them: the northern French Rashi, or Rabbi Sholomo (Solomon) ben Isaac (1030/1040–1105), whose biblical commentaries integrate literal and midrashic (homiletic) interpretations;[33] and the Spanish Abraham Ibn Ezra (1089–1164), whose biblical commentaries stress literal readings and grammatical explanations.[34] Looking at how these medieval and early modern readers of the Hebrew Bible respond to and interpret the biblical story of Jacob and Esau provides an intertextual context that illuminates the response of modern students.

Genesis 25:22–27

The modern performance of *The History of Jacob and Esau* focuses on two central episodes from the biblical text: Rebecca's pregnancy with the twins and their birth; and Jacob's stealing of the firstborn's blessing. The following verses relate to the first episode:

[22] But the children strove together [marginal note: Or, hurt one an other] within her: therefore she said, Seeing it *is* so, why am I thus? [marginal note: That is, with childe, seing one shal destroye another] wherefore she went to aske the Lord [marginal note: For that is the onely refuge in all our miseries]. [23] And the Lord said to her, two nations *are* in thy wombe, and two maner of people shalbe devided out of thy bowels, and the one people, and the one people shall be mightier than the other, and the elder shall serve the yonger. [24] Therefore, when her time of deliverance was fulfilled, beholde, twinnes *were* in her wombe. [25] So he that came out first was red, and he was all over as a rough garment, and they called his name Esáu. [26] And afterwarde came his brother out, and his hand held Esáu by the hele: therefore his name was called Jaakób. Now Izhák was thre score yere olde when Rebekáh bare them. [27] And the boyes grewe, & Esáu *was* a cunning hunter, & lived in the fields [marginal note: Ebr. A man of the field]: but Jaakób was a plaine [marginal note: Or, simple and innocent] man, and dwelt in tentes. (GB, fol. 11v)

The note on verse 22 in the Geneva Bible introduces the message of divine mercy into the narrative of the childless woman, with the comment that the Lord "is the onely refuge in all our miseries." The major concern, however, of the other scholia is with the inborn physical and psychological differences between the brothers. Thus the biblical struggle presented in the phrase "strove together" (verse 22) is amplified with the use of the words "hurt" and "destroye," and the distinctive descriptions of the brothers (verse 27)—the Hebrew words *ish sadeh* ("man of the field") and *tam* ("simple and innocent")—are carefully noted. By doing so, the scholia thereby call attention to these two exegetical cruxes in the Hebrew Bible. Moreover, these cruxes become the focus of an intertextual discussion that is distinguished by an acknowledgment of familial strife bearing cultural and religious import. Rashi sets the stage in his commentary when he explains the unusual Hebrew term *va-yitrotsitsu* ("struggled"), which literally means "run to and fro" (Ibn Ezra, 249):

> You must admit that this verse calls for an interpretation since it leaves unexplained what this struggling was about. . . . Our Rabbis explain that the word *va-yitrotsitsu* has the meaning of running, moving quickly, whenever she [Rebecca] passed by the doors of the Torah [the Pentateuch] of Shem and Eber[35] Jacob moved

> convulsively in his efforts to come to birth, but whenever she passed by the gate of a pagan temple Esau moved convulsively in his efforts to come to birth. (Rashi, 114–15)

Rashi provides the textual issue with a midrashic (homiletic) interpretation that marks Jacob as the studious Jewish son and Esau as an idol worshipper. This is significant because of its wider cultural implications; Jacob is the traditional, quintessential "pale, gentle scholar as favored love-object for [Jewish] women,"[36] whereas Esau, as is stated subsequently, becomes a "cunning hunter" and thereby an image of aggressive masculinity. Luther expediently remarks that "these two brothers struggled in the womb; and later on, after they had been born, they quarrel throughout the entire time of their life. Thus we continually contend with the Pope and the Turk, and it is everlastingly impossible for us to have fellowship or peace with them" (Luther, 4: 368). Rashi's envisioning of the sibling struggle between scholar and pagan is transposed for Luther onto the struggle between Protestant and Catholic, Christian and Muslim infidel. Significantly, the student who played the role of Isaac made the following comments about this relationship:

> I think that this play is very important because while ostensibly depicting a biblical scene, it alludes to the political situation in contemporary England. An interesting point is that, whereas, in Jewish tradition, the Jacob-Esau conflict is viewed in terms of Jewish-Gentile relations, the play sees it in terms of the conflict between Catholicism and Protestantism.
>
> Why is this play appropriate for presentation to an academic audience in Israel? The play is centered around a conflict that is resolved by reconciliation and concession (on the part of Esau, primarily); thus, this dramatic work gives one the hope that even the most severe of disputes can be solved peacefully, as is the case here where Esau transcends himself and makes peace with his new situation.

Echoing Rashi's commentary on the difference between "the doors of the Torah" and "the gate of a pagan temple," the student emphasizes the difference between the Jewish and Christian interpretations of the fraternal struggle. What is more, he singularly looks forward to the meeting between Esau and Jacob in Genesis 33:4, in which "Esau ran to mette him and embraced him, and fel on his necke and kissed him, and thei wept" (GB, fol. 15v). This reconciliation is indeed foreshadowed in the *Historie of*

Jacob and Esau, when in the last scene of the play Esau accepts his mother's request, "Let pass this grudge against thy brother" (*JE* 86). The struggle and its resolution thus become particularly relevant for this reader, as the implications of the biblical passage resonate for him in terms of both sixteenth-century England and his own situation in twenty-first-century Israel.

This struggle continues in verse 27, in which the difference between the two brothers revolves around the issue of honesty and dishonesty. Rashi conceives of Esau not simply as one who tracks animals through deception and trickery (as explained by Ibn Ezra, 251), but also as one who understands "how to entrap and deceive his father with his mouth" (Rashi, 116). Furthermore, Rashi considers Jacob to be one who "as his heart was his mouth [his thoughts and words tallied]. One who is not ingenious in deceiving people is called *tam* plain, simple" (Rashi, 116). Indeed, Rashi's commentary echoes in Luther's own, when Luther explains that the Hebrew word *tam*

> does not denote one who is simple in mind and intellect, that is, without ingenuity and industry. No, it denotes one who is simple, upright, blameless, and sincere in regard to this will. . . . He [Jacob] went to the church and schools often and gladly, learned the Word and good manner, and heard the addresses of the patriarch Shem and the others, just as the Jews have commented. (Luther, 4: 383–84)

This shared emphasis by Rashi and Luther on Jacob's holy studies envisages the difference between the two brothers in terms of religious commitment. It is Calvin, however, who endows this difference with theological significance:

> For after that he [Moses] hath shewed that Esau was a strong man, and a hunter, and a wilde man: he setteth against the same, the milde and gentle disposition of Jacob, because he lived a quiet life at home. To be shorte, the comparison signifieth as muche, as if Moses commended Esau for his puissaunce and might, and said that Jacob was given to live in ease and rest at home: that suche was the inclination of the elder, that it foreshewed him to be in time a man of courage: and the disposition of the other to suche, as that it had nothing worthie of commendation. Seeing by heavenly decree the honour of eldershippe was given to Jacob, why doth God suffer him to lie (as it were) in the dust, but onely because he

will have his election to lie hidde for a time, to the end men might attribute nothing to their preparations. (Calvin, 334–35)[37]

Calvin reads a fascinating ambiguity into the biblical text, which combines a confounded narrative expectation and the doctrine of predestination. How does he bring this ambiguity into effect? Calvin does so by constructing a contemporary, naïve observer of the biblical events—one who is not cognizant of the divine promise made to Rebecca—for whom the expectation of Esau's natural dominance as firstborn belies the eventual "honour of eldershippe" divinely bestowed upon the younger son. To amplify this ambiguity, Calvin emphasizes the distinction between Esau and Jacob in terms of gender characteristics, with that same naïve reader accepting the Bible's seeming approbation of Esau's masculine physical attributes and the disparaging of Jacob's feminine "milde and gentle disposition." In effect, as John Curran notes, "the play alerts us to the dangers of perception by instigating our tendency as an audience to judge the relative merits of the actions of dramatic characters and then exposing this tendency as gravely flawed."[38] Such absence of psychological insight on the part of the naïve reader (subsequently concretized in Isaac's physical blindness) is ultimately resolved for Calvin in a theological context; he explicates the meaning of the biblical text in terms of divine will. In other words, according to Calvin, the biblical narrative generates the mistaken understanding held by that naïve reader, which parallels the human lack of knowledge about and involvement in the process of election; as Calvin states, "Attribute nothing to their preparations." This narrative and theological ambiguity—Who is worthy of mercy? Who is reprobate?—coincide as the naïve reader of the biblical text becomes a realization of human blindness. In this way such ambiguity, both dramatic and narrative, effectively underlines the problems in the interpretive process, thus marking the futility of the reader's efforts to determine the truth and paralleling the predestinatory absence of "man's renewing or will" in determining his fate.

In the context of this discussion of the interpretive process, it is especially interesting to look at the comments made by the student who played Esau. He contemplates in a quite sophisticated manner the dramatic aspect of Calvinist theology—a reading informed by his own studies in early modern English drama:

Esau appears to me like a kind of a tragic character, almost Shakespearean in a way. The twist between meekly accepting his fate and drawing a sword against his brother and carrying it out until

> the tragic end is very small. And only in a Protestant play, a play influenced by a Protestant mentality, a Protestant teaching of the Bible, of predestination, that man's soul is destined to salvation or damnation without man's own involvement, it is all preordained, is expressed in this play in the form of Esau that just accepts his fate because there is nothing else he can do. He bows down to a greater authority.

The student's sense of the fine line of tragedy within the play, which draws on the ambiguity concerning Esau's character, is reflected in the joint decision by the student actors to write an original soliloquy for him. Esau had previously faced Rebecca directly, when she had entreated him to "Forgive, and the Lord shall prosper thee on the land" (*JE* 86). In response he uses strong words of outrage, calling Jacob "that mopish [foolish, stupid] elf" and his mother's "dainty darling . . . prinkox [coxcomb] . . . golpol [golden-haired]" (*JE* 85). The soliloquy was composed with the purpose of filling in the rather sparse details provided in *The Historie of Jacob and Esau* regarding Esau's subsequent change of mind. Thus Esau says:

> Oh boils my blood at this injustice great,
> O how it pains me to think of my fate!
> Twice have I been tricked by my own brother.
> Doth he forget that we are sons of the same mother?
> Yet must I listen to the words of my father dear,
> And the message he doth give me is so clear.
> God's choice must I obediently accept,
> Though the sorrow in my heart be so deep, so abject.
> I am of the seed of Isaac and Abraham, of this I am aware,
> And thus must I acknowledge God's judgment, this I swear!
> The expression on my face change I must,
> I am his own vessel, his will with me I trust.[39]

Esau does indeed yield here to God's judgment (if not specifically to the doctrine of predestination). Yet the student who wrote the soliloquy takes care to let Esau express his feelings of anger, pain, and sorrow, marking in this manner the more dramatically human aspect to his character. Thus Esau's final meeting with his parents becomes more poignant when Isaac commends him by saying, "Son Esau, thou hast thyself well acquitted, / That all quarrel to Jacob thou has remitted" (*JE* 87). In the modern performance the happy family scene maintains a measure of ambiguity; as Esau

Figure 6. Rebecca, Isaac, and Esau.

stoically accepts his father's words, those of his emotion-filled soliloquy still echo for the audience.

Genesis 27:5–30

The second episode on which the modern performance of *The History of Jacob and Esau* focuses is that of the firstborn's blessing. The Geneva Bible relates:

> [6] Then Rebekáh spake unto Jaakób her sonne, saying, Beholde, I have heard thy father talking with Esáu thy brother, saying, [7] Bring me venison, and make me savorie meat, that I maie eat and blesse thee before the Lord, afore my death. [8] Now therefore, my sonne, heare my voyce in that which I commande thee. [9] Get thee now to the flocke [marginal note: this subtiltie is blameworthie because she shulde have tarried till God had performed his promes], & bringe me thence two good kydes of the goates, that I maie make pleasant meat of them for thy father, such as he loveth. [10] Then thou shalt bring it to thy father, and he shal eat, to the

> intent that he maie blesse thee before his death. [11] But Jaakób said to Rebekáh his mother, Beholde Esáu my brother *is* rough, and I am smoothe. [12] My father maie possibly fele me, and I shal seme [marginal note: Ebr. before his eies] to him to be a mocker [marginal note: Or, as though I wolde deceive him]: so shal I bring a curse upon me, and not a blessing. [13] But his mother said unto him, Upon me *be* thy curse [marginal note: The assurance of Gods decree made her bolde], my sonne: onely heare my voyce, and go and bring me *them*. . . . [30] And when Izhák had made an end of blessing Jaakób, and Jaakób was scace gone out from the presence of Izhák his father, then came Esáu his brother from his hunting. (GB, fols. 12r–v)

One primary concern of the Geneva Bible scholia is the careful explication of the Hebrew terms *ve-hayiti ve-einav* (I shall be in his eyes) and *ke-metatei'a*, comprising both the verb "deceiving" and the noun "trickster" (verse 12).[40] This concern marks out Jacob's darker side, remarked upon by the student who played the Poetess:

> The reason I wanted to do the play is because I felt like the characters were very real to life. And I liked the sense of humor that was in it. It's interesting though, because in this play Jacob seems kind of like an innocent pawn and Rebecca is the one that plans the whole thing and she is quite a manipulator, whereas I'm not so sure it shows up that way in the Bible. Jacob isn't such an innocent sweet guy in the Bible, he's a bit of a . . . well, you'd call him a "traveling salesman" or something.

Neither the humor of the Reformation biblical drama nor Jacob's problematic character escapes this student. Indeed, she envisions this character through the modern phrase "traveling salesman," which quite ironically refers to Jacob's subsequent flight from his parents' "tentes" to save himself from Esau's anger as well as his clever transaction (Genesis 30:31–43) with Laban's "great spotted, and little spotted" flocks (GB, fol. 14r).

This ambiguity surrounding Jacob's character also serves a theological purpose, as evident in Calvin's explication of verse 30:

> *Jacob was scarce gone out from the presence.* For if thou compare both their works together, Esau obeyeth his father, bringeth the fruite of his hunting, of the prey gotten by his labour, he dresseth meat for his father, he affirmeth nothing but the truth: to be short,

> thou shalt finde nothing in him, whiche deserveth not praise. Jacob going not from home, appointeth a kid, in sted of Venison, insinuateth himself with many lies, bringeth nothing whiche may rightly commende him, and in many things he deserveth reprehension. Therefore, we must néedes confesse, that the cause of the event dependeth not upon workes but lyeth hid in the everlasting purpose of God [marginal note: Election dependeth not upon workes]. (Calvin, 577)

Calvin's conjecture regarding both Esau and Jacob is duly continued here and used to strengthen the principle stated in the marginal note that "election dependeth not upon works." Calvin does so by developing the distinctly different characteristics of each character, thereby not inconsequentially adding color and depth to the biblical narrative. Indeed, the strength of Calvin's argument rests on the way that he constructs those naïve readers, who on their part "shalt finde nothing in him [Esau], whiche deserveth not praise" and who see Jacob as one "who deserveth reprehension." Such acceptance of these superficial characterizations reveals this reader's basic misunderstanding of divine will, for such characterizations are abrogated in God's previous revelation to Rebecca and in subsequent passages in the biblical text. This confounding of narrative development thus serves to underline the principle of election, which clearly removes the responsibility for action and resolution from the human dimension.

It is the figure of Rebecca, however, that invites the most radical change from traditional to modern responses. The Jewish exegetical response is relatively reticent, explaining that Rebecca's admonishment, "Do not be afraid that your father might curse you," is simply "the way women talk" (Ibn Ezra, 261–62). On their part the Geneva Bible scholia explicate Rebecca's actions as both "blameworthie" and "bold," essentially because of her attempt to precipitate divine will. Because these actions are the moving force in the biblical narrative, Calvin is justifiably concerned with understanding their significance:

> *The cursse be upon my sonne.* Againe, Rebecca sinneth here, in that she burneth with so rash a zeale, that she weigheth not that God disalloweth that, which she having all beganne presenteth. . . . Notwithstanding, no man will denie, that this zeale, though it were preposterous, proceeded both of godlinesse, and also of the special reverence of Gods worde. . . . The fatherly blessing was a seale of Gods grace: I confesse it: but she ought rather to have tarried untill God sent a remedie from heaven, in changing Isaacs

minde, and governing his toung, then to have attempted any unlawful way. (Calvin, 572)

The interesting juxtaposition of the terms "rash" and "preposterous" with "godliness" and "reverence" indicates a confusion in Calvin's response, one that fully indicates an admonition of Rebecca's actions and a wariness in tainting her motives. Perhaps it is his caution in confronting a sacred biblical character, his unwillingness to utterly condemn one of the earliest figures of religious faith and piety from the Hebrew Bible. In doing so, Calvin certainly perceives an ambiguity in Rebecca's character, paralleling what he had read into the biblical descriptions of Jacob and Esau. By preserving such ambiguity, Calvin creates a more complex, even more human, vision of the events, one that looks forward to their dramatic rendering.

One can argue that it is this very ambiguity that leads to a more radical view of Rebecca's character for the modern reader, a view that is already foreshadowed in the comments made in *The Historie of Jacob and Esau* by the boy-servant Mido when he says to his master Isaac:

> I have stood here all this while, list'ning, how you
> And my dame Rebecca have been laying the law;
> But she hath as quick answers as ever I saw.
> Ye could not speak anything unto her so thick,
> But she had her answer as ready and as quick
> (*JE* 24)

Mido's role as comic but perceptive commentator underlines Rebecca's cleverness as well as her appropriation of Isaac's patriarchal, familial authority. Indeed, Michelle Ephraim astutely notes that *The Historie of Jacob and Esau* "lauds Rebecca as the author and agent" of Jacob's usurpation of the firstborn's blessing and furthermore that the play as a whole legitimizes "female authority—Rebecca's and, ultimately, Elizabeth's."[41] It is this aspect that most attracts the modern students and that can clearly be seen in the enthusiastic response of the student who played Rebecca:

> When I first read *Jacob and Esau*, I immediately fell in love with Rebecca. I found her character witty and clever, powerful enough to bring to change and social mobility, and it was really interesting for me to find that a woman could be so powerful in a sixteenth-century play. And I guess that's where it all started, when we all kind of fell in love with her. I am glad I got the opportunity to play Rebecca, I feel honored!

These lines demonstrate how the play catches the student's imagination, emphasizing how her attraction to the figure of Rebecca became the motivating force behind the modern production. It also raises for the modern reader the question of the role and character of women in early modern England, particularly, as Naomi Pasachoff argues, whether Rebecca can be seen as a "revolutionary firebrand . . . who sets in motion the plan to seize from Esau the powers which he now enjoys by virtue of natural but not of divine law."[42] Pasachoff is looking at the play in terms of the religiopolitical struggle of the supporters of Edward and Elizabeth against Mary. The student, on her part, rather discusses the sociocultural issues of "change and social mobility." In both cases the framing of the biblical narrative in terms of relevant contemporary issues successfully highlights the emergence of the figure of wife and mother as a successful force for change. Can one suggest that the highlighting of this figure also produces friction with the analogy to the two childless Tudor queens, effectively underlining the complexity of sixteenth-century responses to a reigning monarch who defies any easy definition?

It is the response of the female student director that draws out another, final issue concerning familial authority:

> To begin with, the story of Jacob and Esau attracted me because of the fact that a prophecy is given to a female, rather than to a male, to Rebecca, rather than to her husband, and the way she doesn't reveal this to her husband (a thing that could justify her deeds). The biblical story raises many questions of gender roles and the strong manipulative female character vs. a blind weak husband.

This passage discloses the way in which the modern reader responds to the biblical text, as she brings to it a perception of issues that are of most interest to her. Not surprisingly, at the center of *The Historie of Jacob and Esau* there is also, as Ephraim argues, "a larger theme of female leadership and male blindness—spiritual and literal."[43] In the modern dramatic re-creation, the characters of Rebecca and Isaac were effectively played by a younger female student as a contradistinction to an older male student. This ability to represent dramatically the difference between the two characters is a modern enhancement of the original use of young boys to perform such roles in the sixteenth-century production. For the audience this physical difference certainly revivifies the biblical characters and animates the familial and theological tension dramatically envisioned between Rebecca and Isaac. What is more, this model of a wise wife and a passive

Figure 7. Rebecca and Isaac.

husband echoes not only the student's singular interest but also a marriage model extant in traditional Jewish culture and literature.[44] Such an extension of biblical themes into wider cultural and contemporary meanings is thus an important consequence of the modern dramatic production.

Conclusion

In the third and final stanza of the "Prologue of the Play," the Poet sets out the way in which performance becomes pedagogy.

> But now for our coming we shall exhibit here,
> Of Jacob and Esau how the story was;
> Whereby God's adoption may plainly appear:
> And also that, whatever God's ordinance was,
> Nothing might defeat, but that it must come to pass.
> That, if this story may your eyes or ears delight,
> We pray you of patience, while we it recite.
> (*JE* 3)

The dramatic realization of the concept of predestination admirably suited the distinct cultural situation of mid-sixteenth-century England. Making apt use of the interest in biblical narrative and in the theater experience, the playwright sets out a satisfying tale of humor, suspense, and divine will. Remarkably, the twenty-first-century students readily comprehended these various aspects, at once reproducing and creatively transforming this situation within a modern university setting. Responding to the play, they transformed its dramatic and theological concerns into their own terms of gender identity, divine judgment, and human compassion. Drawing on their ability to read the Hebrew Bible and the Jewish exegetes, these students were able to establish the authority of their interpretive process, ultimately vying successfully with the Reformation commentators and translators. What is more, the move from the elaborate early modern production to the modern, streamlined version invites a recognition of various issues involved in the encounter of a contemporary reader or audience with an early modern text: the dramatic performance as composing an interpretive act, the modernization of a Reformation text, and the relationship of Jewish and Christian exegetical interpretations.

The Reformation drama *The Historie of Jacob and Esau* thus came alive for a modern audience, providing an exhilarating experience for the actors, audience, and teachers that sustained the power of this dramatic text while encompassing a more extensive range of cultural and religious associations than was possible with the original performance. This, then, is the interpretive incentive of the pedagogical experience: By enabling a twenty-first-century reenactment of the *Jacob and Esau* biblical drama, the students provided the opportunity for themselves and for the members of their department to experience the dramatic and emotional resonances of early modern theological issues—and to transpose these into a reflection on their own cultural and religious discourses. In the end, is this not what experiencing literature is about—a reciprocal move between two historical and cultural situations?

Notes

I would like to thank Alan Rosen for his invaluable comments on this essay.

1. Paul Whitfield White, *Theatre and Reformation: Protestantism, Patronage, and Playing in Tudor England* (Cambridge, UK: Cambridge University Press, 1993), 179.

2. Paul Whitfield White, "Introduction," in *Reformation Biblical Drama: An Old-Spelling Critical Edition*, ed. Paul Whitfield White (New York: Garland, 1992), xx.

3. The only extant complete text of the play is *A New Mery and Wittie Comedie or Enterlude, New Imprinted, Treating upon the Historie of Jacob and Esau Taken out of the XXVII. Chap. of the First Booke of Moses Entituled Genesis* (London: Henrie Bynneman, 1568). The title of the play is cited from *Six Anonymous Plays*, ser. 2, ed. John Stephen Farmer (London: Early English Drama Society, 1906), 2. Hereafter *JE*.

4. White, *Theatre and Reformation*, 112.

5. See the discussion in T. W. Craik, *The Tudor Interlude: Stage, Costume, and Acting* (Leicester, UK: Leicester University Press, 1967), 43–44.

6. Ruth H. Blackburn, *Biblical Drama Under the Tudors* (The Hague: Mouton, 1971), 154.

7. White, "Introduction," xxi.

8. For further discussion, see Michael B. Barbour and Susan Becker Barbour, "A Star Is Born: Staging Choices in *The Nativity* and *The Shepherds*," *Early Theatre* 3 (2000): 210–18; Stephen Johnson, "Historical Text and the Postmodern Aesthetics: Case Study of Handmade Performance's *The Last Judgement*," *Early Theatre* 3 (2000): 259–74; and Gwendolyn Waltz, "Time, Meaning, and Transcendence: Directing *The Incredulity of Thomas*," *Early Theatre* 3 (2000): 240–48.

9. White, "Introduction," xxv. White argues that although *Jacob and Esau* was licensed for printing sometime between June 1557 and June 1558, it was "written toward the end of Edward VI's reign [1547–1553] when two of the play's thematic concerns, the raising of youth and predestinarian theology, were popular subjects . . . and possibly revived under Mary and Elizabeth" (xxxvii).

10. This estimation is informed by the discussion of dramatic performances in the sixteenth century; see Andrew Garr, *The Shakespearean Stage, 1574–1642*, 3rd ed. (Cambridge, UK: Cambridge University Press, 1992), 178–79.

11. John E. Curran Jr., "*Jacob and Esau* and the Iconoclasm of Merit," *Studies in English Literature* 49 (2009): 300.

12. White, *Theatre and Reformation*, 119.

13. Comments by Prof. Yishai Tobin, printed with his permission.

14. *The Bible and Holy Scriptures Conteyned in the Olde and New Testament* (Geneva: Rouland Hall, 1560), fol. 11v. Hereafter GB. Sixteenth-century spelling has been preserved in citing the Geneva Bible, as well as in other contemporary texts, except in the use of long "s," "i" as "j," "u" as "v," replacing the vowel-macron with the succeeding "n" or "m," and replacing superscripted letters over "y" ("e" with "the"; "u" with "you") and "w" ("t" with "with").

15. For summaries of these discussions, see Valerie Traub, "Gender and Sexuality in Shakespeare," in *The Cambridge Companion to Shakespeare*, ed. Margreta De Grazia and Stanley Wells (Cambridge, UK: Cambridge University Press, 2001), 129–46; and Barbara Hodgdon, "Sexual Disguise and the Theatre of Gender," in *The Cambridge Companion to Shakespearean Comedy*, ed. Alexander Leggatt (Cambridge, UK: Cambridge University Press, 2002), 179–97.

16. The comments made by the students who performed in the play were both written and recorded. They are printed in this essay with their permission.

17. The original script contains five acts, with a total of thirty-two scenes.

18. These two passages were composed by Donna Metreger and are printed with her permission.

19. As J. E. Bernard writes, "The whole play is in the dramatic doggerel, which carried on without a break from scene to scene and set to set" (*The*

Prosody of the Tudor Interlude [1939: rpt. Hamden, CT: Archon Books, 1969], 93). Bernard also determines that the play is composed in tetrameter couplets, whereas the prologue and epilogue are composed in tetrameter rhyme royal.

20. The title page lists: "1. The Prologue, A Poet," (*JE* 2), whereas the epilogue (or "Finis") is recited by "The Poet" (*JE* 88).

21. Although published anonymously, both Naomi E. Pasachoff and Paul Whitfield White have argued for the authorship of William Hunnis (d. 1597), schoolmaster, musician, and gentleman of the Chapel Royal. See Naomi E. Pasachoff, *Playwrights, Preachers, and Politicians: A Study of Four Tudor Old Testament Dramas* (Salzburg, Austria: Institut für Englische Sprache und Literatur, Universtät Salzburg, 1975), 40–50; and White, *Theatre and Reformation*, 118–19.

22. "19. Jacob and Esau," in *The Cambridge History of English and American Literature: An Encyclopedia in Eighteen Volumes*, v. 5, *The Drama to 1642, Part One*, ed. Adolphus W. Ward et al. (Cambridge, UK: Cambridge University Press, 1907–1921), online edition January 2000. http://www.bartleby.com/215/0519.html (accessed 23 July 2009).

23. Bernard, *Prosody*, 93.

24. "Rhyme Royal," in *Princeton Encyclopedia of Poetry and Poetics: Enlarged Edition*, ed. Alex Preminger (Princeton, NJ: Princeton University Press, 1965), 710.

25. Helen Thomas, "*Jacob and Esau*—'Rigidly Calvinistic'?" *Studies in English Literature, 1500–1900* 9 (1969): 201.

26. Thomas, "*Jacob and Esau*," 201–2 and 213.

27. This epilogue was composed by Mark Elliott Shapiro and is printed with his permission.

28. For further discussion of the connection between *The Historie of Jacob and Esau* and Elizabeth I (in terms of the figures of both Rebecca and Deborah), see Michelle Karen Ephraim, "Jewish Matriarchs and the Staging of Elizabeth I in 'The History of Jacob and Esau,'" *Studies in English Literature, 1500–1900* 43 (2003): 301–21; Michelle Ephraim, "Maternal Authority in *The Historie of Jacob and Esau*," in her *Reading the Jewish Woman on the Elizabethan Stage* (Aldershot, UK: Ashgate, 2008), 50–67; and Pasachoff, *Playwrights*, 16–56.

29. Julia Kristeva, *Desire in Language: A Semiotic Approach to Literature and Art*, ed. Leon S. Roudiez, trans. Thomas Gora, Alice Jardine, and Leon. S. Roudiez (New York: Columbia University Press, 1980), 15.

30. Martin Luther, *Luther's Works*, v. 4, *Lectures on Genesis: Chapters 21–25*, ed. Jaroslav Pelikan (St. Louis: Concordia, 1964), ix–x. Hereafter Luther.

31. Randall C. Zachman, "Calvin as Commentator on Genesis," in *Calvin and the Bible*, ed. Donald R. McKim (Cambridge, UK: Cambridge University Press, 2006), 1.

32. For further discussion, see David Daiches, *The King James Version of the English Bible* (Chicago: University of Chicago Press, 1941); Chanita Goodblatt,

The Christian Hebraism of John Donne: Written with the Fingers of Man's Hand (Pittsburgh, PA: Duquesne University Press, 2010); and Herman Hailperin, *Rashi and the Christian Scholars* (Pittsburgh, PA: University of Pittsburgh Press, 1963).

33. Rashi, *Pentateuch with Rashi's Commentary: Genesis*, trans. M. Rosenbaum and A. M. Silbermann, in collaboration with A. Blashki and L. Joseph (1929; rpt. Jerusalem: Silbermann Family, 1973). Hereafter Rashi.

34. Abraham ben Meir in Ezra, *Ibn Ezra's Commentary on the Pentateuch: Genesis*, trans. H. Norman Strickman and Arthur M. Silver (New York: Menorah, 1988). Hereafter Ibn Ezra.

35. Shem is one of the sons of Noah, and Eber is Shem's great-grandson. According to rabbinic literature, Shem's "tents" (Genesis 9:27) are identified as an academy, with which Eber becomes associated. See Moses Aberbach, "Shem," in *Encyclopaedia Judaica*, 2nd ed., ed. Michael Berenbaum and Fred Skolnik (Detroit: Macmillan Reference USA), 18: 185.

36. Daniel Boyarin, *Unheroic Conduct: The Rise of Heterosexuality and the Invention of the Jewish Man* (Berkeley: University of California Press, 1977), 68.

37. *A Commentarie of John Calvine, upon the First Book of Moses called Genesis* (London: John Harison and George Bishop, 1578). Hereafter Calvin.

38. Curran, "*Jacob and Esau*," 286.

39. This soliloquy was composed by Donna Metreger and is printed with her permission.

40. The noun *trickster* is cited from *Tanakh: The Holy Scriptures—The New JPS Translation According to the Traditional Hebrew Text* (Philadelphia: Jewish Publication Society, 1985), 40. The Hebrew term *metatei'a* (*ke* means "as" or "like") can, however, also be read as a verb (the *pi'el* verb form), in the singular masculine present tense. *Pi'el* is a verb form whose meaning is "*to busy oneself eagerly* with the action indicated by the stem. This [is an] intensifying of the idea of the stem." See Wilhelm Gesenius, *Gesenius' Hebrew Grammar*, ed. E. Kautzsch, trans. A. E. Cowley (Mineola, NY: Dover, 2006 [1910]), 141.

41. Ephraim, "Maternal Authority," 55, 51.

42. Pasachoff, *Playwrights*, 31.

43. Ephraim, "Maternal Authority," 56.

44. For a discussion of this model, see Boyarin, *Unheroic Conduct*, 68–73.

7

Anne Lake Prescott

Exploiting King Saul in Early Modern England

Good Uses for a Bad King

Some Americans are old enough to remember when a recently defeated politician snarled at reporters in California that soon "you won't have Dick Nixon to kick around anymore." Little did we know. True, kicking kings can be more dangerous than kicking candidates for democratic office, but once the bad ones are safely dead, exploiting their memory can be useful. In this essay I recount how one king—Saul—was put to work in early modern England. That Saul was a bad ruler was generally assumed, although in another culture and in another text (or if he had written the great poetry conventionally ascribed to his son-in-law and successor) he might have found more defenders. The story yields a familiar if uncomfortable *significatio*: History, like fiction, is most compelling when morally or intellectually contradictory, if not to an individual reader then collectively in cultural memory. In this, Saul and David are alike, for David too was a sinner.[1] Yet Saul has drawn less attention from scholars of the period.

Here I look at some high points of Saul's life in more or less chronological order, but first I provide a rapid-fire summary of his career, usefully outlined by Henoch Clapham's *Briefe of the Bible* (1596) in flat verse with prose commentary: The Israelites, heedless of the prophet Samuel's warnings, insist on having a king so as to be more like the heathens. And so God

> doth appoint Samuel to annoynt Saul . . . a tall fellowe to the Kingship. Saul seeking his Fathers Asses, he found a Kingdome: for comming to enquire of Samuel concerning his Asses, . . . Samuel annointeth him, after the which, the Spirit (not of Sanctification, but) of Government and Majestie came upon him. This Saul after-

> wards neglecting his charge concerning the slaughter of Amaleks Cattle and Agag the King [i.e., Saul would not kill Agag, king of the Amalekites, and his cattle], the Lord therefore taketh from him the former Spirit, and put in him a frantick Spirite: commanding Samuel to annoynt David, the youngest sonne of [Jesse] . . . upon whome came the former Majesticall Spirite. After this, Saul ceaseth not to persecute David . . . but David, (though hee had him at vantage) wou'd not hurte him. In the end, consulting with a Witch at Endor . . . hee runneth to the Devill to speake with [the dead] Samuel. Saul, the next daye after, was slaine (togither with his Sonnes) in his warres with the Philistims, running himselfe desperatlie on his swordes pointe. (72–73)

Events also figuring in later exploitations of Saul's name include his sacrifice of cattle before the prophet Samuel arrives to supervise the rite (thus usurping a priestly prerogative); David's musical expulsion of Saul's "frantick Spirite"; Saul's envy of David's victories; his throwing a spear at David; his giving his daughter Michal to David for doubtless slimy political reasons; his demand that David bring him 200 Philistine foreskins; his ordering Doeg to kill priests who had helped David; his going into a cave to defecate, where David sees him and cuts off a piece of his skirt but spares his life because he is an anointed king; Saul's weeping admission that David is the better man; and David's lament for the deaths of Saul and Jonathan. Also notable are the loyalty of most Israelites to Saul, Samuel's grief that God withdrew his spirit from Saul, and God's chilling silence after that withdrawal.

Early modern memories of Saul are not always solemn. An epigram in John Donne Jr.'s *Cabinet of Merry Conceits* (1662) tells how three Oxford students in a pub assault an old man "with flouts and jeers." One calls him "Father Abraham," another "Father Isaac," and the third "Father Jacob." The codger replies that he is none of these: "Wherefore forbear your flouts I you do wish, / For indeed am Saul the Son of Kish, / Who for to seek my Fathers Asses came / From far, and here have found three of the same."[2] Bad verse, good joke. Usually, though, Saul is a guilty tyrant. What was so particularly noxious about Saul's sins? The usual answer was that whereas David broke God's laws against adultery and homicide, Saul ignored a direct personal command—to kill Agag and his people's cattle.[3] Few would have suggested in print that Saul was humane or politic in sparing Agag; better to displace that thought onto Saul. Steven Egerton, introducing a sermon on the scene in 1620, says that Saul defends himself to Samuel "with an impudent face" and appears to think "it a great pity, to kill such a goodly Prince as Agag was," thus "secretly taxing the commandement of the Lord, of too much rigor and severity, & making himselfe more wise & merciful then God."[4] This is not quite in the Bible; Egerton *deduces* it.

The fact remains that Saul disobeyed a direct divine order. Clapham, whom I quoted earlier, allegorizes: "Let Kings beware of sparing any cursed Agag," and because we are "all called to be Kings unto God, Let us spare neither fat sinnes, nor leane sinnes, sinnes lesse or more gainefull and pleasurable, but let us kill them all." This, with or without allegory, is the usual view. Nor did Saul's disobedience lack political relevance. Sparing God's enemy is dangerous, as Queen Elizabeth's advisers reminded her when they begged her to execute Mary Stuart: "They put the Queen in minde of the fearfull examples of Gods Judgements extant in Scripture," writes Sir Richard Baker in 1643, such as "Saul, for sparing of Agag."[5] And in a sermon titled *The Vexation of Saul* (1614), which explains at length why God withdrew his spirit from Saul, Anthony Maxey remarks that Christendom has seen similar downfalls. A marginal note reads, "the King of France but lately murdered" (Henri IV, the Huguenot turned Catholic in 1593, had been assassinated in 1610). Maxey can also be subtle, though, noting how Saul's story shows that the "difference is betweene Morall and Theological virtue, betweene a naturall man and a religious." Saul was a gifted king guilty of a spiritual sin. His tragedy is not the fall of a bad man but of a largely good one. Morality is not religion.

The sin that drew most attention, however, was Saul's envious persecution of David, almost always staged, versified, illustrated, and sermonized from David's viewpoint. In one sense this is logical, for David is the hero and Saul the villain. Yet one can also reflect that for the Renaissance David indeed had a "viewpoint," a lyric subjectivity expressed in the Psalms; if Saul wrote poetry about his own sufferings, a wildly unlikely possibility, it has not survived.

Saul, of course, first meets David when his courtiers summon a youth ("A rosie cheek'd musitian," Anne Bradstreet calls him)[6] whose harping might relieve the madness—melancholy, in Galenic terms—that had come upon him when God withdrew his spirit and sent a malevolent one. How we read that spirit, whether demon, spiritual emptiness, or dried black bile in the brain, is debated, but for Michael Drayton it was indeed severe. His Saul suffers fits,

> With cramps, with stitches and convulsions rackt, . . .
> His eyes were like out of his head to start,
> Fomes at the mouth, and often in his paine

O'r all his Court is heard to roare againe.
("David and Goliah," ll. 207–18)[7]

Cowley's *Davideis* (1656) gives Saul bad hair, brow sweat, breast knocking, and foot stomping.

David cures him, but Saul remains subject to relapse, at one point hurling a spear at the young harpist. This famous musical cure has been widely discussed, so suffice it to say here that the scene provoked debate on the nature of demons and music's effects, helping many to consider the relation of the demonic to bodily dysfunction. Hence one writer's speculation that David's music was in the "Aeolic Mood, . . . which was of a more Airy and soft pleasing sound" and "by its variety and delightfulness, allayeth the Passions and charmeth the Affections into a sweet and pleasing temper"—like that "enchanting Musick of the Harp, provided for King Saul" that made the evil spirit depart.[8] But how? The puzzle was to account for the demon's flight. If music influences the body, and if demons have no bodies, then why did the demon leave? The answer can help determine the place of music in church, if any. If it can expel the demonic, then we should welcome it. But Puritans such as John Spenser, writing in his *Votivae Angliae, Englands Complaint to their King* (1643), insists that if Saul's madness was natural, then he needed a doctor, but if he was, or thought he was, truly possessed by a demon—one of God's creatures—then "I cannot conceive what naturall power musick or melodie can have for the profligation or repulsion of devils . . . but I resolve it thus this musick cured *Saul* not as music, but as *Davids* musick, no musick but *Davids* musick could do it." If Saul had merely wanted music, says Spencer, he had other musicians to send for, not a young man he hated (M2r–v). David's cure of Saul had such relevance to church reform that those who wished to expel music other than Psalms had to interpret their way around it.

The demon's flight did not alleviate Saul's envy. Despite marrying his daughter to David, he set about persecuting him in ways crucial to later political discourse, being also aware, eventually, that David was to replace him and had already been anointed by Samuel. This *replacement*, exploited by any number of writers, is worth pausing over. The pair Saul/David, like that of Esau/Jacob and indeed the later one-man pair Saul/Paul, would seem to show God's taste for replacement or supersession. The second figure, covenant, or identity need not wipe out the first: Christ fulfills yet does not abolish the Law but does supersede it, or so Christians claimed. The superseding figure or arrangement is usually younger—Jacob, David, the new covenant, the new man, the New Testament. Inevitably, Saul was read as the older in the pair Jew/Christian. That is why John Foxe, preaching on "the christening of a certain Jew at London," spends some time on biblical replacements or supersessions, all too predictably scorning the *dépassé* Jews. Thus God "in stead of Cane, Esau, Ismael, Saul, to whom of right apperteineth the ordinary succession & discent of the Priesthode, of the birthright, & inheritance of the kingdome, he made especial choyse of Abel, Isaac, Jacob, & David, who had no interest at all in the right of succession. In like maner forsaking the Jewes, he accepted the Gentiles contrary to all order."[9] The last phrase is significant. God's choices are "contrary to all order" as the English knew order. In England the eldest inherits, but in fairy stories, the Bible, and Christian thought the younger gets the birthright and the elder gets the pottage. After all, that was Esau's choice, just as it was Saul's sin that got him untimely ripped from his throne.

After the Reformation God's power to replace or supersede became even more ideologically weighted, which is why Bishop John Jewell replied to the 1570 papal bull excommunicating Elizabeth by saying that just as God removed the merciless Saul and gave the Israelites David, who loved the people and "put downe Idolatrie," so now he has given us our queen in place of her sister.[10] Do Protestants play Jacob to Catholics' Esau? Not if Protestant faith is in fact *older* than that of the innovating Catholics who press beyond *sola scriptura*. And yet one finds allusions that situate endangered Protestants as fresh Davids and their Catholic persecutors as displaced or displaceable old Sauls.

Those who admired Huguenot political theory, for example, could relish Agrippa d'Aubigné's insistence that Catholic powers are worse than Saul, whom God replaced, and hence deserve an even more direct resistance.[11] And the French civil wars could inspire hopes that once more David would succeed Saul. So says John Phillips in *A friendly larum* (1570): "Let Saule take heede, . . . / For though his Curres a time, / do persecute and spoyle: . . . / In spite of all his crew, / that purpose his advaunce; / Gods truth through knowledge at the last / shall rule and raigne in Fraunce" (B2). David himself might have put it more musically. Anne Dowriche's *French historie* on the "famous bloodie broiles" in France notes hopefully, "Though Saul did persecute gods chosen Prophet long, / Yet did the Lord at length revenge poore David & his wrong." Not that Dowriche's view of geopolitics is live and let live, for she explains that God had "accursed both Agag and his Land, / Commanding Saule without remorse to kil them out of hand" because the Amalekites had impeded the Israelites' passage to the Promised Land. It is time France took the same line with its criminals.[12]

The problem was that Catherine de Medici and other more militant Catholics had come to the same conclusion—on the opposite side.

It was Catherine's son, the duc d'Anjou, who—balancing his family's Catholicism against Flemish resentment of Spain—stars in a related if prematurely triumphalist comparison. One 1582 pageant described in *The joyful and royal entertainment of the Frenche Kings only brother . . . Into his noble citie of Antwerpe* shows Saul scolded by Samuel; the "peece of his garment rent of by him" is "in token that the kingdome should be plucked from Sauls house & given to a better. Whereby was ment, that the soverainetie of those low Countreys was taken from the King of Spaine for his abhominable perjuries, tyrannies, & extortions."[13] In a later pageant David takes on Goliath. A poem explains:

As God bereaving Saul of Crown and Mace,
Did dispossesse him of his kingdome quight,
And after set up David in his place:
so now likewise dispatching from our sight,
The tyrants which oppressed us by might,
Hee giveth thee (O noble Duke) the Reyne
Of these our countreys, over us to reigne.
(*Joyful and royal entertainment*, E2)

But Philip II, busy extending his empire in the New World and replacing ancient paganisms with the Gospel, did not see himself as Saul. Saulness is in the eye of the beholder.

Because the queen whom Anjou had courted in England was so often called another David, praising her invited allusions to what one grateful subject called "the frowning band of cloudie Sauls" or allusions to the days when Mary Tudor was her Saul and Bishop Gardiner the Doeg who killed God's priests.[14] Similarly, in a sermon preached in 1586, John Rainolds celebrated the queen's escapes from danger by offering an extended parallel between Elizabeth and David—if David restored his country's economy, for example, Elizabeth strengthened England's currency. Like David, the queen had suffered persecution: "First (in Queen Maries time) the house of Saul, I mean the brood of them who preferred will-worships before obedience to God, fearing as Saul did, that their seeds succession should not be established as long as David lived." But do not think the pope's sentence against the queen as valid as Samuel's against Saul, for David "did refraine to lay hands on Saul . . . neither out of humanitie only, but of duty"—the duty not to hurt the Lord's anointed.

True, James was also David, as many have noted. Solomon, to whom he was more often compared, makes more sense chronologically, but, as a fairly good poet and psalmist, the king is in this regard a better David than the less often lyrical Elizabeth, able to soften papal wildness with his harp much as David had cured Saul's madness.[15] But Charles I was David, for in that synergy of adulation and instruction that can energize even insipid political flattery, David can replace David, can be a phoenix without the trouble of building a spicy nest. Cromwell, too, was a David, said some, although of course after 1660 he became Saul, and the restored Charles II was David (one who endured the rebellion and treachery of his own Absalom and his own Achitophel).[16] The rhetorical problem is that even if England had an unbroken succession of Davids, from a (chrono)logical point of view, several such Davids might be thought, in retrospect, to have indeed succeeded a Saul. There is an edge to the polemicist John Vicars's comment in *Englands hallelu-jah* (1631) that Spain's Infanta is Saul's daughter Michal and that we are lucky our David (Prince Charles) did not marry her: Spain would well have "spar'd a Daughter" to bring "good Davids slaughter" (B5v). Deflection of blame for the aborted and unpopular Spanish match away from James I and onto Spain makes political sense, but the logic is shaky: Charles/David succeeded *James*, not the king of Spain, but James cannot be Saul. A limited supply of classical and biblical analogues means that soon one has too many moderns for too few ancients.

David escaped Saul's tyranny (thanks in part to Michal) and indeed fought back. That Saul should seek to destroy his designated replacement is understandable in secular terms, but many thought both the attempt and the failure instructive. Modern tyrants beware. "How much the rejection of Saul ought to touch our Christian Princes," exclaims a marginal note (L4v) in Edmund Bunny's *Coronation of David*, published in the Armada year 1588. He means Philip II, presumably, but the Huguenot Philippe Duplessis-Mornay had a more poignant task in dedicating a meditation on Psalm 101 to his old friend Henri IV, now a Catholic but the promulgator in 1598—the year before the translation was published in England—of the Edict of Nantes, which Mornay helped to write. David is Henri's looking glass, says Mornay, for the two kings had parallel careers. Now, like David, Henri must exercise justice and mercy.[17] When Mornay reminds Henri that David was unjustly banished from Saul's presence, the king could not have missed the implied reference to his former coreligionists.

Saul was a tyrant, but not an effective one, so some writers analyze his mistakes. Over and over, in the Psalter's headnotes and marginalia, in sermons, and in Renaissance texts generally, Saul is a Machiavellian and his court a snake pit of cruel, slanderous, and scoffing yes-men who badmouth David and plot his death.[18] The most interesting commentary on how Saul went wrong politically is *David Persecuted* (1637), by the Italian Protestant Virgilio Malvezzi. Malvezzi exploits Saul's misdeeds to meditate on the value of promoting shepherds, the dangers of sailing on the turbulent sea of "Policie," the medicinal value of music, the energizing effect on a fetus of illegitimacy, and much else. Malvezzi spots Saul's political dilemma: The "Tyrant is put to a shrewd pinche [who] is growne jelous of a subject of worth and reputation: If hee kill him, hee feares the rising of the people: If he suffer him, hee doubts his raysing of them. Now hee accounts himselfe happy if, in his oppressing him, he could make the faults of his *will* to be laid upon the ignorance of his *understanding*, and with the imputation of a *madman* smother that of an *ungratefull*." One ruler (Alexander, presumably) "made use of drunkennesse" to protect himself against "the most valorous man of his Armie; and Saul doth the like by his vexation with spirits to make David away" (87–88). A cynical view. Malvezzi's book is less about David persecuted than about Saul baffled.

What may we do in self-defense against a Saul? The default position of the authorities was, inevitably, that no matter how terrible our Saul, we should emulate David's humble loyalty and never, ever, use violence against an anointed monarch (the assumption being that David's military movements were entirely defensive). A pamphlet ascribed to Francis Bacon points out that David, hearing a messenger who claimed to have finished off Saul, condemns him to death for laying hands on the Lord's anointed; how unlike the Jesuits, says Bacon (if Bacon), who are at ease with regicide.[19] Because David was loyal, even when Saul was at his mercy while answering a call of nature in the cave, says a homily printed in 1594, it is an "intolerable ignorance, madnes, and wickedness, for subjects to make any murmuring, rebellions, resistance, or withstanding, commotion, or insurrection against their most deer and most dread sovereign Lord and king."[20] That is throne and episcopacy talking, but in the Geneva Bible, when David finds Saul asleep and does not kill him, a marginal note remarks calmly that this means one should not kill a king "in a private cause: for Jehu slew two Kings at Gods appointment, 2 Kings 9.24." No wonder James reportedly said that some Geneva notes are "untrue, seditious, and savouring too much of dangerous and trayterous conceites."[21] He must have preferred, especially if he did not think too hard about its deeper implications, a sermon—in truth a long metaphysical prose-poem—published the same year that saw the King James Version, 1611. Here Lancelot Andrewes, meditating on stones, cornerstones, rejection, placement, and replacement, stresses that David remained loyal even though "a hard time he had, and many hard termes, and hard usages he endured, for many yeeres together; pursued and followed, and should have bene no *head*, nay should have had no head, if He had bene gotten."[22]

Yet David did resist as well as flee Saul, even if he did not kill him, and this ambiguity helped some in England think about resistance or—as has been noted by one Shakespeare scholar—revenge.[23] Even those who adopt the official view can protest too much. Thus Edwin Sandys's headnotes to his metrical psalms stress royalist fidelity even when others might quietly enjoy the underdog David's refusal to be erased by power. Sandys says that Psalm 94 was probably written when David "was persecuted by King Saul" and "began to think of standing upon his owne defence (being anointed by God for successour in the Kingdom;) yet without any purpose of attempt against Saul, in his person, peace, authoriti, or digniti."[24] Homilies and headnotes do not stop rebels, though. After the Earl of Essex attempted a coup against Elizabeth, William Barlow reminded his congregation that whatever Samuel's disgust with Saul, he did not *remove* him; Barlow recalls that, when asked why he did not obey a royal summons, Essex had replied that "David refused to come to Saul when he sent for him: Ergo I might lawfully refuse to come to Queene Elizabeth." This reminds Barlow of Jacques Clément, the Jacobin friar who defended his assassination of Henri III in 1589 by citing Ehud's killing of King Eglon (Judges 3). Because Eglon is "calve" in Hebrew, Barlow scoffs, and because the present king of France is a "Calvenist, Ergo I may kill him by authoritie of Scripture."[25] In 1601 Henri IV was no longer a "Calvenist," but someone would kill him anyway.

And in 1649 a number of someones killed Charles I. That the magistracy might try and then punish a tyrant was already a familiar claim in Huguenot theory. Theodore Beza, for one, cites David's resistance to Saul to justify the Huguenot side in the French civil wars.[26] Not that one needed to be Huguenot or Cromwellian to think regicidal thoughts: The Catholic William Allen claims that "as the whole body is of more authoritie then the only head, and may cure the head if it be out of tune, so may the wealpublique cure or cutt of their heades, if they infest the rest." A marginal note says, unconvincingly, "Nothing heer spoken against dew respect to Princes," and the next page cites as examples of excised diseased heads those of "Saul and Amon (though both of them were lawfully placed in that dignity) and the bringing in of David and Josias in their roomes."[27] Even more remarkable, though, is a pamphlet opposing a Saulish Charles while claiming a Davidic loyalty. In the anonymous *Englands third alarm to warre stirring up the whole land as one man to help the Lord, and His servant David . . .* (1643) the argument takes the form of a long recitation of "Davids story, & Sauls persecution." The author calls this a "tragedy," and seems to mean this in a quasi-Aristotelian sense: Saul was a great man with a flawed will. What drove him? The devil. And what drives Charles? The devil. David was no rebel, for he battled the devil, not Saul. Neither are *we* rebels, for Charles is not only wickedly counseled but demon-possessed. So "if the King doe not his duty his people must doe theirs"—liberate England's monarch from his inner imp. This is demonizing the enemy as an act of charity.[28]

Saul's penultimate sin was to disguise himself and visit the witch of Endor, who summoned the ghost of Samuel so Saul might ask about the future, a scene often figuring in discussions of witchcraft and necromancy (1 Samuel 28). Is the witch (or, to put it more kindly, medium) real or a con artist? Is the summoned figure of Samuel a ghost, a demon, or a fraud? What are the theological implications? If David's adultery and homicide provoked an array of moral, amatory, and political treatments, Saul's venture into the occult offered more intellectual interest—and political interest too, granted James I's fascination with demonology.

It is God's terrible silence that drives Saul to the imprudent hope that a ghost might be more informative. Francis Quarles finds a moral.

> When *Saul* receiv'd no *answer* down from *heav'n*
> How quickly was his jealous *passion* driven
> A despr'ate Course! He needs must cure the *Itch*
> Of his extreame desiers, by a *Witch*:
> *When we have lost our way to* God, *how levell,*
> *How easie to be found's the way toth' Divell.*[29]

Hatred and God's silence are a lethal combination.

Other writers attended more closely to the intersection of theology and epistemology: Can the dead in fact reappear? Hamlet's dilemma. If no one can leave Hell, then Samuel's ghost must be demonic or delusional. But what of Christ's Harrowing of Hell? Thomas Bilson, bishop of Winchester, writing in the waning days of Henry VIII's reign, mulls over Samuel's postmortem whereabouts: Samuel says to Saul, tomorrow you and your sons will be with me, but Saul was a reprobate. "It is likelier that Samuel was in hell with Saul till he were delivered thence," argues Bilson, "than that Saul was in Abrahams bosome with Samuel." So did Saul see the real Samuel? Or was this a demon tempting Saul to despair? We cannot think that Samuel's soul was truly in Hell. All Samuel meant, concludes Bilson, was that the king would soon be dead too.

Many commentators thought this Samuel illusory. Thomas Adams's eloquent sermon, *The Blacke Devill* (1615), suggests that the devil took "to himselfe an airy body" so as to appear "in the shape of Samuel" (F3).[30] Such a devil, adds Adams, is best fought by picking up the stones with which David killed Goliath (G1). To consult a witch is indeed horrible, says Thomas Jackson in *The eternall truth of Scriptures* (1613–1614), an intelligent work with many comments on literature and fiction, and yet what this Samuel told Saul—that he and his sons would die—was true (G4). The devil can speak truth for his purpose. In James I's *Daemonologie* (1597), though, one speaker suggests that Saul fantasized Samuel merely because he had been fasting, had a bad conscience, and heard the witch's cry of recognition. Nor would God permit the devil "to come in the shape of his Saintes." Granted, says a friend, yet Saul saw *something* like Samuel, and the Bible says, "Sathan can trans-forme himselfe into an Angell of light." Milton agreed.[31]

But were Satan and witches truly present? No, says Reginald Scot's *Discoverie of witchcraft* (1584), a lengthy debunking with amusing anecdotes and brisk logic. It "is not likelie," argues Scot, "that god would answer Saule by dead Samuell, when he would not answer him by living Samuell: and most unlikely of all, that God would answer him by a divell" after he "denied to doo it by a prophet." Saul's story is tragic, but Scot nudges it into comedy: "But now forsooth Saule," because he "would not be knowne, he put on other garments. But to bring that matter to passe, he must have been cut shorter by the head and shoulders, for by so much was he higher than any of the people. And therefore whatsoever face the craftie quene did set upon it, she knew him well enough." She hears Saul's request, says Scot, then nips "into her closet, where doubtless she had hir familiar; to wit, some lewd craftie preest, and made Saule stand at the doore like a foole (as it were with his finger in a hole) to heare the cousening answers, but not to see the cousening handling thereof." She uses "ordinarie words of conjuration," Scot goes on, such as "*Hay, fortune furie, nunque; credo, passe, passe, when come you sirra*" and then acts up a storm: "Lo . . . I see woonderfull things. So as *Saule* hearing these words, longed to know all, and asked hir what she sawe. Whereby you may know that Saule saw nothing, but stood without like a mome, whilest she plaied hir part in hir closet."[32] Saul's adventure in Endor, then, helped many think about the spirit world, the nature of its denizens, and our access—or lack of access—to its nether reaches.

The next day Saul loses to the Philistines and falls on his sword after his armor bearer refuses to kill him. This would seem the end point of an unpardonable despair, although the Jesuit Robert Southwell found it in his heart (and perhaps in the Fathers) to allegorize the deed: Saul's suicide with his own sword, he says, is a sword effecting justice, and so by analogy Saul's death parallels that of Jesus, whose willing self-sacrifice justified mankind by satisfying the law.[33] Is Southwell troubled? He knew, and almost with pleasure, that being in the Catholic underground could be suicidal. And John Davies of Hereford, born Catholic but with a taste for such Protestant writers as Duplessis-Mornay and Du Bartas, says something similar: "Then sith our Saule [that's Jesus] falles on his Justice Sword / For us, wee die should, likewise, for our Lord."[34] There is suicide, and then there is allegorical suicide. John Donne, though, needed no allegory to justify Saul, who figures in *Biathanatos*, a meditation on self-slaughter and the canons fixed against it. Donne too pairs the dying Israelite king and the crucified king of the Jews. Citing patristic precedent for the claim, he remarks—but this is, notes the title page, a "paradox"—that Christ died when he chose to, and so did Saul, "thinking it dishonourable to dye by the hand of his and Gods enemies."[35]

May one pray for Saul? Protestants do not, in theory, pray for the dead, and praying for Saul would seem especially futile. And, as William Burton pointed out in a 1594 sermon, it would be impious to pray for a reprobate who, if restored to life, would still be a man God had rejected. He adds, if David curses God's enemies, why should we "pray God to blesse and save those that go about to destroy his Church, his truth, his annoynted, and his children?"[36] And yet, says the poet and moralist Richard Brathwaite, that Samuel *wept* for Saul is further evidence that weeping and moderate mourning befit a Christian.[37] But those tears were antemortem; what of the dead Saul? Writing of the pelican—symbol of charity—Thomas Dekker urges us to pray for those who plot against our lives: "Following the steps of Samuel, let us even pray for king Saul, albeit king Saul be an enemy to [Christ's] servants."[38] To the strict, this is some loving-kindness but little theology. To help Saul's soul without pelican allegory, one probably should be Catholic, like Jane Owen, who in her *Antidote against purgatory* (St.-Omer, 1634) approvingly quotes Bellarmine's claim that David's fast after hearing about the death of Saul and Jonathan was "a satisfactory worke," which "being applied for the dead, doth helpe the dead" (L4v).

Going beyond this weeping charity are some surprising royalist comparisons of the Stuarts to Saul. Charles Cotton's panegyric to Charles II calls the returning monarch "a King like *Saul*, in the stature of his Vertues, more conspicuous then all the potent Princes of the earth."[39] A couple of years later, Charles's dead father received a more extended comparison:

Charles I merged Saul's might and Jonathan's sweetness into one person, says Arthur Bury in *The Bow: or The Lamentation of David over Saul and Jonathan* (1662). Saul, he says, died not at the hands of the Philistines, nor from age, nor from luxury, but rather "by the hands of his own Subjects" (so much for the suicide), and Charles fell "in the name of the people, under formalities of justice, by the hands of mushrooms, under [his] own window." But, adds Bury with sarcastic parody, "Tell it not in Amsterdam publish it not in the conventicles of the Schismaticks, lest they boast against the Episcopal discipline as a nurse of prophanesse" (C4v–D3, E4).[40]

That is the end of this much abbreviated tale of Saul in Renaissance England, one more valuable for its ambiguities and contradictions than for the simplicities of perfumed goodness or snarling evil. Early modern England turned to Saul's story for pious reflection but also for a language in which to think about political, religious, social, and even medical and musical questions. The discourse could also be constricting: so long as it matters how one reads David's refusal to kill Saul, discussion of revolution is tethered to ancient precedent. Significantly, a civil war pamphlet that seems like something Jefferson or Paine could have written—*Salus populi solus Rex, The Peoples Safety Is the sole Soveraignty* (1648)—argues for popular sovereignty with no reference to Saul's tyranny and only passing allusions to Goliath and Absalom. For good or ill, we enter a more familiar world, one in which even the devout, on election day, seldom ask what would David do. Yet the psalmist king's melancholy and envious persecutor, sparer of Agag and murderer of priests, is a haunting figure, and I end with some lines from a poem by Judith Wright.

> Old king without a throne,
> the hollow of despair
> behind his obstinate unyielding stare,
> knows only, God is gone:
> and, fingers clenching on his chair,
> feels night and the soul's terror coming on.
> Bring me that harp, that singer. Let him sing. . . .
> Comfort me.
> Make me believe the meaning in the rhyme.
> The world's a traitor to the self-betrayed;
> but once I thought there was a truth in time,
> while now my terror is eternity.
> So do not take me outside time.
> Make me believe in my mortality,
> since that is all I have, the old king said.[41]

Wright gives the harp some bracing yet hopeful answers, but it is Saul's lonely and empty melancholy that requires and in a way facilitates such hope. David may need Saul.

Notes

1. David's very sins could be turned to good moral use. See, for example, A. Simson, *A sacred Septenarie* (1623): "for Davids sin turnes to the glorie of God, the comfort of the Church, and his owne salvation: so that as dung and excrements of nature are profitable to fatten the ground, so is his sinne to better and make him more fruitfull to God" (B2v).

2. John Donne [Jr.], *Donne's Satyr, containing... a cabinet of merry conceits...* (1662), F3v.

3. Simson, *A sacred Septenarie*, condemns Saul but is softer on David: "for Davids sin turnes to the glorie of God, the comfort of the Church, and his owne salvation: so that as dung and excrements of nature are profitable to fatten the ground, so is his sinne to better and make him more fruitfull to God" (B2v). Sins by the good are fertility-promoting dung, sins by the wicked are growth-impeding poison. Simson sees the danger of his argument, hastening to warn licentious libertines not to cite David as an excuse.

4. Richard Rogers, *Samuels Encounter with Saul* (1620), A6v–A7, a posthumously published sermon. Edgerton's Saul is primarily a hypocrite.

5. Sir Richard Baker's magnificent *Chronicle of the Kings of England* (London: Daniel Frere, 1643), 4L4. Saul's sacrifice of the fat Amalekite cattle when he had been ordered simply to kill them, even if performed with good intentions, is an unlawful overstepping of religious lines and, like the sparing of Agag, worse than witchcraft and idolatry (see 1 Samuel 15:23), so Englishmen should obey the law of God, not the pope. See Heinrich Bullinger, *A confutation of he Popes bull*, trans. Arthur Golding (1572), P4.

6. I thank Margaret Hannay for this reference.

7. Michael Drayton, "David and Goliah," in *The Works of Michael Drayton*, ed. William Hebel (Oxford, UK: Blackwell, 1961), 3: 418–39; published in *The Muses Elizium* (1630).

8. John Playford, *An Introduction to the skill of musick* (1682), 59, a multi-authored volume written in part well before the publication date. "Airy" music would aerate blood and dissolve the brain's dried black bile. On such theories and their relevance to Saul, see Anne Lake Prescott, "'Formes of Joy and Art': Donne, David, and the Power of Music," *John Donne Journal* 25 (2006): 3–36, which cites much earlier material.

9. John Foxe, *A Sermon preached at the christening of a certaine Jew at London*, trans. from Latin by James Bell (1578), C3v. Later Foxe affects bafflement that Jews reject Christ, for he was one of their own on his mother's side (C7).

10. John Jewell, *A vewe of a seditious bul sent into Englande, from Pius Quintus Bishop of Rome...* (1582, a sermon preached in 1570), F8.

11. Agrippa d'Aubigné, *Du Debvoir mutuel des royes et des subjects*, in *Oeuvres*, ed. Henri Weber (Paris: Gallimard, 1969), 470–73.

12. Anne Dowriche, *The French historie*... (1589), B1v–B2. There can be friendlier replacements. Writing on "the happie union of the kingdoms of England and Scotland" (1603), Francis Bacon notes that David reigned first over the small kingdom of Judea and then, after the death of Saul's son, over the larger Israel as well. Scotland has been replaced by, absorbed by, Great Britain (C4v–C5); or, as a contemporary pun had it, the kingdom was now Al-be/i-on[e]. Alexander Craig, *Poeticall essayes* (1604), C2v; and Alexander Gardyne, *A garden of grave and godlie flowers* (Edinburgh, 1609), B1v.

13. Translated from French by Arthur Golding (1582), E2.

14. E. Hutchins, *Davids sling against great Goliah* (1581), B8v; William Leigh, *Queene Elizabeth, paralleled in her princely virtues* (London, 1612, preached before 1603), esp. D8–D8v. Thomas Jackson, in *Davids Pastorall poeme or Sheepeheards Song* (1603), preached on the day of James's accession, says that young Elizabeth had been hunted "like a Partridge upon the mountains, as David said"; the margin cites 1 Samuel 26:20. Jackson was among those calling the new king a Solomon.

15. James Doelman, *King James I and the Religious Culture of England* (Cambridge, UK: D. S. Brewer, 2000), 76.

16. Joseph A. Mazzeo, "Cromwell as Davidic King," in *Renaissance and Seventeenth Century Studies*, ed. J. A. Mazzeo (New York: Columbia University Press, 1964), 183–208.

17. Philippe Duplessis-Mornay, *Meditations upon Psal. 101*, trans. T. Wilcox (1599).

18. See Anne Lake Prescott, "Evil Tongues at the Court of Saul: David as a Slandered Courtier," *Journal of Medieval and Renaissance Studies* 21 (1991): 163–86.

19. *A Letter written out of England to an English gentleman* (1599), B2v. One supposed plot was to poison the pommel of the queen's saddle so that when mounting or dismounting, she would absorb the venom (A4).

20. *Certaine Sermons* (1594; STC 13658), I7v–I8. The authors would have been touched by *Mercurius Davidicus, or A Patterne of Loyall Devotion, Taken out of King Davids Psalmes* (Oxford, 1634), a pastiche of psalm verses reworded a little and applied to the beleaguered Charles.

21. Quoted by Hardin Craig Jr., "The Geneva Bible as a Political Document," *Pacific Historical Review* 7 (1938): 40–49.

22. Lancelot Andrewes, *A sermon preached before his Majestie at White-Hall, on 24. of March last, being Easter day, and being, also the day of the Beginning of His Majesties most Gracious Reigne* (1611), D2. The text is Psalm 118:22: "The Stone, which the Builder refused, the same Stone, is become (or made) the Head of the Corner."

23. Gene Edward Veith Jr., "'Wait upon the Lord': David, *Hamlet*, and the Problem of Revenge," in *The David Myth in Western Literature*, ed. Raymond-

Jean Frontain and Jan Wojcik (West Lafayette, IN: Purdue University Press, 1980), 70–85.

24. Sir Edwin Sandys, *Sacred hymns Consisting of fifti select psalms of David and others, paraphrastically turned into English verse . . .* (1615), 77.

25. William Barlow, *A Sermon preached at Paules Crosse, on the first Sunday in Lent, Martii 1. 1600* (1601), C5.

26. John Calvin, *The sermons of M. John Calvin upon the fifth booke of Moses*, trans. Arthur Golding (1583), 316. See also Edward Gosselin, "David in Tempore Belli: Beza's David in the Service of the Huguenots," *Sixteenth Century Journal* 7 (1976): 31–54.

27. William Allen (and others, under the name R. Doleman), *A conference about the next succession to the crowne of Ingland* (Antwerp, 1595), D8v–E1.

28. *Englands third alarm to warre* (1643), esp. the preface and A1–C1v.

29. Francis Quarles, *Divine Fancies* (1632), I2v.

30. Cf. *Davids Meditation of Gods Word* (1616) on how Satan disguised himself as Samuel so as to bewitch Saul and later men into thinking that witches have power over the dead (Y4v).

31. James I, *Daemonologie* (1597), ed. G. B. Harrison (1924; rpt. with new material, San Diego: Book Tree, 2002), 2–4. Ludwig Lavater, in *Of ghostes and spirites, walking by night*, trans. Robert Harrison (1596 ed.), Z2, observes that if we call the pagan gods "gods," even though they were devils, we may also call this devil "Samuel" and not mean the *real* Samuel.

32. Reginald Scot, *The Discoverie of Witchcraft*, intro. Montague Summers (1930; rpt., New York: Dover, 1972), 82–83. Scot several times cites Jean Bodin, who argues, for example, that "Samuel" could not have been a demon because in his conversation with Saul the name "Jehovah" is "five times repeated, of which the name the divell cannot abide the hearing" (81). Yet Bodin, says Scot, places Saul among the elect (80).

33. Robert Southwell, *An Epistle of Comfort* (Paris [really London], 1587), G5.

34. "The Holy Rood" (1609), 16, in John Davies of Hereford, *Complete Works*, ed. Alexander B. Grosart (rpt., New York: AMS Press, 1967). A few pages earlier Davies had exclaimed that, although David cured Saul with his harp, Christ must die before he can bring health, there being "so many Sauls possest with Sathans store." Not for the first time, Saul and David seem oddly close, not quite alternatives but conjoined siblings, "frenemies," in the shifting dynamics of comparison and analogue.

35. John Donne, *Biathanatos* (published posthumously in 1644), 135, 191, 203.

36. William Burton, *An exposition of the Lords Prayer . . .* (1594), C3v–C5. In 1592 Burton had cited Saul as a warning to those with many talents but no integrity; see his *Davids Evidence* (1592), F6v.

37. Richard Brathwaite, *An exquisite discourse of epitaphs*, published with Patrick Hannay's *A happy husband* (1619), K8. Jan van der Noot likewise re-

calls Samuel's charitable lament for his sinful king, associating it with the semiprecious stone beryl, symbol of those who "through compassion & pitie, sorrowfully have bewailed & lamented the fall of their brethren." See Jan van der Noot, *Theatre [of] voluptuous worldlings* (1569), P4.

38. Thomas Dekker, *Foure birds of Noahs arke* (1609), H4. Dekker adds that we should also pray for the Jews.

39. Charles Cotton, *A panegyrick to the King's Most Excellent Majesty* (1660), B2v.

40. The sermon was preached on January 30, anniversary of Charles's execution. For Bury, Charles I is David, as well as Saul and Jonathan, so he has his bases covered.

41. From Judith Wright, "The Harp and the King," in *The Two Fires* (1955); I thank John Shawcross for showing me this poem. See *A Human Pattern: Selected Poems* (ETT Imprint: Sydney, 2010); my thanks to the publisher for permission to quote these lines.

8

Elliott M. Simon

Prophetic Voices

Joachim de Fiore, Moses Maimonides, Philip Sidney, Mary Herbert, and the Psalms

In the *Defence of Poesy* (c. 1581), Sir Philip Sidney (1554–1586) identifies poetic creativity with the prophetic tradition of David's Psalms in which preexisting texts considered sacred are translated into edifying ethical and spiritual precepts for the present or are interpreted as prescripted consequences for the future. This conception of prophecy is found in the works of two radically different medieval religious and philosophical thinkers: the Cistercian abbot Joachim de Fiore (1135–1202) and the Jewish Talmudist and philosopher Moses Maimonides (1135–1204). For Joachim the prophetic message of God was transmitted from the Hebraic and Aramaic Old Testament into the Septuagint Bible. The Christian Gospels of the apostles and the interpretations of St. Paul's Epistles and John of Patmos's book of Revelation were added and translated into the Vulgate Bible, which was eventually canonized by the early church fathers and successive Catholic Church councils. Joachim argues that the Bible is a "historical narrative" from the beginning of time projected into a vision of the End of Days. It traces the ultimate evolution of humanity through its tribulations and divinely inspired consolations from generation to generation, culminating in a state of spiritual perfectibility that is prerequisite for the Second Coming. For Maimonides the word of God from Moses in the Hebrew written Torah, the oral Torah of Sinaitic origin, and the prophetic tradition were interpreted and illuminated by successive generations of the *Anshei Knesset Hagadol, Tanaim, Amoraim, Sevoraim,* and *Geonim.* He believed that although there is an authoritative difference between the prophetic tradition and the Oral Law tradition, sages with great learning in each generation should aspire to clarify and understand the holy laws of the Torah according to their capabilities.

Whereas Joachim was concerned with translating historical periods into stages of spiritual enlightenment, Maimonides was concerned with translating the equivocal literal and figurative language of biblical expression into an intellectual apprehension of truth in the Bible. Although the Psalms are not considered formally prophetic literature, in both the Jewish and Christian traditions David preceded the prophets and was considered "divinely inspired." Those who composed Davidic psalms shared that inspiration and believed that from the House of David a messiah would eventually appear. Psalms represent the most profound and universal artistic expression of the personal interaction between the human and the divine. Joachim and his Christian followers linked the idea of human creativity with the arduous study of prior biblical texts to express a progressively higher spiritual consciousness. Following the Jewish Talmudic tradition, Maimonides also linked human creativity with the study of prior biblical and philosophical texts to illuminate an intellectual understanding of biblical language and to identify the true meaning of the "divine Word" and its application to the changing circumstance of Jews in each generation. Both Joachim and Maimonides argued that each person in every generation can translate the Psalms into the spiritual, intellectual, and artistic expression of their pious devotion to God. These theories of historical continuity and requisite transmission of sacred texts promoted by subsequent theologians and religious philosophers and later Protestant biblical translators appealed to Philip Sidney and Mary Sidney Herbert, who created their own prophetic voices in their translation of the Psalms.

Throughout the later Middle Ages and well into the Renaissance Joachim's theory of the Bible as a prophetic narrative had a profound influence on Christian movements dealing with spiritual and ecclesiastical reform. Similarly, Maimonides' conceptions of scriptural exegesis and prophetic transmission had a profound influence on Jewish biblical commentators and on Christian Hebraists, who turned to Hebraic hermeneutics to justify their assertions of divine continuity and authority for their versions of the biblical revelations. With Joachim translators of the Psalms could see themselves as historical incarnations of David speaking to their own people with a voice of higher spiritual illumination; with Maimonides they could see themselves interpreting the equivocal language of the biblical texts and translating their particular idioms of spiritual signification into concrete linguistic images.

For Sidney prophecy aspires to communicate a divine wisdom akin to Joachim's interpretation of the Bible as a "sacred spiritual history" and

Maimonides' exegesis of biblical poetic language as a revelation of God's word. Sidney believed that Psalms could be used as a literary model for the poet-prophet in his emerging creative theory of Protestant poetics.

> Among the Romans a poet was called *vates*, which is as much as a diviner, foreseer, or prophet. . . . And may I not presume a little further, to show the reasonableness of this word *vates*, and say that the holy David's Psalms are a divine poem? If I do, I shall not do it without the testimony of great learned men, both ancient and modern. But even the name Psalms will speak for me, which being interpreted, is nothing but songs; then that it is fully written in metre, as all learned Hebricians agree, although the rules be not yet fully found; lastly and principally, *his handling his prophecy, which is merely poetical*; for what else is the awakening his musical instruments, the often and free changing of persons, his notable *prosopopoeias*, when he maketh you, as it were, see God coming in His majesty, his telling of the beasts' joyfulness and hills leaping, but a heavenly poesy, wherein he most showeth himself a passionate lover of that unspeakable and everlasting beauty to be seen by the eyes of the mind, only cleared by faith?[1]

Similar to Clément Marot (c. 1496–1554) and Philippe Du Plessis Mornay (1549–1623), Sidney believed that David's poetry "scaled the heights of literary achievement surpassing the Greeks and the Romans."[2] In *The Trewness of the Christian Religion* (1587), Mornay argues that "the ancient Greeks and Romans sang vauntings of men, counterfetted praises, and discourses of Love Songs." In David's poetry *Eros* and *Deus* are so deeply embedded in the psyche that they are "songs of the very Love itself . . . [such that] the arte of them is so excellent that it is an excellencie even to translate them."[3] Throughout the Renaissance, however, there was no comprehensive understanding about how biblical Hebrew verse was composed.[4] Sidney and his sister, Mary Sidney Herbert, the Countess of Pembroke (1561–1621), did not read Hebrew, but it is clear that they used scholarly biblical commentaries of those who could and who attempted to reveal Christian prefigurations within the Hebrew original.[5] They carefully compared their translations with versions of the Psalms found in the *Whole Booke of Psalmes* (1562) by Thomas Sternhold (1500–1549) and John Hopkins (d. 1570), *The Book of Common Prayer* (1549, rev. 1559), the Geneva Bible (1560), the Bishops' Bible (1568), the *Hymnes* of Martin Luther (1483–1546), and the influential commentaries of John Calvin (1509–1564) and Théodore Bèza (1519–1605).[6]

All art is referential to previous art forms. In David's Psalms the relationship between God and the Hebrews was predicated on the divine covenant of obedience and blessing between God and Abraham reaffirmed by Moses. David and other psalmists composed meditations on the glory of God, the sinful tribulations of Israel, and suppliant assertions of their faith in God's redemption of Israel that became the universal prophetic paradigm repeated by later prophets.[7] For Sidney the psalmist expresses his adoration of God and perceptions of the inherent fallibilities of human nature in terms of the Protestant assertion that redemption can be achieved only through faith in Jesus's prophetic message in scripture and the intervention of grace.

Sidney also identifies the poet as a craftsman, and the Sidney-Herbert Psalter is appreciated for its inventive meters, disjunctive imagery, and complex syntax that capture the emotional intensity of the poet-prophet who struggles with his desire to be a pious lover of God.[8] Herbert identifies their Psalter as "a translation into divers and sundry kinds of verse, more rare and excellent for the method and variety than ever yet hath been done in English" (Sidney-Herbert Psalms, xxxiii [title page]). From Francesco Petrarca's (1304–1377) *De ignorantia* to Sidney's *Defence*, poets assumed that rhetorical eloquence could create a semblance of a divine revelation; eloquence was not merely an ornament to knowledge and piety, it was its telos.[9] Herbert emphasizes the eloquence of their metrical rendering into English of David's verses by using a variety of forms and tropes that had been recommended by George Puttenham (1529–1590) in his *Arte of English Poesie* (1589). They recast their biblical persona to speak in their newly fashioned Protestant prophetic voice concerning their faith in the ideals of spiritual redemption.[10] For example, in Psalm 140:1–3, David says, "Deliver me, O Lord, from the evil men: preserve me from the violent man; who devise mischiefs in their hearts; continually they stir up wars."[11] Herbert translates this passage:

Protect me Lord, preserve me, sett me free
  From men that be so vile, soe violent:
    In whose entent both force and fraud doth lurk
  My bane to work: whose tongues are sharper things
Than Adders stings: whose rusty lips enclose
A poisons hoorde, such in the Aspick growes.

. . . .

  Whose thoughts are spent in thinking how they may
  My stepps betray: how nett of fowle misshape
May me entrapp: how hidd in traitor grasse
Their conning cord may catch me as I passe.
    (Psalm 140:1–6, 9–12; Sidney-Herbert *Psalms*, 322)

Whereas David prays to be protected from violent men of war, Herbert desires to be protected from lascivious men who want to degrade her poetry and denigrate her piety with their courtly decadence. Herbert seems to imitate David, but she translates the prior text of a Hebrew warrior king in terms of her feminine sense of social vulnerability, religious integrity, and literary creativity.[12]

Joachim de Fiore never called himself a prophet in the sense of one who foretells the future according to supernatural (astrological or visionary) revelations. Instead, in *Liber Concordie, novi ac veteris Testamenti* (c. 1184, published in Venice 1519) and *Expositio in Apocalypsim* (c. 1184, published in Venice 1527), he asserts that the Old and New Testaments provide a prophetic historical narrative from Genesis through the Hebrew prophets to Jesus and his apostles, culminating in the book of Revelation. Each incarnation of the prophetic voice represents the progressive spiritual development of the *spiritualis intellectus* who will ultimately triumph over the Antichrist at the End of Days. Whereas Moses builds on the narrative of the patriarchs, Jesus builds on the narrative of Moses and the Hebrew prophets, and the apostles build on the teachings of Jesus, all set in terms of the eternal present of God.[13] For Joachim each prophet must struggle with the subtle historical and theological issues of the biblical texts, and "like Elijah . . . build the altar of the Old Testament," "pour out the water of the New Testament," and penetrate the hidden mysteries of scripture (*Liber Concordie*, fol. 7r). True spiritual understanding is a process wherein the Intellect, "following the Spirit," informs the Imagination, "going from illumination to illumination," and translates the shared moral, ethical, and intellectual values expressed in scripture to achieve "the jubilation of psalmody" as a correct interpretation of the divine plan in the *seventh status* (*Liber Concordie*, fol. 7).[14]

The *spiritualis intellectus* illuminates the necessary spiritual discipline for the general reformation of ecclesiastical and social orders. The spiritual man will

> clear the eyes of the mind from all dust of the earth; leave the tumults of crowds and the clamor of words; follow the angel in spirit into the desert; ascend with the same angel into the great and high mountain; there you will behold high truths hidden from the beginning of time and from all generations. . . . For we, called in these latest times to follow the spirit rather than the letter, ought to obey, going from illumination to illumination, from the first heaven to the second, and from the second to the third, from the place of darkness into the light of the moon, that at last we may

> come out of the moonlight into the glory of the full sun. (*Liber Concordie*, fols. 5v–6r)

Only after periods of great ecclesiastical, political, and social tribulations will the "spiritual man" as angelic pope or world emperor emerge and translate the symbolism of sacred history that reveals a true and coherent *renovatio mundi*. "Upon the spiritual men, therefore, is laid the heavy burden of meditation. They must be able to intercede for souls like Abraham for Sodom (*Liber Concordie*, fol. 76); like Moses, the spiritual man descends from the mountain of contemplation to an active life and must know how to deliver to Aaron the words for the people (*Liber Concordie*, fol. 93); like Elijah they must call down rain for thirsty souls, supplanting fears with hope for the future (*Liber Concordie*, fol. 103v). The rise of the mendicant Franciscan and Dominican orders in the early thirteenth century was seen as a partial fulfillment of Joachim's conception of the spiritual man, although Augustinians, Jesuits, and Protestant reformers also claimed this title.[15]

With Martin Luther, Protestant reformers such as William Tyndale (c. 1494–1536), John Bale (1495–1563), and John Foxe (1517–87) identified the *spiritualis intellectus* in their own terms and used Joachim's *Expositio in Apocalypsim* as a paradigm for ecclesiastical reform.[16] They translated Joachim's seventh status in terms of their faith in the ascendancy of reformed doctrines and portrayed the Catholic establishment as the corrupt forces of the Antichrist. William Perkins (1558–1602), in *Idolatrie of the Last Times* (1605), wrote:

> Abbat Ioachim in his commentarie upon the Revelation hath these words: Some that carry a shew of the seat of God, that is the Catholic Church are made the seat of the beast, which is the Kingdome of Antichrist, reigning everywhere in his members from the beginning of the Church. Againe, we have, by tradition from our Fathers, that Rome is spiritually Babylon. Againe, Marchants of the earth are Priests themselves who sell prayers and Masses for pence [*pro denariis*], making the house of prayer a place of merchandise. Againe, we know that not onely Bishops and Priests are intangled in the affairs of Babylon that they may grow rich; but also some Abbats, Monkes, and religious persons or rather which seeme to be so and are not.[17]

Similar to Joachim, Sidney emphasizes the role of the poet-prophet to interpret historical events that illuminate a coherent pattern of spiritual development and argues that literary creativity must surpass historical experience.[18] Although humanist translators and editors of classical and biblical texts emphasized philological precision in their quest to capture historical truth, they found that linguistic accuracy alone may not reveal what should be understood as spiritual Truth. Joachim emphasized how historical events illuminated the progressive development of the prophet's spiritual consciousness of that higher order of Truth. For Sidney the poet becomes an authentic prophetic voice to the extent that he or she becomes a part of an evolving spiritual process, not laboring to tell merely what was or what is but what should or should not be held as true.[19] In his interpretive translation of Psalm 2:1–5 he writes:

> What ayles this heathenish rage? What doe these people meane
> To mutter murmurs vaine?
> Why doe these earthly kinges, and lordes such meeting make
> And counsell joyntly take
> Against the lorde of lordes, the lorde of every thinge
> And his anointed kinge?
> (Sidney-Herbert *Psalms*, 4)

Whereas David refers to the Hebrews who oppose the teachings of God and rebel against his authority as "the king" chosen by God to rule in Judea, Sidney refers to the religious discord within the Reformation and Counter-Reformation counsels. Similar to the Protestant apologists John Bale, in *Images of Both Churches* (1547), and John Foxe, in *Acts and Monuments* (1563), Sidney argues that the doctrinal reforms of the Protestants represent a spiritual reformation that justifies their rejection of Catholicism. The emotional language and vivid dramatic imagery in the book of Revelation could be interpreted as echoes of David's spiritual crises in Psalms. Sidney's analogy does not merely focus on historical similarities but emphasizes the validity of the spiritual advance to a higher *status of revelation* embodied by the reformed church as a fulfillment of Joachim's paradigm in his exegesis of Revelation. The tribulations of an errant humanity will be amended by the greater wisdom of the spiritual man who bears the blessed Protestant understanding of the Lord. Sidney's *spiritualis intellectus* knows how to serve God with fear, rejoices in him with trembling (awe), and places his faith in him, "their only trust," to receive the divine blessing; otherwise God's wrath in the end will destroy them all (Psalm 2: 25–32; Sidney-Herbert *Psalms*, 4–5).

Joachim's concept of historical continuity is also found in Herbert's translation of Psalm 76:1–6.

Only to Juda God his will doth signify;
    Only in Jacob is his name notorious;
His restfull tent doth only Salem dignify;
    On Syon only stands his dwelling glorious;
Their bow, and shaft, and shield, and sword he shivered,
Drave warr from us, and us from warr delivered.
    (Sidney-Herbert *Psalms*, 177)

In the Hebrew version, A Psalm of Asaf, the psalmist declares: "In Yehuda is God known: his name is great in Yisra'el. In Shalem also is his tabernacle, and his dwelling place is in Ziyon. There he broke the flashing arrows, the shield, and the sword, and the battle. (Sela) Thou art glorious and excellent, coming down from the mountains of prey [mountains inhabited by wild animals]" (*KJB* 763). God is known in David's Judea; his name is great among all the children of Jacob, also called Yisra'el (Genesis 32:29) and applied to all the united tribes under David and later Solomon. David restored the Tabernacle (the Holy Ark) to Jerusalem by conquering the violent Philistines. Jerusalem is also called the City of David (2 Samuel 6:12–19), which he conquered from the Jebusites (2 Samuel 5:6–10). From the Old Testament, Herbert identifies God's will with David's Judeans as God's chosen people. However, in the next line she makes a pun on "notorious," which means "well known," maintaining the Old Testament idea that God's name is revered by Jacob (Yisra'el). However, it also means "evil and wicked," as used in the *Book of Common Prayer* and other contemporary texts, implying that only in Jacob (Yisra'el) has the name of God, now identified as Jesus, become notorious; Jews do not recognize Jesus as the son of God. God's Temple was destroyed, first by the Babylonians as a punishment for Judea's departure from God's laws, resulting in the Babylonian exile, and then by the Romans, interpreted by Christians as a punishment for the Jews' failure to accept Jesus, resulting in their exile and notoriety in Christian Europe. Furthermore, Jesus declared that "my kingdom is not of this world" (John 18:36) and that the "kingdom of God shall be taken from you [the Pharisees], and given to a nation bringing forth the fruits thereof" (Matthew 21:43). Herbert believes that the divine covenant is now preserved in "true Jacobs sole devotion" (Psalm 76:13; Sidney-Herbert *Psalms*, 177), meaning her version of Protestant faith residing in the new "Syon" of England that stands against the coming wrath of God's final judgment (Psalm 76:19–30; Sidney-Herbert *Psalms*, 177–78).[20] Joachim's prophetic model of the *spiritualis intellectus* allows Sidney and Herbert to translate Psalms as though their poetic voices continue the biblical narrative of progressive spiritual development, emphasizing their English Protestant faith that fulfills the requisite spiritual wisdom of the Davidic messiah.

If prophecy involves the exegesis of prior sacred texts, how can people translate (and perhaps transform) those texts into their own idiom, time, and place? In *The Guide of the Perplexed*,[21] Maimonides argues that prophetic writings are textual versions of the divine Word that necessitate continuous interpretation, a proposition that was certainly approved by John Calvin, Théodore Bèza, William Tyndale, and other Protestant biblical translators in Geneva and Leiden. Maimonides believes that God is ineffable and that his attributes are incomprehensible. Unlike Joachim, Maimonides argues that prophecy can neither deal with the mystery of first cause nor with final ends. "Know that the final end of all that exists ought not to be sought—neither according to our opinion who asserts that the world have been produced in time nor according to the opinion of Aristotle who holds that the world is eternal. For according to his opinion as to the eternity of the world, no ultimate end should be sought for any part of the world" (*Guide*, III.13, 2: 448–50; III.25, 2: 505–6).[22] Maimonides argues that Creation was the sublime overflow of God's essence that gives form to inferior matter and initiates its coming into being. In his interpretation of Genesis wherein God says that "it was good" after each day of Creation (Genesis 1:4, 10, 13, 18, 22, and 31), the mystery of God's essence is differentiated from his creations, but those creations are made "good" under the influence of the divine overflow (*Guide*, III.13, 2: 453–54).

Maimonides uses the same term, *overflow*, to define prophecy and describe its mental processes.

> Know that the true reality and quiddity of prophecy consists in its being an overflow overflowing from God, may He be cherished and honored, through the intermediation of the Active Intellect, toward the rational faculty in the first place and thereafter toward the imaginative faculty. This is the highest degree of man and the ultimate perfection for the imaginative faculty. This is something that cannot be attained solely through perfection in the speculative sciences and through improvement of moral habits, even if all of them have become as fine and good as can be. There still is needed in addition the highest possible degree of perfection of the imaginative faculty in respect of its original natural disposition. . . . You know, too, the actions of the imaginative faculty that are in its nature, such as retaining things perceived by the senses, combining

> these things, and imitating them. And you know that its greatest and noblest action takes place only when the senses rest and do not perform their actions. It is then that a certain overflow overflows to this faculty according to its disposition, and it is the cause of the veridical dreams. This same overflow is the cause of the prophecy. There is only a difference in degree, not in kind. (*Guide*, II.36, 2: 369–70)

Maimonides' concept of the "overflow of God" erases all anthropomorphic attributes associated with the conception of God's being. God causes his knowledge to overflow to the prophets.[23] The divine overflow shapes the prophet's moral and intellectual nature and is manifest in his aspiration to master the prior texts recorded in the Torah, thereby giving his "prophetic words" the attribution of a holy spirit (*Guide*, II.32, 2: 361; II.41, 2: 385).[24]

Maimonides argues that the divine overflow reaches both the rational and imaginative faculty in harmony.

> For the very overflow that affects the imaginative faculty—with the result of rendering it perfect so that its acts bring about its giving information about what will happen and its apprehending those future events as if they were things that had been perceived by the senses and had reached the imaginative faculty from the senses—is also the overflow that renders perfect the act of the rational faculty, so that its act brings about its knowing things that are in their existence, and it achieves this apprehension as if it had apprehended it by starting from speculative premises. . . . For the overflow of the Active Intellect goes in its true reality to it (that is, to the rational faculty), causing it to pass from potentiality to actuality. It is from the rational faculty that that overflow comes to the imaginative faculty. (*Guide*, II.38, 2: 377–78; III.24, 2: 501)[25]

Maimonides defines the Imagination as the "creative faculty of the mind" working in harmony with reason to illuminate the proper correspondence between intelligible ideas and their existent or nonexistent material forms. The individual that perfects his intellect through scholarly training and correctly interprets the configurations of his imagination, translating "potentiality into actuality," will become a prophet. "This is the highest degree of man and the ultimate term of perfection that can exist for his species; and this state is the ultimate term of perfection for the imaginative faculty" (*Guide*, II.41, 2: 385). However, Maimonides qualifies this point, arguing that even the perfected intellect may be deceived unless the divine will empowers his capacity to understand such an exalted apprehension.[26] Everything that is imagined exists or can exist, and that which does not enter within the net of the Imagination is incapable of existing (*Guide*, I.49, 1: 109). To create a superior spiritual reality, one should give preference to the Imagination unfettered by the need for a referential concrete object (*Guide*, II.2, 2: 279–80).[27] The overflow of the Intellect to the Imaginative faculty enables it to create a reality as it should be passing from potentiality to actuality and instills in known things a higher order of being as if they were apprehended from abstract speculative premises (*Guide*, II.38, 2: 377–78; III.20, 2: 481–85).

Following Maimonides' theory of divine overflow, Yohanan Alemanno (1435–1504?), the Jewish-Italian humanist philosopher and biblical exegete, in his "Song of Solomon's Ascents" (*Shir ha-ma'alot li-Shlomo*, ca. 1488), equates the gift of prophecy with artists who use their crafts of perspective and symbolism to make truthful images that illuminate the higher intelligible beauty embedded in material objects.[28] For Maimonides, Alemanno, and Sidney the superior artistic operations of the Imagination posit an alternative to the "mimetic reality principle" in which "potentialities" may be conceptualized as "actualities" and the actualities of the past and present may be projected as comprehensible paradigms of the future.[29] The prophetic imagination is commonly described as a critical agent that necessarily mystifies everyday reality by creating another order of possibility; it establishes a critical distance from the world as it is and reveals new patterns of a creative order that might be or should be. Sidney argues that "nature never set forth the earth in so rich a tapestry as divers poets have done; neither with so pleasant rivers, fruitful trees, sweet-smelling flowers, nor whatsoever else may make the too much loved earth more lovely. Her world is brazen, the poets only deliver a golden" (*Defence*, 216, ll. 182–85). The poet-prophet offers a "golden world" based on prior texts that are translated in terms of newly interpreted moral myths to guide people to create their own "perfected" moral landscape (*Defence*, 216, ll. 175–85).[30]

In his translation of Psalm 19:1–16, Sidney assumes that God exists as a "thundering" judgmental power manifest in nature.

The heav'nly frame, setts foorth the fame
  Of him that only thunders;
The firmament so strangly bent
  Showes his hand-working wonders.
Day unto day, it doth display,
  Their course doth it acknowledge:
And night to night, succeeding right,

In darkness teach cleare knowledge.
There is no speach, nor language, which
Is soe of skill bereaved,
But of the skies the teaching cries,
They have heard and conceaved.
There be no eyne, but read the line
From soe faire booke proceeding:
Their wordes be sett in letters greate
For ev'ry bodies reading.
(Sidney-Herbert *Psalms*, 39)

The divine design of Nature constitutes a mysterious magnificence for which a suitable language must be found to interpret it so that all people may understand it. However, people find that the significant revelations of the wondrous world are often perplexing. This perplexity is engendered by Christian doctrines that link the fall of humanity with the fall of Nature, now "strangely bent" (wrought or inclined) but still assumed to possess its initial mysterious perfection. Sidney believes that poetry can clarify such perplexity through its *eikastiké* arts, defined as "figuring forth good things" (*Defence*, 236, ll. 988–96).[31] Similar to Maimonides, Sidney believes that the ability to understand the divinity within the natural world is dependent on God first redeeming the moral flaws of the sinner's "natural disposition," a correction that the sinner cannot do on his own.

Who is the man, that ever can
His faultes know and acknowledge!
O Lord, cleane me from faultes that be
Most secret from all knowledge.
(Psalm 19:49–52; Sidney-Herbert *Psalms*, 40)

Sidney's moral self-examination and pious supplication are prerequisite for his self-enhancement as a poet and paramount in his prophetic vision. For the poet the psalmist's belief that the "Heavens declare the glory of God" must be accepted as an act of faith; whatever may be the will of God, it can only be for the good. Thus the poetic idealization of earthly existence, which may appear to be a fictional view of the world, is intended to express one's faith in the divine perfection that still resides in Nature and in humanity.[32] Sidney concludes the psalm with the hope that he will be able to translate the mysterious language of the heavens adequately in his words. "So lett wordes sproong from my weake tongue / And my hartes meditation, / My saving might, Lord, in thy sight / Receave good acceptation" (Psalm 19:61–64; Sidney-Herbert *Psalms*, 41).[33] David, uninhibited by the Christian dogma of original sin, is concerned that his verbal expression of God's majesty in nature is inadequate; his words do not express the transcendent glory of God that he apprehends in Nature. Sidney, aware of the poet's divided moral nature, interprets David's supplication in such a way that he prays that his words generated by the meditations of his heart—the seat of his imagination—can create images of an idealized Nature that illuminate in comprehensible forms the divine perfection that by faith he assumes exists within Nature.

For Sidney the superior artistic operation of the imagination provides a transcendent experience; it offers a golden world liberated from the constraints of the real world.

> Only the poet, disdaining to be tied to any such subjection, lifted up with the vigour of his own invention, doth grow in effect another nature, in making things better than nature bringeth forth, or quite anew, forms such as never were in nature, as the Heroes, Demigods, Cyclops, Chimeras, Furies, and such like: so as he goeth hand in hand with nature, not enclosed within the narrow warrant of her gifts, but freely ranging only within the zodiac of his own wit. (*Defence*, 216, ll. 175–82)

Sidney argues that the poet can be considered a "second creator" aspiring to express the "ineffable excellence of God," qualities attributed to David in his Psalms, to Solomon in Song of Songs, and to Moses and Deborah in their hymns (*Defence*, 217, ll. 222–35). Through his "shaping spirit of the imagination" and "critical reason" working on prior sacred texts, the poet-prophet creates an artistic apprehension of a higher truth of enlightened possibilities that constitute an alternative to the temporal realities of his society.[34] Maimonides attributed that high aspiration to the divine will working through the Active Intellect overflowing to the rational and then to the imaginative faculties. Medieval philosophers such as al-Farabi (Abū Nasr al-Fārābi, c. 872–950/951) and Avicenna (Ibn Sīnā, c. 980–1037) claimed that the imagination was responsible for creating myths and fables that were indispensable for the prophet to present divine truth to those lacking a proper intellectual preparation (*Guide*, II.45, 2: 395–403).[35] Sidney also argues that one may balance the "highest point of man's wit" (Intellect) with the efficacy of the imagination to render nature in a semblance of its perfected forms. Assuming that God created man in his own likeness, "with the force of a divine breath" (overflow), he also inspired the poet "to bring forth things surpassing nature," which are best expressed in his poetry. For Sidney such inspiration is an attribute of divine providence working through the poet's natural disposition in terms of the Protestant concept of calling. However, he also believes that the human's natural disposition is divided: The poet's "erected wit" allows him "to know what perfection is," but his "infected will" (sin and perplexity) inhibits him from reaching it (*Defence*, 217, ll. 201–10). Both the natural world and the human being are still responsive to heavenly powers, and the imagination rendering spiritual ideas into corporeal forms enables the poet-prophet to comprehend the divine presence in the world.[36]

For Maimonides and Sidney the equivocal nature of words creates its own kind of perplexity. Maimonides frequently cites the Talmudic axiom that "God speaks in the language of men" (*Guide*, I.26, 1: 56),[37] but after the formative episode of the tower of Babel (Genesis 11:1–9), he argues that every effort to understand the oral and written "word of God" involves interpretations of its literal and figurative meanings, and each interpretation results in translations that may create semantic confusion.[38] Maimonides believes that Moses received the Ten Commandments, indeed the whole Pentateuch, directly on Mount Sinai (Exodus 19:3–31:18).[39] However, God "speaking" and "saying" are equivocal terms denoting emanations of the divine will, which in essence are unknowable (*Guide*, I.63, 1: 153–54; I.65, 1: 158–59; I.66, 1: 160–61). The biblical narrative includes numerous examples of Moses paraphrasing and explicating the "divine word" into the language of the perplexed Hebrews. Similarly, Maimonides demonstrates that the later prophets speak in their unique figurative language of "dark sayings" and poetic conceits that approximate the original sacred text translated for successive generations in their own terms of signification. "Know that every prophet has a kind of speech peculiar to him, which is, as it were, the language of that individual, which the prophetic revelation peculiar to him causes him to speak to those who understand" (*Guide*, II.29, 2: 336–37).[40]

The prophets' revisions and rationalizations had a profound effect on Maimonides' *Mishnah Torah* and *Guide* and on other notable Jewish biblical exegetes and poets: Rashi (Rabbi Shlomo Yitzaki, 1040–1105), Abraham Ibn Ezra (1089–c.1164) and David Kimhi (RaDak, 1160–1235).[41] Biblical Hebrew was believed to be God's undoubted idiom, but there was considerable debate among Jewish exegetes about many of its esoteric meanings. Although the loss of the "divine language" of Creation is part of the fundamental differentiation between the divine and the human,[42] Christian Hebraists turned to the Jewish biblical exegetes whose philological interpretations could be used to clarify some of the ambiguous expressions in the Bible.[43] Maimonides states that the purpose of his *Guide* is to explain the meaning of those equivocal terms in the Pentateuch that render the Law and the injunctions of the prophets perplexing (*Guide*, Introduction to Part I, 1: 5–6; II.2, 2: 253).

In the Psalms David speaks in his own words referential to prior oral versions of the biblical narrative. His meditations express his profound desire to perfect his "intertextual self" to speak wisely concerning divine matter. For Maimonides, the exegete, sensitive to the oral tradition and written Bible and Jewish biblical commentary, must determine whether the parables and riddles in the Psalms serve as literal figures of speech using conventional meanings or are used figuratively to denote a higher order of spiritual signification (*Guide*, II.47, 2: 409). "Know that the key to the understanding of all the prophets, peace be on them, and to the knowledge of its truth, is an understanding of the parables, of their import, and of the meaning of their words occurring in them" (*Guide*, Introduction to Part I, 1: 10–11). If the distinction between literal and figurative meaning is not acknowledged, then perplexing incongruities arise, making it difficult to understand the "subtle allegorical expressions of metaphysical [divine] matters" (*Guide*, I.32, 1: 68–69; I.34, 1: 73).[44] This was a particular problem for Protestant biblical translators who were concerned with recovering the "literal meaning" of words in the scriptures, which they believed were the "true (absolute) words of God." Maimonides shows that when it is written that "God speaks to the heart," an organ common to all animals, it refers to that part of the body in which the "principle of life" resides. It also denotes "thought" (2 Kings 5:26, Numbers 15:39, Deuteronomy 29:17), "opinion" (Proverbs 10:21), "the will" (Jeremiah 3:15, 2 Kings 10:15), or "the intellect" (Kohelet [Ecclesiastes] 10:2), and when a person is commanded "to love the Lord thy God with all thy heart" (Deuteronomy 6:5), "it signifies that such love must engage all the forces of the body and the soul, for the animating principle of all of them derives from the heart" (*Guide*, I.39, 1: 88–89). The "soul" is also an equivocal term: It is the animal spirit in all sentient beings; it denotes the rational faculty in human beings; it is an entity that remains after death; and, "in all cases in which the term soul is applied to God, it has the meaning of the ineffable divine will" (*Guide*, I.41, 1: 91). The prophet speaks in an equivocal language not to obfuscate divine commandments but to allow his words to assume a more comprehensive dimension of expression. Whereas human understanding begins with literal sense perception, it is through the intellect and the imagination interpreting the figurative signification of those perceptions that one achieves a greater measure of spiritual comprehension (*Guide*, I.4, 1: 27–28).

Maimonides asserts that to love God is a testimony to his existence and is consequent upon the knowledge of God, which is based on the study of Torah (*Guide*, III.28, 2: 512). However, when asked, "What is the love of God that is befitting," Maimonides argues that it is "to love God . . . such that one is enraptured . . . like love-sick individuals whose minds [*da'atam*] are at no time free from passion for a particular woman, and are enraptured by her at all times."[45] Maimonides intended his analogy to be understood figuratively. His idea of a perfected humanity emphasizes the primal harmony between masculine and feminine attributes assumed to have been present at the divine creation of the hermaphrodite Adam (Genesis 1:26–27) as an "image and likeness of God" or from Plato's version of the myth of the androgyne in the *Symposium* (189d–191d). The all-consuming mystery of "loving God" is conceived as an intellectual and emotional process of reconciling all contraries, eliminating all perplexing binary gender opposition, and uniting the body and the soul into a comprehensible form of human wholeness.

Furthermore, Maimonides addresses the perplexing relationship between language and Truth when words are equivocal and Truth is identified as an immutable emanation from God. Even the most perfected intellectual in natural and divine sciences is unable to articulate with complete clarity the portion of that divine wisdom he has apprehended. At what point can one's faith in that higher wisdom actually constitute a superior reality? Maimonides cites the dictum in Psalms 65:1–2—"Silence is praise to Thee"—in that however we acknowledge the majesty of God, we perceive some deficiency in our expression.[46] "We are dazzled by His beauty, and He is hidden from us because of the intensity with which He becomes manifest, just as the sun is hidden to the eyes that are too weak to apprehend it" (*Guide*, I.59, 1: 139).[47] Such epiphanies may illuminate the psalmist's process of self-transformation, but for the reader of the Psalms those revelations are not so easily comprehended.[48]

David and the other psalmists praise God in a cycle of approximations of their passionate love and desire for redemption and enlightenment in a language that seems inadequate both for their subject (God) and their intention (redemption). In his translation of Psalm 39:1–12 Sidney writes:

Thus did I thinck, I well will marke my way
  Least by my tongue I happ to stray;
I musle will my mouth while in the sight
  I do abide of wicked wight.
And so I nothing said, I muett stood,
  I silence kept, even in the good.
But, still, the more that I did hold my peace,
  The more my sorrow did encrease,

The more me thought, my hart was hott in me;
  And as I mus'd such world to see,
The fire tooke fire, and forcibly out brake;
  My tongue would needes and thus I spake.
    (Sidney-Herbert *Psalms*, 89)

The poet writes lyrical songs praising the imagined beauty and goodness of God for which he has the wit to conceive of such a sublime vision of biblical Truth, but he doubts the adequacy of his words to express it. For Sidney the poet-prophet must invest that Truth with a compensatory emotional forcefulness or *energeia* (*Defence*, 246, ll. 1379–93).[49] Maimonides emphasizes the overflow of the Active Intellect on the Rational Intellect and Imagination to resolve the perplexity of textual perceptions. Protestant biblical exegetes emphasize the recovery of the literal signification of words to make biblical Truth comprehensible. Sidney insists that the poet must add the rhetorical power of *energeia* to express his intended meaning as an independent and vivid apprehension of his counterreality. Although we may say that Truth refers to "what is actual" and that falsity or fiction refers to "what is not actual," we may also say that the imagination manifests a subjective, intuitive, and creative insight into a higher ontological order defining Truth as "what should be or could be" through *poiesis* (*Defence*, 235, ll. 935–53). Sidney's fiction expresses a dialectical counterreality in a figurative and emotional charged poetic language. Powerful writing exposes the cognitive struggle of the poet-prophet to find coherence in prior texts that can enlighten the reader. In the Psalms Sidney incorporates his social life as an ambitious courtier in Elizabeth's court and his political and religious struggles as a Protestant patriot with David's conflict with Saul and the Philistines. By translating David's passion into his own poetic voice, Sidney reveals the emotional contradictions that he cannot completely understand, spoken in an equivocal language within which he struggles to locate himself.[50]

Sidney focuses on the problem of equivocal language approximating Truth and true feeling in the rhetorical strategies of both his love sonnets (*Astrophil and Stella*) and Psalms.[51] The emotional sincerity of his subjective intention must compensate for his conflicted mental and moral state that produces the equivocal double message of "loving in truth" tainted by wickedness rather than virtue. Margaret Ferguson suggests that the problem for Sidney is that "a written medium" implies that the reader cannot or will not understand the poet's words and that Sidney's allegorical intention of winning the mind from wickedness to virtue cannot be realized until it is confirmed by the reader.[52] For Maimonides and Sidney everyone reads differently according to their intellect and sensibility. Both the prophet and the poet must enable words to say more than they usually say so that the enlightened reader can appreciate their higher significance.

In Psalm 6:1–8 Sidney's psalmist is refashioned as a penitent Christian fearful of his moral and spiritual blindness and verbal confusion for which only his faith in the mitigating "reading" by God will transform his meditation into a model of Christian redemption. Psalm 6 is the first of the seven penitential psalms in the Christian tradition associated with David's sin of sexual transgression with Bathsheba contrasting the themes of earthly and divine love.[53]

> Lord, lett not mee, a worm, by thee be shent
> While thou art in the heate of thy displeasure:
> Ne let thy rage, of my due punishment
> Become the measure.
> But mercy, Lord, lett mercy thine descend,
> For I am weake, and in my weakness languish:
> Lord, help, for ev'n my bones their marrow spend
> With cruell anguish.
> (Sidney-Herbert *Psalms*, 12)

Sidney's psalmist hopes that his emotional "weeping sobbing voice" will clarify his faith in God's Creation and laws and mitigate his faults and perplexity so that he will not be left as an "unrequited" supplicant. Similar to the poet-lover, Sidney's poet-psalmist is concerned with his equivocal moral nature and how that equivocation can be clarified in his conflicted messages of earthly and divine love. In Psalm 19, after celebrating the magnificence of the universe that illuminates the glory of God, Sidney returns to his assertions regarding the inadequacy of his language to make him worthy of redemption: "Soe lett wordes sproong from my weake tongue / And my hartes meditation, / My saving might, Lord, in thy sight / Receave good acceptation" (Psalm 19:61–64, Sidney-Herbert *Psalms*, 41). Again in Psalm 39:37–42 he declares:

> Heare, Lord, my suites, and cries: stopp not thine eares
> At these my wordes, all cloth'd in teares:
> For I, with thee, on earth a stranger am,
> But baiting, as my fathers came.
> Stay then thy wrath, that I maie strength receave
> Ere I my earthly being leave.
> (Sidney-Herbert *Psalms*, 90)

The poet-prophet finds that his lack of inner harmony separates his intellect from his subjective emotional intention manifest in his equivocal language, which in turn may or may not be acceptable to God, whose "reader-response" is impossible to know.[54]

To overcome the problem of equivocal language, Sidney aspires to create a unique "alchemy of words," poetic transformations of rhetorical tropes that would verbally and pictorially express a heightened "spiritual" level of consciousness.[55] Like Ezekiel (Ezekiel 37:1–14), Sidney wants to breathe new life into the valley of dry bones of conventional language and give it a new life that will be worthy of God's approbation.[56] Although he uses well-known rhetorical expressions from Virgil, Dante, Petrarca, Pietro Bembo, and the Pléiade poets, the power of his language comes from his disjunctive imagery, which forces his readers to interpret his distorted syntax and semantic irony and appreciate the evocativeness of those images and the sounds of words.[57] Maimonides argues that one must resolve the perplexity engendered by the equivocal nature of language to achieve a clear understanding of biblical truth. In general, Sidney and Herbert believe that equivocal language expands the "potential" meanings of words and provides new forms of aesthetic expression that will inspire readers to reinterpret the poetic-prophetic text for their personal edification.

However, what is the correlation between sacred Truth and personal edification? For Sidney any realization of truth must be able to cope with "falsity," defined not as a falsehood but as a creative process that asserts a critical justification of enlightened potentialities.[58] The poet-prophet must go beyond the mere imitation of factual experience as it is and aspire to a higher ontological order of "falsity" as the articulation of potentiality in terms of what should be or what could be. Sidney argues that the skill of the poet is based on the "*idea* or fore-conceit" of the work and not on the work itself.

> And that the poet hath that *idea* is manifest, by delivering them forth in such excellency as he had imagined them. Which delivering them forth also is not wholely imaginative, as we are wont to say by them that build castles in the air; but so far substantially it worketh, not only to make a Cyrus, which had been but a particular excellency as nature might have done, but to bestow a Cyrus upon the world to make many Cyruses, if they will learn aright why and how that maker made him. (*Defence*, 216, ll. 191–201)[59]

Such falsity is crucial to the power of creating counterrealities through language. For Sidney equivocality and falsity are not pathologies of language; they are the roots of prophetic genius. They expand the evocative power of language to illuminate a higher order of apprehension and understanding and to allow true ideas possessing a sacred authority to appear as actual possibilities in life experiences.

Herbert's well-known manipulations of language and versification also attempt to establish an aesthetic reality for the psalmist's wisdom. She combines her courtly grace with her pious intentions as she makes her personal devotions beautiful as well as doctrinaire. In her tribute to Philip as "co-author" of the *Psalms*, "To the Angell Spirit," Herbert combines her adoration of her brother, her reverence for David, and her pious Protestant faith in God's Truth illuminated by prior biblical commentaries.

> Oh! When to this Accompt, this cast upp Summe,
>   this Reckoning made, this Audit of my woe,
>   I call my thoughts, when so strange passions flowe;
> Howe works my hart, my sences striken dumbe?
>   that would thee more, then ever hart could showe,
>   and all too short who knew thee best doth knowe
> There lives no witt that may thy praise become.
> Truth I invoke (who scorne else where to move
>   or here in ought my blood should partialize)
>   Truth, sacred Truth, Thee sole to solemnize
> Those precious rights well knowne best mindes approve.
>   (Sidney-Herbert *Psalms*, xxxvi–xxxvii, ll. 43–53)

Such equivocal terms as "account," "reckoning," and "audit" emphasize the psalmist's self-examination and critical evaluation of her poetic translation intended to praise the Holy Spirit that inspired David, which is now linked to Philip as an "angelic spirit" who inspires her to express the elusive truth and beauty of her faith in God. Barbara K. Lewalski argues that through her varieties of stanzas, metrical patterns, and contemporary metaphors, Herbert creates a new persona for the psalmist and a variable addressee for the psalms.[60] In Psalm 49:1–6 Herbert bravely declares:

> World-dwellers all give heede to what I saie;
> To all I speake, to rich, poore, high and low;
> Knowledg the subject is my hart conceaves,
> Wisdome the wordes shall from my mouth proceed:
> Which I will measure by melodious eare,
> And ridled speech to tuned harp accord.
>   (Sidney-Herbert *Psalms*, 115)

Her "ridled" (allegorical) speech allows words to say more than they usually do. The spiritual reflections of David are imaginatively expressed in the beautiful melody of her English verses and yet maintain the equivocal nature of prophetic speech intended to expand the spiritual consciousness of the diverse audience she addresses.[61] Herbert confronts the problem of equivocal language in many of her psalms with the rhetorical question: "Who of his force can utter what is true? / Who all his praise in praises comprehend" (Psalm 106:3–4; Sidney-Herbert *Psalms*, 248). Her psalmist praises God yet solicits a reward for herself; her self-asserted goodness suffers the evil distortions and envy of others, but her confessed sinfulness is an invitation for divine blessings; her reverence stands in fear, and her truth in words appeals to the authority of her faith in God: "Well I thy wisdom may adore, / But never reach with earthly mind" (Psalm 139:20–21; Sidney-Herbert *Psalms*, 319). Although imitating the prophetic voice of Hebraic David, Herbert's voice resonates with her equivocal apprehension in Protestant terms of being a sinner, albeit with virtuous intentions, uncertain of how her language will appeal to God.

Ironically, the chief impediment to Herbert's prophetic enlightenment lies in the equivocal nature of literary eloquence with which she initially intended to promote her translations. In her "Dialogue Between Two Shepherds, Thenot and Piers" (1599),[62] Thenot defends elegant hyperbole and courtly conceits as a means to achieve a verbal eloquence that raises the literal meaning of words and images into the domain of higher Neoplatonic ideas simulating divine expression. However, similar to Maimonides and Rashi, Piers defends heartfelt plain speaking that is aware of its limitations such that the ultimate speech act is silence, reflecting the inexpressible attributes of God (ll. 58–60).[63] In Psalm 120:5–9 Herbert prays:

> Lord ridd my soule from treasonous eloquence
> Of filthy forgers craftily fraudulent:
> And from the tongue where lodg'd resideth
> Poison'd abuse, ruine of believers.
> (Sidney-Herbert *Psalms*, 293)

Maimonides argues that the prophet must clarify the significance of prophetic texts expressed in hyperbole or literal terms (*Guide*, II.47, 2: 407). Rashi glosses this passage: "O Lord deliver my soul from *treacherous lips*, from deceitful tongue," identifying treacherous lips as a metaphor for the descendants of Esau, who hunt down people with malicious slander. Slander is a characteristic vice of "wicked kingdoms" such as Edom and Rome.[64] David Kimhi renders the passage: "Deliver me, O Lord, [from] the people in whose midst we are, for they are lying and deceitful men."[65] Miles Coverdale (1488–1569) translates the passage as "Delyver my soule, O Lord, from *lyenge lippes*, and from a deceitful tongue," and similarly the Geneva Bible (1560) translates the passage as "Deliver my soule, ô Lord, frō *lying lippes*, and from a deceitful tongue."[66] Herbert's translation of "lying lips" to "treasonous eloquence" is significant. She seems fearful of the seductive power of literary eloquence emanating from others who are essentially wicked and identifies such eloquence with the rhetorical strategies of Elizabethan courtly decadence that may infect her pious intentions.[67] She may also identify herself with David's desire to escape the evil influence of deceit and violence while in exile in the lands of Meshech and Kedar that might affect his speech, pervert his soul, and inhibit his ascension to Jerusalem.[68] Although her translations are generally noted for their eloquent verbal inventions, such eloquence may distort the true splendor of divine wisdom with its artificial and hyperbolic exaggerations that disguise the moral nature of the speaker and thereby create further perplexities. Herbert's eloquence emanates from within herself, but which self—the Protestant sinner or the pious psalmist? Her psalms focus on the inner life of the penitent Christian whose suffering may be attributed to her moral weakness or to the mysterious nature of divine justice. For example, in Psalm 120 (Sidney-Herbert *Psalms*, 293) she confesses her moral inadequacies in the context of a pervasive evil in the world. She finds that her sublime desire for salvation through grace cannot be evoked by her equivocal language addressed to God whose commandments may prove impossible to meet.

For Maimonides eloquence is a manifestation of the Intellect overflowing into the Imagination of the prophet so that divine Truth may be embodied in beautiful expressions "addressed to the people to teach them and let his own perfection overflow towards them" (*Guide*, II.37, 2: 374–75). Eloquence must reflect the moral perfection of the speaker whose intellectual and imaginative expression takes on the semblance of words inspired by the holy spirit (*Guide*, II.45, 2: 398). Similarly, Plato's Socrates argues that we become like the divine as far as we can through righteousness with the help of wisdom: "In the divine there is no shadow of unrighteousness, and nothing is more like the divine than anyone of us who becomes as righteous as possible."[69] Erudition and eloquence informed by piety are the hallmark of Petrarca's theory of human perfectibility and Erasmus's theory of the ideal education of a Christian prince.[70] For Maimonides erudition is based on a thorough knowledge of the Torah and the Talmud; for Herbert erudition is based on her knowledge of the Bible enhanced by her understanding of Protestant doctrines concerning faith and grace. Herbert's psalmist prays that God will protect her from internal and external evils and that her equivocal language will be "interpreted" by God as an expression of the true nature of her pious intention that comes from her heart. Like Sidney, she uses the equivocal meaning of the word "heart" as the seat of true feeling and the seat of the imagination.

> Ward well my words, O Lord, (for that it is I pray)
> A watchfull Sentinell at my mouthes passage lay,
>   At wicket of my lipps stand ay a faithfull porter;
> Incline me not to ill, nor lett me loosly goe
> A mate in work with such, whence no good work doth grow,
> And in their flattring baites, lett me be no consorter.
> . . . .
> O soe direct my feete they may escape the hands
> Of their entangling snare, which for me pitched stands;
>   And from the wicked netts for me with craft they cover,
> Nay for these fowlers, once, thy self a fowler be,
> And make them fowly fall where netts are laid by thee;
>   But where for me they lay, let me leap freely over.
>   (Psalm 141:7–12, 25–30; Sidney-Herbert *Psalms*, 324–25)

Maimonides argues that through the performance of mitzvot the Intellect can imitate *in actu* all intelligible manifestations of God's providence by following his laws "with all thy heart, and with all thy soul, and with all thy might" (*Guide*, III.28, 2: 512; III.52, 2: 629–30; III.54, 2: 636–38).[71] The perfection of moral virtues attains its ultimate excellence as rational virtues, which teach true opinions concerning divine things.[72] In Psalm 141 David prays that God will protect his mind and heart from evil thoughts and deeds and his mouth from expressing iniquity. The righteous may rebuke him, but their correction is likened to the holy oil used to anoint him: "Let not my head refuse it" (Psalm 141:5, *KJB* 795). In Maimonides' terms that oil is like the divine overflow investing him with the blessing of kingship, perfected rational virtues, and true eloquent speech. David prays that when the false judges are overthrown, only his "sweet word," his eloquent testimony of God's providential power, will prevail, and he alone will escape their nets of iniquity.

Herbert conceptualizes grace as a divine overflow, which is essential to her Protestant faith, so that she will be guided by the Holy Spirit and so that her psalms will have the same rhetorical power of sanctity as those of David. Herbert makes her supplication to a providential God to be her "watchful Sentinell" who will guard her words, guide her virtuous deeds, and protect her from flatterers who threaten her virtues and her "divine poems." She knows that God commands her to "do justly, to love mercy, and walk humbly with God" (Micah 6:8), but her humility is foregrounded in the Christian doctrine of being a sinner with an inadequate intellect prone to backsliding. Grace is the ultimate *desiderium*, but it is also the ultimate mystery. She knows that her prophetic-poet as penitent Christian is dependent on heavenly powers beyond her control. Thus she asserts her pious faith in God to direct her "feete"—literally, her virtuous intentions and deeds, and figuratively, her eloquent poetic verses—to be worthy of a blessed reception.[73]

For Sidney and Herbert translating the Psalms was an act of intertextual creativity. They transformed the Hebraic David into their Protestant prophetic voice using prior Latin, French, and English translations of the Psalms and an extensive body of biblical exegeses by Jewish and Christian commentators. They considered themselves participants in what Joachim de Fiore called the grand theodicy of the Bible's historical narrative as Protestant versions of his *spiritualis intellectus* expressing a higher order of spiritual consciousness for their English-speaking readers. Similar to Maimonides' conception of the prophet and prophecy in the *Guide of the Perplexed*, Sidney believed that the poet as prophet, using his Intellect and Imagination, could illuminate the perplexing relationship between religious Truth and the inherent equivocal nature of biblical language.[74] In every generation the poet-prophet who aspires to apprehend the superior wisdom and authority of a divine revelation in his creative writing must deal with the equivocal nature of biblical language to find his own effective manner of expression. Sidney and Herbert believed that they could establish an aesthetic reality for the psalmist's wisdom through their manipulations of the English language and versification. Hebraic David prays that God will approve of his enlightened spiritual meditations. Sidney and Herbert pray that their words will say more than they usually say and that their readers will appreciate the subjective and emotional poignancy of their psalmody and the reformed spiritual significance of their Protestant prophetic voices.

Notes

1. Philip Sidney, *Defence of Poesy*, in *Sir Philip Sidney: The Major Works*, ed. Katherine Duncan-Jones (Oxford, UK: Oxford University Press, 2002), 214–15, ll. 112–13, 131–45. All citations to the *Defence* are taken from this edition.

2. Anne Lake Prescott, *French Poets and the English Renaissance: Studies in Fame and Transformation* (New Haven, CT: Yale University Press, 1978), 17.

3. Philippe Du Plessis Mornay, *A woorke concerning the Trewnesse of the Christian Religion*, trans. Sir Philip Sidney and finished by Arthur Golding (London: Thomas Cadman, 1587), sigs. Dd5–Dd5v. Also see Hannibal Hamlin, *Psalm Culture and Early Modern English Literature* (Cambridge, UK: Cambridge University Press, 2004), 112; Lily Campbell, *Divine Poetry and Drama in Sixteenth Century England* (Cambridge, UK: Cambridge University Press, 1959), 35–38; and Margaret P. Hannay, "'So May I with the Psalmist Truly Say': Early Modern Englishwomen's Psalm Discourse," in *Written or Be Written: Early Modern Women Poets and Cultural Constraints*, ed. Barbara Smith and Ursala Appelt (Burlington, VT: Ashgate, 2001), 109–11.

4. Biblical poetry, designated as songs with cantillation marks, was identified with Psalms, Job, Proverbs, Lamentations, the "Song of the Sea" (Exodus 15), the "Song of Moses" (Deuteronomy 32), the "Song of Deborah" (Judges 5), the "Song of David" (2 Samuel 22), Song of Songs, Isaiah's "Song of the Vineyard" (Isaiah 5), and parts of Ezekiel. But such a designation is too general. Josephus, Philo, the early church fathers Origen and Jerome, and the historian Eusebius of Caesarea thought that the "Song of the Sea" was written in hexameters and that the psalmists used iambs, alcaics, and sapphics, like Horace and Pindar did. Azariah de' Rossi (c. 1511?–1578?) argued that one must not count syllables or words but the number of ideas per clause. To show how biblical poetry served as a precedent for contemporary poetry, de' Rossi proposed the concept of biblical parallelism. See Azariah de' Rossi, *Me'or Enayim* (Light of the Eyes) (1571–1572), trans. Joanna Weinberg, Yale Judaica Series 31 (New Haven, CT: Yale University Press, 2001), 710–16. Also see Arthur M. Lesley, "Sixteenth-Century Italian Jewish Analysis of Biblical Poetics," paper delivered at the "Colloque Poésie et Religion 1540–1600" (McGill University, Montréal, 1985); and G. Lloyd Jones, *The Discovery of Hebrew in Tudor England: A Third Language* (Manchester, UK: Manchester University Press, 1983), 239–43.

5. Although Philip's and Mary's knowledge of Hebrew is highly speculative, Mary probably had more exposure to the language through the Herbert family chaplain, Gervase Babington (1549/50–1610). Babington studied at Cambridge University (BA in 1571, MA in 1573) under John Whitgift (c. 1530–1604) as a student in theology, Hebrew, and Greek. See Chanita Goodblatt, "'High Holy Muse': Christian Hebraism and Jewish Exegesis in the Sidneian *Psalmes*," in *Tradition, Heterodoxy, and Religious Culture: Judaism and Christianity in the Early Modern Period*, ed. Chanita Goodblatt and Howard Kreisel, Goldstein-Goren Library of Jewish Thought 6 (Beer Sheva, Israel: Ben Gurion University of the Negev Press, 2006), 289–92; Margaret P. Hannay, *Philip's Phoenix: Mary Sidney, Countess of Pembroke* (New York: Oxford University Press, 1990), 132–35; and Hamlin, *Psalm Culture*, 101.

6. See Anne Lake Prescott, "King David as a 'Right Poet': Sidney and the Psalmist," *English Literary History* 19 (1989): 131–51; Anne Lake Prescott, "Evil Tongues at the Court of Saul: The Renaissance David as a Slandered Courtier," *Journal of Medieval and Renaissance Studies* 21 (1991): 163–86; and Prescott,

French Poets, 16–17. Also see Roland Greene, "Sir Philip Sidney's Psalms, the Sixteenth-Century Psalter, and the Nature of Lyric," *Studies in English Literature* 30 (1990): 19–40.

7. Numerous Jewish and Christian biblical commentators have noted this pattern of disobedience and sin, punishment, and the promise of redemption in the prophetic texts of Jonah (fl. 750–730 BCE), Isaiah (fl. 740–687 BCE), and Micah (fl. 740–686 BCE), which deal with the fall of the Northern Kingdom of Israel to the Assyrians in 722 and King Hezekiah's reform and Judea's victory over the Assyrian king Sennasherib, and in Jeremiah (fl. 626–570 BCE) and Ezekiel (fl. 593–571 BCE), which deal with the fall of Judea to the Babylonian king Nebuchadnezzar, the exile, and the promise of return and the rebuilding of the Temple.

8. See Deborah Shugar, *The Renaissance Bible: Scholarship, Sacrifice, and Subjectivity* (Berkeley: University of California Press, 1994), 105. Also see J. C. A. Rathmell, "Introduction," in *The Psalms of Sir Philip Sidney and the Countess of Pembroke*, ed. J. C. A. Rathmell (Garden City, NY: Anchor, 1963), xiv and xix–xxvii. All citations to the Psalms of Sidney and Herbert refer to this edition (hereafter referred to as the Sidney-Herbert *Psalms*). Readers may also refer to the newer edition in *The Collected Works of Mary Sidney Herbert, Countess of Pembroke*, v. 2, *The Psalmes of David*, ed. Margaret P. Hannay, Noel J. Kinnamont, and Michael G. Brennan (New York: Oxford University Press, 1998).

9. Francesco Petrarca, "On His Own Ignorance and That of Many Others," trans. Hans Nachod, in *The Renaissance Philosophy of Man*, ed. Ernst Cassirer, Paul O. Kristeller, and John H. Randall Jr. (Chicago: University of Chicago Press, 1948), 115. Also see Aaron W. Hughes, "Transforming the Maimonidean Imagination: Aesthetics in the Renaissance Thought of Judah Abravanel," *Harvard Theological Review* 97.4 (2004): 467; and Brian Vickers, "Rhetoric and Poetics," in *The Cambridge History of Renaissance Philosophy*, ed. Charles B. Schmitt, Quentin Skinner, Eckhard Kessler, and Jill Kraye. (Cambridge, UK: Cambridge University Press, 1988), 715.

10. See Hannay, "So May I," 124; Suzanne Woods, *Natural Emphasis: English Versification from Chaucer to Dryden* (San Marino, CA: Huntington Library, 1984), 169–75. In the *Defence of Poesy* Sidney cites the biblical episode (2 Samuel 12:1–15) when Nathan the prophet criticizes King David for forsaking God by committing adultery with Bathsheba and murdering Uriah, which made David, "as in a glass see his own filthiness, as that heavenly psalm of mercy [Psalm 51] well testifieth" (*Defence*, 228, ll. 664–71). For Sidney, the prophet, like the psalmist, speaking directly or through parable, must assert the righteousness of God, reveal to people their sinfulness, and inspire them to repent.

11. *The Koren Jerusalem Bible: The Hebrew/English Tanakh*, ed. and trans. Harold Fisch (Jerusalem: Koren, 2008), 795. All English translations from the Hebrew version of Psalms are taken from this work, hereafter notated *KJB*.

12. See Louis L. Martz, *The Poetry of Meditation: A Study in English Religious Literature of the Seventeenth Century* (New Haven, CT: Yale University

Press, 1962), 278; A. C. Hamilton, *Sir Philip Sidney: A Study of His Life and His Works* (Cambridge, UK: Cambridge University Press, 1977), 72–73; and Hannay, "So May I," 107.

13. God's communion in the Garden of Eden with Adam and Eve (Genesis 1:26–31) is reaffirmed through Noah (Genesis 8:15–9:17), Abraham (Genesis 22:1–19), Jacob (Genesis 32:25–31), Moses (Exodus 3:3–22, and 19:3–31:18), David (2 Samuel 7:1–29), Daniel (10:1–12:13), and Jesus (Matthew 1:1–25, 24:4, 25:46, 28:16–20), culminating in John's Revelation.

14. Marjorie Reeves, *The Influence of Prophecy in the Later Middle Ages: A Study in Joachimism* (Oxford, UK: Clarendon Press, 1969), 16–17. On Elijah's altar, see 1 Kings 18:31–39. Also see Norman Cohn, *The Pursuit of the Millennium: Revolutionary Messianism in Medieval and Reformation Europe*, 2nd ed. (New York: Harper Torchbooks, 1961), 151–52. John Colet (1467–1519), in his lectures on St. Paul's Epistles, argues that one must place the Bible before his audience as a record of real events in the daily lives and teaching of living men instead of regarding it as a closed "arsenal of texts." See Frederic Seebohm, *The Oxford Reformers* (London: J. M. Dent, 1929), 17. Such had been the desire of St. Jerome when he translated the Bible from Greek-Aramaic (possibly Hebrew) into Latin and of Erasmus in his paraphrase and annotations of Jerome's Bible. Also see Campbell, *Divine Poetry*, 15–20.

15. See Reeves, *Influence of Prophecy*, 141–42, 145–47, 156–507. Later followers of Joachim, for example, Pietro Columna (Petrus Galatinus, 1460–1540), based their interpretations of enigmatic prophets and their prophecies on the symbolism of Joachim's biblical history. Egidio of Viterbo (Aegidius of Viterbo, 1470–1532), who is often linked with Giovanni Pico della Mirandola (1463–1494) and Johann Reuchlin (1455–1522) in their interest in Jewish Kabbalah drawn from the *Zohar* (c. 1280) of Moses de Leon (1250–1305), believed that kabbalistic biblical exegesis could reveal a hidden truth within the Christian religion that substantiates Joachim's faith in the "age of the spirit" and the *renovatio mundi*. See Reeves, *Influence of Prophecy*, 235–37, 268–71, 364, 366, and 442. Also see Cohn, *Pursuit of the Millennium*, 151–52.

16. See David Weil Baker's insightful essay, "The Historical Faith of William Tyndale: Non-Salvific Reading of Scripture at the Outset of the English Reformation," *Renaissance Quarterly* 62.3 (2009): 661–92.

17. William Perkins, *Works* (Cambridge, 1605), 841. Talmudists also made the connection between Babylon and Rome as evil powers that destroyed the First and Second Temples, resulting in the exile of the Jews. Franciscan spirituals made the same connection between Babylon and Rome in their campaign for ecclesiastical reform. See Reeves, *Influence of Prophecy*, 489–90.

18. John Donne noted this attribute in the Sidney-Herbert Psalter. "The songs are these, which heaven's high holy Muse / Whispered to David, David to the Jews: / And David's successors, in holy zeal, / In forms of joy and art do re-reveal / To us so sweetly and sincerely too." Donne identifies Sidney and Herbert as David's "successors." John Donne, "Upon the translation of the Psalms

by Sir Philip Sidney, and the Countess of Pembroke his sister" (1621), in *John Donne: The Major Works*, ed. John Carey (Oxford, UK: Oxford University Press, 1990), 304, ll. 31–35. See Goodblatt, "High Holy Muse," 287–88.

19. Sidney, *Defence*, 214, ll. 87–90. "The historian scarcely giveth leisure to the moralist to say so much, but that he, laden with old mouse-eaten records, authorizing himself (for the most part) upon other histories, whose greatest authorities are built upon the notable foundation of hearsay; having much ado to accord differing writers and to pick truth out of the partiality; better acquainted with a thousand years ago than with the present age, and yet better knowing how this world goeth than how his own wit runneth; curious for antiquities and inquisitive novelties; a wonder to young folks and a tyrant in table talk, denieth, in a great chafe, that any man for teaching of virtue, and virtuous action is comparable to him" (*Defence*, 200, ll. 342–52). Also see *Defence*, 235, ll. 935–44.

20. Also see Psalm 46, in which Herbert repeats the idea: "Our rock on Jacobs God wee found / Above the reach of harmes" (Sidney-Herbert *Psalms*, 110–11, ll. 23–24, 39–40).

21. Moses Maimonides, *The Guide of the Perplexed*, trans. Shlomo Pines, 2 vols. (Chicago: University of Chicago Press, 1963). All citations to the *Guide* are taken from this edition and are noted by Maimonides' book and chapter numbers followed by the volume and page numbers in the modern edition. The *Guide* was translated into Latin (from Arabic and Hebrew editions) by Agostino Giustiniani in Paris (1520) and later by Johannes Buxtorf the Younger in Basle (1629).

22. Maimonides thought that the great mysteries of life are not known: "We are like someone in a very dark night over whom lightening flashes time and time again." However, divine apprehension comes to each person according to his abilities, and "all this in equivocal terms so that the multitude might comprehend them according to the capacity of their understanding." Prophecy takes on a semblance of a divine revelation when "the prophet illuminates something sublime in sacred texts that can serve as a guide for those who aspire to their greatest possible perfection." See Maimonides, *Guide*, Introduction to Part I, 1: 7–10.

23. "It has been said that the world derives from the overflow of God and that He has caused to overflow to it everything in it that is produced in time. In the same way it is said that He caused His knowledge to overflow to the prophets" (Maimonides, *Guide*, I.69, 1: 169; II.12, 2: 279–80). See Menachem Kellner, *Dogma in Medieval Jewish Thought: From Maimonides to Abravanel* (Oxford, UK: Oxford University Press, 1986), 50–51. Also see Arthur M. Lesley, "The Place of the *Dialoghi d'Amore* in Contemporaneous Jewish Thought," in *Essential Papers on Jewish Culture in Renaissance and Baroque Italy*, ed. David B. Ruderman (New York: New York University Press, 1992), 170–88; and Arthur M. Lesley, "Proverbs, Figures, and Riddles: The Dialogues of Love as a Humanist Composition," in *The Midrashic Imagination: Jewish Exegesis, Thought, and*

History, ed. Michael Fishbane (Albany: State University of New York Press, 1993), 204–5.

24. This attribution of a holy spirit speaking prophecy is similar to both Joachim's theory of spiritual understanding, in which the Intellect "follows the Spirit" and informs the imagination to create its illumination, and the conception of the Shechinah in the works of later kabbalists. In Moses de Leon's (1250–1305) *Book of the Zohar* (c. 1280), the Shechinah is the divine presence within *Knesset Israel* and King David in the tenth *spheria, Malkut*. All references to the *Zohar* are from *The Zohar* (*Sefer Ha'zohar*), Pritzker ed., trans. Daniel C. Matt, 11 vols. (Stanford, CA: Stanford University Press, 2004– [later volumes still in press]).

25. Without the interaction of the rational faculty on the imaginative faculty, the sensual images produced by the imagination alone would be faulty. See Howard Kreisel, *Prophecy: The History of an Idea in Medieval Jewish Philosophy* (Dordrecht: Kluwer, 2001), 221–89.

26. "Human beings do not will themselves into a status of prophet, the divine will must inspire [initiate] the perfected person into the miraculous calling for prophet" (Maimonides, *Guide*, II.32, 2: 361–62).

27. The imagination retains things perceived by the senses in memory and combines them through its creative faculty (Maimonides, *Guide*, I.73, 1: 209–11). See Harold Bloom, *A Map of Misreading* (1975; rpt. Oxford, UK: Oxford University Press, 2003), 48. Also see Robert Gordis, *Poets, Prophets, and Sages: Essays in Biblical Interpretation* (Bloomington: Indiana University Press, 1971), 341.

28. See Arthur M. Lesley, *'The Song of Solomon's Ascents' by Yohanan Alemanno: Love and Human Perfection According to a Jewish Colleague of Giovanni Pico della Mirandola* (Ph.D. diss., University of California, Berkeley, 1976), 210. Also see B. C. Novak, "Giovanni Pico della Mirandola and Yohanan Alemanno," *Journal of the Warburg and Courtauld Institutes* 45 (1982): 130–32. Alemanno's influence on Pico's theories of love and interest in the Kabbalah are well known. Along with Yehudah Abravanel's (Leone Ebreo, 1460/1465–c. 1530) *Dialoghi d'Amore* they provide a traceable background to Sidney's concept of love and mystical union (*unio mystica*) with God in prophecy and in the Psalms.

29. See Seth Weiner, "Sidney and the Rabbis: A Note on the Psalms of David and Renaissance Hebraica," in *Sir Philip Sidney's Achievements*, ed. Michael J. B. Allen, Dominic Baker-Smith, Arthur F. Kinney, and Margaret M. Sullivan (New York: AMS Press, 1990), 161.

30. See Maurice Evans, "Divided Aims in the Revised Arcadia," in *Sir Philip Sidney and the Interpretation of Renaissance Culture: The Poet in His Time and in Ours*, ed. Gary Waller and Michael D. Moore (London: Croom Helm; and Totowa, NJ: Barnes & Noble, 1984), 34–36. Sidney's mythopoeic imagination produces a vision of his self-justification and worthiness before God in his version of the Psalms. See David Daiches, *God and the Poets: The*

Gifford Lectures, 1983 (Oxford, UK: Clarendon Press, 1984), 182; and Charles Russell, *Poets, Prophets, and Revolutionaries: The Literary Avant-Garde from Rimbaud Through Postmodernism* (New York: Oxford University Press, 1985), 19–23.

31. See Michael J. B. Allen, "Sidney's *Defence* and the Image Making of Plato's *Sophist*," in *Sir Philip Sidney's Achievements*, ed. Michael J. B. Allen, Dominic Baker-Smith, Arthur F. Kinney, and Margaret M. Sullivan (New York: AMS Press, 1990), 93–103.

32. See Daiches, *God and the Poets*, 56. Also see Francesco Petrarca, "Ascent of Mont Ventoux," trans. Hans Nachod, in *The Renaissance Philosophy of Man*, ed. Ernst Cassirer, Paul O. Kristeller, and John H. Randall Jr. (Chicago: University of Chicago Press, 1948), 42–44.

33. "Let the words of my mouth, and the meditation of my heart, be acceptable in thy sight, O Lord, my rock, and my redeemer" (Psalm 19:15; *KJB* 735).

34. See Russell, *Poets*, 27. Critical reason is a process of revealing and understanding social change and personal otherness (21–23). Also see Octavio Paz, *Children of the Mire*, trans. Rachel Philips (Cambridge, MA: Harvard University Press, 1974), 26; and Daiches, *God and the Poets*, 58, 60–61, 69.

35. See Jeffrey Macy, "Prophecy in al-Farabi and Maimonides: The Imaginative and Rational Faculties," in *Maimonides and Philosophy: Papers Presented at the Sixth Jerusalem Philosophical Encounter, May 1985*, ed. Shlomo Pines and Yirmiyahu Yovel (Dordrecht: Martinus Nijhoff, 1986), 185–201; and Howard Kreisel, *Maimonides' Political Thought: Studies in Ethics, Law, and the Human Ideal* (Albany: State University of New York Press, 1999), 63–92.

36. The world is a gigantic mirror that reflects spiritual beauty through which one can grasp divine intelligibles albeit in perplexing expressions. See Abraham Melamed, "The Transformation of the Love-of-the-Noble Motif in Albo, Alemanno, Judah Abravanel, and Moscato" (Hebrew), in *The Philosophy of Leone Ebreo: Four Lectures*, ed. Menachem Dorman and Ze'ev Levy (Haifa: Hakibbutz Hameuchad, 1985), 62–66.

37. Babylonian Talmud, Yebamoth 71a; Baba Mesi'a 31b.

38. Mikhail Bakhtin argues that language always exists in relation to another; they interact; they rewrite one another, and in doing so may deviate from one another and produce a complex and ideologically contrary text. Thus even the canonical "word of God" calls into question the notion of a finished or formally closable text. See Mikhail Bakhtin, *The Dialogic Imagination: Four Essays*, trans. Carl Emerson and Michael Holyquist (Austin: University of Texas Press, 1981), 47.

39. On the uniqueness of Moses's revelations, see Maimonides, *Guide*, II.35, 2: 367–8; II.37, 2: 373; and II.39, 2: 379–80.

40. Maimonides shows that one can find the use of "similitude" in Hosea 12:11; use of "parables" in Ezekiel 17:2 and 21:5; and "dark sayings" in Proverbs 1:5–6 (*Guide*, III.43, 2: 573).

41. Although Maimonides' works were considered controversial, they did influence the transmission of Rashi's exegeses. The well-known expression "from Moses to Moses there were none like Moses" evidences the importance of Maimonides' explications of biblical and Talmudic texts. See Ilil Arbel, *Maimonides: A Spiritual Biography* (New York: Crossroads/Herder & Herder, 2001); Yitzhak Avishur, *Shivchē ha-Rambam* (Praises of the Rambam) (Jerusalem: Magnes Press, 1998); Alfred Ivry, "Neoplatonic Currents in Maimonides' Thought," in *Perspectives on Maimonides*, ed. Joel. L. Kraemer (Oxford, UK: Oxford University Press, 1991), 135; and Daniel Boyarin, *Intertextuality and Reading of Midrash* (1990; rpt. Bloomington: Indiana University Press, 1994), 1–11.

42. Meister Eckhart (1260–1327/28), Nicholas of Cusa (1401–1464), Heinrich Cornelius Agrippa (1486–1535), Paracelsus (Theophrastus Bombastus von Hohenheim, 1493–1541), Jakob Böhme (1575–1624), and Angelus Silesius (1624–1677) argued that although Hebrew was a uniquely privileged language, it was corrupted by the Fall and only obscurely revelatory of the divine presence. See George Steiner, *After Babel: Aspects of Language and Translation*, 3rd ed. (Oxford, UK: Oxford University Press, 1994), 59–62.

43. Goodblatt, "High Holy Muse," 292–93. On the availability of the works of Rashi, Ibn Ezra, Kimhi, and other medieval rabbis to Christian scholars, see Louis Newman, *Jewish Influence on Christian Reform Movements* (1925; rpt. New York: Columbia University Press, 1966), 99. Also see Cecil Roth, "The Latin Renaissance and the Jewish Translators" and "The Christian Hebraists," in his *Jews in the Renaissance* (New York: Harper & Row [Harper Torchbook], 1965), 64–85 and 137–65. On the transmission of Jewish exegesis in the English Reformation, see David Daiches, *The King James Version of the English Bible* (Chicago: University of Chicago Press, 1941); Jason P. Rosenblatt, *Torah and the Law in Paradise Lost* (Princeton, NJ: Princeton University Press, 1994); Jason P. Rosenblatt, *Renaissance England's Chief Rabbi: John Seldon's Cultural Influence* (Oxford, UK: Oxford University Press, 2006); Chanita Goodblatt, "From 'Tav' to the Cross: John Donne's Protestant Exegesis and Polemics," in *John Donne and the Protestant Reformation*, ed. Mary Papazian (Detroit: Wayne State University Press, 2003), 221–46; and Chanita Goodblatt, *John Donne's Christian Hebraism: Written with the Finger of Man's Hand* (Pittsburgh, PA: Duquesne University Press, 2010).

44. Babylonian Talmud, Hullin 90a, Tamid 2a. See Maimonides, *Guide*, II.47, 2: 407–9. Allegorical interpretation based on philosophical and religious practice was used by Philo of Alexandria in the first century CE. See Gordis, *Poets*, 4–6, 17–19, 37.

45. See Moses Maimonides, *The Book of Knowledge*, ed. and trans. Moses Hyamson (Jerusalem: Feldheim, 1974), 92b. Also see Maimonides, *Guide*, III.52, 2: 620; and Maimonides, *The Codes of Maimonides (Mishnah Torah)*, bk. 2, *The Book of Love*, trans. Menachem Kellner (New Haven, CT: Yale University

Press, 2004), xiv and xvi. Whether or not the love of a woman stands in opposition to the love of God is a strongly debated issue in the *Guide*.

46. Maimonides follows Rashi's meaning of *dumiyyāh* as "silence," as in "to be silent." "Whoever multiplies Your praise, for which there is no end, only detracts from your praise." See Mayer I. Gruber, ed., *Rashi's Commentary on Psalms* (Leiden: Brill, 2004), 436–37. Abraham Ibn Ezra suggests that *dumiyyāh* derives from the verb *dāmāh* (wait), a point followed by David Kimhi. See David Kimhi, *The Commentary of Rabbi David Kimhi on Psalms CXX–CL*, ed. and trans. Joshua Baker and Ernest W. Nicholson (Cambridge, UK: Cambridge University Press, 1973), 5. It was also repeated by the translators of the Geneva Bible (*The Geneva Bible: A Facsimile of the 1560 Edition*, ed. Lloyd E. Berry [Madison: University of Wisconsin Press, 1969], 248a); by the translators of the King James Bible (1611) (New York: Watchtower Bible and Tract Society, n.d.), 537b; and in the Jewish English version, "Praise awaits thee, O God" (*KJB* 756).

47. Dante Alighieri (c. 1265–1321) uses a similar conceit as he attempts to contemplate the "supernal face" in the Empyrean: "What then I saw is more than tongue can say. / Our human speech is dark before the vision. / The ravished memory swoons and falls away. . . . I yearned to know just how our image merges / into that circle, and how it there finds place; / but mine were not the wings for such a flight. / Yet, as I wished, the truth I wished for came / Cleaving my mind in a great flash of light. / Here my powers rest from their high fantasy, / but already I could feel my being turned— / instinct and intellect balanced equally / as in a wheel whose motion nothing jars—by the Love that moves the Sun and the other stars" (*Paradiso*, trans. John Ciardi [New York: W. W. Norton, 1977], 599 [canto 33, ll. 55–58], 601 [canto 33, ll. 137–46]).

48. See Russell, *Poets*, 49, 51–54.

49. As Geoffrey Shepherd has noted, *energeia* is the emotional power of presenting subject matter, not so much limited to truth in words but to the vivid mental apprehension of the things themselves. Geoffrey Shepherd, ed., "Introduction," in *An Apology for Poetry* (London: Nelson, 1965), 55–61.

50. Pierre Macherey argues that the writer is not an autonomous producer of materials he expresses; he may be the material agent of writing, but the "great writer" is one whose writings reveal the contradictions of the language of his source texts and his own. Pierre Macherey, *A Theory of Literary Production*, trans. Geoffrey Wall (London: Routledge, 2006), 41. Also see Gary F. Waller, "The Rewriting of Petrarch: Sidney and the Language of Sixteenth-Century Poetry," in *Sir Philip Sidney and the Interpretation of Renaissance Culture: The Poet in His Time and in Ours*, ed. Gary Waller and Michael D. Moore (London: Croom Helm; and Totowa, NJ: Barnes & Noble, 1984), 80–81.

51. Astrophil declares: "What may words say, or what may words not say, / Where truth itself must speak like flattery?" (*Astrophil and Stella*, in *Sir Philip Sidney: The Major Works*, ed. Katherine Duncan Jones [Oxford, UK: Oxford University Press, 1989/2002], 166, 35:1–2). All citations to *Astrophil and Stella*

are taken from the Oxford edition. The indeterminacy of words, their lack of an absolute referent, reveals Astrophil's inability to enforce any single meaning on his language. Astrophil laments that "my words, I know do well set forth my mind; / My mind bemoans his sense of inward smart; / Such smart may pity claim of any heart" (*Astrophil and Stella*, 170, 44:1–3).

52. Margaret Ferguson, "Sidney's *A Defence of Poetry*: A Retrial," *Boundary* 2.7 (1979): 75, 79. Also see Jacqueline Miller, "'What May Words Say': The Limits of Language in *Astrophil and Stella*," in *Sir Philip Sidney and the Interpretation of Renaissance Culture: The Poet in His Time and in Ours*, ed. Gary Waller and Michael D. Moore (London: Croom Helm; and Totowa, NJ: Barnes & Noble, 1984), 95–99; Jacqueline Miller, "'Love doth hold my hand': Writing and Wooing in the Sonnets of Sidney and Spenser," *English Literary History* 46 (1979): 541–58; Murray Krieger, "Poetic Presence and Illusion I: Renaissance Theory and Duplicity of Metaphor," in his *Poetic Presence and Illusion: Essays in Critical History and Theory* (Baltimore: Johns Hopkins University Press, 1979), 13; and Richard Young, "English Petrarke: A Study of Sidney's *Astrophil and Stella*," in *Three Studies in the Renaissance: Sidney, Jonson, Milton*, Yale Studies in English 138 (New Haven, CT: Yale University Press, 1958), 55.

53. For an insightful analysis of Christian Hebraic motifs in Sidney's Psalm 6, see Goodblatt, "High Holy Muse," 293–98 (on Psalm 6 as a penitential psalm, 298).

54. George Steiner argues that all understanding is at the same time a misunderstanding; words are devalued between private and public aspects of language for which the imaginative and expressive resources of most men and women are limited (*After Babel*, 181–83, 193).

55. Sidney argues that the "purifying wit [of the poet]—this enriching of memory, enabling of judgment, and enlarging of conceit—which commonly we call learning, under what name soever it come forth, or to what immediate end soever it be directed, the final end is to lead and draw us to as high a perfection as our degenerate souls, made worse by their clayey lodgings, can be capable of" (*Defence*, 217–19, ll. 219–21 to ll. 292–98).

56. Such seems to be the intention behind the development of Tuscan Italian in the quatrocento of Dante and Petrarca, the sixteenth-century development of French by the Pléiade poets Du Bellay and Ronsard, and the linguistic experiments in English of Sidney and Edmund Spenser. See Russell, *Poets*, 24, 35–36.

57. In the *Defence* Sidney argues that writers must explore the truly excellent qualities of English. "I know some will say it is a mingled language. And why not so much the better, taking the best of both the other? Another will say it wanteth grammar. Nay truly, it hath that praise, that it wants not grammar: for grammar it might have, but it needs it not, being so easily in itself, and so void of those cumbersome differences of cases, genders, moods, and tenses, which I think was a piece of the Tower of Babylon's curse, that a man should be put to school to learn his mother tongue. But for the uttering sweetly and

properly the conceits of the mind (which is the end of speech), that hath it equally with any other tongue in the world; and is particularly happy in compositions of two or three words together, near the Greek, far beyond Latin, which is one of the greatest beauties can be in a language" (*Defence*, 248, ll. 1460–71).

58. See Daiches, *God and the Poets*, 60–61, 69.

59. Sidney is referring to Xenophon's *Cyropaedia*. "Xenophon's work was regularly used in the education of young princes, such as Edward IV and James VI of Scotland . . . as well as forming part of the curriculum of Shrewsbury School when Sidney was there." See *Sir Philip Sidney: The Major Works*, ed. Katherine Duncan-Jones (Oxford, UK: Oxford University Press, 2002), 374, no. 216, ll. 198, 220.

60. Barbara K. Lewalski, *Protestant Poetics and the Seventeenth-Century Religious Lyric* (Princeton, NJ: Princeton University Press, 1979), 4, 241. Also see Shannon Miller, "Mary Sidney and Gendered Strategies for the Writing of Psalms," in *Write or Be Written: Early Modern Women Poets and Cultural Constraints*, ed. Barbara Smith and Ursala Appelt (Aldershot, UK: Ashgate, 2001), 160–61, 163–70.

61. Herbert manipulates her equivocal language to transform the male Davidic psalmist and the female translator into a hermaphroditic poetic-prophetic voice of divine and human wisdom. See Herbert's translations of Psalms 45, 55, 61, 63, 64, 66, 71, 73, 77, 86, 88, 95, 102, 104, 107, 108, 109, 111, 116, 118, 130, 135, 136, 142, and 145.

62. M. H. Abrams, ed., *The Norton Anthology of English Literature*, 6th ed. (New York: W. W. Norton, 1993), v. 1, 1048.

63. On the principle of silence as a manifestation of piety and praise, see Maimonides, *Guide*, I.59, 1: 139. Also see Gruber, *Rashi's Commentary*, 436–37; and Kimhi, *Commentary on Psalms CXX–CL*, 5.

64. See Gruber, *Rashi's Commentary*, 698–99.

65. See Kimhi, *Commentary on Psalms CXX–CL*, 5.

66. See *The Book of Psalms from the Version of Miles Coverdale* (1535), in *The Great Bible of 1539* (London: Haymarket Press, 1930); *The Coverdale Bible* (1535) (Donetsk, Ukraine: StudyLight.org, 2003); and *Geneva Bible* (facsimile ed.), 263.

67. In the *Defence* Sidney also raised the problematic aspects of literary eloquence: "Eloquence appareled, or rather disguised, in a courtesan-like painted affectation: one time, with so far-fet words that may seem monsters but must seem strangers to any poor Englishman; another time, with coursing of a letter, as if they were bound to follow the method of a dictionary; another time, with figures and flowers, extremely winter-starved. But I would this fault were only peculiar to versifiers, and had not as large possession among prose-printers; and (which is to be marveled) among many scholars; and (which is to be pitied) among some preachers. . . . So these men bringing in such a kind of eloquence, well may they obtain an opinion of a seeming finesse, but persuade few—which should be the end of their finesse" (*Defence*, 246–47, ll. 1397–1444).

68. Meshech has many identities in the Bible: the son of Noah's son Jepheth (Genesis 10:2), the son of Shem (1 Chronicles 1:17), and a man identified with evil men (Ezekiel 32:26, 38:2–3, 39:1). Kedar also has several identities, one of which is as the son of Ishmael (Genesis 25:13); in addition, Isaiah prophesized against Kedar's archers (Isaiah 21:16–17), Jeremiah preached against Kedar as followers of false gods (Jeremiah 2:10), and Kedar's kingdom was destroyed by Nebuchadnezzar (Ezekiel 27:21, 49:28).

69. Plato, *Theaetetus*, trans. F. M. Cornford, in *Collected Dialogues of Plato*, ed. Edith Hamilton and Huntington Cairns, Bollingen Series 71 (New York: Bollingen Foundation, 1961), 881, 176a–c.

70. In his critique of Cicero, Petrarca argues: "Everything he [Cicero] displays with great care and eloquence. I wonder whether any writer ever treated these matters with greater heed and keener insight. And all this he does merely to lead us to this conclusion: whatever we behold with our eyes or perceive with our intellect is made by God for the well-being of man and governed by divine providence and counsel. . . . Cicero adds: 'We must believe that without the aid of God none of them was the man he was,' and 'without divine inspiration no one was ever a great man.'" Petrarca, "His Own Ignorance," 86–87. For Cicero's citations, see *De natura deorum*, ii.66. Also see Desiderius Erasmus, *The Education of a Christian Prince*, trans. and ed. Lester K. Born (New York: Columbia University Press, Octagon Books, 1965), 133–34, 140–42.

71. Intellectual perfection depends on antecedent moral perfection. Maimonides links moral perfection to *kedoshim* (holiness): "You shall be holy; for I the Lord your God am holy" (Leviticus 19:2). Also see Deuteronomy 6:5, Jeremiah 9:22–23, Micah 6:8, and Isaiah 35:5 ("then the eyes of the blind shall be opened, and the ears of the deaf shall be unstopped"). Maimonides' view of mitzvot affirms the superiority of intellectual and moral perfection over simple obedience to the commandments. See Menachem Kellner, *Maimonides on Human Perfection*, Brown University Judaic Studies 202 (Atlanta: Scholars Press, 1990), 41–43, 55–57, and 59–60.

72. See Julius Guttmann, *Philosophies of Judaism: The History of Jewish Philosophy from Biblical Times to Franz Rosenzweig*, trans. David W. Silverman (New York: Holt, Rinehart & Winston, 1964), 200.

73. See Hannay, "So May I," 106; and Hannay, *Philip's Phoenix*, 84–105. Also see W. Stanford Reid, "The Battle Hymns of the Lord: Calvinist Psalmody of the Sixteenth Century," *Sixteenth Century Essays and Studies* 2 (1971): 36–54; Prescott, "Evil Tongues," 163–86; and Rivka Zim, *English Metrical Psalms: Poetry as Praise and Prayer, 1553–1601* (Cambridge, UK: Cambridge University Press, 1987).

74. Variations in semantics and figurative imagery in ancient Hebrew, which created perplexing expressions used by David, Solomon, the prophets, and later writers of biblical "wisdom literature," were apparent in their historical periods.

9

Noam Flinker

Biblical and Rabbinic Intertextuality in George Herbert's "The Collar" and "The Pearl"

Although it is a commonplace of Herbert scholarship that there is a strong connection between his verse and the Bible, many scholars have been satisfied to make this observation in passing or else, in some important cases, to detail how specific biblical texts help us to understand Herbert's works. In most of these instances, however, Herbert's readers have regarded the Bible as a text primarily connected with doctrine and belief, a means of determining the nature of truth for the poet. In this essay I wish to widen the scope of the discussion in terms of intertextuality and some relevant implications of Julia Kristeva's presentation of that concept for reading Herbert. This will add to a theoretical view of the relative stability of Herbert's texts and likewise include associations between narratives and motifs in the Hebrew Bible and in the New Testament that are not explicitly connected to a doctrine or text that the poet mentions. Although scholars have long recognized the underlying Christian intertexts beneath the surface of Herbert's poetry, little attention has been given to indirect ways in which some of the Hebraic sources are submerged even deeper in the texture of his verse.

The intertextual echoes between the various books of the Bible itself are complex and multileveled. Centuries after the ancient Hebrew texts were first put together, postbiblical Jewish sources quote and interpret them for a variety of exegetical, doctrinal, and literary purposes. Likewise, the New Testament refers back to the Hebrew Bible, as do the early patristic writers. Any attempt to account for all the possible understandings of even a single biblical verse would thus present an individual reader with serious difficulty. A poet like Herbert often picked up some of these echoes and used them for his own purposes. In the analyses of "The Collar" and "The Pearl" that follow I trace a few of these indirect intertextual echoes in an effort to expand and extend the range of potential references examined by the various perceptive scholars who have treated these issues.

Recent accounts of the Hebrew Bible often stress the plethora of voices that can be heard, complicating the message conveyed by the text. Harold Toliver makes the obvious point that such a view of the Bible is clearly different from one that Herbert could have entertained: "He [i.e., Herbert] would have found strange, for instance, the proposition that the Hebrew Bible is an account of a developing nation governed by intricate codes and laws similar in ideology to other mesopotamian countries."[1] Likewise, the claims of Michael Fishbane would have been quite foreign to Herbert: "We shall explore some of the types of textual interpretation in ancient Israel—that is, within the Hebrew Bible itself—paying particular attention to how the texts that comprise it were revised and even reauthorized during the course of many centuries, and to how older traditions fostered new insights which, in turn, thickened the intertextual matrix of the culture and conditioned its imagination."[2] On the other hand, the meticulous care with which Meir Sternberg treats "the striking systemacity of biblical narrative" might not have surprised the poet.[3] That is, one must distinguish between the various voices that contributed to the formation of a text and the way in which these were carefully shaped and edited at some later date.

Although the general concept of intertextuality is much broader than many of its applications I wish to consider, there is an important level at which the concept as developed by Kristeva is quite relevant. Jonathan Culler explains that "literary works are to be considered not as autonomous entities, 'organic wholes,' but as intertextual constructs: sequences which have meaning in relation to other texts which they take up, cite, parody, refute, or generally transform. A text can be read only in relation to other texts, and it is made possible by the codes which animate the discursive space of a culture."[4] Kristeva's concept stipulates that "the passage from one signifying system to another demands a new articulation of the thetic—of enunciative and denotative positionality. If one grants that every signifying practice is a field of transpositions of various signifying systems (an inter-textuality), one then understands that its 'place' of enunciation and its denoted 'object' are never single, complete, and identical to themselves, but always plural, shattered, capable of being tabulated."[5] All texts then evince the conflicts and tensions of the different levels on which they convey message or meaning. They likewise reflect the various tensions implicit in the very nature of signification: oedipal, spiritual, sexual, and so on.

Kristeva's notion of shattered texts is relevant to a discussion of the psychic and spiritual makeup of the speakers in poems by George Herbert. In a review of Kristeva's *La Révolution du langage poétique* Philip Lewis examines her view that "the poetic subject is a dialectical process in which the structured language of the ego comes into contact with a violent, heterogeneous force which is its ground, with the flow of psychic instincts."[6] With regard to Herbert this means that the speakers in his poems can be understood as describing aspects of their lives in language that communicates some specific event or experience to the reader. The very words they use, however, likewise call up biblical events that convey their meaning on an intertextual level. This availability of various signifying systems in Herbert's verse implies, from this perspective, a series of instinctual conflicts that to some extent destabilize the writing and the poetic voices. The plural, multivoiced intertextualities of Kristeva point to the conflicted world beneath the surface of Herbert's verse. This, of course, is what most readers assume about Herbert and his work, but it provides a textual means to acknowledge it. I would argue, however, that Herbert was conscious of this yet nevertheless managed to shape his intertextualities in poetic ways that suited him, his moods, and his texts. His work is not unlike the Hebrew Bible, which can be read as a record of the struggles of conflicting ancient texts that suggest a multiplicity of voices but can likewise be seen from the perspective of the editor or redactor who found ways to accommodate the original texts into the systemacity on which Sternberg insists. If this is ultimately based on a conflicted and unstable human personality, so much the better for the verisimilitude of the textual experience. A calm, simple view of Herbert as a personality contributes little to an understanding of his complexly fascinating poems.

A good deal of fruitful scholarly attention has been given to Herbert's use of the Hebrew Bible. Mary Ellen Rickey, Rosemond Tuve, Joseph H. Summers, Arnold Stein, Coburn Freer, Stanley Fish, Barbara Lewalski, Barbara Leah Harman, Richard Strier, Chana Bloch, Gene E. Veith, Stanley Stewart, and Harold E. Toliver are only a few of the important critics of Herbert who have treated his use of biblical materials in depth.[7] Likewise, some recent attention has been given to Herbert's attitudes toward the Jews, which I discuss later. My concern, however, is to consider the largely unconscious intertextual connections in Herbert's verse that echo earlier Hebraic texts and in some cases seem almost unaware of the voices that lie beneath so many biblical passages. For every verse from either the Hebrew Bible or the New Testament that critics claim Herbert might have had in mind, there are countless others that may or may not have deliberate echoes in a specific poem. It is striking that some of these possibilities are acknowledged in Herbert's prose discussion of the duties of a country parson. In the discussions that follow I move from echoes that are explicitly relevant to Herbert to those whose aptness might have surprised even the poet himself.

Herbert makes the intertextual possibilities of biblical texts quite explicit in his prose work, *A Priest to the Temple, Or, The Countrey Parson.* In his chapter on "The Parsons Knowledg" he comments on how the parson should read scripture and recommends:

> a diligent Collation of Scripture with Scripture. For all Truth being consonant to it self, and all being penn'd by one and the selfsame Spirit, it cannot be, but that an industrious, and judicious comparing of place with place must be a singular help for the right understanding of the Scriptures. To this may be added the consideration of any text with the coherence thereof, touching what goes before, and what follows after, as also the scope of the Holy Ghost.[8]

This method of reading is crucial for understanding Herbert. It suggests that, like the country parson, readers should collate different biblical texts to understand their significance, but it implies that this is likewise a useful way to approach Herbert's own poetry. The final words of the passage require that in addition to the meaning of any specific biblical text, we should consider what precedes and what follows it. In the explications that follow, I try to apply this method to my reading of Herbert's "Collar" and then extend it further to include the relevance of rabbinic parallels to the parable of the pearl in Matthew (13:45–46) as relevant to Herbert's "Pearl."

Before proceeding with the poems, however, I want to illustrate the method with an example of biblically charged language from the text of Herbert's *Countrey Parson.* In Chapter 8, "The Parson on Sundays," Herbert is discussing the way the parson should communicate with his flock outside the church. He would have those who cannot or will not follow the message of the sermon preached earlier in church approached in different ways, so as to make the words and example of the parson clarify the deeper meaning of his message.

> The rest of the day he spends either in reconciling neighbours that are at variance, or in visiting the sick, or in exhortations to some of his flock by themselves, whom his Sermons cannot, or doe not reach. And every one is more awaked, when we come, and say, *Thou art the man.* This way he findes exceeding usefull, and winning; and these exhortations he cals his privy purse, even as

> Princes have theirs, besides their publick disbursments. (Herbert, *Works*, 236)

As John Wall suggests in a short note in his edition of *The Country Parson* and *The Temple*, Herbert expects his reader to recognize the biblical language in the phrase "Thou art the man."[9] The words are those of Nathan the prophet (2 Samuel 12:7), when he decided to confront King David, who had slept with Bathsheba, the wife of Uriah the Hittite, and subsequently arranged for the husband to be killed in battle. Nathan told David a parable about a rich man who took unfair advantage of his poor neighbor, and when David indignantly demanded that the man be punished, Nathan made it clear that the king himself was the subject of the parable: "Thou art the man," Nathan exclaimed. Herbert comments on Nathan's manner of speaking in a later passage.

> Those that the Parson findes idle, or ill imployed, he chides not at first, for that were neither civill, nor profitable; but always in the close, before he departs from them: yet in this he distinguisheth; for if he be a plaine countryman, he reproves him plainly; for they are not sensible of finenesse: if they be of higher quality, they commonly are quick, and sensible, and very tender of reproof: and therefore he lays his discourse so, that he comes to the point very leasurely, and oftentimes, as *Nathan* did, in the person of another, making them to reprove themselves. (Herbert, *Works*, 248)

Thus the biblical narrative of 2 Samuel 12 serves Herbert both as a source with which to charge his own language with biblical significance and as a model for pastoral work. Nevertheless, the reader must recognize the phrase "Thou art the man," and then its narrative context needs to be probed. Doing so explains the significance of Herbert's reference to Nathan's "leasurely" or parabolic style. The prophet tells the king a story about "the person of another" with a moral point that is not immediately clear to the listener. David is so taken with Nathan's narrative that he responds intuitively with no apparent sense of its implications with regard to his own situation. When Nathan finally reaches his conclusion, David is mortified and has no choice but to confess his sin. This kind of close examination of a biblical text with the explicit relevance of the narrative that surrounds it is similar to the mode of reading Herbert's poetry used in this essay. It is not, however, much like most other treatments of Herbert's use of the Bible in that it concerns biblical narrative rather than theology or belief.

"The Collar"

Herbert's well-known poem "The Collar" recounts the momentary rebellion of a speaker who wants to enjoy the ordinary pleasures of earthly life rather than submit to the disciplines required of a Christian clergyman. His language is wild and excited as Herbert's persona rebukes himself for past failures to enjoy this world.

> I Struck the board, and cry'd, No more.
>   I will abroad.
>   What? Shall I ever sigh and pine?
> My lines and life are free, free as the rode,
>   Loose as the winde, as large as store.
> . . . .
>   Sure there was wine
> Before my sighs did drie it: there was corn
>   Before my tears did drown it.

The poem concludes in a very different spirit as the speaker suddenly imagines that in the midst of this tirade he hears a softly chiding voice.

> But as I rav'd and grew more fierce and wilde
>   At every word,
> Me thoughts I heard one calling, *Child!*
>   And I reply'd, *My Lord.*
>
>   (Herbert, *Works*, 153–54)

Perceptive critics have often shown just how many of these lines support the Christian resolution of the conclusion long before the speaker has heard the voice and responded. The wine, along with the corn that he could have enjoyed, suggests, we are told, the Eucharist. The freedom of the road becomes a kind of Via Dolorosa from a Christian perspective. That is, beneath the surface of the speaker's tirade lies a deeper understanding of the Christian significance of what he is trying to embrace for its simple, sensuous appeal.[10]

In addition to the implicit Christianity in such images, however, there are other biblical echoes with associations that are closely aligned to the speaker's mood before he hears the voice calling "Child." Corn and wine recur together throughout the Hebrew Bible, generally in the context of indicators of prosperity and material well-being. A series of passages from the book of Deuteronomy makes this clear. When Moses tells the Israelites of the material benefits associated with obedience to God, he uses corn and wine to illustrate: "And he will love thee, and bless thee, and multiply thee: he will also bless the fruit of thy womb, and the fruit of thy land, thy *corn*, and thy *wine*, and thine oil, the increase of thy kine, and the flocks of thy sheep, in the land which he sware unto thy fathers to give thee" (emphasis added).[11] An implicit connection is set up between religious observance and the fullness of earthly pleasure that will follow such practice: "Thou shalt observe the feast of tabernacles seven days, after that thou hast gathered in thy *corn* and thy *wine*" (Deuteronomy 16:13; emphasis added). Likewise, when Moses wishes to emphasize the terrible consequences of disobedience, he threatens his listeners with the loss of their material possessions, as symbolized by the absence of corn and wine: "And he shall eat the fruit of thy cattle, and the fruit of thy land, until thou be destroyed: which also shall not leave thee either *corn*, *wine*, or oil, or the increase of thy kine, or flocks of thy sheep, until he have destroyed thee" (Deuteronomy 28:51; emphasis added).

Often, however, such straightforward reference to material well-being appears in a more complex context. Isaac blesses his son Jacob (thinking that he is Esau): "Therefore God give thee of the dew of heaven, and the fatness of the earth, and plenty of corn and wine" (Genesis 27:28). There is surely an irony here because Isaac does not know that he is addressing Jacob and not Esau. By providing his second son with the blessing he thought he was giving to his favorite, Isaac is perpetuating the dysfunction of his relationship with his wife and sons. When he gives the blessing for corn and wine to Jacob, Isaac is contributing to the growing fraternal strife between his sons and apparently attempting to hurt or anger Rebecca, his wife. He then goes on to spell out the implications of his blessing: "Let people serve thee, and nations bow down to thee: be lord over thy brethren, and let thy mother's sons bow down to thee: cursed be every one that curseth thee, and blessed be every one that blesseth thee" (Genesis 27:29).

This passage in Genesis can evoke different responses. A simplistic reading might regard the story as a glorification of Rebecca and Jacob, who may seem to be anticipating God's wishes for the future. The conflict between Jacob and Esau might then appear as part of the divine plan. Clearly, however, such a reading ignores the many problems implicit in the narrative. Why does Jacob resort to trickery to gain his father's blessing? Why does Isaac frame his blessing in such a discriminatory manner? The material well-being signified by corn and wine did not have to be something reserved for only one of the brothers. Isaac needlessly chooses to impose his desire for Esau's dominance over Jacob onto the blessing and thus manages to hurt his favorite and incite even more fraternal strife. The pain this causes Esau is plain enough in the ensuing colloquy.

> "Hast thou not reserved a blessing for me?" And Isaac answered and said unto Esau: "Behold, I have made him thy lord, and all his brethren have I given to him for servants; and with corn and wine have I sustained him; and what shall I do now unto thee, my son?" And Esau said unto his father: "Hast thou but one blessing, my father? bless me, even me also, O my father." And Esau lifted up his voice, and wept. And Isaac his father answered and said unto him: Behold, thy dwelling shall be the fatness of the earth, and of the dew of heaven from above; And by thy sword shalt thou live, and shalt serve thy brother; and it shall come to pass when thou shalt have the dominion, that thou shalt break his yoke from off thy neck. And Esau hated Jacob because of the blessing wherewith his father blessed him. (Genesis 27:36–41)

It is not insignificant that in the aftermath of this story both Esau and Jacob prosper. Isaac believes that his blessing will deny corn and wine to one of his sons, but this does not come to be. On the other hand, Jacob clearly internalizes his father's favoritism and allows his own preference for his son Joseph to incite the same sort of fraternal hatred that Isaac and Rebecca allow to develop between their sons. The material concern for corn and wine becomes an excuse for playing favorites with love, which almost causes the deaths of Jacob (at the hands of Esau) and of Joseph (at the hands of his brothers). In a later biblical text it is the psalmist who sums up a biblical perspective about the distinction between the pleasures of material wealth and a more spiritual kind of joy: "Thou hast put gladness in my heart, more than in the time that their *corn* and their *wine* increased" (Psalm 4:7; emphasis added).

These biblical passages all shed light on Herbert's poem. The desire of the rebellious speaker to indulge in wine and corn first appears as a natural rejection of asceticism. The speaker wants to enjoy the wine and the corn and believes that he has hitherto ruined these delights. He decides that he will recover all his "sigh-blown age / On double pleasures." The speaker's rhetoric justifies the pursuit of material delight (double pleasures), even though it should be clear that such a life would be less than satisfying. The biblical intertexts help to clarify this. Isaac's misuse of the blessing for bread and wine almost leads to disaster. It takes the spiritual insight of the psalmist to point to the redemptive possibilities in these symbols of material well-being. The contexts from the Hebrew Bible thus help to explain and articulate the apparently abrupt shift in Herbert's speaker as the dramatic action of the poem brings him back to God.

The issue that needs attention here concerns the relationship between different signifying systems at work in Herbert's verse. Leah Harman has isolated a series of texts by Herbert that she describes as "'collapsing poems'—speakers both protect and dismantle their own narratives, and because they do they raise questions about the values we attach to stories, about the costs we are willing to support in order to maintain them, and about the difficulties we undergo when stories fail to represent us in traditional ways."[12] She views poems such as "The Collar" as failing to provide what she describes as "adequate self-representation."[13] Nevertheless Harman points to biblical materials in other Herbert texts that function in a manner similar to the intertextuality of "The Collar": "The alignment of biblical with personal stories provides, in other words, access to representation, though it is in the nature of such representation that it makes persons inseparable from the sequences they join."[14] Likewise, I would argue, the intertextual echoes in "The Collar" connect personal narrative with biblical ones and, in so doing, help to prevent the collapsing Harman discerns. The speaker's concern for the loss of corn and wine connects him with the fate of the Israelites if they fail to observe the "commandments of the Lord." He is likewise associated with the dysfunctional behavior of Isaac and Jacob. The biblical intertext from Psalms provides an implicit corrective that acts to deepen the dramatic conclusion of the poem. As the speaker replies "My Lord," he has unconsciously followed the lead of the psalmist in rejecting the materiality of the corn and wine, just as he more consciously identifies with their eucharistic suggestiveness.

The echoes of Genesis and the Psalms in the language of wine and corn thus provide fragments of an earlier culture that begin by supporting the psychic destabilization and rebellion of the speaker. The materiality of the language of "The Collar" sets up echoes of a subversion of the final vision without which the poem cannot function. In the end, however, the intertextual echoes help to support the final resolution of the poem. They call into question any simple reading but, in so doing, point to the intensity of the reader's experience.

"The Pearl"

Although my point in this essay concerns Hebraic intertexts that Herbert may not have considered explicitly, it is, perhaps, not irrelevant that his attitudes toward the Jews were more sympathetic than those of most seventeenth-century Englishmen. Scholars such as Harold Fisch have made this point: "George Herbert's poem, 'The Jews' with its extremely cordial opening lines . . . is to my knowledge the first clearly sympathetic reference to post-biblical Jews in the annals of English Literature."[15] Ariane M. Balizet has extended this somewhat: "In his poetry, Herbert confronts all aspects of Jews in the English cultural imagination, falling prey to prejudice and vilification of Jews even as he offers nuanced and even sympathetic depictions."[16] She cites John Donne's famous sonnet that begins "Spit in my face yee Jewes" as an illustration of the ordinary "villainous" representation of Jews in seventeenth-century England.[17]

Greg Miller likewise discusses what he calls Herbert's "philo-semitism" and concludes, "Though in comparison with his contemporaries Herbert reads Jews and Jewish history sympathetically, criticizing Christians for their easy pride, his imaginative sympathies are nevertheless seriously limited."[18] A significant indicator of Herbert's views can be seen in the poem that immediately precedes "The Collar" in *The Temple.* In "The Jews" the speaker pities them, writing:

> POore nation, whose sweet sap and juice
> Our cyens have purloin'd, and left you drie:
> Whose streams we got by the Apostles sluce,
> And use in baptisme, while ye pine and die:
> Who by not keeping once, became a debter;
> And now by keeping lose the letter.
> (Herbert, *Works*, 152)

That is, Christians can be saved while the Jews "pine and die" without benefit of Christian salvation. Herbert is sympathetic to the situation of the Jews but remains convinced of their fate as rejecters of Christianity.

Although this might indeed have been Herbert's attitude toward the Jews, some of his poems remain strikingly open to readings that depend to some extent on Jewish texts, rabbinic as well as biblical. In what follows I develop my argument on the basis of Herbert's "Pearl." Before doing so, however, a brief summary of some of the complex issues about Herbert and biblical scholarship will prove useful.

David S. Katz has sketched out the parameters of sixteenth- and early-seventeenth-century Christian Hebraism in Europe and Britain. He points to the important contributions to the study of Hebrew in Tudor and Jacobean England by Jews who converted to Christianity. He goes on, however, to indicate that "it was only several generations later, by the outbreak of the English Civil War in the 1640s that English scholars were ready to expand their interests in any sort of systematic way to include other aspects of the Jewish tradition, both the kabbalah (Jewish mysticism) and the Talmud (the 'oral' law)."[19] These later developments were published too late to have been relevant for Herbert. Nevertheless, Joseph Mede, a renowned biblical scholar and Hebraist, was an older contemporary at Cambridge while Herbert was there, and the two may have been in contact. Mede's copy of Johannes Buxtorf's *Biblia Sacra Hebraica & Chaldaica cum Masora* may have interested Herbert and could have provided access to Hebraic sources.[20]

Chauncey Wood has recently discussed Herbert's ownership of a rare sixteenth-century Latin commentary on the Gospels by Lucas Franciscus Brugensis.[21] This work includes a great deal of information about classical and Hebraic contexts relevant for understanding the Gospels in general and Matthew in particular. For example, early in his Gospel, Matthew tells how "many of the Pharisees and Sadducees" came to see John baptizing in the Jordan (Matthew 3:7). Brugensis devotes almost two entire pages to a detailed description of the significance of these terms, including their Hebrew roots, meanings, and historical contexts up through the early first century CE. His discussion makes it clear that his expertise about the period (including many of the somewhat arcane Jewish subtexts) was wide and deep. On the other hand, he is careful to avoid any reference to later Jewish developments that are likewise relevant. This seems to have been a practice that he maintained throughout his commentary. Brugensis clarifies his agenda in a key sentence in the "Prolegomena" to his commentary: "Disputationes denique longas, siue de explicandis dogmatis ecclesiasticis, siue de refellendis haeresibus, euitauimus, nec nisi coacti aliquando breuibus perstrinximus huiusmodi"[22] (In sum, we avoided long disputations, whether about explaining church dogmas or about refuting heresies, and unless occasionally forced with short *remarks*, we did not criticize *matters* of this sort).[23] I take this to mean that Brugensis knows much more than he writes but wishes to avoid matters of dogma. He does not criticize ("nec . . . perstrinximus") issues that might open him to controversy that he wishes to avoid.

The approach of Brugensis is even clearer as reflected in Matthew Poole's massive *Synopsis Criticorum Aliorumque*. Poole collected various comments by different early modern scholars and identified his sources with minimal marginal notes. For example, where Matthew describes how "Jesus went about all Galilee, teaching in their synagogues" (Matthew 4:23), Poole cites a comment by Brugensis to the effect that the Jews had one Temple but numerous synagogues, often with many in a single town. When it comes to a more detailed account of the synagogue and the practices associated with it, Poole must go elsewhere, citing Abraham Scultetus (1566–1625) and Maimonides as well as various Talmudic passages.[24]

In short, one can document Herbert's potential familiarity with Hebraic sources relevant to the times of Jesus and before. The much more complicated question of Herbert's familiarity with rabbinic materials remains speculative. As Katz suggests, Poole's work did not appear until later in the seventeenth century (1669), as did John Lightfoot's *Horae Hebraicae et Talmudicae. Impensae I. In Chorographiam aliquam terrae Israeliticae II. In Evangelium S. Matthae* (Hebrew and Talmudical exercitations upon . . . Matthew) (1658), and even John Selden's important publications on rabbinic materials did not appear until just after Herbert had died. Herbert might have had access to Talmudic works and to the commentaries of Maimonides and others through Joseph Mede, but there is no clear indication that this was the case. It is nevertheless crucial to note that Jewish texts, such as those to be discussed later, were available for curious readers during the late seventeenth century and perhaps before. Not unlike the biblical materials that reverberate in a poem such as "The Collar," their intertextual pressures would have simultaneously threatened the stability and orthodoxy of the works of such men as Brugensis and Herbert while lending extra textual support for the insights they provided.

In light of all this, Herbert's oft anthologized "The Pearl. Matth. 13:45" raises a series of fascinating issues and problems. In this poem Herbert sets up a hermeneutic struggle to determine the spiritual meaning of a valuable stone. The reference to Matthew in the title is to a passage where Jesus compares the kingdom of heaven to "a merchant man seeking goodly pearls: who when he had found one pearl of great price, went and sold all that he had and bought it" (Matthew 13:45–46). This parable surely echoes the many references to pearls in rabbinic literature. The language and images that Jesus used must have reflected the oral traditions of his contemporaries and teachers. It is, however, quite difficult to document this orality exactly. Although many of the comments, ideas, and conversations of the classical rabbis were eventually written down, the original date and version is almost impossible to determine. A text that first appears in the Babylonian Talmud, which was most probably first preserved in written form as late as the sixth century CE, might reflect an oral tradition dating back hundreds of years.

The classical rabbis were concerned with connections between material things and the elusive world of the spirit. They made different kinds of references to pearls. In some cases the gems are part of a discussion of down-to-earth material value. In one passage they treat the question of the shifting values of a thing like a pearl in terms of geographic location. The pearl might be worth more in a city than in a small town.[25] More relevant to Matthew's Gospel, however, are parables told by various rabbis. In many cases the pearls are part of a comparison between material wealth and faith or knowledge of the Torah. In one passage it is reported that R. Joshua asked some younger colleagues about new developments in recent Torah discussions. At first they claimed that nothing could compare to R. Joshua's learning, but he insisted on hearing of the discussion.

> He said to them, "And what was the topic of the narrative today?" They said to him, "It was the passage that begins, Assemble the people, the men, women, and children" (Deut. 31:12); He said to them, "And what did he expound in that connection?" They said to him, "This is how he interpreted it: 'The men come to learn, the women to listen, but why do the children come? It is to provide the occasion for the gaining of a reward for those who bring them.'" He said to them, "You had a good pearl in your hands, and you wanted to make me lose it."[26]

In these expressions the rabbis are using the pearl as a referent for hermeneutic insight. The valuable stone connects the world of material culture to that of scriptural interpretation. For the rabbis this was not a movement from one world to another but a perception of the interconnectedness of the various levels of God's creation.

Other "pearls" in various traditional explanations expand the possibilities of the metaphor. Most striking is a comment on a passage from the Song of Songs: "Thy two breasts are like two young roes that are twins, which feed among the lilies" (4:5). The rabbis explain that the breasts of the beloved really refer to Moses and Aaron. This allegorical explanation does not, however, look away from the breasts. For the Midrash explains: "Just as the breasts are the beauty and the ornament of a woman, so Moses and Aaron were the beauty and ornament of Israel."[27] This pattern repeats itself in terms of charm, glory and pride, abundance of milk, and so on. Finally R. Akiba is quoted, when he explains: "They were like two fine pearls belonging to a king which he put in a balance, finding that neither weighed down the other. So were Moses and Aaron just equal."[28]

The various levels of the allegory are interconnected. The pearls are material things known for their beauty and value but likewise associated with the spirituality of the Torah. There is then a continuum between the flesh and sexuality of the breasts, the balanced beauty of the pearls, and Moses and Aaron. The woman and the pearls are real, but they also signify something higher. This is part of the insight of Jesus in his parable. He focuses on the attraction of the pearl for the merchant but then emphasizes the leap to the higher level. When he found the pearl, the merchant "sold all that he had, and bought it." Jesus focuses on the way in which the valuable pearl points to something else that requires his followers to reject the world of materiality and embrace a spiritual reality. Nevertheless, the way to that reality is through the materiality of the pearl.

Chauncey Wood regards "The Pearl" as a poem about relinquishment of this world. He sees the commentary of Brugensis on Matthew 13:45 in terms of metaphor: "For Lucas, the Kingdom of Heaven is not to be bought as the Merchant bought pearls, but rather purchased in a metaphorical way."[29] Brugensis is quite specific about avoiding the materiality of the language of the parable. As Wood points out, he uses words such as *emere* (purchase) and *pretium* (price) but does so "in order to stress their metaphorical nature."[30] This approach should be associated with Brugensis's avoidance of the specific rabbinic context in which Jesus couched his parable. Herbert probably could not have realized this. Nevertheless, "The Pearl" requires its readers to focus on the materiality of the title and on the way in which the body of the poem avoids the image. Wood may be right about relinquishment here, but even that depends on the literal jewel in the rabbinic parable.

The same is the point in Herbert's poems. In "The Collar" the stuff of rebellion is dramatically juxtaposed against the speaker's perception of the one who calls. Still the richness of the poem is in its imagery and rhetoric of rebellion. "The Pearl" sets up a contrast between what the speaker knows of the world and his wish to love God. The poem is primarily concerned with what the speaker knows: "Learning," "Honour," "Pleasure," and all the experiences he connects to these abstractions. At the end of each stanza, however, Herbert clarifies that he chooses God over everything previously described, writing "Yet I love thee." One can argue that the need to distinguish between the material world and God is clear in the poem but not necessarily in terms of the rabbinic parable. Although the "fine pearl" of R. Joshua is available to anyone willing to listen to the thoughts of the other rabbis, in Matthew it is necessary to sell everything to buy the valuable pearl. Herbert continues this dichotomy and articulates the awareness of the value of learning, honor, and pleasure even as he subsequently rejects them for God. Nevertheless, beneath the surface of the poem one can sense the availability of the other material possibilities of the pearl. Herbert begins with what we would call the humanities: "the wayes of Learning" in terms of rationality and nature shaped ("spunne") into laws and politics.

> I Know the wayes of Learning; both the head
> And pipes that feed the presse, and make it runne;

What reason hath from nature borrowed,
Or of it self, like a good huswife, spunne
In laws and policie; what the starres conspire,
What willing nature speaks, what forc'd by fire;
Both th' old discoveries, and the new-found seas,
The stock and surplus, cause and historie;
All these stand open, or I have the keyes:
  Yet I love thee.
    (Herbert, *Works*, 88–89)

Herbert touches on stars, nature, and recent navigational discoveries, recognizing that he has the wherewithal (the "keyes") to experience all this. When he avers, "Yet I love thee," the immediate impression is that he has somehow rejected all for the love of God. On the other hand, however, nine of the ten lines in the stanza are devoted to the details of learning. There is no explicit mention of a specific pearl, but the reference to Matthew 13 in the title makes it clear that the parable of Jesus is meant in some way to shape or direct the poem. The materiality of the pearl is silently present in the accounts of "Learning" and subsequently of "Honour" and "Pleasure." The rabbinic analogues to the pearl of Jesus provide an important context for articulating this silence. Like the imagery of Herbert's poem, the concluding leap to love of God requires an awareness of the literal appeal of the pearl, just as the various rabbinic contexts suggest.

The oral tradition within which Jesus was operating provides important cultural contexts for understanding his parable. Pharisaic Judaism juxtaposed the written Torah (Pentateuch) with the oral interpretation that developed about it. There was even a claim that both of these Torahs had been revealed to Moses on Mount Sinai. In the context of first-century Jewish culture this means that intertextual echoes of other uses of pearl imagery would have been available in one form or another. In the context of seventeenth-century England it is likewise clear that some of Herbert's contemporaries (e.g., Abraham Scultetus, John Selden, John Lightfoot, and Matthew Poole) were intensely interested in rabbinic echoes in the Gospels. Although Brugensis appears to have imposed a silence about this in the commentary that Herbert owned, the poet was not necessarily unaware of these traditions. In any case the Brugensian effort to silence the rabbinic traditions would nevertheless have had its effect on the intertextual tensions in his commentary and thus on the cultural world of his readers. The different echoes of the pearl in Matthew's Gospel constitute what Kristeva might see as part of the plural and shattered instinctual conflicts that result from the presence of different signifying systems in the same text. On this level the effort to silence a system must be reflected in the text.

The intertextual echoes of the Hebrew Bible and rabbinic lore are clearly of distinctly different levels of intensity. It is quite reasonable to assume that Herbert would have heard the echoes of Genesis and the Psalms in the language of wine and corn. The chances that he was conscious of the pearls of rabbis such as Yehoshua and Akiba are much slimmer. On the other hand, the materiality of the language of "The Collar" and "The Pearl" sets up echoes of a subversion of the final vision without which the poems cannot function. In the end the intertextual echoes help to destabilize the poems just enough to convey their dramatic intensity and power. Whether or not Herbert was aware of the rabbinic echoes of the parable, his title makes it difficult to avoid the insights of the rabbis, who were more concerned with the movement from materiality to spirituality than with disregarding the physical source of the insight. The intertextual echoes thus call into question any simple reading of the poems but, in so doing, help to articulate the intensity of the reader's experience.

Notes

1. Harold E. Toliver, *George Herbert's Christian Narrative* (University Park: Pennsylvania State University Press, 1993), 19–20.

2. Michael Fishbane, "Inner Biblical Exegesis: Types and Strategies of Interpretation in Ancient Israel," in *Midrash and Literature*, ed. Geoffrey H. Hartman and Sanford Budick (New Haven, CT: Yale University Press, 1986), 20.

3. Meir Sternberg, *The Poetics of Biblical Narrative: Ideological Literature and the Drama of Reading* (Bloomington: Indiana University Press, 1985), 11.

4. Jonathan Culler, *The Pursuit of Signs: Semiotics, Literature, Deconstruction* (Ithaca, NY: Cornell University Press, 1981), 38.

5. Julia Kristeva, *Revolution in Poetic Language*, trans. Margaret Waller (New York: Columbia University Press, 1984), 60.

6. Philip E. Lewis, "Review: Revolutionary Semiotics," *Diacritics* 4.3 (1974): 31.

7. Mary Ellen Rickey, in *Utmost Art: Complexity in the Verse of George Herbert* (Lexington: University of Kentucky Press, 1966), deals with the complex mix of classical and biblical materials in Herbert's poems. Rosemond Tuve, in *A Reading of George Herbert* (Chicago: University of Chicago Press, 1952), is primarily concerned with Roman Catholic religious traditions in relation to Herbert. Both Joseph H. Summers (*George Herbert: His Religion and Art* [1954; rpt. Binghamton, NY: Medieval and Renaissance Texts and Studies, 1981]) and Arnold Stein (*George Herbert's Lyrics* [Baltimore: Johns Hopkins University Press, 1968]) trace many biblical sources that they use (quite differently) to analyze the complexity of Herbert's verse. Coburn Freer, in *Music for a King:*

George Herbert's Style and the Metrical Psalms (Baltimore: Johns Hopkins University Press, 1972), focuses on Herbert's use of the Psalms. In the course of articulating his thesis about Herbert and catechizing in *The Living Temple: George Herbert and Catechizing* (Berkeley: University of California Press, 1978), Stanley Fish often refers back to biblical passages. Barbara Lewalski's monumental *Protestant Poetics and the Seventeenth-Century Religious Lyric* (Princeton, NJ: Princeton University Press, 1979) presents a detailed account of Herbert's use of biblical models for many of his poems. Barbara Leah Harman's *Costly Monuments: Representations of the Self in George Herbert's Poetry* (Cambridge, MA: Harvard University Press, 1982) introduces a more theoretical element to the discussion as she deals with Herbert's presentation of the self and the ways that the Bible complicates that practice. Richard Strier's *Love Known: Theology and Experience in George Herbert's Poetry* (Chicago: University of Chicago Press, 1983) provides an account of Herbert's doctrinal commitment to justification by faith and includes a wealth of thoughtful analyses of ways in which the poems make use of biblical texts and related theological materials. Chana Bloch devotes an entire book (*Spelling the Word: George Herbert and the Bible* [Berkeley: University of California Press, 1985]) to Herbert's use of the Bible. Her thoughtful, sensitive readings are largely responsible for helping me to develop the material in this essay. Gene E. Veith's treatment of Herbert's Protestant spirituality (*Reformation Spirituality: The Religion of George Herbert* [Lewisburg, PA: Bucknell University Press and Associated University Presses, 1985]) necessarily deals with a great many biblical passages in the poems that testify to the congruence between belief and literary practice. Stanley Stewart, in *George Herbert* (Boston: Twayne, 1986), returns to the insights of Tuve as he points to the importance of Roman Catholic traditions in understanding Herbert's use of the Bible. In *Christian Narrative* Harold Toliver sets up a mythos or fable that attempts to account for the various developments of Christianity throughout *The Temple.* Toliver is closest in his reading of Herbert's use of the Bible to my view of the intertextuality of biblical materials.

8. George Herbert, *A Priest to the Temple, or, the Countrey Parson, His Character, and Rule of Holy Life,* in George Herbert, *The Works of George Herbert,* ed. F. E. Hutchinson (1941; rpt. Oxford, UK: Clarendon Press, 1964), 229. All subsequent citations to Herbert's prose and poems are to the Hutchinson edition.

9. John N. Wall, ed., *George Herbert: The Country Parson; The Temple* (New York: Paulist Press, 1981), 65n33. The phrase is not italicized in Herbert's *Remains* (1652) or in the second edition of 1671. Hutchinson relies on the third edition of 1675 for the use of italics. There is no note about the biblical allusion in Hutchinson.

10. Jeffrey Hart long ago pointed to "the controlling imagery of the poem as Eucharistic" in "Herbert's *The Collar* Re-Read," in *Essential Articles for the Study of George Herbert's Poetry,* ed. John R. Roberts (Hamden, CT: Archon,

1979), 457. Notes in the editions of Herbert by C. A. Patrides (*The English Poems of George Herbert* [Totowa NJ: Rowman & Littlefield, 1974], 161) and Helen Wilcox (*The English Poems of George Herbert* [Cambridge, UK: Cambridge University Press, 2007], 527–28) develop this insight. Gene Veith's comment is especially relevant: "The irony of 'The Collar' in which the imagery employed to express rebellion has a double-edged religious meaning, is well known. . . . The speaker's desire for wine and corn (10–13) assumes a complicated resonance when they are recognized also as sacramental symbols" (Veith, *Reformation Spirituality*, 108). Nevertheless the general trend in Herbert scholarship has been to stress the typological and theological implications of the imagery. My point is that there are also other intertextual echoes at work here.

11. All citations from the Bible are to the Authorized (i.e., King James) Version. This specific passage is from Deuteronomy 7:13.

12. Harman, *Costly Monuments*, 35.

13. Harman, *Costly Monuments*, 86.

14. Harman, *Costly Monuments*, 181.

15. Harold Fisch, *Jerusalem and Albion: The Hebraic Factor in Seventeenth-Century Literature* (London: Routledge & Kegan Paul, 1964), 189.

16. Ariane M. Balizet, "'A Jewish Choice': The Judaic Past and Present in the Poetry of George Herbert," *George Herbert Journal* 26 (2002): 48.

17. Balizet, "A Jewish Choice," 50.

18. Greg Miller, *George Herbert's "Holy Patterns": Reforming Individuals in Community* (New York: Continuum, 2007), 134.

19. David S. Katz, "The Abendanna Brothers and the Christian Hebraists of Seventeenth-Century England," *Journal of Ecclesiastical History* 40 (1989): 30.

20. See Jeffrey K. Jue, *Heaven Upon Earth: Joseph Mede (1586–1638) and the Legacy of Millenarianism*, International Archives of the History of Ideas, no. 194 (Dordrecht: Springer, 2006), 128: "Mede's library contained a volume of Johannes Buxtorf's edited Hebrew and Chaldee Bible with a commentary on the Masora (textual apparatus) composed from the writings of prominent rabbis. Buxtorf devoted his entire academic career to making Jewish writings and language more accessible for non-Jews."

21. Chauncey Wood, "Herbert's 'The Pearl' and the *Commentary* by Franciscus Lucas Brugensis," *George Herbert Journal* 27 (2003–2004): 32–42. Wood cites from the first volume of the Brugensis commentary in connection to "The Pearl."

22. Franciscus Lucas Brugensis, *In Sacrosancta Quatuor Iesu Christi Evangelia Francisci Lucas Brugensis Ecclesiae Cathedralis Audomaropolitanae Theologi & Decani Commentarius* (Antwerp, 1606), v. 1, sig. B1r.

23. I am indebted to my esteemed colleague, Dr. Ivor Ludlam, for his help and advice in translating this passage.

24. Matthew Poole, *Synopsis Criticorum Aliorumque S. Scripturae Interpretum*, 5 vols. (London, 1669), v. 4, A, col. 111.

25. In a discussion of the actual value of items pledged to the Temple treasury, the Mishnah determines that "in the case of a pearl: if they bring it up to a city, it fetches a better price--the sanctuary [nonetheless] has a claim only in its own place and in its own time." See 'Arakin 24A, in *The Talmud of Babylonia: An American Translation*, trans. Jacob Neusner, Brown Judaic Studies no. 63 (Chico, CA: Scholars Press, 1984), v. 32, 184.

26. Hagigah [3a], in *The Talmud of Babylonia: An American Translation*, trans. Jacob Neusner, Brown Judaic Studies no. 280 (Atlanta: Scholars Press, 1993), v. 12, 10. The Hebrew phrase that refers to the pearl is *margalit tova hayta beyedchem ubikashtem le-ovda mimeni* (there was a fine pearl in your hands, and you attempted to deprive me of it).

This kind of use of "pearl" recurs in at least two other passages. One is in *Midrash Rabbah*, v. 6, *Numbers*, trans. Judah J. Slotki, ed. H. Freedman and Maurice Simon (London: Soncino, 1939), 575, which repeats the account from Tractate Hagigah. The other is in Tractate Baba Bathra, where R. Hiyya b. Abba also uses the phrase to refer to a novel interpretation of the Torah:

> *Abba Halipa of Qeruya asked R. Hiyya bar Abba*: "When the summary figure of those who entered Egypt with Jacob is given, they are counted as seventy, but when they are named one by one [Genesis 46:8 ff.] they number seventy minus one!" He said to him, "There was a twin girl with Dinah: 'With [expressed by the accusative particle et] his daughter Dinah' (Gen. 46.15)." *Well then*, there should have been a twin girl with Benjamin, for it is written "With [expressed by the accusative particle et] Benjamin, his brother, his mother's son" (Gen. 43:29). He said to him, "I had a valuable pearl in my hands, and you want to take it away from me." (*Talmud of Babylonia*, Tractate Baba Batra [123a–b], v. 22D, chaps. 7 and 8, 73)

27. *Midrash Rabbah*, v. 9, *Song of Songs*, trans. Maurice Simon (London: Soncino, 1939), 198.

28. *Midrash Rabbah*, v. 9, *Song of Songs*, 199.

29. Wood, "Herbert's 'The Pearl,'" 38.

30. Wood, "Herbert's 'The Pearl,'" 39.

IV

Women and Religion

10

Yaakov Mascetti

"This Pretious Passeover Feed Upon"

Poetic Eucharist and Feminine Vision in Aemilia Lanyer's Salve Deus Rex Judaeorum

Hyt semes quite [white], and is red
Hyt is quike, and seemes dede:
Hyt is flesche and semes brede
Hyt is on and semes too;
Hyt is God body and no more.
British Library Royal 17 A.XVI, fol. 27v

Eucharist and Image/Sight

Early modern theological disputes over the true significance of the Eucharist grew out of the fundamental differences between Catholics and Protestants in their conceptions of human-made signs and their representation of the Divine. The discourses of religious reformation that shaped the English church during the sixteenth and seventeenth centuries often focused on the physical perception of signs and on the belief that they could, or could not, represent or convey God's presence to the human observer. Indeed, theologians in England and on the Continent invested considerable effort in the definition or the confutation of the "power and pre-eminent sanctity of the Eucharist."[1] The discrepancy between what one saw and what one was called to believe one saw in the church during the Mass led to the stiffening of two diametrically opposed conceptions of faith: human perception and the meaning of signs. Just as late medieval Catholic believers were called to perceive the divine substance of the Host with the eyes of faith, despite its being hidden beneath the material accident of the bread, Protestant theologians stressed the discrepancy and irreconcilable difference between the thing seen and what it was supposed to mean.[2]

An exemplification of the two opposite perspectives on what can be termed spiritual perception is provided by the prayer quoted as the epigraph to this essay, a fifteenth-century text that was used in pre-Reformation England for the doctrinal instruction of the Mass. This prayer presents four paradoxes, all related to the inability to see the truth beyond the apparent. The writer presents an unqualified "it," namely, the Eucharist, as the thing seen by the believer in the church during Mass: Although it *appears to be* white, it *really is* red; it is alive, although it appears to be dead; it is flesh, although it appears to be bread; and ultimately it is one, although it seems to be made up of two. The mid-fifteenth-century distinction between what really is and what appears to the eye is based on a pre-Reformation conception of the "scopic relationship" between the believer and the object of faith.[3] Gazing at the host during Mass was part of the Roman Catholic eucharistic faith and liturgy; by virtue of this optic bond the individual believer could be blessed and redeemed.[4] Grace came through the fixed gaze on the Host. Yet these four paradoxes point to the fact that what was visible to the eye was not the Christly truth but a misleading appearance, for the "Host did not look like the thing it was."[5] Consequently, the eye had to be educated to see properly, without getting caught in the tempting distinctions of doubt between appearance and truth.

The English Reformation brought a significant shift in local conceptions of truth, vision, and the role of representation in liturgy, relocating the emphasis of theological discourses from the visible and material to the verbal and metaphysical.[6] As Margaret Aston has argued, discourses of iconoclasm in England and on the Continent addressed with growing emphasis the "role of the arts in the Christian worship," whereas the "changes in the doctrine of the Eucharist" brought about by Protestant theological works modified the "fate of imagery."[7] The matter of the use of images in religious cult was tainted with the "iniquitous sin of idolatry," and the iconoclasts were thus determined to "to erase not simply the idols defiling God's churches but also the idols defiling people's thoughts."[8] Patrick Collinson, who is more extreme in his historical narrative, sees a clear-cut change in the religious sensibility of English Christendom, a veritable "iconoclastic holocaust" in the local visual culture, only the vessel of truth was not the icon but the biblical text, the sole, "plain, honest, even artless" conveyer of the divine message.[9] Between 1580 and the mid-1600s English Protestantism directed "the eye, that potentially idolatrous eye, inward, rejecting realistic religious pictures."[10] Protestant England thus moved "from a cultural phase which may be described as iconoclastic" to the "iconophobic" rejection of "all images."[11]

These historical narratives delineate the traits of a clear-cut paradigm shift or change in episteme, leaving little or no space for the fuzziness of theological ambivalences like that of Lanyer's religious conceptions, trapping their complexity in the simplicity of the transition from iconophilia, iconoclasm, and iconophobia. As Tessa Watt has argued, "this vision of a major cultural cleavage" may be "misleading in several important ways."[12] Although Watt does work comfortably with the idea of a "reformation of images" in England during the sixteenth and seventeenth centuries and with the idea of a shift away from the "ocularcentrism" of medieval religious sensibility, she objects to Collinson's portrayal of a "major cultural watershed" dated "fairly precisely to the years around 1580."[13] Watt states that in the theological sources of the time there is "nothing to indicate a sudden break, or a 'total repudiation' of images," although she concedes that the discourses of iconoclasm certainly had a crucial "effect on the English *mentalité*."[14] More than the mere shattering of external images, this gradual change was accompanied by a "reaction against the role of the visual and sensual in religious perception," the manifestation of a "desire to purify the mind itself of the inner idols."[15] Watt reads into this period a "continuing process of substituting acceptable images for unacceptable," even within the "increasingly constrictive boundaries" of the sixteenth and seventeenth centuries.[16] While "painters and printers continued to cater to the demand for religious figure subjects" for the more moderate Protestants in England, the more extreme currents were developing a "hostility to art in general," attacking both the material representations of divinity and the idols of the mind. These unseen cognitive idols were the target of what Watt calls the "profound mental revolution" of the more extreme strands of English Protestantism, which reacted "against the role of the visual and sensual in religious perception" and pursued an "inward-looking iconoclasm" and the "purification, even mortification, of the visual imagination."[17] As William Perkins wrote in his 1601 *Warning Against the Idolatry of the Last Times*, "the right way to conceive God, is not conceive any form, but to conceive . . . his properties and proper effects," for as "soon as the mind frames unto itself any form of God . . . an idol is set up in the mind."[18] Changes took place, but they were "more subtle" than the modern scholar may think, and that "visual culture continued to play a role in mainstream Protestant culture."[19]

This was the complex background of theological disputes over the role of images, representation, and the physical perception of Divinity in which Aemilia Lanyer conceived her poetic utterance on feminine faith as a statement on the appropriate way to see things invisible to the eye. Her gendered conception of sight and religious truth gave place to a feminine renarration of biblical accounts. Lanyer calls her feminine reader to see the nonobvious presence of the Eucharist within her poetry, as opposed to the obtuse blindness of the male reader who ignores the presence of the imperceptible. As such, I present Lanyer's gendered sight and religious poetry in *Salve Deus Rex Judaeorum* as a feminine response to the male-centeredness of contemporary Protestant lexica of belief and sight.

As I argue and demonstrate, Lanyer conceived of sight as the physical and cognitive bond that links the feminine reader, the text, and its feminine author; this bond is manifested in a moment of hermeneutic encounter, as the eucharistic union of the three in one, as I explain later. Although recent scholarship has tended to emphasize the proximity of Lanyer's unique hermeneutic model to the queen's pro-Catholic ideas, I argue here that Lanyer's poetry was based on a solidly Lutheran and Calvinist theological substratum.[20] When seen against the background of contemporary seventeenth-century theological discourses of sight, cognition, and communion, Lanyer's gendered conception of vision and hermeneutics takes on the traits of what John Pocock calls a "move" performed by an author to endorse and rearrange "the possibilities of language open to the author and [her] co-users of language."[21] Considering the range of theological conceptions of sight available to Lanyer in early-seventeenth-century England, her definition of a feminine way to *see* and cognize the truth of scriptures can be seen as a gendered engagement with the ambivalent early Protestant conceptions of the visual sphere. Engaging contextual languages of Calvinist iconophobia, where the icon was suspiciously kept "in a [perpetual] state of remove" and understood to signify "by visual means that what it shows is elsewhere and invisible," Lanyer fashioned her feminine poetics and her response to contemporary Protestant discourses of textual iconography, presenting her poetry as the mirror in which the (exclusively feminine) reader could visually perceive the iconic manifestation of Christ's self-sacrifice.[22]

By displacing the image of the crucifix from the visual sphere to the textual one, Lanyer merges the act of reading with a visual perception of the Passion, ultimately inviting the reader to see her poetry as a mirror in which she may see both herself and Christ. In doing so, the poet not only uses but also *questions* contemporary theological languages of vision, reading, and interpretation, presenting her feminine *poesis* as an alternative model of scopic communion between reading subject and textual object. In an ideal moment of cognitive communion between reader and text, Lanyer's hermeneutic act ceases to be one of visual contemplation and becomes one of consumption. In that moment poetry is no longer a text to interpret but the locus of eucharistic presence, to be consumed and assimilated: "Here," Lanyer states, "I have prepar'd my Paschal Lambe" ("To the Queens Most Excellent Majestie," l. 85). Seeing the text and reading it are necessary operations for the reader to be able to encounter Christ's presence visually, as subject and object meet in a point of communion. Lanyer's unique reading mode, though, is exclusive to a feminine readership; only women possess the "judiciall view" that allows them to see, in Lanyer's narration, the true meaning of the scriptures.

Lanyer's Eucharistic Vision in Context

Lanyer's only volume of poems is an early modern woman's public engagement with contemporary theological disputes over the nature and role of human artifacts in the religious sphere. In this section I wish to delineate the traits of the contextual web of theological languages games in which Lanyer lived and wrote her poetry. The early seventeenth century was, both in England and on the Continent, a time of significant change in religious habits of thought, mostly because of the growing influence of Lutheran and Calvinist theologies in northern European religious discourses. The Lutheran theses and subsequent development of a theological discourse that could "resurrect Christian faith from a supposed state of decrepitude," led, as Joseph Koerner has shown, to the reformation of visual religiosity.[23] Although Luther's judgment of images and of the role of visual perception in religious cult was "pivotal," it was the work of following generations of English and continental Protestant thinkers who developed Calvin's iconoclastic lexica and gave a strong impetus to the reformation of the image and of its religious meaning.[24]

The redefinition of hermeneutics as one of the three paths to redemption led to what Susanne Woods has called the "Protestant focus on word," which informed English religious poetry from the second half of the sixteenth century to the Civil War, and, as I wish to demonstrate in this section, contributed to the formation of Lanyer's poetry as the image of Christ. The two factors shaping Lanyer's emphasis on gendered hermeneutics as the path leading the feminine reader to a communion with Christ were Luther's statement that "scripture is its own interpreter" and "is itself its own light" (*scriptura sui ipsius interpres*) and Calvin's concept of the text being the sole acceptable living image of God.[25] In this complex habit of thought, scriptures and exegesis were, so to speak, one and the same thing; the biblical word was at once the witness of God's visual absence and semantic presence. It was this synthesis that the Protestant believer would adopt in constructing a relationship with God and that led to the development of the aesthetic system reflected in Lanyer's work, in which Christ could be perceived visually only in the text, only within the word.

As in Christ's advent and teachings, the Lutheran reconception of biblical exegesis was focused on a movement from the outer to the inner, from the external codification of the Law to the internal spirit of the original scriptural text, changing the hermeneutical habits of theologians from the systematic imposition of meaning onto the text to what Luther defined as the tasting of the Word's "most delicious kernel."[26] The sole focus of the scriptures was Christ: To find in them any other signified element meant performing a forceful exegetic insertion of spurious interpretations. The Lutheran religious pedagogy was thus composed of scriptural reading, prayer, and homiletics, by means of which the individual believer would be educated to discover Christ both in the word (scripture) and in the world: "On earth you will neither see him nor reach him with your senses or thought. Rather, as St. Paul says, you will see him covered in dark word and image—that is in word and sacrament. Those are like his mask or clothing under which he conceals himself. But certainly he is there, since he himself works miracles, preaches, administers sacrament, consoles, strengthens and aids."[27]

Luther postulated, therefore, that "through faith" the individual could reveal "the invisible things . . . hidden in the word."[28] *Sola scriptura* was the individual's path to redemption by virtue of the interpretation of scriptures and their vast range of meanings, leading eventually to the perception of Christ in the words. Christ being the "universal scope of Scripture," he becomes enclosed in the verbal message of the Bible, and the crucifix is "linguistified, i.e. transformed from an object in the world to a reference of words."[29] A further change took place with Calvin; whereas Luther limited himself to the transposition of divine presence into the semantic sphere of human words, for Calvin divine presence ceased to be a matter of some*thing* hidden in the word, "the res itself," and thus elaborated the idea of preaching as the reiteration of the divine message and the hallowing of God's name in the sermon and the prayer.[30] Besides being interpreted by exegesis, the Word also had to be preached, for, as Luther argued, "God's name, when read or heard, engenders in the heart a picture of the crucifix."[31]

This internalized presence of Christ was a semantic transposition of the sacramental real presence, a visual understanding of Christ on the cross and the reader's "tasting" of the scriptural word and of its divine message as the kernel of a nut. With regard to early-seventeenth-century English religious habits of thought, Calvin's further elaboration of this process, namely, the semantics of sacramental symbolism, is particularly pertinent, considering that during the late Tudor and early Stuart periods "British sacramental theology" positioned itself to a large extent against the background of continental Calvinism.[32] The theological debates in that complex and variegated context revolved around questions on the true nature of sacraments, the interpretation of the Eucharist, and the understanding of religious signs as humanward or Godward.[33] Calvin rejected any form of "human attempt to create signs and symbols of God's presence on earth."[34] With his emphasis on the *potentially* idolatrous nature of manmade signs, seals, and symbols, in his writings the French reformer nevertheless accepted some form of mimesis in fashioning the liturgical means to relate to the Divine, distinguishing between the "living icons of God" and the idolatrous "dead images."[35] In this logocentric and staunchly iconoclastic theological system, the word of God as revealed in the scriptures was the "life and soul of images and symbols"—the human signs that lacked the Word, lacked life and so were to be considered dead.[36] Conceived and formed in the "field of tension" between the "essentially invisible, infinite, and spiritual God" and his becoming somewhat visible in the sign, the living image, albeit physically present in front of the believer, could never lapse into the illusion of signifying, enclosing, or containing God.[37] If the dead images were artifacts made by man to "drag God down from heaven," Calvin's concept of a living image represented the God-granted ladder given to man by grace and by means of which he could, ultimately, ascend to him.[38]

This ascent to God was, of course, a strictly textual one. Reading God's word in the Bible, Calvin's ideal reader would thus *see* the living image of the Christian truth, not perceive it physically, as in the "spectacle of too much weight" in John Donne's "Goodfriday 1613," but intellectually and spiritually. This visual contact would thus take place as part of the reader's hermeneutic effort; reading, seeing, and cognizing the Word were all necessary actions for the individual to undergo a process of transformation, which would lead him from one degree of glory to another, gradually bringing him to a closer similitude with God. Far from being a merely inert and passive object, the living image was an artifact with an active force of its own, which could glorify the believer by virtue of his "visual" contemplation of God's image.[39] The dead image, on the other hand, was the simple result of the individual's fashioning of God in his own image, making the "spiritual and infinite God" into a "finite and carnal" one, "a prisoner of a man-made image conceived to represent God."[40]

The living image was therefore both an aesthetic and a religious paradox; in it the invisible God could be seen by virtue of exegesis while nonetheless remaining invisible. This theological *iconoclash*, to use Bruno Latour's term, combined the irreconcilable elements of aesthetics and deity, not only representing and portraying God while not portraying him but also presenting him to the believer for him to cling on and unite to.[41] Seeking to remove dead images from places of worship, Calvin placed the "living icons" that God uses to represent himself to human beings at the center of his catechism; only in this way would the believer's sensibility be trained to perceive the Divine only in images made by God for our use.

> When I consider for what use temples are ordained, me thinks it is very ill beseeming the holiness thereof, to receiue any other images than these liuely and naturall images, which the Lord by his word hath consecrate. I meane Baptisme, and the Lords supper, and other ceremonies wherewith our eies ought both more earnestly to be occupied, and more liuely to be mooued, then that they should need any other images framed by the wit of men.[42]

Calvin's pugnacious resistance to what he considered the idolatrous tendency of those who wanted to perceive God in human artifacts (painting, statues, poems, etc.) continued to develop throughout his career. As his earliest works confirm, this iconoclastic endeavor developed together with an interest in the evocative power of words and on the reflection of God's image in the Gospels. The latter motif led him, later in his career, to meditate on the relationship between the believer and the text of sacred scriptures, comparing their study to the visual contemplation of an image in a mirror.[43]

Basing his work on Seneca and Cicero, Calvin became aware of the similarities between the classical ideas of reflective textuality and the Christian dogma of Christ's presence in the Gospel.[44] As Cicero writes in his *De Oratore*, the "keenest of all our senses is the sense of sight," and for the orator to attain the best possible results through his speech, the use of visual metaphors obtains a penetration of ideas into the mind of the hearer/reader.[45] The most effective words were, for the Latin author, those that portray the reality they are treating before the eyes of the listener, words describing a visual sphere capable of "encountering and speedily penetrating the mind."[46] A similar emphasis on the importance of the use of sight in texts and speeches was found by Calvin in Augustine's description of the sacraments as "visible words." In the *Institutes of the Christian Religion*, which defines the sacraments as the seals of the Christian faith, Calvin elaborated on the Augustinian conception of signs and their meaning. A sign, Augustine explained in his *De Doctrina Christiana*, is a "thing which of itself makes some other thing come to mind, besides the impression that it presents to the senses."[47] Sacramental signs were thus to be conceived as the visible representations of God's word, the exemplification, as Calvin later elaborated, of "the promises of God, as it were painted in a table" and "setteth them before our sight cunningly expressed and as in an image."[48] Calvin's theology pushed the "faithfull man" to avoid stopping at the "fleshly sight" of the sacramental sign but to use the things seen or read as "degrees of proportion" to rise "up with godly consideration to the high mysteries which lie hidden in the sacraments."[49] But for this sign to "become a sacrament," Augustine added, the "Word" had to be added "to the element."[50] The Word became a central element in Calvin's theological aesthetics; the material sacramental sign could acquire the status of a "visible word" only when accompanied by the impalpable semantics of the Gospel's Word.

Similarly to Cicero's use of words for the portrayal of ideas as *things seen* by the eyes, Calvin adopted Augustinian theology to define sacraments as *things seen* used to portray "in a graphic and iconic way the words that God proclaims" in the Gospels.[51] Sacrament reflected the image of God's word as in a mirror, making visible the invisible and inconceivable semantics of divine will; by contemplating it, the believer could thus see the reflected image of God's word, a "visible word." And although Calvin pushed in his *Institutes* to extend the Augustinian understanding of sacraments "to all forms of divine self-manifestation," whereby the individual's gaze upon creation could contemplate the visible signs of divine will, the vision of the Gospels remained in his theology the main channel for a visual contemplation of God. The written word was a visible representation of the invisible semantics of divine presence.

Relying on Ciceronian literature, Erasmus of Rotterdam developed a similar concept of textual reflection, presenting his writing as a mirror image of the reader himself, a "kind of likeness of yourself, as in a painting," conceived to lead the individual to "a clear knowledge of what you are on the inside and what you are skin-deep."[52] When dealing with the Gospels, the reader would be presented in the text with both a specular image of his psyche and the very image of Christ, himself the "reflection of the glory of the Father."[53] The act of faith was for Erasmus a visual one, a hermeneutic and visual encounter between the individual and the Gospel, in which one could choose to gaze upon the scriptures as the "image of his [Christ's] mind" reproduced by the "artistry of the Holy Spirit."[54] For both Erasmus and Calvin the reader's "reverent eyes" were called to scan the texts of the Gospels, treasuring in the mind not only the "living image" of "His holy mind" but the "speaking, healing, dying, rising Christ Himself," making him "so fully present" that the reader "would see less if [he] gazed upon Him with [his] very eyes."[55] The absence is therefore more immediately significant than the true physical presence; the displacement of truth in the hermeneutic endeavor is more significant than the eucharistic real presence.

This was therefore the discourse of eucharistic hermeneutics fashioned partly by Erasmus and by Calvin that led to the representation of the Gospel as the locus of the "visual self-manifestation of Christ and all his benefits." Faith, described in the Letter to the Hebrews 11:1 as "the substance of things hoped for, the evidence of things not seen," is presented in Calvin's *Institutes* with similar words, as the "seeing of things not seene, a plainnesse of darke things: a presence of things absent, an open showing of hidden things."[56] Upon contemplating himself, the world, and the Gospel with the new eyes of faith, the believer gazes upon the mysteries of God "onely in his word."[57] As Calvin elaborated on Paul's words, reading the Gospel was to be engaged "with uncovered face," in the unmediated cognitive stance in which there are "no veil[s]" betweene him and it, and leading to a transformation of the reader into the Christly icon he perceives in the Gospels.[58] The Gospel is a mirror in which the reader, to use Erasmus's words, sees his own image merging with that of Christ, who is himself the image of God. A contemplation of these three personae in one, reading is a veritable act of transformation, a moment in which the individual, gazing upon the text, sees God's semantic icon in the words and then, while seeing himself reflected in the scriptures, sees himself in God. To use Wendy Wall's words, in *Salve Deus* not only do "subject and object blend" but also Lanyer performs a veritable deconstruction of the dichotomous distinction between gazing subject and inert object.[59] The subjective reader merges with the objective text, and the text acquires subjective qualities and approaches the reader as an objective entity; in this way the act of reading is re-presented as a eucharistic moment of union and interpenetration of human and divine, in which subject and object not only invert places, but become one and the same thing.

"Who sees this Bridegroome, never can be sad": Seeing Christ in Lanyer's Text

One cannot "find out what a man means by simply studying his spoken or written statements," R. G. Collingwood once wrote, without trying to reconstruct and know "what the question was (a question in his own mind, and presumed by him to be in yours) to which the thing he has said or written was meant as an answer."[60] Similarly, it appears to me that a scholar cannot aspire to recover the possible range of intentions of Lanyer's use of eucharistic theology and Calvinist hermeneutics in the poetry of *Salve Deus* without presenting it as a feminine and gendered answer to contemporary discourses of divine presence and absence in man-made artifacts. In the preceding section I presented Calvin's conceptions of the text as a living image of God and the act of interpretation as a moment of religious encounter between reader and text as the theological substratum of Lanyer's opus in *Salve Deus*.[61] The invitation she addresses to the reader over and over again is to gaze upon the text, to read it carefully, and to enjoy the religious work it performs, presenting its hermeneutical act as the veritable consumption of a ritual meal. Her poetry is the living image of Christ, and in it the reader perceives the figure of Christ's living sacrifice. To ignore the theological significance of Christic optics in *Salve Deus* means to fail to *see* what Lanyer wants her reader to see, consume, and digest: the crucified Christ.

As a first step toward this encounter, the reader is called to relinquish what Donne would have called her "vulgar sight," the incapacity to perceive or cognize things hidden and to acquire the "better eyes" of she who can see Christ within the text.[62] Similarly, Lanyer's invitation addressed to Queen Anne to see that "which is seldome seene, / A Womans writing of divinest things" can also be considered a requested effort to perceive beyond what is apparently not perceivable, namely, a woman reinterpreting and writing on sacred issues. The two operations, that of seeing Christ's presence in the scriptures and that of seeing a woman's writing are, needless to say, two very different kinds of visual perception; nevertheless, it is interesting to note the function in similar, if not parallel, ways. For a reader to acquire the "better eyes" and see Lanyer's gendered religious sight, there has to be an act of will, without which, the poet seems to imply, the rare spectacle can go unseen. *Looking* and *reading* the first of the dedicatory poems, Lanyer's reader is called to *see* the text as the "Mirrour of a worthy Mind," the reflection of the Queen's virtues ("To the Queens Most Excellent Majestie," l. 37). But this reflection is not the final aim of the poet's textual optics, because in the mirror image of her own monarchic glory the queen will contemplate, within and beyond the text's "here," an image of Christ, "behold[ing] / That mightie Monarch both of heav'n and earth" ("To the Queens Most Excellent Majestie," ll. 33–34).

As seen in Calvin's model of hermeneutic contemplation of the living image of Christ in the *Scriptura*, Lanyer, I wish to argue, presents the reader with her poetry as a renarrated version of parts of the Gospels, the result of her feminine priestly "Worke," which she "was appointed to performe" by God. Upon reading the poems, the feminine reader perceives in the text, as in Erasmus's reading model, a reflected image of herself, in which, through a careful engagement with the scriptures/poems, she perceives Christ's presence in the words; at this instant the reader, the text, and Christ merge in a moment of communion. Lanyer's text reflects back to her reader not the mere mirror image of herself but one in which Christ's figure and that of the queen overlap. This intersection between divine and human, between physical text and supernal presence, gives Lanyer's *poesis* a hypostatical connotation, bringing the human "flesh" of "base and meanest berth" to an intersection with the image of the "Crown and Crowner of all Kings" ("To the Queens Most Excellent Majestie," ll. 46, 49).[63] As seen in Calvin's theology, the transformative power of sight in the mirror of the Gospel is of central importance; for there to be a moment of refinement in the reader, there has to be a voluntary act of seeing *beyond* one's reflection in the "seeing-glass" of the Gospel, into the mysteries of God.[64] Lanyer's mirror poetics are not a locus of narcissistic reflection of the subject, a moment of textual reflection in which the image is nothing but a mendacious and thus feminine replica of the gazing individual.[65] Gazing upon the text, the reader sees both God and herself in the text and thus sees herself in God in the poetic fabric composed by Lanyer.

Once empowered, this reader becomes capable of judging whether Lanyer's new narration of the Gospels agrees "with the Text" or not ("To the Queens Most Excellent Majestie," l. 76). In this process of interpretation, though, meaning is not imposed on the text, as in the aggressive readings of the male reader where the active subjectivity is always opposed to the passive objectivity of the text. Lanyer's feminine hermeneutic act in the opening verses of her dedicatory poem to Queen Anne is an invitation to "entertaine" the reader at the poem's "Feast" ("To the Queens Most Excellent Majestie," l. 83). In this way, seeing and reading are no longer perceptive acts preceding cognition but acts of encounter and consumption, for the text is a semantic vessel containing the poet's "Paschal Lambe" ("To the Queens Most Excellent Majestie," l. 85). Seeing the text means feeding upon the text, an act through which the feminine reader voluntarily reveals the visual and material presence of the "living Sacrifice" in the reflected image of herself in the author's "Glasse" ("To the Queens Most Excellent Majestie," l. 40).

Starting with the title, the poem *Salve Deus Rex Judaeorum* (hereafter *SDRJ*) is built on a substratum of optic images and metaphors, where the symbolism of sight and cognition intertwines with the poet's intent to convey through her verses a displaced, though real, Christic presence. The poet titles her work as a salutation to Christ, the crucified and dead messiah, self-sacrificed and thus proved to be God and king of the Jews. As Janel Mueller has convincingly argued, Lanyer's salutation is a respectfully distorted and feminine version of the mocking exclamation, reported in Matthew 27:29, of the Roman soldiers upon having placed a crown of thorns on Jesus's head before his crucifixion: "salve rex Iudaeorum," or as the King James Bible translated it, "Hail, King of the Jews!"[66] This "verbal gesture of mockery" reported by the Gospels, concludes Mueller, is both embraced and rejected by Lanyer, who adds "just one word in apposition, *Deus*," and thus "makes fully explicit" to her reader that the poetic text is an "expression of personal faith in the divinity" of Christ.[67] Before this recognition of Christ as the God of the Jews, the salutation of Lanyer's title entails, however, a proper sight and perception of reality. The apposed Deus brings the poet to a true perception and understanding of historical facts, not simply to religious faith; the ensuing poems undertake the visual representation of the Passion for the reader to see, understand, and ultimately assimilate. This true vision of the crucifixion, as Lanyer writes in her letter to the doubtful reader, was dreamt of together with the title of the book years before performing "this Worke," which thus retells that narrative as perceived in its true light (citation). *Poesis*, Lanyer seems to be stating, is not a mere artistic elaboration but a re-creation of communion, the true reproduction of a moment of visual contact, a verbal representation of a scene seen and understood.

As Lanyer explains to Lady Margaret, Countess Dowager of Cumberland, upon dedicating her book to her, poetry is the result of the light of inspiration ("To the Ladie Margaret Countesse Dowager of Cumberland," ll. 34–35). And although *Salve Deus* is not the poem her addressee may (or may not) have requested from Lanyer, that moment in which the patron is enlightened with the light of wisdom is portrayed as a "faire night" of full moon where "shining *Phoebe*" presents to Lady Margaret a view of "*Paradice* to your sweet sight" (*SDRJ*, l. 21). The moon, represented in the Greek mythological persona of Phoebe, is she

> Whose Eagles eyes behold the glorious Sunne
> Of th'all-creating Providence, reflecting
> His blessed beames on all by him, begunne;
> Increasing, strengthning, guiding and directing
> All wordly creatures their due course to runne,
> Unto His powrefull pleasure all subjecting:
> And thou (deere Ladie) by his speciall grace,
> In these his creatures dost behold his face.
> (*SDRJ*, ll. 25–32)

The context of that night in which Lanyer was supposedly asked to write poetry by her potential patron is represented as a moment in which the moon was full and reflected the sun's light to the world's creatures. Seeing the sun's blinding light is something that only the moon can do; with its "eagles eyes" it "behold[s] the glorious Sunne." The cosmological optics of this line would be rather straightforward, were it not for the fact that the "Sunne" here is not only the celestial sphere but also a widely used seventeenth-century allegory of Christ, the son/sun whose visage cannot be contemplated and whose light is an "all-creating Providence."[68] The moon reflects, therefore, the light of the sun "on all," just as the countess inspires her interlocutor with her reflection of the divine imperative. By virtue of the moon's reflected light, "all worldly creatures" see and know where and what their "due course" is; by virtue of this reflection, the "Sunne" subjects all to his "powerfull pleasure" and allows the observer "in these his creatures to behold his [the Sunne's] face." This optic model, where a source of light is reflected in a secondary body and in which that reflected light can allow a third person to see the importance of the source of light, provides Lanyer with a visual allegory for her *poesis*. Just like Lady Margaret, the poetry of *Salve Deus* plays a lunar role, reflecting for its readers the scene of Christ's self-sacrifice and conveying the blinding scene, described by Donne as a "spectacle of too much weight," in a form apt to be beheld.[69] "Here," writes Lanyer earlier on in her dedicatory poems, in the poems of *Salve Deus* the reader "may . . . behold / That mightie Monarch both of heav'n and earth" ("To the Queens Most Excellent Majestie," ll. 43–44).

The reflection of Christ's image in Lanyer's poem is meant to mediate between divine and human, conveying to the reader that which is "exceeding glorious to behold" (*SDRJ*, l. 87), which "none lives that can his wondrous workes declare" (*SDRJ*, l. 78), he "whose wondrous works no mortall eie can see" (*SDRJ*, l. 148). If the reader herself cannot see Christ, the poet certainly can and has and thus describes how "with Majestie and Honor is He clad," struggling to convey to her reader the bliss of such a sight, for "who sees this Bridegroome, never can be sad" (*SDRJ*, l. 77). Sight, though, does not just work in one direction. Within the verses of the poems the reader visually perceives a mediated representation of the Divine, and the Divine examines and judges the human. In this way, as the reader beholds the "Bridegroom" represented in Lanyer's poems, she is herself beheld by Christ in the "inward cares" of her soul (*SDRJ*, l. 49). Christ's sight perceives and brings to light the true nature of "them that double-hearted bee" (*SDRJ*, l. 105), those who see the world around them in one way while, on the other hand, they "secretly doe let their arrowes flee, / To wound true hearted people any way" (*SDRJ*, ll. 109–10). Sin is visual dissimulation, a deviation of the senses, and thus in Christ's "sight abhorr'd" (*SDRJ*, l. 96) for his "countenance will behold the thing that's just" (*SDRJ*, l. 122). If dissimulation is a thing possible and accepted in Lanyer's post-lapsarian world, the model she adopts for her conception of sight, and ultimately of cognition too, dismisses as the superficiality of an "outward Beautie" the esthetic values and virtues of "the world" (*SDRJ*, l. 185). The "vulgar sight," as Donne would have called it, of those whose eyes perceive nothing but the "gawdie colors" (*SDRJ*, l. 188) and "perfit features in a fading face" and whose bliss is solely in the "due proportion pleasing to the sight" is ultimately a masculine prerogative.[70] Physical beauty is the "Pride of Nature which adornes the faire," which when "unaccompanied with virtue" is to Lanyer nothing but a source of temptation for those who "seeke, attempt, plot and devise, / How they may overthrow the chastest Dame" (*SDRJ*, ll. 201–7). The "hight of all perfection" is thus feminine beauty adorned by a "noble mind" ready to "scorne the base subjection / Of Feares, or Favors" imposed on her by a male counterpart who sees nothing and aims at nothing else but the "White" beauty of a woman's skin (*SDRJ*, ll. 241–44, 208).

It is this subtle combination of physical beauty and moral virtues that makes a woman worthy, in Lanyer's words, of being "pleasing in thy Makers sight"; in stark opposition to the lascivious gazes of worldly men, Christ's sight perceives the true and inner beauty of a woman's "Grace" (*SDRJ*, ll. 249, 250). The true relationship between a woman's beauteous soul and the divine male counterpart is one in which each can see the other as "most pretious" with a "glorious sight" that perceives the true virtue of the other (*SDRJ*, ll. 249–54). Just as Christ the man sees both woman's outward beauty and her soul's "heavenly grace," in the same way the feminine counterpart is invited to see the truth about Christ's Passion, beyond the male-authored narrative of the Gospels (*SDRJ*, l. 245). Lanyer's feminine reader is invited to see his "Death and Passion" as rewritten by a woman, beyond the outward traits of the male-centered tradition (*SDRJ*, l. 271). If men failed to see the redeemer in Christ the man, obsessed as they are with outward signs and physical traits, with their "glorious sight" women will succeed to see him and know him as the savior and true God (*SDRJ*, l. 1095).

A woman's renarration of the Passion was nevertheless not an easy task to engage in in early-seventeenth-century England. "A woman's writing of divinest things" was not merely a cliché in the manner of the self-effacing and apologetic tones typical of early modern women writers; it was for Lanyer a veritable paradox ("To the Queens Most Excellent Majestie," l. 4). Without the financial support of aristocratic patrons, middle-class women such as Lanyer lacked the education to undertake such a task, and they certainly lacked the authority to propose different perspectives on the traditional and canonical narrative of Christ's crucifixion. Like Icarus flying with "waxen wings" and trying to reach an unreachable sun, the speaker's "deare Muse" is thus seen as unable to soar above the "pitch" of her "appointed straine," if not by virtue of a divine and "powerfull Grace" whose love infuses the "few humble lines" of *Salve Deus* (*SDRJ*, ll. 273–80, 291, 292). The source of her poetic and religious authority is thus divine inspiration, godly revelation, and grace. Empowered and strengthened in her writing by "his Grace," Lanyer thus engages her poetic work, "the manner of his Passion to unfold"; her poetry will "unfold" the story of the Passion by reinterpreting it, showing to the eyes of the reader the true story and image of Christ's death (*SDRJ*, ll. 298, 304).[71] The poet's "Worke," as she calls it in her closing letter "To the doubtfull Reader," will be accomplished by grace alone (*sola gratia*), overcoming the "blindest Weaknesse" of a male-imposed ignorance and lack of education and presenting Christ's glory as "more bright" in the eyes of her readers (*SDRJ*, ll. 303, 300).

As the source of her authority is relocated from the "deare Muse" to God's "Grace," Lanyer provides her reader with the necessary tools to accept the work she is about to begin, for the story will not be renarrated with the same words of the Gospels but with the simple words of a personal endeavor to "unfold" the light of Christ in the story of the Passion.

> In other Phrases than may well agree
> With his pure Doctrine, and most holy Writ,
> That Heavens cleare eye, and all the World may see,
> I seeke his Glory, rather than to get
> The Vulgars breath, the seed of Vanitie,
> Nor Fames lowd Trumpet care I to admit;
> But rather strive in plainest Words to showe,
> The Matter which I seeke to undergoe.
> (*SDRJ*, ll. 305–12)

The poet's choice of words marks the difference with the accepted canon of the Gospels and exemplifies the significance of Lanyer's endeavor to attain Christ's glory and to oppose the passive approval of male-authored versions of the sacred writ. *Salve Deus*, though, is not simply, as Guibbory has argued, Lanyer's "oppositional alternative to the monumental biblical project of [King] James," namely, the accepted translated version of the biblical canon.[72] This new gospel is the *visual demonstration* against the weight of custom and of the accepted canon that only in her "plainest Words" is the sole true "Glory" of Christ. This fact is presented as visually self-evident to both "Heavens cleare eye" and for "all the World" to see. Rewriting "This Storie" is certainly not a simple task for Lanyer, for its truth is found on a "mightie Hill"; and yet, as high, cragged, and steep as that hill may be, the poet can always resort to an optic contemplation of it from afar, "behold[ing] it with the eye of Faith" (*SDRJ*, ll. 315, 317–18). The story is, for Lanyer, Christ himself, and her renarration "present[s] [the reader] this pure unspotted Lambe" (*SDRJ*, l. 319). As the result of a clear act of faith and after having asked Christ "t'illuminate [her] Spirit," Lanyer's poetry literally shows the reader "his Death" and asks her to contemplate, in the midst of "that blacke fac'd Night," the "Paschal Lambe" and the "figure of that living Sacrifice" as they are represented "in plainest Words" of her narration (*SDRJ*, ll. 321, 325, 327; "To the Queens most Excellent Majestie," l. 86).

"In your heart I leave / His perfect picture": Lanyer's Feminine Icon of Christ

Throughout her novel narration of the Passion, Lanyer's plain words focus on a basic dichotomy between, on the one hand, the masculine incapacity of the disciples, the priests of the Temple, and the Roman authorities to see Christ's divinity and, on the other, the feminine impotence of the daughters of Jerusalem and the Virgin Mary to stop the Romans from killing Christ. In this section I wish to demonstrate how pivotal the visual metaphor is in Lanyer's exposition of this dichotomy, focusing on the ways in which the poet both endorses the contemporary conception of feminine vision as lacking objective clarity and presents it as the sole alternative to the sinful optics of male post-lapsarian misdemeanors. The "tearfull eyes" of the weeping daughters of Jerusalem, upon their contemplating what John Donne would have called the "spectacle of too much weight" of Christ's crucified body, paradoxically see Christ's "eies more bright" than their male counterparts do (*SDRJ*, l. 988; John Donne, "Goodfriday 1613: Riding Westward," l. 16). It is "Faith and Love" and not knowledge and wisdom that allow these women to become the "reflection from this Heav'nly Light" (*SDRJ*, ll. 989–90).

The renarration begins with the night before Christ's crucifixion, as he tells his disciples of the upcoming betrayal before the "Cocke did crowe" (*SDRJ*, l. 346). Working on the trope of light as knowledge versus night as ignorance, in the first part of her "unfolding" of the Passion Lanyer lovingly accompanies her "most blessed Lord" (*SDRJ*, l. 331) through the "Indurements" (*SDRJ*, l. 397), the "Suffrings" (*SDRJ*, l. 404), and the "agony" (*SDRJ*, l.

405) of his self-sacrifice. And as he returns to his disciples, after having prayed to the Father "Not my will, but thy will Lord be done," Christ does not find twelve concerned men but twelve "sleeping Friends," who, unable or unwilling to "watch one hour for love of thee," prefer to slumber and ignore the upcoming death of their master (*SDRJ*, ll. 401, 417–18). It is the shutting of the disciples "Eies" that allegorizes Lanyer's conception of a masculine incapacity to see, perceive, and cognize Christ's divinity: "Yet shut those Eies that should their Maker see" (*SDRJ*, l. 420). Seeing Christ entails a voluntary act of cognitive acceptance, of understanding, and of encounter with the truth. The disciples' closed eyes represented, therefore, the slumbering unwillingness to accept Christ and thus the voluntary closing of the mind to truth.

> But now thy friends whom thou didst call to goe,
> Heavy Spectators of thy haplesse case,
> See thy Betrayer, whom too well they knowe,
> One of the twelve, now object of disgrace,
> A trothlesse traytor, and a mortall foe,
> With fained kindnesse seekes thee to imbrace;
> And gives a kisse, whereby he may deceive thee,
> That in the hands of Sinners he might leave thee.
> (*SDRJ*, ll. 481–88)

Lanyer is careful to present the disciples as Christ's friends, those who follow him faithfully and who ultimately fail to save him because they lapse into a state of apathetic cognitive slumber. This state of consciousness they voluntarily fall into, in which "their eyes were heavie, and their hearts asleepe" turns them from *agents* of redemption to "Heavy *Spectators* of thy [Christ's] haplesse case" (*SDRJ*, l. 482, my italics). In this removed state the individual contemplating Christ turns into a spectator of events that do not involve him; the betrayer "imbraces" and "gives [Christ] a kiss," whereas the disciples assist in the scene but do not interfere; they are passive spectators.

This voyeuristic sense of distance from the betrayal of Christ is followed by the fierce misjudgment on the part of "High Priests and Scribes, and Elders of the Land": those Jews, all men, who failed to see the divine nature of Jesus (*SDRJ*, l. 490). The poet describes a distinct incapacity of the part of "these Monsters" to *know* Jesus, for, she emphasizes, "they could not know him, whom their eyes did see" (*SDRJ*, l. 504). These men physically perceive Jesus, they seek his name, and they judge him, but they cannot know the truth he embodies.

How blinde were they could not discerne the Light!
How dull! if not to understand the truth,
How weake! if meekenesse overcame their might;
How stony hearted, if not mov'd to ruth:
How void of Pitie, and how full of Spight,
Gainst him that was the Lord of Light and Truth:
Here insolent Boldnesse checkt by Love and Grace,
Retires, and falls before our Makers face.
(*SDRJ*, ll. 505–12)

The dullness, blindness, and weakness of the Jewish masculine figures allow Lanyer to elaborate further on the paradox of sight and cognition: Those who see are truly blind, the wise misunderstand the truth, and the mighty are overcome by meekness. If Jesus's true nature is apparently human but truly divine, apparently weak but truly almighty, and apparently mortal but truly immortal, then those who judge him are apparently powerful but truly dull, blind, and weak. Only by virtue of a moment of visual encounter with Jesus, where the "insolent Boldnesse" of these men meets his "Love and Grace" and "falls before our Makers face," is the hidden truth revealed, in its undeniable visual immediacy, to those who could not see but now cannot refrain from doing so (*SDRJ*, ll. 511, 512). In this way, Lanyer's Jesus reveals himself to the "stony-hearted" Jews with the phrase "I am hee," not in order to hand himself over to the might of the "accursed crew" but for them to see clearly that he is Christ (*SDRJ*, ll. 513, 518, 508). The poet thus presents the masculine doubt as dispelled by the true visual self-revelation of Christ, bringing together his "Pure Innocencie" and their "Sinne" while causing the world "Torments" and "Joyes" (*SDRJ*, ll. 527–28). But men remain blinded by the "ugly mists" of sin, and upon encountering Christ, the light of truth, "they could discerne no Light" (*SDRJ*, ll. 681–82). Lanyer addresses the primary culprit, the Jewish high priest, and delineates his incapacity to understand the truth of his prisoner's words: Unable to "apprehend it [truth] to be so," in asking Jesus if he is the son of God, Caiaphas poses a question that contains the answer hidden within, but his "malice" prevents him from perceiving it (*SDRJ*, ll. 710, 707).

To thee O *Caiphas* doth he answere give,
That thou hast said, what thou desir'st to know,
And yet thy malice will not let him live,
So much thou art unto thy selfe a foe;
He speaketh truth, but thou wilt not beleeve,

Nor canst thou apprehend it to be so:
   Though he expresse his Glory unto thee,
   Thy Owly eies are blind, and cannot see.

Thou rend'st thy cloathes, in stead of thy false heart,
And on the guiltlesse lai'st thy guilty crime;
For thou blasphem'st, and he must feele the smart:
To sentence death, thou think'st it now high time;
No witnesse now thou need'st, for this fowle part,
Thou to the height of wickednesse canst clime:
   And give occasion to the ruder sort,
   To make afflictions, sorrows, follies sport.
   (*SDRJ*, ll. 705–20)

When the human word is articulated in the presence of the Word, of the *Verbum*, the cognitive process of knowing things conveyed by means of semantics no longer passes through inquiry but is immediately apprehended; seeing Christ means knowing truth without mediation of any kind. The carnal meaningfulness of the Christic word leaves no space, no gaps for questions, for the sign and its meaning are one and the same thing. Yet Caiaphas asks, and Lanyer speculates on the fact that he inquires in the presence of the answer to all. Albeit his hunger to know is motivated more by a gratuitous desire than a sincere need to cognize, Caiaphas is a blind man with "Owly eies," a judge who should be empowered to understand the reality in front of him and yet "cannot see" (*SDRJ*, l. 712). Caiaphas is for Lanyer more than a historical figure; he is the allegory of masculine perceptual ignorance that will not allow the Christic undermining of all interrogations, of all doubts. Although Christ projects onto Caiaphas his glory—"he expresse his Glory unto thee"—Caiaphas, despite his big and penetrating eyes, cannot "apprehend it to be so"; he cannot see the presence of the divine in its immediate fullness.

Moving on to her description of Christ's betrayal, of his arrest and of his trial, and working her way toward his crucifixion, Lanyer addresses the fall of men and provides her reader with a type of masculine disbelief and misdemeanor.

By this Example, what can be expected
From wicked Man, which on the Earth doth live?
But faithlesse dealing, feare of God neglected;
Who for their private gaine cares not to sell
The Innocent Blood of Gods most deere elected,

As did that caytife wretch, now damn'd in Hell:
If in Christs Schoole, he tooke so great a fall,
What will they doe, that come not there at all.
(*SDRJ*, ll. 737–44)

The neglectful and faithless attitude of the disciples and Caiaphas is a voluntary sin, an intentional misperception of Jesus, a self-imposed blindness to divinity that is, for the poetess, a paradigm of the masculine incapacity to cognize things hidden, to apprehend that which is true and eternal. Man is blind to Christ's divinity because he is "wicked" and "faithlesse" and neglects "feare of God," valuing only the monetary worth of a person whose value is that of "the Innocent Blood of Gods most deere elected" (*SDRJ*, ll. 739, 741). The male figures in Lanyer's narration of the Passion are unwilling to see the truth; they are blinded by their own pride, by their own malice—and their fall is a visual one. In stark opposition to Caiaphas stands Pontius Pilate, the Roman governor presented as the one who must "Judge the Cause / Of faultlesse *Jesus*." The subject whose future he will have to decide on "before him stands" just like he stood before Caiaphas, yet this time a feminine voice, that of Pilate's wife, begs for the judge to have pity of the "Saviors life."

Let barb'rous crueltie farre depart from thee,
And in true Justice take afflictions part;
Open thine eies, that thou the truth mai'st see,
Doe not the thing that goes against thy heart,
Condemne not him that must thy Saviour be;
But view his holy Life, his good desert.
Let not us Women glory in Mens fall,
Who had power given to over-rule us all.
(*SDRJ*, ll. 753–60)

From Lanyer's perspective feminine superiority is evident; male blindness is, quite simply, the incapacity to make a connection between what can be seen and what cannot, between the external reality of truth ("open thine eyes") and the truth that is in one's heart ("Doe not the thing that goes against thy heart"). Compared with the blindness of men, the "former fault" of the feminine sex, that of Eve in the Garden of Eden, appears as "much lesse" important. The poet's apology in favor of Eve's innocence is interpolated into her renarration of Christ's crucifixion, with the precise intention of comparing the two sins, of man and of woman. In this way Lanyer manages to create a stark contrast between masculine sight and cognition and those of the feminine protagonist of history.

Till now your indiscretion sets us free,
And makes our former fault much lesse appeare;
Our Mother Eve, who tasted of the Tree,
Giving to Adam what shee held most deare,
Was simply good, and had no powre to see,
The after-comming harme did not appeare:
The subtile Serpent that our Sex betraide,
Before our fall so sure a plot had laide.
(*SDRJ*, ll. 761–68)

By opposing the traditionally subaltern role assigned to women because of Eve's sin and rejecting the predicament of the feminine sex as the cause for human damnation, Lanyer redefines Adam's fall as a cognitive one. Men have misapprehended Christ; they have intentionally ignored the truth of his redemption. Eve's sin, on the other hand, is for Lanyer the type of feminine cognition rooted in an "undiscerning ignorance," an inherent incapacity to *see* the consequences of her actions (*SDRJ*, l. 769). If Lanyer's Eve errs "for knowledge sake" because she lacks and thus desires the cognitive capacity to judge and discern, then Adam is beguiled into his fall by the visual beauty of the fruit, which "being *faire* perswaded him to fall" (*SDRJ*, ll. 797–98). Women sin because of their innocence and their ignorance, whereas men sin because of their irrational and blind attraction for physical beauty. Both fall because of their blindness.

Lanyer's objective is to recover from that primigenial state of blindness, returning to the innocent sight and pure cognition of Eve's prelapsarian state. The poet represents the scene of the dying Christ from the perspective of the weeping daughters of Jerusalem, who cried as they followed Jesus to Golgotha. Crucified and dying, Jesus ignores all the "Questions that they [the men] could devise," refusing to look on those who failed to see his redemptive truth, but immediately "turne[s] about his face" toward the weeping women, to comfort them "whose teares powr'd forth apace" (*SDRJ*, ll. 979, 971, 973). Taking compassion in their "hearts . . . ready now to breake," Jesus answers the "piteous cries" of these "thrice happy women" with the look of his eyes while the poet binds divine "grace" to Jesus's "face" (*SDRJ*, ll. 984, 969).

Most blessed daughters of Jerusalem,
Who found such favour in your Saviors sight,
To turne his face when you did pitie him;
Your tearefull eyes, beheld his eies more bright;
Your Faith and Love unto such grace did clime,

To have reflection from this Heav'nly Light:
Your Eagles eyes did gaze against this Sunne,
Your hearts did thinke, he dead, the world were done.
(*SDRJ*, ll. 985–92)

The crucifixion is a scene of inconceivable suffering and self-sacrifice, which men refuse to perceive. In this stanza Lanyer presents to her reader the soteriological dynamics of her feminine optics; as the daughters of Jerusalem weep for the crucifixion of Jesus, he turns his face toward them, redeeming and comforting them in his sight. Looking is knowing—seeing is redeeming. Yet in this moment of visual communion between women and Christ, Lanyer presents feminine sight as paradoxically filtered and blurred by tears. It is not that their eyes see Christ despite the tears—it is *because* of the pity, *because* of the tears, that women *see* Christ's "eies more bright" (*SDRJ*, l. 988). True vision is, paradoxically, an unclear vision, thanks to which women ascend to a cognitive communion with God, illumined by "Heav'nly Light" and reflecting it as the moon does in the first verses of the book (*SDRJ*, l. 990). Tears are the allegory of an emotional blurring of intellectual clarity and allow women's eyes to become, in Lanyer's words, "Eagles eyes" that "gaze against this Sunne" (*SDRJ*, l. 991). Tears of pity make Lanyer's feminine sight paradoxically sharp, allowing her to gaze, see, and represent the Passion in her poetry. Tears of pity of the "woefull Mother" wash away the blood shed by Christ's wounds, "that sinners might not tread it under feet," and "teares of joy" flow from her eyes "when God look'd downe upon" her "poore degree" (*SDRJ*, ll. 1009, 1018, 1085–86).

When spightfull men with torments did oppresse
Th'afflicted body of this innocent Dove,
Poore women seeing how much they did transgresse,
By teares, by sighes, by cries intreat, nay prove,
What may be done among the thickest presse,
They labour still these tyrants hearts to move;
In pitie and compassion to forbeare
Their whipping, spurning, tearing of his haire.
(*SDRJ*, ll. 993–1000)

The weeping daughters of Jerusalem together with Mary shed their tears as they look at the spectacle of Christ crucified, perceiving in an unmediated way the full visual meaning of the scene. Christ, moved by their pain, looks down on these women and makes them, by virtue of his sight, at once true servants and true lovers of his redeeming figure. With this exchange of glances, in this quasi-erotic moment of visual communion, Lanyer concludes her narration of the Passion, presenting to her reader a final, extremely graphic representation of Christ's "alabaster breast," his "bloody side, / His members torne, and on his head a Crowne / Of sharpest Thorns" (*SDRJ*, ll. 1162–64). This is the image represented in the poem and presented in all its visual goriness to Lanyer's reader.

> This with the eie of Faith thou maist behold,
> Deere Spouse of Christ, and more than I can write;
> And here both Griefe and Joy thou maist unfold,
> To view thy Love in this most heavy plight,
> Bowing his head, his bloodlesse body cold;
> Those eies waxe dimme that gave us all our light,
> His count'nance pale, yet still continues sweet,
> His blessed blood watring his pierced feet.
> (*SDRJ*, ll. 1169–76)

Addressing "my Ladie of Cumberland," Lanyer presents the scene of the Passion and postulates how the image represented should be perceived: not with the physical eye, which failed the disciples and the Jews, but with the "eie of Faith" (*SDRJ*, l. 1169). When using the proper sense, the feminine beholder is not a "heavy spectator" like her masculine counterpart but a veritable "Spouse of Christ," who sees in the text more than there is or maybe more than there seems to be (*SDRJ*, ll. 482, 1170). In this iconographic text Lanyer's feminine reader perceives the "most heavy plight," a moment of suffering that brings together, in a paradoxical and hypostatical way, "both Griefe and Joy" so that the reader can "unfold" the mystery of a "glorious miracle without compare" (*SDRJ*, ll. 1172, 1171, 1177). The crucifixion is a moment of redemption and of sorrow, a "union of contraries" that the reader may behold and understand with the eye of faith, to be gazed at in the poetic text (*SDRJ*, l. 1258). The image of the Christ "upon the Crosse depriv'd of life and breath" is presented to Lady Margaret Countess Dowager of Cumberland for her to "view" and know (*SDRJ*, ll. 1265–66). Lanyer's "This" is *this* text, *this* image in *this* text—this is the image that when reflected in the reader's eyes represents "that Bridegroome that appears so faire," a spectacle "beauteous to behold" (*SDRJ*, ll. 1305, 1312).

Lanyer's eucharistic aesthetics are not mimetically effective, though, and the poet must, for obvious theological reasons related to the iconophobia of her cultural context, refrain from delineating the exact traits of the crucified Christ. What she does instead is to state that her poetry is that icon, Calvin's living image, the reading of which will instill in the reader's heart a representation of Christ crucified.

Ah! give me leave (good Lady) now to leave
This taske of Beauty which I tooke in hand,
I cannot wade so deepe, I may deceave
My selfe, before I can attaine the land;
Therefore (good Madame) in your heart I leave
His perfect picture, where it still shall stand,
Deepely engraved in that holy shrine,
Environed with Love and Thoughts divine

There may you see him as a God in glory,
And as a man in miserable case;
There may you reade his true and perfect storie,
His bleeding body there you may embrace,
And kisse his dying cheekes with teares of sorrow,
With joyfull griefe, you may intreat for grace;
And all your prayers, and your almes-deeds
May bring to stop his cruell wounds that bleeds.
(*SDRJ*, ll. 1321–36)

The representation of Christ on the cross by means of a renarration of the Passion is for Lanyer ultimately a "taske of Beauty" that she cannot complete, for she "cannot wade so deepe" through the immense sea of Christ's self-sacrifice (*SDRJ*, ll. 1322–23). To wade in such a sea and to reach thereby "the land" on the other side would mean, to use Lanyer's marine allegory, accomplishing the true representation of a scene that cannot be represented or understood (*SDRJ*, l. 1324). The textual icon cannot accomplish this representation, but it can instill in the heart of the reader "His perfect picture," turning it into a locus of liturgical passion, a "holy shrine" where the thoughts and the love of the feminine reader envelop this icon (*SDRJ*, ll. 1326–27). Lanyer thus accomplishes the transposition of the Christic icon from the visual objective sphere to the subjective sphere of the believer's thoughts. The text of her Christic poetry serves as a living icon, conceived and fashioned in the paradoxical tension defined by Calvin between the urge to iconize and the obligation to obliterate the visual. This textual icon is by no means univocally trapped in this Calvinist iconoclastic tension, though; it is presented as an active artifact conceived to perform a work on its reader/viewer. Once reflected in the reader's understanding, Lanyer's poetry turns the reader into a holy vessel, apt to contain the "perfect picture" and mimesis of Christ (*SDRJ*, l. 1326). "There," in the glorified heart of her enlightened feminine reader, the Countess will be able to "see him," perceive the Christic presence in all its paradoxical duality, both as "God in glory" and as "a man in miserable case" (*SDRJ*, ll. 1329–30). In the double nature of her poetry the imperfection of feminine authorship merges with the perfection of the subject, just like the imperfection of Jesus's human nature mingled in hypostatical harmony with his divine essence, and thus presents to the reader the "true and perfect storie" of Christ's Passion (*SDRJ*, l. 1331).

Lanyer's poetic work ends with her exhausted "weake Muse" finally wishing "to rest" after having placed all the "Beauties" of her new gospel in the reader's "breast" (*SDRJ*, ll. 1831–32). The task of portraying the icon of Christ's crucifixion and visually representing the last moments of his life has both failed and been accomplished; the text wishes to present to the reader's sight a scene it cannot fully represent. Thus I conclude that Lanyer's paradoxical combination of iconodulism and iconophobia is rooted in the discourses of Calvinist anxiety of early modern English Protestant theology with the potentially idolatrous nature of human artifacts: her conception of a textual icon. To use Calvin's lexicon, the iconicity of Lanyer's *Salve Deus Rex Judaeorum* is that of a "living image," of an empty artifact that paradoxically contains the Word of God as revealed to her in a dream. Lanyer's poetry is not presented as a mere sign, an artifact lacking the Word and life and thus to be considered dead.[73] Placed in the "field of tension" between the "essentially invisible, infinite, and spiritual God" and his becoming somewhat visible in the sign, *Salve Deus* could therefore never lapse into the illusion of signifying, enclosing, or containing God in itself.[74] Lanyer's poetry was thus the presentation to the reader of the "Paschal Lambe" not as a mere eucharistic signifier made to "drag God down from heaven" but as a paradoxically visible and invisible representation of Christ, presented to her feminine reader as a locus of ascent to God.[75]

As I have emphasized throughout this essay, Lanyer's conception of poetry was intended to provide the reader with a visual and cognitive contact with Christ's *living image*. The text contains and performs a process of transformation of the reader, leading her from one degree of vision to another, gradually bringing her to a closer similitude and ultimately to a union with Christ. *Salve Deus Rex Judaeorum* undermines contemporary expectations for a feminine (and thus passive or inert) artifact, presenting itself to the reader first as a living mirror image of Christ and then as a performative text that could glorify the reader by virtue of a visual contemplation. Just as in Calvin's living images, the invisible God could thus become somewhat visible while nonetheless remaining invisible. Lanyer's poetry contained both Christ's "perfect image" and its absence, relocating the contemplation of it in the heart of the glorified reader. In this way the poems of *Salve Deus* provide their readers with a semantic icon of Christ that they contemplate while reading the text. As the reader, poem, and Christ come together in a moment of communion and as the reading act becomes one of consumption, what were the eucharistic aesthetics transform the reader, perfecting the imperfect cognition and turning the reader's heart into a "holy shrine, / Environed with Love and Thoughts divine."

Notes

1. Eamon Duffy, *The Stripping of the Altars: Traditional Religion in England, c. 1400–c. 1500* (New Haven, CT: Yale University Press, 1992), 102.

2. Duffy, *Stripping of the Altars*, 102.

3. Regina M. Schwartz, "Through the Optic Glass: Voyeurism and Paradise Lost," in *Desire in the Renaissance: Psychoanalysis and Literature*, ed. Valeria Finucci and Regina Schwartz (Princeton, NJ: Princeton University Press, 1994), 146.

4. Duffy, *Stripping of the Altars*, 102.

5. Duffy, *Stripping of the Altars*, 102.

6. Margaret Aston, *England's Iconoclasts*, v. 1, *Laws Against the Images* (Oxford, UK: Clarendon Press, 1988), 1.

7. Aston, *Laws Against the Images*, 2.

8. Aston, *Laws Against the Images*, 2.

9. Patrick Collinson, *The Birthpangs of Protestant England* (London: Macmillan Press, 1988), 95, 97.

10. Collinson, *Birthpangs*, 117.

11. Collinson, *Birthpangs*, 117.

12. Tessa Watt, *Cheap Print and Popular Piety, 1550–1660* (Cambridge, UK: Cambridge University Press, 1991), 133.

13. Watt, *Cheap Print*, 134. The concept of ocularcentrism was coined and used by Martin Jay, *Downcast Eyes: The Denigration of Vision in Twentieth-Century French Thought* (Los Angeles: University of California Press, 1993), 27–29.

14. Watt, *Cheap Print*, 135.

15. Watt, *Cheap Print*, 135.

16. Watt, *Cheap Print*, 135.

17. Watt, *Cheap Print*, 135.

18. William Perkins, *Warning Against the Idolatrie of the Last Times* (Cambridge, 1601), 107–8.

19. James A. Knapp, *Illustrating the Past in Early-Modern England: The Representation of History in Printed Books* (Aldershot, UK: Ashgate, 2003), 18.

20. See, for example, Gerald Scott Harp, *Sense Metaphors of Cognition in Early-Modern Texts* (Ph.D. diss., University of Iowa, 2002); B. R. Siegfried, "An Apology for Knowledge: Gender and the Hermeneutics of Incarnation in the Works of Aemilia Lanyer and Sor Juana Ines dela Cruz," *Early Modern Literary Studies* 6.3 (2001): 1–47; Theresa DiPasquale, *Refiguring the Sacred Feminine: The Poems of John Donne, Aemilia Lanyer, and John Milton* (Pittsburgh, PA: Duquesne University Press, 2008); and Catherine Keohane, "'That Blindest Weakness Be Not Over-Bold': Aemilia Lanyer's Radical Unfolding of the Passion," *English Literary History* 64.2 (summer 1997): 359–89.

21. J. G. A. Pocock, "Introduction: The State of the Art," in his *Virtue, Commerce, and History: Essays on Political Thought and History, Chiefly in the Eighteenth Century* (Cambridge, UK: Cambridge University Press, 1985), 15.

22. Joseph L. Koerner, *The Reformation of the Image* (Chicago: University of Chicago Press, 2004), 11–12.

23. Koerner, *Reformation of the Image*, 27.

24. Koerner, *Reformation of the Image*, 27. Koerner presents Luther as the breaking point of religious iconodulism in European Christianity, emphasizing his ambivalent conception of the role of images.

25. Susanne Woods, *Lanyer: A Renaissance Woman Poet* (Oxford, UK: Oxford University Press, 1999), 126; Luther, quoted in Koerner, *Reformation of the Image*, 201.

26. Luther, quoted in Koerner, *Reformation of the Image*, 202. Cited from Martin Luther, *D. Martin Luthers Werke: Kritische Gesammtausgabe*, 72 vols. (Weimar: Hermann Boehlau, 1883), 55: 6. Hereafter, this edition of Luther's complete works will be referred to as *MLW*.

27. Koerner, *Reformation of the Image*, 202–3. *MLW* 45: 522.

28. Koerner, *Reformation of the Image*, 203. *MLW* 45: 522.

29. Koerner, *Reformation of the Image*, 204. *MLW* 24: 16.

30. Brian D. Spinks, *Sacraments, Ceremonies, and the Stuart Divines: Sacramental Theology and Liturgy in England and Scotland, 1603–1662.* (Aldershot, UK: Ashgate, 2002), xiii.

31. Koerner, *Reformation of the Image*, 253.

32. John J. Larocca, "Review of *Sacraments, Ceremonies and Stuart Divines: Sacramental Theology and Liturgy in England and Scotland, 1603–1662* by Bryan D. Spinks," *Albion* 35.3 (2003): 481.

33. Larocca, "Review," 481.

34. Randall C. Zachman, *Image and Word in the Theology of John Calvin* (Notre Dame, IN: University of Notre Dame Press, 2007), 1.

35. Zachman, *Image and Word*, 2.

36. Zachman, *Image and Word*, 8.

37. Zachman, *Image and Word*, 8.

38. Zachman, *Image and Word*, 8.

39. I use the term *performative* in the sense given to it by J. L. Austin in his *How to Do Things with Words* (Oxford, UK: Clarendon, 1962) and used in

Quentin Skinner's explanation of the illocutionary force of an author's work in "Motives, Intentions, and Interpretation," *New Literary History* 3.2 (1972): 393–408. On pages 401–4 Skinner delves into the ways in which, following the work of the Oxford school of philosophy of language, one can talk about the "illocutionary force" of a text, of its contextual meaning, and of the ways a reader can follow to retrieve the range of possible meanings of an utterance.

40. Zachman, *Image and Word*, 8.

41. Bruno Latour and Peter Weibel, eds., *Iconoclash: Beyond the Image Wars in Science, Religion, and Art* (Cambridge, MA: MIT Press, 2002).

42. John Calvin, *The institution of Christian religion, written in Latine by M. Iohn Caluine, translated into English according to the authors last edition; with sundry tables to finde the principall matters intreated of in this booke, and also the declaration of places of Scripture therein expounded: by Thomas Norton. Whereunto there are newly added in the margin of the booke, notes conteining in briefe the substance of the matter handled in ech section*, trans. T. Norton (London, 1611), I.11.xiii.39.

43. Zachman, *Image and Word*, 9.

44. Zachman, *Image and Word*, 13.

45. Cicero, *De Oratore*, trans. E. W. Sutton (Cambridge, MA: Harvard University Press, 1967), II.lxxxvii.357–58.

46. Cicero, *De Oratore*, II.lxxxvii.357–58.

47. Augustine, *De Doctrina Christiana*, ed. and trans. R. P. H. Green (Oxford, UK: Clarendon Press, 1995), II.I.1.57.

48. Calvin, *Institution*, IV.14.vi.631.

49. Calvin, *Institution*, IV.14.vi.631.

50. Augustine, "In Joannis Evangelium," in *Patrologiae Cursus Completus, Series Latina*, ed. J.-P. Migne (Paris: Garnier Fratres, 1844–91), v. 35, tract. LXXX, 3: 1840.

51. Zachman, *Image and Word*, 13.

52. Erasmus, *Enchiridion*, in *Collected Works of Erasmus*, v. 66, *Spiritualia*, ed. John O'Malley (Toronto: University of Toronto Press, 1988), 41.

53. Erasmus, *Enchiridion*, 41.

54. Erasmus, *Enchiridion*, 72.

55. John C. Olin, ed., *Christian Humanism and the Reformation: Selected Writings of Erasmus*, 3rd ed. (New York: Fordham University Press, 1987), 108.

56. Calvin, *Institution*, III.41.ii.279.

57. Calvin, *Institution*, III.41.ii.279.

58. Calvin, *Institution*, III.20.ii.267.

59. Wendy Wall, "Our Bodies/Our Texts? Renaissance Women and the Trials of Authorship," in *Anxious Power: Reading, Writing, and Ambivalence in Narrative by Women*, ed. Carol J. Singley and Susan F. Sweeney (Albany: State University of New York Press, 1993), 51–71, at 66–67.

60. R. G. Collingwood, *An Autobiography* (Oxford, UK: Oxford University Press, 1939), 31.

61. All references from Aemilia Lanyer's collection are taken from *The Poems of Aemilia Lanyer: Salve Deus Rex Judaeorum*, ed. Susanne Woods (Oxford, UK: Oxford University Press, 1993). References to poems are indicated in the text with poem title and line number. References to dedicatory letters are indicated with title and page number referring to this edition.

62. See John Donne, "The Harbinger to the Progresse," in *The Epithalamions, Anniversaries, and Epicedes of John Donne*, ed. W. Milgate (Oxford, UK: Clarendon Press, 1978), 40, ll. 24–25.

63. In a recently published essay of mine on Lanyer's *Salve Deus*, I have generally addressed issues of feminine priesthood and of the gendered renarration of the Gospels (see Yaakov Mascetti, "'Here I Have Prepar'd My Paschal Lambe': Reading and Seeing the Eucharistic Presence in Aemilia Lanyer's *Salve Deus Rex Judaeorum*," *Partial Answers* 9.1 [January 2011]: 1–15). In the present essay I am addressing Lanyer's eucharistic poetry not de facto, as a literary phenomenon as is, but as a textual gesture conceived and formulated within and in reaction to a specific context. In this way I hope to be able to propose a compelling reconstruction of the possible range of intentions the author may have had in conceiving this feminine renarration of the Gospels.

64. Calvin, *Commentary to James, I:23–25*, in *Calvin's New Testament Commentaries*, 12 vols., ed. David W. Torrance and Thomas F. Torrance (Grand Rapids, MI: Eerdmans, 1959–1972), 3: 273.

65. On the subject of reflected mendacity and the way in which the mirror is seen as a representation of feminine reification, see Frederick Goldin, *The Mirror of Narcissus in the Courtly Love Lyric* (Ithaca, NY: Cornell University Press, 1967). Gary F. Waller noted that "the logic of love-poetry in the Renaissance is that of the gaze, the discrimination of form and the rendering open and passive of the beautiful object—the woman perceived as territory." See Gary F. Waller, "Struggling into Discourse: The Emergence of Renaissance Women's Writing," in *Silent But for the Word: Tudor Women as Patrons, Translators, and Writers of Religious Works*, ed. Margaret P. Hannay (Kent, OH: Kent State University Press, 1985), 239–56, at 250.

66. Janel Mueller, "The Feminist Poetics of Aemilia Lanyer's *Salve Deus Rex Judaeorum*," in *Feminist Measures: Soundings in Poetry and Theory*, ed. Lynn Keller and Christanne Miller (Ann Arbor: University of Michigan Press, 1995), 226–27.

67. Mueller, "Feminist Poetics," 226–27.

68. Although I am conscious of the potentially straightforward patriarchal overtones of this imagery of the sun and the moon, wherein the solar source of light is the man and the lunar reflection of it is the woman, it appears to me that Lanyer is more intent on engaging a theological lexicon, highlighting the sun/Son binome rather than what may seem, from a modern perspective, a standard reiteration of traditional patriarchal paradigms.

69. John Donne, "Goodfriday 1613: Riding Westward," in *The Poems of John Donne*, 2 vols., ed. Herbert J. C. Grierson (Oxford, UK: Oxford University Press, 1968), 1: 336–67, l. 16.

70. John Donne uses the concept of vulgar sight in "The Harbinger to the Progresse," in *The Poems of John Donne*, 2 vols., ed. Herbert J. C. Grierson (Oxford, UK: Oxford University Press, 1968), 1: 250, l. 24.

71. See *Oxford English Dictionary*, s.v. unfold, defs. 3 and 4.

72. Achsah Guibbory, "The Gospel According to Aemilia: Women and the Sacred," in *Aemilia Lanyer: Gender, Genre, and the Canon*, ed. Marshall Grossman (Lexington: University Press of Kentucky, 1998), 193.

73. Zachman, *Image and Word*, 8.

74. Zachman, *Image and Word*, 8.

75. Zachman, *Image and Word*, 8.

11

JEANNE SHAMI

Reading Funeral Sermons for Early Modern English Women

Some Literary and Historiographical Challenges

Edward Rainbowe's final testimony to the greatness of his subject, Lady Anne Clifford, is that a "History" is more appropriate than a "Sermon" to honor "this great *wise Woman*; who while she lived was the Honour of her Sex and Age."[1] I concur. In what follows I illustrate how a literary-historical study of sermons enables recovery of the lives, experiences, and thoughts of early modern women, and I initiate interpretive methodologies for doing so.

After the Reformation sermons became perhaps the most significant official expression of the English church's values and authority. Their increased importance was due to several factors: vernacular translations of scripture, increased patronage of an educated clergy, increased liturgical prominence of sermons, emphasis on sermons as conduits of grace, and, at least in part, the proliferation of religious controversy. It has generally been assumed, however, that even as the priesthood of all believers raised women's status as men's spiritual equals, women were excluded from this emerging religious culture because of the Pauline scriptural injunction against women's public speaking and teaching and its concomitant social enforcement within a patriarchal society.[2] The corollary of this assumption is that with regard to sermons, women exercised largely *passive* roles within a *domestic* context: hearing, copying, memorizing, and repeating sermons for the instruction of children and servants and reading them privately to foster personal and domestic religious devotion.

Such assumptions are no longer tenable, especially if we reimagine this scholarly field by examining how women participated in the religious, political, and literary culture enlarged by vernacular preaching: first, as subjects, but then as patrons, consumers, and preachers of sermons.[3] We can think of these four categories as occupying a spectrum ranging from women as subjects of discourse, particularly in marriage and funeral sermons, on the one end, to women as agents of discourse, or preachers, at the other end, particularly through the records of Quaker women, who occupied public roles and wielded the authority of biblical interpretation normally accorded to preachers. Both of these areas raise complex questions of terminology and methodology and have been treated extensively in the secondary literature. At present the most elusive area is the middle ground of this spectrum: women as patrons of preachers and women as collectors, consumers, and transmitters of particular religious cultures. In this essay I survey briefly these four areas of study but focus primarily on historiographical and literary problems created within just one of these fields: women as represented in sermons, primarily those preached at funerals.

It is a truism that women preachers were not part of mainstream religious culture, although they flourished briefly (despite vociferous opposition) among radical, nonconforming, and marginal groups during the 1640s and 1650s in England and as missionaries to Ireland, Barbados, and Massachusetts and (in the case of Mary Fisher) to the sultan of Turkey himself.[4] The Quakers were the most advanced supporters of women preachers, in theory and practice, applying the term *preaching* not only to women who expounded scriptures in public but also to "a general class of activity which consisted of any voicing of religious opinion—in print, in the church or congregation, in the company of others anywhere, and even in the home in disagreement with one's husband."[5] Margaret Fell Fox's *Women's Speaking Justified* (1646), a theoretical justification of women's public speaking, tackles the question of such speech head on; however, no sermons by Fox survive to illustrate this tract's "stunning self-assurance about her own ability to preach, theologize, or adjudicate equally with men, a real sense of herself as an equal that is very rare even in the most active seventeenth-century women."[6] By the end of the seventeenth century, even Quakerism was less open to female participation; the women's meetings declined, and "women preachers seemed unnatural even to women."[7] Those who persisted in their preaching activities endured constant surveillance, were imprisoned, fined, ducked, put in the stocks, searched for signs of witchcraft, whipped, attacked, beaten to death, threatened with butcher knives, and led through the streets with iron bridles, the latter punishment normally reserved for scolds who undermined their husbands' authority. In extreme cases they were transported to Jamaica for their intransigence.[8] Despite a period of intense experimentation among nonconformists in the 1640s and 1650s, then, women's preaching remained largely in the domestic sphere in early modern England.

That said, numerous miscellanies containing women's sermon notes survive, as well as exercises in scriptural interpretation with personal application resembling sermons. The most stunning example of these is a sermonic text by Anna Walker, court lady to James I's queen consort, Anne of Denmark. This text follows many of the sermon's generic codes, including self-conscious choice of text (in Walker's case, introducing a pun on her surname that is interwoven throughout the entire manuscript), division and application of that text, and a dedication to the queen (in a bid for patronage). In addition, the manuscript reveals its history of transmission to at least one other female reader (Elizabeth Wilbraham), although, in the end, we have no evidence that the sermon was read by anyone (including its intended female auditor, Queen Anne) or that it was preached or read publicly, either in the queen's household chapel or elsewhere.[9]

The examples of Margaret Fell Fox and Anna Walker expose problems associated with the available archive for scholarly study of women and sermons. In the case of Fox we have no sermons to accompany the theoretical power of her tract defending women's public speech, and in the case of Anna Walker we have a "sermon" that may never have been read even in silence, much less preached in public. A related problem involves definitions of preaching that limit the term to mean only public scriptural interpretation, usually as part of an official worship service, by an ordained minister, thus excluding activities that we—and some contemporaries—construed as preaching, including repetition of sermons, domestic instruction based on sermons, and biblical exegesis in public circumstances outside official worship services. In fact, these activities could and did exert tremendous influence, epitomized in Becon's *Catechism*, which concluded that women (especially "old and ancient matrons") were not only *allowed* to but "straitly commanded to preach and teach in their own houses" in their role as "bishops in their own house."[10]

If we move beyond these domestic intersections of public preaching and private teaching to activities in which women participated in the creation and transmission of healthy sermon cultures, we find that women's reach is staggering, though the evidence is fragmentary. It extends first to patronage of preachers and domestic chaplains, a practice that influenced the orientation of parish and household communities. It extends further to public, official patronage by queens and queen consorts. No one can doubt the influence of Mary and Elizabeth on preaching during their reigns, but the more complex effects achieved by the Catholic consorts of ostensibly reformed monarchs (e.g., Anne of Denmark and Henrietta Maria) await further study. Finally, we are only beginning to appreciate the influence of women as consumers of sermons: collectors, readers and annotators, transmitters, and hearers. This field is both fertile and seeded with landmines for the unwary, inasmuch as these extensions of the study of women and sermons turn on the crucial paradox of women as both passive receivers and active propagators of sermons.

❖

The study of women as *subjects* of funeral sermons has generated vigorous historiographical debate about their value as historical and biographical sources. Tracing their origins in classical funeral orations filtered through Erasmian humanism, Patrick Collinson found their biographical portions too conventional: "The qualities most often admired in the spiritual biographies are humility, modesty, and, once again, a sure instinct for the safe sure middle way, expressed in a wide variety of clichés."[11] This rhetorical appetite for an Aristotelian "middle way" was exacerbated by a tendency to eulogize all women in their social roles as virgins, wives, and widows as patterns of perfect piety.[12] Moreover, the rhetorical situation invited overpraising, a fact that made funeral sermons suspect to many Church of England divines, including John Carter who—having delivered funeral sermons for noble parishioners such as Frances Stanley Egerton, Countess of Bridgewater—himself attempted unsuccessfully to prevent his own life from becoming the subject of a sermon at his funeral.[13]

Moreover, the surviving archive of funeral sermons provides only a limited and idiosyncratic account of a few women, mostly of the literate upper classes and primarily of a puritan cast, the issue of gender compounding problems of access and interpretation. In fact, the cost of a funeral sermon, which was not an ordinary part of the liturgy, meant that most funerals did not include one.[14] The methodological problems common to the study of sermons in general exacerbate these challenges: (1) the disjunction between sermons as delivered and as subsequently published; (2) the limits of the archive (not all preached sermons survived either in print or in manuscript, thus calling into question the exemplary function of the deceased); (3) the difficulty in re-creating the occasional context and impact of the sermons, either to their auditors or to those who read, copied, or transmitted them; and (4) the difficulty in assessing the cultural impact of these sermons (did they reflect social realities or social fantasies about human behavior?).

Moreover, the debate about the ideological value of funeral sermons continues. Whose ends did they serve? Who was their intended audience? Were men as well as women expected to follow the exemplary lives celebrated there? These questions are complicated by the uniquely liminal status of funeral sermons, which formed bridges between the living subject's private life and the deceased subject's exemplary and didactic public life,[15] and are further complicated by differences between the didactic and exemplary functions of funeral sermons preached for men (often clergymen) and women. Certainly, however, differences between the kinds of funeral sermons addressed to these separate audiences—the sermons for men emphasizing civic virtues, those for women emphasizing domestic virtues—exist, even though the lines between them are blurred.[16]

Peter Lake's analysis of John Ley's funeral sermon for Mrs. Jane Ratcliffe offers a paradigm for extracting information from funeral sermons despite their generic conventionality and the "intentions and attitudes" of their authors.[17] However, perhaps the first thing to say about this *sermon* is that—at 198 pages divided into 27 chapters—it is hardly a sermon as we understand the term. Ley calls it a "Funerall remembrance"[18] intended to keep alive the memory of Chester's "Ruth" (from which book Ley takes his text [Ruth 3:11, "All the Citie of my people doth know that thou art a virtuous Woman"]). Only a portion of Ley's text was preached in Chester (in part because Mrs. Ratcliffe's funeral sermon was preached in London, where she died), and it more closely resembles a biography than a sermon, the biblical text serving as a thematic unifying device rather than as the basis for scriptural exegesis. The printed text also obscures the dramatic occasion of this sermon's delivery, although we can imagine that Ley's stress on Mrs. Ratcliffe's moderation in matters of ceremonial conformity corresponded to a tension in that congregation between Brownists and conformists and provided "living (or only recently dead) proof that, . . . an ardent but moderate puritan zeal was entirely compatible with a full and loyal membership of the national church."[19] It is precisely the stress on moderation (in this and other funeral sermons) that Collinson identifies as the residue of the classical encomium, leading to the overwhelming fixation on the virtues of a transposed Aristotelian "mediocrity" and the evacuation of anything that could distinguish the admirable qualities of the puritan saints from those associated "with Christian perfection in almost any age."[20] Consequently, even Foxe's martyrs became "men and women of dispassionate moderation, temperate in speech, given to no extremes of behaviour, even in their utter extremity."[21]

Lake disagrees. While acknowledging the conventionality of the form of biography attached to most (especially puritan) sermons, he observes: "Idealized they may be but they had also to be recognizable" to their neighbors in the congregation, which is why not all godly lives are the same.[22] He demonstrates the point by interpreting an incident involving a new dress (in which Mrs. Ratcliffe's reluctance to wear finery is pitted against obedience to her husband's wish that she wear the dress). Clearly fascinated by the conflict, Ley narrates this incident over several pages in almost voyeuristic fashion. Lake interprets this incident to show how Ley turns Mrs. Ratcliffe's apparent defeat (obedience to her husband) into a moral victory (the achievement of even greater godly charisma and potency) without openly defying patriarchy: "There could hardly be a better example of the contrast between the formally patriarchal content of puritan ideology and the subtle ways in which the personal godliness of individual women could be invoked to subvert that patriarchalism," exemplified by Ley's rhetorical use of the incident to demonstrate Jane's moral superiority to her husband, paradoxically demonstrated by the conflict between her humility and her wish to obey her husband.[23] In this and other cases of conscience, Lake reveals how Mrs. Ratcliffe was exemplary in part because she exemplified godly expectations for women's religious behavior and in part because audiences could recognize her particular and individualized qualities. The sermon does not offer her merely as an exemplar of the godly obedient matron but exposes the "tension between the claims of godliness and the normal social roles assigned to her as a married woman."[24]

In fact, Mrs. Ratcliffe's chosen role as a godly woman generated, "through her feminine acquaintances and clerical clients, a position of real potency or charisma," a position achieved—paradoxically—by "a sort of extreme moderation."[25] She offered no direct challenge to "conventional views regarding women's subordination," leading Lake to admit that his reading of Mrs. Ratcliffe as a woman emancipated by her charismatic godliness is not the only one possible from existing evidence: Attention to "fleeting hints culled from almost incidental asides and vignettes inserted into Ley's narrative" and to "silences, omissions, divergences from the norm" can, "taken with other material, be made to yield a certain significance."[26] In fact, the sermon could just as easily support other "perfectly accurate, if partial" alternatives: Jane Ratcliffe as a woman personally emancipated through the extremity of her chosen (moderate) style of godliness, a "woman of spirit and ability broken by the constraints of marriage and the horrors of childbirth" in a patriarchal system, or "a shrew and know-all" recuperated after death for godliness and for posterity as a "quiescent model of female behaviour."[27] Lake's essay demonstrates how Jane Ratcliffe and other subjects "being dead yet speaking" present a "godly paradigm intended for inspiration and imitation,"[28] as he exposes through practices of close reading the interpretive hazards and almost total lack of certainty regarding the exemplary power of the discourse.

Finally, the issue of gender compounds problems of access and interpretation to this surviving archive of funeral sermons. To complicate matters further, even this limited sermon archive exhibits great generic variety, making it difficult to recognize the reading practices best suited to interpret individual sermons. Many funeral sermons are perfectly orthodox and impersonal exegeses of scriptural texts with a godly life appended, so that sermon and life—while connected and intended to be taken together—function separately as well as in tandem. Many were revised and amplified for publication, sometimes many years after the funeral, thus complicating our sense of funeral sermons as occasional performances. Some godly lives, though written by clergymen and *called* sermons, are printed with no sermon at all. Some—in many ways the most interesting—include direct quotations from these women's writings, including scriptural interpretations and devotional meditations. These latter sermons are uniquely challenging in that these women's words of biblical exegesis are known to us only as they are excerpted, cited indirectly, or ventriloquized by their preachers after their authors' deaths, selected, spoken, and published by preachers for their own ideological purposes. However, few, if any, of these alleged volumes of manuscript material are extant, except as cited indirectly by their preachers after their authors' deaths. As Charles Fitz-Jeffrey said in his funeral sermon for Lady Phillipa Rous: "Shee being dead, yet preacheth vnto vs a sensible Sermon,"[29] invoking not only the text of her dead body but also the speaking and printed texts of the sermon. Discrepancies between sermons and subjects challenge us to extract the maximum historical value from these disputed documents. And paradoxically it is only when we do so that we appreciate their literary complexity. In what follows I use a number of case studies to examine the scholarly significance of the discrepancies between sermons and subjects and conclude with provisional methodologies for extracting the maximum historical value from these disputed documents.

For those women whose lives are well documented, the disjunction between the apparent conventionality of their lives depicted in their funeral sermons and the known circumstances of their lives available in other documents is particularly frustrating. The sermon preached by Edward Rainbowe, bishop of Carlisle, for Lady Anne Clifford, Countess Dowager of Pembroke, Dorset, and Montgomery, is perhaps the best known of these. It has stirred controversy among readers seeking to reconcile the woman revealed in this sermon with the woman so recently the subject of feminist historians who admire her resistance to patriarchal authority reflected in her lifelong legal battle to secure inheritance of her father's estates. Lucinda Becker epitomizes the frustrations of those who know the history of Anne Clifford's courageous legal battles and her single-minded campaign for justice. Becker writes that "despite Clifford's forthright views, her assertive fight for her rights to vast tracts of family land, and the determined energy with which she sought to improve and expand her properties right up to the end of her life," the sermon reduces her to "a mirror in which other women may view a purely domestic sphere of action."[30]

If we accept Lake's contention—that the ideology of such sermons depended on the fit between the known subject and an idealized version of that subject appropriated to the ideological intentions of the preacher—then the text from Proverbs 14:1 ("Every wise Woman buildeth her House") is uniquely chosen to test that fit. The scriptural text's focus on building resonates against the backdrop of Anne Clifford's restorations of her family estates and her construction of chapels and almshouses, activities that became possible only after all possible male heirs and her third husband died in 1649 or 1650. Anne did not so much succeed in her legal battles as outlive all claimants to her possessions, a providential fact that is intimated by the sermon's emphasis on her building projects but is never made explicit. With its focus on building, the text from Proverbs sets up an anticipated personal application in which Lady Clifford in death is not so much extolled as gathered up into the typological history of salvation narrated in the Bible. Nonetheless, the choice of text pays homage to her achievements in this realm, which *are* celebrated in the sermon.

Despite the subversive possibilities of Rainbowe's chosen text, the sermon fails, for some readers, to celebrate Clifford's unique independence, courage, and persistence. Rainbowe interprets her most courageous actions as examples of virtues conventionally associated with women, such as meekness, humility, and constancy, where building becomes a form of praiseworthy "housewifery" motivated by charity, gratitude, kindness, and piety (rather than, one presumes, the more masculine virtues of honor and public service) as the products of love rather than power. All of this is disappointing to some readers, in part because they read her life so differently: as a protofeminist crusade for women's rights as landowners. Although the sermon alludes to her legal battles, it subsumes them within the "ethos of the home."[31] Even Lady Clifford's courage in openly supporting the king before the occupying parliamentary forces headed by Colonel Harrison is contained as an example of her womanly "constancy," and her personal diaries are read to signify "religious" virtue rather than self-fashioning. Mary Ellen Lamb protests: "Rather than the painful and sometimes obsessive creation of herself as an agent in a hostile culture, Clifford's writings were read [by Rainbowe] to reveal her 'serenity,' an absence of sin, a void rather than a presence. To the Bishop of Carlisle, Clifford's diary was in a sense composed of blank pages."[32] But Rainbowe's sermon could equally be seen as honoring his subject by recognizing and establishing in painstaking detail the connections between Lady Clifford's body, her architectural projects, and her peculiar diaries (which disappoint many readers as autobiography or life writing, even as Rainbowe's sermon disappoints as biography). Anne M. Myers demonstrates that the diaries are organized by architectural landmarks rather than by time, moments where past, present, and future intersect (as in the repeated descriptions of Brougham Castle as both birthplace and grave). Their repetitions, like those inscribed in the funeral monuments and inscriptions she composes, builds, and records or in the medals she strikes, succeed in multiplying Lady Clifford so that she inhabits her castles verbally and memorially at the same time, thus demonstrating her right to them.[33]

In a reading that resists the domestication of Lady Clifford's virtues, Barbara K. Lewalski finds Rainbowe's "interpretive key" in his statement that Lady Clifford was "absolute Mistris of her Self, her Resolutions, Actions, and Time" (53), qualities that emphasize the "extraordinary completeness and autonomy of her life" and that he finds "especially remarkable in a woman."[34] The sentence is part of a series of paradoxes, however: Lady Clifford is pleasing to all yet like to none; her manner of dress was not disliked by any but imitated by none, and so on. Lady Clifford's autonomy and completeness, then, are qualified by the statement that she "yet allowed a time for every purpose, for all *Addresses*, for any *Persons*" (53). Rainbowe is likely not referring to her ontological integrity or core identity, as the partial quotation suggests, but perhaps only to her hospitality and accessibility.

The sermon is more profitably understood as a witty exegetical exercise, with *paradox* as its interpretive key, a device of rhetorical invention to be distinguished from the moderating rhetoric Collinson observed in funeral sermons that collapsed every personal trait toward a neutral middle ground and evacuated individual personalities and characters. Moderating rhetoric of the type Collinson dislikes gives us Samuel Crook, who was "grave without austerity, pleasant without levity," or John Carter, who "never made Feasts, yet always had wholesome full and liberal Diet in his house."[35] Lady Clifford is also described, in the famous words of Dr. Donne, as a person who could discourse as ably on predestination as on slea-silk, but that phrase resonates with the complexity of this woman capable of discourse on the most theoretical and practical levels, equally comfortable with both and presumably with the full range of topics in between. Such an interpretation accords with Rainbowe's description of her "sharpness of Wit, a faithful Memory, [and] deep Judgment," or, more eloquently, "a clear Soul shining through a *Vivid* Body" (38, 16). More important, it concurs with his account of the apparent "*Paradoxes* and *Contradictions* in her Life; She lived, and conversed, *outwardly* with the *World*, as easily as might be; yet her Guise *inward* and *reflex'd*, was quite as one of another World" (52).

An equally paradoxical and mysterious key to Lady Clifford is found in Rainbowe's summation of her character: "None disliked what she did, or was, because she was like her self in all things" (53). And what did it entail to be "like her self"? The answer appears to be that she was a wise woman, a "great Patterne of Virtue, and an eminent Benefactor to her Generation"—a pattern to both men and women because in "Scripture-philosophy" "all souls are equal," and a pattern because she was a good "housewife" (sig. A2, 7, 12). This rhetorical move—a pretty piece of wit that joins Lady Clifford's domestic and public persons—has appeared reductive and trivializing to many modern readers, but Rainbowe makes explicit the honor of Clifford's station as well as the consequences of "the well-ordering of a *Family*" (25) for the commonwealth. He measures her integrity not simply, or literally, by the houses that she built but by her impact on those who inhabit them, "Families being the first Principles of Bodies publick, the Seminaries which stock cities, out of which Kingdoms and Commonwealths do grow" (27). Chief among Lady Clifford's achievements was the education of her children and servants, evidenced by her practice of strewing her bedchamber with sayings copied from memory and pinned up by her servants in the manner of a giant commonplace book, her habit of supplying each servant with books of religious devotion four times a year, her reading of books on theology and religious controversy (thus edifying her own "building"), and her conformity to the Church of England. Certainly there is much here to distinguish Lady Clifford from the conventionally pious women of many funeral sermons, and there is no contradiction between the woman whose conversation is seasoned with salt, "savoury, but never bitter," and the woman whose chief virtue is "humility" or whose public actions were examples of "Good Housewifery" (44, 12). The totality of these claims shows Lady Clifford "like her self" by exemplifying just how forward-looking, courageous, and edifying her womanly humility, good housewifery, and maintenance of a well-ordered family could be. Rainbowe redeems the terms, filling them to capacity, rather than discarding them for words of a more "masculine" tenor, all the while reminding us that Anne Clifford comprehends both sexes and stands in for all virtues, with biblical warrant for doing so.

◆

John Donne's sermon for Lady Magdalen Danvers—called by Lewalski his "most conventional" funeral sermon[36]—challenges modern readers to find the woman behind the conventional façade, a response that is complicated by the known relationship between Donne and Lady Danvers (formerly Mrs. Herbert) over many years, the obvious affection they shared, and his close relationship with her children and with her much younger husband, Sir John Danvers. Further obstructing our ability to discover Magdalen Danvers *in* this sermon is the fact that the sermon itself became part of the record of her life incorporated into Izaak Walton's life of George Herbert so that—in a circular way—what we know of Mrs. Herbert as biography relies heavily on Donne's sermon.[37] Finally, the sermon shares many of the generic characteristics of funeral sermons: its division into exegesis of a scriptural text and application of that text to the deceased; its choice of a scriptural text that inspires hope and removes the sting of death; its biographical emphasis on birth, breeding, education, and manner of death; and its treatment of the subject's most notable personal qualities. Together these qualities create a sense of detachment from the raw pain of loss that underwrites the sermon.

At the heart of the sermon's application of the heavenly vision of the text is Donne's estimation of Mrs. Danvers's distinguishing quality—"Her *rule* was *mediocrity*"[38]—and herein lies the paradox. It is precisely this word *mediocrity* that has led commentators to describe the sermon as "conventional," especially because that mediocrity is embodied in domestic virtues. As Arnold Stein observes, "All of Lady Danvers's actions move from the center of domestic virtue: the civil virtue of her charity and her religious virtue move out but circle that center. No sins are mentioned but potential flaws are brought up in passing, and careful discriminations answer and dissipate questions that are never quite formed."[39] Donne appears detached to some, despite Izaak Walton's claim that he delivered the sermon weeping.[40]

The first thing to observe is that the sermon is delivered a month after the funeral, Donne being committed elsewhere and unable to preach her funeral sermon. Understandably, this state of affairs undermines the immediacy of his vision of the new heavens and new earth in which righteousness dwells called for by his scriptural text. Lady Danvers is already there and so must be invoked as she was a month ago, content for the moment "to bee one of this Congregation, and to heare some parts of this *Text* re-applied unto thee" (8: 86). In this reapplication, Donne makes explicit that Lady Danvers's mediocrity is a vibrant state, achieved strenuously and maintained actively in every aspect of her life. Emotionally, it is a cheerful and holy mediocrity somewhere between the occasional melancholy from which she suffered and her inclination to be "naturally cheerfull, and merry, and loving facetiousnesse, and sharpnesse of wit" (8: 86). Physically, it is a comeliness distinguishable from pride on the one hand and careless indifference to her appearance on the other. Religiously, it is the rule of her religion—scripturally based and mediated through the established church—that places her, for Donne, between the papists who undervalue scripture and the separatists who undervalue the church. Even her dying revealed this rule of mediocrity: "she "died without any change of *countenance*, or *posture*; without any *strugling*, any *disorder*; but her *Death-bed* was as quiet, as her *Grave*" (8: 91).

The most celebrated example of Lady Danvers's mediocrity is her socially scandalous marriage to John Danvers, which in Donne's witty handling becomes a consequence of cosmic "mediocrity" moderating the marriage of a widowed mother of ten in her forties to a man twenty years her junior: "For, as the well tuning of an *Instrument*, makes *higher* and *lower* strings, of one sound, so the inequality of their yeeres, was thus reduc't to an evennesse, that shee had a cheerfulnesse, agreeable to his youth, and he a sober staidnesse, conformable to her more yeeres. So that, I would not consider her, at so much more then forty, nor him, at so much lesse then thirty, at that time, but as their persons were made one, and their fortunes made one, by marriage, so I would put their yeeres into one number, and finding a sixty betweene them, thinke them thirty a peece" (8: 88). This explanation may be just a witty compliment—to both the deceased and her widower—of a piece with other characteristically witty allusions (such as Donne's first-person statement that his mother was a Hittite [8: 72]), but even a month after Lady Danvers's death, the sermon aches with the memory of her personal beauty, her religious conformity, her cheerful and affable character, her love of family, her generosity, her courage (in shielding him and others in a plague year), and her struggles with melancholy. Many of Donne's sermons resonate with desire for the new heavens and the new earth, which he always imagines as immediate, and present, and possible, but this sermon interweaves the scriptural text with the text of his deceased friend seamlessly and without compromise. This enfolding of Lady Danvers's life and that of her family, friends, and congregation into the scriptural promises is a work of consolation both personal and communal.

◆

John Carter's sermon preached at the funeral of Lady Frances Stanley Egerton, Countess of Bridgewater, wife of John Egerton, first Earl of Bridgewater (hereafter referred to as Lady Bridgewater), although never printed, survives in manuscript and provides a particularly instructive case study of the discrepancies between the known (and to modern eyes) most important aspects of a woman's biography and her funeral commemorations. As Heidi Brayman Hackel has observed, "Frances Bridgewater left only one record of her learning and intellectual interests: her library [of 241 books]," a substantial and intriguing collection in which she emerges as "altogether more vigorous and educated than she seems to her contemporaries."[41] Although her sister, the Countess of Huntingdon (Elizabeth Stanley), two of her daughters, and her son are extolled as readers and book collectors and for their learning, Lady Bridgewater "does not ripple the historical record with curiosity, resistance, or exceptional intelligence."[42] Just as Rainbowe argued that Lady Clifford could be judged by her "Companions" (i.e., her books) (60), so Hackel argues that Lady Bridgewater's library offers glimpses of her person and interests.

That said, however, Lady Bridgewater's funeral sermon, preached on April 2, 1636, offers some tantalizing hints of the woman behind the conventional generic portrait afforded by funeral sermons and the godly lives connected with them.[43] It takes as its text Psalm 37:37 ("Marke the perfect man and Behould the upright, for the end of that man is peace"), a text remarkable for its simultaneous evocation and cancellation of Frances Egerton's sex: "Change but the Sexe and make it woman, or take the word in its full latitude, as it comprehends the woman; and this sad Spectacle, applyes the Doctrine which my Texte delivers: The Psalmist long since gaue the Thesis, and this dayes Funerall exhibits the Hypothesis: this spectacle present you with an example for this Rule; and this Rule, with the Morall of this Example." As with many funeral sermons, this one claims exemplary status for its subject for both men and women, playing on the equality before Christ of all Christian souls.[44] Moreover, Carter spends considerable time at the sermon's outset justifying personal application to Lady Bridgewater, citing the examples of the church fathers Basil and Gregory Nazienzen and of biblical mourners such as David, Zacheus, and the apostles.

Having established that there is "none so greate an healpe, to healpe a Soule to Heaven, as a good Example," Carter divides his exegesis into a precept, a pattern, and a reason before applying these parts to his dead subject. Although it is true that Lady Bridgewater's learning and love of books are nowhere mentioned in the sermon, some passing references to these matters suggest that they were appropriate, maybe even implicit, in speaking of her. Explication of "Behould," for example, leads to a comparison between the creatures we behold and the books we annotate with a marginal hand that "directs our reading to an higher reference and though it selfe is Earthy, it reads vs a Divinity Lecture, and preaches to vs in a Speaking Silence, that Deity, which made it for us." Lessons taught by particular creatures—the ant, the ox, the serpent, the dove—are called "perticuler Scholes," and the conclusions we draw from them are as the conclusions of a syllogism. The life of a Christian is a living comment upon the Bible, Carter says, and the dead are good copies laid before us not only to read but so that we may "write after" them, particularly their virtues rather than their vices.

In keeping with this scholarly, bookish emphasis, the sermon abounds with allusions to the secular and mythical as well as to scriptural examples and authors—Pliny, Pythagoras, Hermes Trismegistus, Florus (author of a book owned by Lady Bridgewater), Alexander the Great, Aristotle, Plato, Hercules, and Procrustes, along with Abraham, Isaiah, David, Rebecca, and Paul. And the countess's interest in natural history could have inspired the comparison of the virtuous man wrapped in integrity to "a Porcupine in his quills; or a Tortoyse in his shell." Hackel has noted the breadth of the countess's library, particularly in works of controversial divinity, as well as devotional works, and the sermon assumes such knowledge, alluding easily, for example, to Pelagians and Catharists—heretics both—in a single sentence. Carter's praise for Lady Bridgewater's firm allegiance to the "Truth of Religion" is reflected in the number of conformist Protestant works in her library, although she also possessed books with Marian or recusant connections befitting the "dangerous times" in which she lived.[45]

These oblique connections aside, particular mention of Lady Bridgewater's learning and love of books is subsumed in a fairly conventional panegyrical discourse focused on her piety, although Carter adds "ready apprehension and sound judgment" to her honorable birth. He praises her especially for her spiritual humility, the extent of her public and private devotions, her love of sermons (which she had repeated to her if she had to miss because of illness), and her practices of prayer and attending sermons.

One gets a real sense of her charity and discretion: Not only was there no one who would speak ill of her, but she attained her own heights without bringing others down. Lady Bridgewater was meticulous about her household accounts, paying her debts punctually. Although she valued virtue in people, she was not censorious: "If she beheld a virtue, she would comend it, if she spy'd a vice, like Constantine, she would cast her mantle over it; if it was too perspicuous to be hid, she would make noe other use of it, than this; let him that thinketh he stands, take heede least he falls; this man hath slipp'd to day, and we may falle to morrow." Conventionally, Carter speaks of Lady Bridgewater's role as wife, mother, and mistress to her servants, ending with a description of the manner of her death, and, in particular, the conventionality of a quiet death: "But this ever honoured Lady moov'd neither head, nor hand, nor foote, death could not move a jointe of her; we knew not that her soule had lefte her body, but by the wante of breath." Her virtues—while conventional in funeral sermons—are not particularly domestic. They are the virtues of charity and discretion, expressed in her piety, in the generosity of her speech, and in her social relations with family, servants, neighbors, and chaplains in the church and in her community. It is true that we hear many conventional praises of her piety and devotion, but the idiosyncrasies of her social relations shine through her chaplain's words, and her obvious delight in secular and sacred learning—learning of all sorts—is intimated by the freedom of allusion with which Carter addresses her husband, family, and those attending the funeral.

One last example of the discrepancy between life and funeral sermon must suffice. Martha Moulsworth wrote one of the first autobiographical poems in the English language ("Memorandum," dated 1632). The poem is a significant social and literary artifact that communicates in a strikingly candid, graceful, and human way the social constraints and the subtle emotions Moulsworth experienced concerning her upbringing, three marriages, children, and lack of a man's education.[46] Like the poem, Moulsworth's funeral sermon, preached by Thomas Hassall, reveals her extraordinary self-consciousness as author, wife, and patron of her commemorator (whom she handpicked to preach her sermon). Together, "Memorandum" and the funeral sermon provide a rich store of materials for comparing Moulsworth's self-depiction with the portrait painted by her preacher, and they are a unique example of the ways in which autobiography and biography are transformed by the genres in which they are expressed.[47] Neither can be said to present the authentic or "real" Martha Moulsworth, although the poem's unconventional complexity makes one realize what has been glossed over in Hassall's sermon. In fact, if verifiable "fact" were the criterion by which "reality" were determined, one would have to conclude that the poem—with its factual anomalies—is more accurate than the sermon, but what we seem to have is a self-conscious and personal authenticity—an authenticity of emotion and feeling—sometimes at odds with the known historical facts of Moulsworth's life.

A crucial incident exposing this conflict involves Moulsworth's claim in "Memorandum" that her father "Beyond my sex & kind / he did with learninge Lattin deck mind [*sic*]" (ll. 29–30). Although Moulsworth confesses that she has lost the language through lack of use (commenting cryptically in the margin that "Lattin is nott the most marketable mariadge mettall" [l. 38]), she justifies her early exposure to it: "And whie nott so? the muses ffemalls are / and therfore of Vs ffemales take some care / Two Vniuersities we haue of men / o thatt we had but one of women then" (ll. 31–34). Various explanations for the claim that Moulsworth's father taught her Latin reveal the unease generated by notes of inauthenticity in the poem (as if we expect someone who is telling her life story, even in a poem, to do so only through verifiable facts). Germaine Greer disposes of the incident summarily by exposing how Moulsworth's father, a tutor to Sir Philip Sidney, apparently died in relative poverty when she was only 3 years old and therefore could not have taught her Latin or left her any financial resources. After her mother's death less than a year later, Moulsworth was probably raised by Helena and Ralph Johnson, her grandmother and step-grandfather. "The truth is that any education Moulsworth had, and we know from Hassall's funeral sermon that she read and wrote copiously, had come from her guardians, who are not mentioned in 'The Memorandum.'"[48]

Inclined to be more generous to Moulsworth but still feeling the need to explain this discrepancy, Robert Evans speculates that "Dorsett's [Martha's father] letters corroborate many of Martha's claims about him; he seems to have been the kind of intelligent, virtuous man whom Sidney could respect"[49] and who would have been competent to instruct his daughter had he lived. He also had connections to many important people through the Sidneys. "Perhaps he left detailed instructions for her upbringing; perhaps he asked his many learned friends to make sure that the girl was properly raised and taught,"[50] but he could not have personally supervised her education. Although Hassall may have used the poem as a source for his funeral sermon, he attributes her education to unspecified others, suggesting that "the more complex truth about her education was something she must have discussed with Hassall or with members of her family."[51] The "exaggerated claims"[52] that Moulsworth makes in her poem raise questions about why she felt the need to make them.

Hassall's final summary idealizes Moulsworth. Jimmy Hull observes: "The Moulsworth who could propose a women's university, or boast about the intellectual capacities of women, or reflect wryly on the marriage market, or allude to sexual pleasures, or fight and beat a vicar in court, is altogether missing here."[53] Partly, this idealization reflects the nature of the funeral sermon and the fact that it was delivered some fourteen years after Moulsworth wrote the poem, but without the poem "it would be easy enough to view Moulsworth as a 'model' Renaissance woman, rather than as one who had begun to break the mold."[54] Yet that early introduction to "Arts and Letters"[55] paid dividends during her sickness, when she passed the time "with reading good Bookes, / her constant Companions, / and faythfull Cownsellers." Even in that final illness, Martha read the Bible, took note of particular places in it, which she commended to others, and read both civil and ecclesiastical histories, finding in both "concurrences / with the present tymes."[56]

Because Hassall's sermon confirms information that Moulsworth provided in her poem and introduces other traits that she may have been too modest to mention, it appears to be "a reliable source of information" about her.[57] Hull conjectures that the sermon talks about what is dearest to Moulsworth's own heart (one wonders, then, about her dismissal of her children in one line), whereas the sermon "focuses more on her importance to the community." The result, however, is that Hassall makes Moulsworth a much more conventional figure than she seems from "Memorandum" by ignoring "some of the most interesting aspects of her personality" and emphasizing others.[58]

On the topic of marriage, Moulsworth's poem suggests that although she saw her life falling into the sequential (and conventional) roles of daughter, wife, and widow, she also articulated "the actual complexity of such roles and how they might be subject to change or even challenge."[59] Her depiction of her three marriages combines "charity and truth, idealism and realism,"[60] especially when she distinguishes her third marriage by emphasizing her partner's special characteristics or when she mixes resentment at the necessity of marriage with realistic acceptance of it as an institution. Of her first marriage Moulsworth notes that "I did nott bind my selfe in Mariadge" (l. 50) until the age of 21, concluding that "my first knott held fiue yeares, & eight months more" (l. 52). Her second husband is dispatched in two lines. Her third husband, Bevill Moulsworth, however, was "a louely man, & kind" (l. 57), and Moulsworth devotes sixteen lines to describing their special relationship: "was neuer man so Buxome to his wife / with him I led an easie darlings life. / I had my will in house, in purse in Store / whatt would a weomen old or yong haue more?" (ll. 65–68). Indeed, Moulsworth's poem demonstrates that sometimes companionate marriages were achieved, while it "exemplifies (and in some cases subtly modifies) many of the ideals championed by Renaissance advocates of worthy wives and marriages."[61] The sermon also occludes Moulsworth's determination at the end of her poem to remain in the "siluer" state of widowhood rather than marry again.

Hassall's sermon confirms the image of the "good and decent woman"[62] that emerges from Moulsworth's poem but only by idealizing her.[63] Hassall's portrait of her as a conventional woman (exemplifying the virtues of "Integrity, Iustice, Pietye, / and well formed Charitye" to make her life a "patterne of / Modesty, discression, / Hospitality, Frugality / to others of her Sexe") erases her determination not to marry until the age of 21 and her evident partiality toward her third husband (Hassall insists that "shee / would many tymes saye / They were all so good, / that she knew not / which was the better").[64] The cumulative effect of Hassall's idealizations of his subject layered with the self-portrait presented in "Memorandum" demonstrates the difficulties that funeral sermons pose as records of women's lives.

As the funeral sermon for Jane Ratcliffe also demonstrates, the spiritual lives described in this genre were often tied to a profound, intelligent, and probing habit of biblical interpretation. In Ratcliffe's case this tie was generated by her "continual and attentive hearing of Sermons / and reading good bookes, the Bible especially." But, more important, her questions about scripture indicated her "deepe insight into the sacred Text, and an especiall acquaintance with the Spirit that indited it," an insight that prompted Ley to seek her advice on "points of religion" based on her observations of the Bible that he encouraged her to write down.[65] As Lake demonstrates, although Mrs. Ratcliffe could not compete with university-educated ministers in terms of formal learning, her ardent devotion and profession of true religion enabled her to gain entrance into "the literate and scholarly protestant culture propagated by the universities and their clerical alumni."[66] The residue of patriarchy prevails in Ley's account, however. Jane Ratcliffe agrees to write down her interpretations only if Ley agrees to supervise and correct them, and she uses them for her own devotion or to teach her children and servants, although "an eloquent man and mighty in the Scriptures . . . might not disdain to learn of this *Priscilla*."[67]

Several sermons for women repeat this theme, offering tantalizing glimpses into a religious culture in which women not only heard sermons but also repeated them, took notes that then contributed to their commonplace books, and used them as means of instruction of children and servants. Some of these women also developed the habit of writing down their own biblical interpretations, often in discursive consultation with their chaplains (much in the same fashion as Catholic women and their confessors), and in some cases—less extraordinary than at first sight—preparing their own sermons, some of which are quoted for the first time in their funeral sermons.[68] Elizabeth Machell "hanged upon the mouth of [God's] messengers, as Chickens hang upon the mouth of the Hen,"[69] and Lady Strode "was a Notary, and tooke the Sermons which she heard, by her own penne."[70] Lady Strode used these notes to reconstruct the sermons and preach them to her maidservants, a practice repeated in many households. Rebekka Crisp is remembered gratefully by her relative Thomas Gataker as a "great Questionist" and a "whetstone" to his own spiritual growth.[71] The most remarkable sermon of all—Anna Walker's sermon composed for her mistress, Anne of Denmark—is the only known case of a sermon composed by a literate and witty court lady (as part of a bid for patronage but arguably serving other needs of self-expression). What we know about women's practices of putting their scriptural interpretations into writing makes this "sermon" (if indeed that is what it is) less anomalous, although its originality ought not to be underestimated.[72] A culture for such activity already existed. Such practices also help to explain the apparently sudden flourishing of female preaching and prophecy in the 1640s and 1650s among radical sects, especially the Quakers.

One particularly interesting woman was Lady Frances Hobart, daughter of Lady Frances Stanley Egerton and her husband, Sir John Egerton, first Earl of Bridgewater. Most of our knowledge of her life comes from her funeral sermon, a partisan performance by a long-time friend and spiritual adviser who connived with her to establish a spiritual discipline in her household, comprising prayers three times daily, scripture readings twice daily, catechizing, and a regimen of sermons and lectures that—in her widowhood—was astounding. She regularly heard seven or more sermons a week—four during the week and three on Sundays. As John Collinges claims, Lady Hobart was "unweariable in her attendance upon Sermons, such especially where the Truths of God were opened most lively, and with least vanity, and in fullest evidence of Scripture."[73] She also endowed one lecture a week by Mr. Collinges and arranged for repetitions of one or both sermons on Sunday night after the more public sermons in the town were finished. In addition to this regimen, Lady Hobart engaged Collinges to preach a morning sermon, except for those days when he was administering public communion. Most astonishing, she converted some rooms in her house into a chapel seating more than 200 people, which Collinges claims was full every Sunday for the last sixteen years of her life. Although Collinges reports that Lady Hobart spent several hours a day discoursing on these sermons, we have no surviving evidence of her responses to them. Certainly, however, we can conclude that her life centered on a biblical and sermon-centered piety that she established, maintained, and modeled for her children and servants.

Examples of women's writings, including scriptural interpretation, abound in their funeral sermons, and some are published there. Edmund Calamy preached Elizabeth Moore's funeral sermon on a text chosen by her (Psalm 119:92: "Unless thy Law had been my delights, I should then have perished in mine affliction") and published it along with four others preached on the same text, a short account of her life, and finally her seventeen "evidences for heaven"—scriptural texts culled by Mrs. Moore from her scriptural reading, aided by her clearer vision following the hearing of sermons and the action of the spirit. These "evidences" consist of seventeen verses accompanied by a short explication and personal application, confirming that she was well versed in scriptures that served as cordials during her year-long battle with breast cancer.[74] Henry Wilkinson's narrative of Margaret Corbet's life (appended to her funeral sermon) reports that "she wrote the Sermons she heard . . . and she hath left many volumes of Sermons of her own handwriting, taken with great dexterity, and these are so many choice monuments of her industry."[75] We have no way of knowing what these volumes contained, although Wilkinson also informs us that Mrs. Corbet could discourse on all material points of religion, and "search't Expositors, and Practicall Divines" to assist her interpretations.[76] It is likely, however, that Wilkinson's emphasis on her "industry" in leaving these volumes means that she left us primarily the "Sermon notes . . . which she took at Church" and read to her servants rather than her own scriptural interpretations.[77] Nonetheless, Corbet's industry in note taking, sermon repetition, and examination of her servants on the sermons they heard offers a glimpse of a life permeated by sermons.

Funeral sermons reveal just how prevalent was the habit of being a "Writer of sermons" (as Calamy described Lady Anne Waller), noting her folio commonplace book crammed with observations out of scriptures and fed by her habit of hearing sermons twice a day.[78] Calamy says that Waller wrote them "in her *Heart* as well as in her *Book*, and her life was an *exact Commentary* upon the Sermons she heard." Her commonplace book—a large folio—contained the observations of her reading in "Scripture, divines, and her own experiences."[79] Moreover, Waller took it upon herself to explain obscure points of doctrine from Sunday sermons to her household. This work was enhanced by her establishment of lectures in her parishes and her bequests to support ministers.[80]

The same habit of writing out scriptural observations was passed down to Waller's stepdaughter (and subsequently daughter-in-law), Anne Harcourt, who along with her servants attended public sermons on the Sabbath, after which she examined her servants on the sermon and repeated it for their edification.[81] The sermon further reveals that Anne Harcourt—only 20 when she died—kept a large paper book secretly in her chamber, "designed to be her souls looking-glass."[82] Hall quotes verbatim from the page for April 14, 1664, nine days before Harcourt's death, written as her confession of faith and testimony of her assurance of her salvation in Christ.[83]

Similarly, Stephen Denison published the writings of Elizabeth Juxon, the wife of John Juxon, who heard "nine or ten Sermons euery weeke."[84] Not only did Mrs. Juxon select the text for the sermon (Job 7:3–4), a text that Denison applies in detail to the circumstances of her life, but also the last part of the book records Mrs. Juxon's twenty marks of election, accompanied by Denison's commentary, analysis, and application of these marks to the larger audience of this sermon.[85] Nehemiah Wallington's copy of this text confirms that Christians strove to identify and lay claim to those marks of election and that he applied them personally to his own spiritual life, confirming that the lives of women commemorated in sermons were exemplary to men as well as to women.

Finally, Lady Strode not only copied out sermons that she heard, but more provocatively, "she hath left (and that in no small volume) diuers disputations, that shee had with Separatists and Papists; her answeres; and what was her owne resolution in the controuerted opinions; annexing her reasons,"[86] one more testimony to the common practice of scriptural exegesis among godly women.[87]

Early modern funeral sermons for women are only one body of texts illuminating women's roles as exegetes, preachers, and patterns for imitation. Frustrating in their ties to conventional forms of hagiography, these sermons nonetheless offer glimpses of the ways in which women engaged with post-Reformation sermon culture both publicly and domestically. To further this study of women and sermons, we need to take these first steps: (1) Compile a broad comprehensive public archive of printed and manuscript funeral sermons, building on excellent foundational work by Ralph Houlbrooke and others; (2) develop a generic paradigm for the sermon that distinguishes between the life commemorated as exegesis and that documented as biography; (3) maintain a sensitivity to the linguistic, generic, and structural *differences* between sermons to offset their conventionality; (4) analyze letters, diaries, sermon notes, passages of scriptural exegesis in commonplace books, and other manuscript and printed sources to recover audience responses; (5) provide more detailed historical contextualization of these sermons, paying attention to their multiple occasions as preached, written, heard, published, and read; and (6) engage in further comparative analysis of sermons by the same author. These and other initiatives will develop a more complete and balanced account of the intersections and collaborations between women and their funeral sermons and will sustain the history that informs these often unconventional paragons of moderation.

Notes

1. Edward Rainbowe, *A Sermon Preached at the Funeral of the Right Honorable Anne Countess of Pembroke, Dorset, and Montgomery* (1677), 67. Subsequent references to this sermon are indicated by page number in the text of the essay.

2. The primary texts cited were 1 Corinthians 14:34, 35 and 1 Timothy 2:11, 12.

3. I have mapped out these four areas of the field in "Women and Sermons," in *Oxford Companion to the Early Modern Sermon*, ed. Hugh Adlington, Peter McCullough, and Emma Rhatigan (Oxford, UK: Oxford University Press, 2011), 155–77.

4. Richard L. Greaves, "Foundation Builders: The Role of Women in Early English Nonconformity," in *Triumph over Silence: Women in Protestant History*, ed. Richard Greaves (Westport, CT: Greenwood Press, 1985), 85; Keith Thomas, "Women and the Civil War Sects," *Past and Present* 13 (1958): 47.

5. Dorothy Ludlow, *"Arise and be Doing": English Preaching Women, 1640–1660* (Ph.D. diss., Indiana University, 1978), 8.

6. Judith Kegan Gardiner, "Re-Gendering Individualism: Margaret Fell Fox and Quaker Rhetoric," in *Privileging Gender in Early Modern England: Sixteenth Century Essays and Studies*, ed. Jean R. Brink (Kirksville, MO: Sixteenth Century Journal, 1993), 224, 220.

7. Patricia Crawford, *Women and Religion in England, 1500–1720* (London: Routledge, 1993), 207.

8. Dorothy Ludlow, "Shaking Patriarchy's Foundations: Sectarian Women in England, 1641–1700," in *Triumph over Silence: Women in Protestant History*, ed. Richard L. Greaves (Westport, CT: Greenwood Press, 1985), 110.

9. See Suzanne Trill, "A Feminist Critic in the Archives: Reading Anna Walker's *A Sweete Savor for Woman* (c. 1606)," *Women's Writing* 9.2 (2002): 199–214.

10. Thomas Becon, *The Catechism of Thomas Becon, S.T.P. Chaplain to Archbishop Cranmer, Prebendary of Canterbury &c. With Other Pieces Written by Him in the Reign of King Edward the Sixt*, ed. Rev. John Ayre (Cambridge, UK: Cambridge University Press for the Parker Society, 1844), 376.

11. Patrick Collinson, "'A Magazine of Religious Patterns': An Erasmian Topic Transposed in English Protestantism," in his *Godly People: Essays on English Protestantism and Puritanism* (London: Hambledon Press, 1983), 513.

12. For the most recent, comprehensive treatment of these subjects, see Lyndell O'Hara, *"Far Beyond Her Nature and Her Sex": The Creation of a Protestant Hagiography in England, 1590–1640* (Ph.D. diss., Fordham University, 2006), *passim.*

13. Collinson, "Religious Patterns," 520.

14. Eric Carlson, "English Funeral Sermons as Sources: The Example of Female Piety in pre-1640 Sermons," *Albion* 32.4 (2000): 577, 578n53, identified twenty-nine funeral sermons for women before 1640 that contained biographical information, whereas O'Hara (*Far Beyond Her Nature*) examined twenty-seven sermons. Their cutoff date means that the great period in which funeral sermons and the eulogies attached to them flourished (after 1640) has not been adequately studied. For the most detailed historical introduction to the early modern funeral sermon, see Ralph Houlbrooke, *Death, Religion, and the Family in England, 1480–1750* (Oxford, UK: Oxford University Press, 1998), 294–330.

15. O'Hara, *Far Beyond Her Nature*, 2.

16. O'Hara, *Far Beyond Her Nature*, 21–24.

17. Peter Lake, "Feminine Piety and Personal Potency: The Emancipation of Mrs. Jane Ratcliffe," *The Seventeenth Century* 2 (1987): 144. Carlson finds these sermons to be "fruitful, revealing, and trustworthy sources for studying the behaviours and practices of some segments of English society" ("English Funeral Sermons," 569), and Houlbrooke notes that close reading gives a strong impression "of their rich variety, of the adaptation of conventional patterns to meet particular circumstances, and of the extent to which authors treasured distinctive elements of personal character" (*Death*, 320).

18. John Ley, *A Patterne of Pietie, or the Religious Life and Death of That Grave and Gracious Mrs. Jane Ratcliffe Widow and Citizen of Chester* (1640), 1.

19. Lake, "Feminine Piety," 146.

20. Collinson, "Religious Patterns," 516.

21. Collinson, "Religious Patterns," 512.

22. Lake, "Feminine Piety," 160.

23. Lake, "Feminine Piety," 151.

24. Lake, "Feminine Piety," 151.

25. Lake, "Feminine Piety," 158.

26. Lake, "Feminine Piety," 154, 160, 161.

27. Lake, "Feminine Piety," 160.

28. O'Hara, *Far Beyond Her Nature*, 42, 8.

29. Charles Fitz-Geffrey, *Deaths Sermon unto the Liuing Delivered at the Funerals of the Religious Ladie Philippe, Late wife vnto the Right Worshipfull Sr. Anthonie Rous of Halton in Cornwall Knight* (1620), 30.

30. Lucinda Becker, *Death and the Early Modern Englishwoman* (Aldershot, UK: Ashgate, 2003), 97–98.

31. Heidi Brayman Hackel, *Reading Material in Early Modern England* (Cambridge, UK: Cambridge University Press, 2005), 229.

32. Mary Ellen Lamb, "The Agency of the Split Subject: Lady Anne Clifford and the Uses of Reading," *English Literary Renaissance* 22 (1992): 367.

33. Anne M. Myers, "Construction Sites: The Architecture of Anne Clifford's Diaries," *English Literary History* 73 (2006): 588–89.

34. Barbara K. Lewalski, *Writing Women in Jacobean England* (Cambridge, MA: Harvard University Press, 1993), 130.

35. Samuel Clark, *A Collection of the Lives of Ten Eminent Divines* (1662), 44, 8.

36. Barbara K. Lewalski, *Donne's "Anniversaries" and the Poetry of Praise: The Creation of a Symbolic Mode* (Princeton, NJ: Princeton University Press, 1973), 209.

37. Surprisingly, there is no life of Magdalen Newport Herbert Danvers in the new *Oxford Dictionary of National Biography*.

38. John Donne, *A Sermon of Commemoration of the Lady Danvers*, in *The Sermons of John Donne*, 10 vols., ed. George Potter and Evelyn Simpson (Berkeley: University of California Press, 1953–1962), 8: 89. Subsequent references to this sermon will be indicated by volume and page number in the text.

39. Arnold Stein, *The House of Death: Messages from the English Renaissance* (Baltimore: Johns Hopkins University Press, 1986), 55.

40. Izaak Walton, *Life of Mr. George Herbert* (1670), 19.

41. Hackel, *Reading Material*, 243, 244.

42. Hackel, *Reading Material*, 253. For example, Elizabeth Stanley, Countess of Huntingdon, is praised for her "understanding" and "perspicacity," notably in "occasions and affairs" (Joseph Fletcher, *A Sermon Preached at Ashby De-la-Zouche in the Countie of Leicester: At the Funerall of the Truly Noble and Vertuous Lady Elizabeth Stanley*... [1633]), 34), and like so many virtuous women, is commended for her diligence in searching the scriptures for evidences of her salvation, observations that she committed to writing until her death (41).

43. Huntington Library, MS EL 6883, facsimile, unfoliated. Quoted by kind permission of the Duke of Sutherland.

44. Carlson observes that in such cases the message was twofold: "First, women could not use their sex as an excuse for spiritual failings. . . . Second, if women—the weaker vessel—could overcome Satan, there was no excuse for men not to do so. Indeed, women were the best possible example for men" ("English Funeral Sermons," 587).

45. Hackel, *Reading Material*, 248.

46. Although funeral sermons for women rarely praise their education (although their qualities of mind and apprehension are noted), Stephen Geree's funeral sermon for Elizabeth Machell says, "She was so good a scholar in CHRIST'S Schoole, that she was called to take her highest degree, to wit, in heauen, long before the usuall time, as some doe in the Vniversity *propter excellentiam*, for their excellencie above their fellowes" (Stephen Geree, *The Ornament of Women. Or, A Description of the True Excellency of Women. Delivered in a Sermon at the Funerall of M. Elizabeth Machell, on Easter Munday Being the 15. of April 1639* [1639], 65). This comparison likely struck no one in the audience as odd, although we hear it today as deeply ironic. Similarly, Geree praises Machell, also with no apparent irony, as having a "masculine, heroicke, and invincible spirit" (*Ornament of Women*, 74).

47. Martha Moulsworth's "Memorandum" and Thomas Hassall's funeral sermon are printed in Robert C. Evans and Anne C. Little, eds., *"The Muses Females Are": Martha Moulsworth and Other Women Writers of the English Renaissance* (West Cornwall, CT: Locust Hill Press, 1995), app. 1, app. 3.

48. Germaine Greer, "'Backward Springs': The Self-Invention of Martha Moulsworth," in *"The Muses Females Are": Martha Moulsworth and Other Women Writers of the English Renaissance*, ed. Robert C. Evans and Anne C. Little (West Cornwall, CT: Locust Hill Press, 1995), 7.

49. Robert C. Evans, "Life and Times of Martha Moulsworth," in *"The Muses Female Are": Martha Moulsworth and Other Women Writers of the English Renaissance*, ed. Robert C. Evans and Anne C. Little (West Cornwall, CT: Locust Hill Press, 1995), 21.

50. Evans and Little, *The Muses Females Are*, 23.

51. Evans and Little, *The Muses Females Are*, 69.

52. Evans and Little, *The Muses Females Are*, 23.

53. Jimmy K. Hull, "Convention and Unconventionality in Hassall's Sermon and Moulsworth's 'Memorandum,'" *Critical Matrix: The Princeton Journal of Women, Gender, and Culture* 10 (1996): 70.

54. Thomas Hassall, "Thomas Hassall's Funeral Sermon on Martha Moulsworth," in *"The Muses Females Are": Martha Moulsworth and Other Women Writers of the English Renaissance*, ed. Robert C. Evans and Anne C. Little (West Cornwall, CT: Locust Hill Press, 1995), 71.

55. Hassall, "Funeral Sermon," 252.

56. Hassall, "Funeral Sermon," 253.

57. Hull, "Convention," 44.

58. Hull, "Convention," 45.

59. Evans, "Life and Times of Martha Moulsworth," 39.

60. Evans, "Life and Times of Martha Moulsworth," 23.

61. Evans, "Life and Times of Martha Moulsworth," 55.

62. Evans, "Life and Times of Martha Moulsworth," 68.

63. Hull, "Convention," 70.

64. Hassall, "Funeral Sermon," 252.

65. Ley, *Patterne of Pietie*, 25–26.

66. Lake, "Feminine Piety," 150.

67. Ley, *Patterne of Pietie*, 27.

68. Several of these sermons are surveyed in Debra L. Parish, "The Power of Female Pietism: Women as Spiritual Authorities and Religious Role Models in Seventeenth-Century England," *Journal of Religious History* 17.1 (1992): 33–46. Parish was looking for evidence of female "pietism" during the Civil War period, but I have scoured these and other sermons (both earlier and later) for evidence of the ways in which sermons were absorbed into early modern culture through women, thus extending their spiritual and polemical reach far beyond their occasion, but in ways that cannot always be measured.

69. Geree, *Ornament of Women*, 78–79.

70. John Barlow, *The True Guide to Glory: A Sermon Preached at Plympton-Mary in Devon, at the Funerals of the Right Worshipull, and Truly Religious Lady, the Lady Strode of Newingham [and Other Sermons]* (1632), 48.

71. Thomas Gataker, *Pauls Desire of Dissolution, and Deaths Advantage* (1620), sig. Bv.

72. Trill notes three distinctive qualities of this sermon that contribute to its originality: (1) the choice of text that enables a personalizing strategy based on a pun on her surname (Walker); (2) the use of this punning to connect the sermon to other parts of the manuscript, indicating her self-conscious insertion into all the materials presented; and (3) the coherence of the apparently miscellaneous contents of the manuscript as a whole ("Feminist Critic," 201). Trill's essay provides a detailed preliminary analysis of the manuscript's contents, including the sermon (206–7). The remarkable generic and personal self-consciousness of this entire manuscript, but particularly the sermon, will repay further analysis. Trill's essay opens up several areas: the significance of the secretary, gothic, and italic hands; Walker's choice of an anti-Catholic subject in her bid for patronage from an overtly Catholic queen; the style of the sermon, which anticipates the prophetic style of seventeenth-century preacher-prophets such as Eleanor Davies and Anna Trapnel; and the overt female consciousness of the manuscript.

73. John Collinges, *The Excellent Woman: Discourse More Privately from Proverbs 31.29, 30, 31. Upon the Occasion of the Death of the Right Honourable, The Lady Frances Hobart* (1669), 27.

74. Edmund Calamy, *The Godly Mans Ark, Or, City of Refuge in the Day of His Distresses*, 3rd ed. (1661).

75. Henry Wilkinson, *The Hope of Glory or Christs Indwelling in True Believers . . . March 5. 1656. At the Funerall of That Eminently-Religious-Gentlewoman Mris Margaret Corbet* (Oxford, 1657), 64.

76. Wilkinson, *Hope of Glory*, 64.

77. Wilkinson, *Hope of Glory*, 64.

78. Edmund Calamy, *The Happinesse of Those Who Sleep in Jesus . . . October 31. 1661* (1662), 28.

79. Calamy, *Happinesse*, 28.

80. Calamy, *Happinesse*, 29.

81. Edmund Hall, *A Sermon Preached at Stanton-Harcourt Church, at the Funerall of the Honourable the Lady Anne Harcourt, Who Deceased Aug. 23. 1664. Together with Her Funerall Speech* (Oxford, 1664), 55–56.

82. Hall, *Sermon*, 56.

83. Hall, *Sermon*, 57.

84. Stephen Denison, *The Monvment or Tombe-Stone . . .* (1620), 85.

85. Denison, *Monvment*, 78–82, 85–123.

86. Barlow, *True Guide to Glory*, 49.

87. Time does not permit, but the sermon preached at the funeral of Susanna, Countess of Suffolk, merits analysis for its remarkable interweaving of scriptural exegesis and biography. See Edward Rainbowe, *A Sermon Preached at Walden in Essex, at the Interrment of the Corps of the Right Honorable SUSANNA, Countesse of SUFFOLKE* (1649).

V

Religion and Secularization

12

Noam Reisner

Framing Religion

Marlovian Policy and the Pluralism of Art

Cultural historians often turn to the plays of Christopher Marlowe to contextualize the religious tensions between Catholics and Protestants in Elizabethan society and the persecution of other religious minorities on its cultural margins. Such studies, often conducted under the aegis of New Historicist approaches, detect a powerful voice of cultural resistance and dissent in the Marlovian ethos explored in such politically charged plays as *Tamburlaine the Great, The Jew of Malta,* or *The Massacre at Paris.*[1] Behind these scholarly meditations on the historical permeability of text and context, however, Marlowe the author consistently refuses to die. The darkly elusive persona of the Canterbury-born and Cambridge-educated poet-playwright—who probably spied for the English crown on the Catholic community at Rheims and was brutally murdered under suspicious circumstances while being investigated by the same crown for atheism—continues to enliven critical debate about the plays and poems left in his name.

Marlowe's alleged atheism is especially relevant in this context. Cultural historians have helpfully moved the debate about the atheist Marlowe away from hypothetical biographical speculations about the poet's religious unbelief to wider questions about what Marlowe's undeniable atheistic *reputation* actually connotes in a wider sociocultural context.[2] But even the most scrupulous historian weighing in on this debate has had to concede that Marlowe's plays are uniquely uniform in the gratuitous blasphemy that runs throughout them as a dark thread of sinister relativism and skepticism. Whether such relativism connotes outright atheism or merely the sharp satire of a poet disaffected with an irreligious world, there is no question that the overriding irreverence and frivolity of the plays in the face of religious certitudes is always framed by profound reflections on contemporary religious habits of thought and the violence attached to them in practice.[3]

The so-called Baines Note that Richard Baines delivered to the Privy Council close to the time of Marlowe's death famously attributes to Marlowe outrageous opinions on all forms of religious, particularly Christian, belief. Among the more colorful highlights are the accusations that Marlowe promulgates "into every company he cometh" the views that Moses was but a "juggler," that "Christ was a bastard and his mother dishonest," and that "St John the Evangelist was bedfellow to Christ and . . . used him as the sinners of Sodoma."[4] Yet there is one allegation in the Baines Note that is particularly striking in relation to how we presently perceive the status of Marlowe's craft as a poet and dramatist engaging with the dominant religious consensus of his day. This is the claim that Marlowe allegedly professed that "if he were put to write a new religion, he would undertake both a more excellent and admirable method."[5] What is striking about the suggestion that Marlowe bragged he was able to write into existence a more "admirable method" of religion is the genuinely Protestant notion that views the expression of religious belief as a textual transaction that depends on acts of reading and writing. The implication that such a religious construction might then depend for its success on literary aesthetic values can be read as blasphemously cynical, but it is not in fact that remote from the fundamental assumptions of Erasmian literary theology, which indirectly inspired and then facilitated the hermeneutical methods of the reformers themselves.[6] In England in the late 1580s the line between a cynic who might note that state religion is a matter of policy designed "only to keep men in awe"[7] and a devout Protestant who insists on reforming the old faith *as* a matter of policy was a very fine one. Marlowe, like many of his contemporaries who had to negotiate the violent cross-currents of reform and counterreform, used the art of writing and its theatrical expression to tread this line carefully, even as he exposed the hypocrisies that kept it in place.

Behind the premise that religious reform is a radical act of rewriting lies humanist literary concerns for the power of eloquence to move minds and shape opinions. In this respect Marlowe's poetic style is not incidental to its cultural implications but fundamentally implicated in them. When Ben Jonson alluded (in "To the Memory of My Beloved, the Author Mr William Shakespeare") to Marlowe's "mighty line,"[8] he not only set up the inevitable comparison that would haunt Marlowe's reputation but also gave a name to a rhetorical-poetic style that he recognized as distinctly characterizing Marlowe. "Mighty" connotes many possible stylistic associations, but above all it evokes the aggressive power and dark beauty of Marlowe's blank verse with its distinct stop-ended lines—a style we recognize throughout much of Marlowe's surviving poetry and drama without having to belabor the question with biographical speculations. Yet it remains difficult to do so without slipping back into the now apparently anachronistic tendency to then also speak of the poet Marlowe addressing us directly through his texts as a subversive essayist in complete control of his medium and its implied heretical arguments.

Despite this danger, it is vital that some effort be made to reclaim the study of Marlovian poetics as the center of our critical engagement with the Marlovian text, in order to sharpen and complement the valid contextual claims of New Historicism. Speaking of Marlowe's Barabas, for example, Stephen Greenblatt famously phrased the New Historicist axiom that has since dominated the study of Marlovian drama, especially where contemporary religious schism and paranoia are concerned.

> Like all of Marlowe's heroes, Barabas defines himself by negating cherished values, but his identity is itself . . . a social construction, a fiction composed of the sleaziest materials in his culture. If Marlowe questions the notion of literature as cautionary tale, if his very use of admonitory fictions subverts them, he cannot dismiss the immense power of the social system in which such fictions play their part.[9]

Few scholars have taken issue with Greenblatt's claim or with the careful manner in which he works his way to reach it.[10] It is quite glaring, however, that having identified a central conceptual tension in Marlowe's plays, Greenblatt goes on to list the exploits of Tamburlaine, Barabas, and Faustus as exemplifying such tension without noting the obvious differences in poetic and rhetorical style. It is as though style has nothing to say to the emerging context being illuminated. Marlowe's mighty lines come in many shapes and forms, however; as Harry Levin noted, long before Greenblatt shifted the debate to social paradigms, whereas "*Tamburlaine* is an aesthetic spectacle" of unbridled power (where power translates into aggressive rhetorical bombast and hyperbole), Barabas's capitalist cynicism finds expression in a more consciously controlled theatrical style, "lighted with scriptural grandeur," that "out-Herods Tamburlaine by making hyperboles sound like understatements."[11] If Greenblatt has exposed the limitations of Levin's methodology, this school of thought (to which we can add Paul Kocher, Clifford Leech, J. B. Steane, Eugene Waith, and Judith

Weil) is conspicuously and detrimentally absent from the subsequent New Historicist discussions.[12] It is therefore my central premise in this essay that only the superimposition of Levin onto Greenblatt can make possible a more comprehensive reassessment of Marlowe's art and its engagement with prevailing cultural-religious paradigms. The contextual and thematic concerns in Marlovian drama are finally inseparable from the formal concerns of the rhetorical art sustaining the central ideas, where declamatory poetry—especially in the famous Marlovian soliloquy of power—emerges not merely as an instrument for self-fashioning against the power constructs generated by religious and theological ideas but finally as an alternative metaphysical and societal ordering principle. To claim this is not to indulge in what W. L. Godshalk dismissed quite a while ago as Levin's anachronistic post-Victorian romanticism,[13] but to reengage with the New Historicist debate about Marlowe and religious culture at the deepest rhetorical and poetic level of the texts that now stand as an enigmatic testimony to the contested habits of thought that shaped them.

The heightened metatheatricality of Marlovian drama, whereby it constantly references the mimetic and ethical instability of the theatrical medium itself, indicates that there is an intimate connection between the implied ethics of the playwright's craft in theory and Marlowe's distinctly religious subversiveness *as* a playwright in practice.[14] Yet the Marlovian play text is one where characters are first defined by the hyperbolic poetry and vibrant dialogue that animates them and only then in relation to the theatrical and metatheatrical spaces they inhabit. Indeed, the rhetorical energy that defines a Tamburlaine, a Barabas, or a Guise allows them to create a meta-Euclidean space in which to act out their gargantuan defiance to a received social order that would otherwise seek to contain them and impose upon them fixed identities.

The character of the Guise in what is the badly corrupt 1602 octavo text of *The Massacre at Paris* is particularly relevant as an example of this spatial amplification through rhetoric working against delimiting religious ideologies. The Guise—probably the last of Marlowe's creations in a short but memorable line of overreachers—delivers a dazzling soliloquy (the longest of its kind in the surviving Marlowe canon) in which he reveals his true ambitions to steal, lie, bribe, and murder his way to the "diadem of France" (2.44). English Protestant propaganda at the time consistently represented the Guise as a religious fanatic—a bogeyman of the French wars

of religion driven to murderous violence by his zealotry. Had Marlowe faithfully stuck to this outline, it would have sufficed to deliver a sober critique of the violence underpinning religious fanaticism or to feed (as some think) sanguine Protestant anti-Catholic, anti-French propaganda.[15] It is true that in its current form the soliloquy is something of a fossil of Marlovian stylistic grandeur in a text that at best preserves only rough outlines of the original play penned by Marlowe. Nevertheless, the Guise that emerges from this fossilized speech reaches for far darker and more daring territory than a mere harangue of French Catholic aggression would have warranted. In fact, the Catholic faith (at least the religious orthodoxy for which it stood) is quietly and ironically excused for the massacre when we discover that the Guise only *pretends* to religion; the Guise is not a Catholic zealot but a closet atheist and Machiavellian plotter who cynically exploits religious prejudices between French Catholics and Huguenots to orchestrate a political massacre of rivals. In a moment of defiant bravado the Guise declares:

> My policy hath framed religion.
> Religion: *O Diabole*!
> Fie, I am ashamed, how ever that I seem,
> To think a word of such a simple sound,
> Of so great matter should be made the ground.
> (*The Massacre at Paris*, 2.65–69)

Religious hypocrites in Marlowe's works—and there are many of them—use religion as "ground" for any number of crimes. When the Christian authorities of Malta rob Barabas of all his wealth in the earlier play, *The Jew of Malta*, there is a tone of entirely serious indignation when Barabas hurls a perfectly rhetorical question at the governor, Ferneze: "Is theft the ground of your religion?" (1.2.96). In the Guise's soliloquy, however, the irony of this idea is compounded, because even the godless plotter is ashamed to think that such a "simple" word as "religion" could be used with such cavalier ease to advance diabolic and murderous plots. Strikingly, what offends the Guise is the simplicity of *sound* conjured by the word *religion.* Aesthetic and spiritual-religious concerns uncomfortably intersect in the Guise's atheist fantasy of power; the word *religion,* which ought perhaps to be simple as its "sound" suggests, silently brings up associations of plain eloquence and plain Protestant spirituality that weigh against the Guise's heretical bombast. Consequently, when we are confronted by such bombast, we moreover realize that such mock "religion" can only be made the ground of "great matter" in a Machiavellian arena of temporal power struggles, which tend toward the arbitrary greatness of state in the first place.

At this point it could be said that, as Judith Weil has argued, Marlowe's poetry creates provocative ironies that subtly mock the Guise, even as the sheer energy of his rhetoric invites us to admire and envy his power.[16] The object of the emerging irony in this case, however, is not to offer a simplistic satire of the Guise's religious hypocrisy; Marlowe's Guise is many things, but he is never merely ridiculous. His religious hypocrisy is extraordinary for the astonishing poetic energy, sustaining what Levin has described as its "sheer appetency" above and beyond the subtle ironies it generates in our ears.[17] The insatiable desire erupting to the surface in the Guise's relentless poetic bombast draws attention away from the failure of institutional religion to impose a vision of justice and order on the world. Rather, it focuses attention on the implications of such a breakdown on the individual man of ambition, carving a place for himself in a wild, irreligious world by *religiously* appealing to extravagant modes of rhetorical power, forever hovering on the edge of a primordial chaos. The Guise opens his soliloquy by declaring that he is not merely about to share his secret thoughts with us but to unleash in the process the very force of his relentless ambition.

> Now, Guise, begin those deep-engendered thoughts
> To burst abroad those never-dying flames
> Which cannot be extinguished but by blood.
> (*The Massacre at Paris*, 2.34–36)

Hyperbole produces in this case odd syntax because it seems to imply that the deeply engendered thoughts the Guise has are somehow not the same as "those never-dying flames" of ambition, fanned, as it were, by thinking ambitiously. As always with Marlowe there is a distinct metapoetic conceit at work. What bursts forth as the Guise soliloquizes and transforms dark incipient desires into blank verse are the never-dying flames of the Guise's borrowed rhetorical skills—that is, borrowed from his playwright-creator lurking in the wings. What then follows is a torrent of frightening transgressive fantasies that, as the Guise darkly concedes, may be "aimed at by many / Yet understood by none."

> That like I best that flies beyond my reach.
> Set me to scale the high pyramides,
> And thereon set the diadem of France;
> I'll either rend it with my nails to naught,

Or mount the top with my aspiring wings,
Although my downfall be the deepest hell.
For *this* I wake, when others think I sleep,
For *this* I wait, that scorn attendance else,
For *this*, my quenchless thirst whereon I build,
Hath often pleaded kindred to the king.
For *this*, *this* head, *this* heart, *this* hand and sword,
Contrives, imagines, and fully executes
Matters of import aimed at by many,
Yet understood by none.
For *this*, hath heaven engendered me of earth,
For *this*, *this* earth sustains my body's weight,
And with *this* weight I'll counterpoise a crown,
Or with seditions weary all the world.
For *this*, from Spain the stately Catholics
Sends Indian gold to coin me French *écues*;
For *this*, have I a largess from the Pope,
A pension and a dispensation too;
And by that privilege to work upon,
My policy hath framed religion.
(*The Massacre at Paris*, 2.42–65, my emphases)

The power of the soliloquy comes from the repetition of the pronominal adjective *this* suspended between two engendering processes: on the one hand, the man engendered by heaven of earth; and on the other, the inner man of limitless ambition engendered by dark but also vigorously creative thoughts, trapped in the metaphysical and physical constraints of a created body. The pronoun *this* should be demonstrative in this context, but in the emerging rhetorical space between what the Guise's thoughts *will* him to do and what divine providence working through creation will *allow* him to do, *this* becomes strangely indefinite. Grammatically, *this* does not point to the French crown but abstractly to the Guise's ambition *for* the crown, described periphrastically over eighteen mighty lines of poetry as the desire to have that which "flies beyond my reach" (1.2.42). This is entirely appropriate, because ambition in Marlovian psychology is indeed not a definite noun but an intangible chthonic force that persists in human affairs as latent presence. It is not, indeed, a noun one can point to as "this head," "this heart," or "this hand and sword" by which the earthly Guise otherwise defines himself. The use of anaphora creates a rhetorical effect of elusive dark power that takes us far beyond historical contexts and European politics to a Faustian world of dark metaphysics and hubristic possibilities. It is an alternative Marlovian world that for a brief, mesmerizing moment, sustained by poetry and desire, exists entirely independent of the theatrical space failing to contain it. At the same time, however, that failure of theatrical-spatial containment nevertheless allows for the grim realities of corrupt human affairs to persist as threatening certainties in the offstage inferred reality.

This unsettling metatheatrical movement in Marlowe's drama often hinges on the poetic placing of the word *policy* in key speeches. For example, Barabas congratulates himself on his scheming that eventually lands him the governorship of Malta, saying: "Thus hast thou gotten, by thy policy, / No simple place, no small authority" (*The Jew of Malta*, 5.2.27–28). Here and elsewhere in Marlowe's plays, *policy* is a wonderfully multivalent word, alive with Marlovian possibilities of action, artfulness, and ingenuity. All the senses of *policy* available in Marlowe's time—policy as art of government, as an expedient, as a stratagem or trick, as a desirable course of action, or as cunning or shrewd conduct—coalesce into a single protean word, which points to the irruption of ruthless Machiavellian pragmatism in a social and political world otherwise shaped by theories of providence and religious dogma as well as by the racial and class stereotypes that they sustain. At the same time, the word *policy* also conjures up associations of the dramatist's craft and cunning plotting, eliciting our admiration for Marlowe's art and sympathy for his outrageous villains, all the while simultaneously ventilating genuine concerns about the ethical viability of the theatrical medium itself. In *The Massacre at Paris*, as in *The Jew of Malta* (where it recurs thirteen times), *policy* thus becomes shorthand for the overreacher's ability to impose his will on the world through careful political and rhetorical-poetic plotting, which shows itself to be all too aware of the theatrics underpinning the political will to power.[18] Such power, however, is always untenable in the social spheres to which it aspires, precisely because of its theatrical precariousness. By the time Barabas secures for himself a political place through his theatrical policy, it is a place lacking any real ontological viability, which he is therefore forced to disavow. As a consummate actor-playwright, Barabas increasingly finds that it is the means of policy rather than its political end that his transgressive imagination translates into political capital.[19] Therefore, when in *The Massacre* the Guise's speech winds down to find its rhetorical summation in the aphorism "my policy hath framed religion," we know we have been witnessing in dramatic terms the framing—that is, the embellishment and adaptation but also pure theatrical contrivance—not of a Machiavellian political stratagem masquerading as religion but of Marlovian declamatory poetry elevating the deeply ambivalent truth of theatrical spectacle, hyperbole, and fancy to a metatheatrical point where it can begin to compete for the cultural spaces inhabited by the tyranny of religious dogma.

The question here of the importance of place in relation to both the poetry and dramaturgy of Marlovian drama is therefore paramount. Metatheatrically speaking, ingenuous dramatic policy and plotting allow for the rhetorical assertion of power to interact with the spatial permeability of the stage on which the Marlovian overreacher struts. For example, it has long been noticed that Marlovian drama, especially in *The Jew of Malta,* is obsessed with the conceptual and theatrical manipulation of enclosed spaces. Yet the most that has been advanced in relation to such observations is abstract New Historicist claims about what such onstage manipulation of space, mirrored in the villain's boundless ambition, connotes in the wider cultural contexts with which the plays are said to interact.[20] There is something to be said, however, for the way in which Marlowe uses onstage spatial boundaries to enclose in a mimetic frame the poetry that gives his overreaching villains their sense of dangerous power. It is precisely at the flashpoint where declamatory poetry interacts and clashes with the theatrical spaces that would contain the poetry's mimetic relationship with the audience, willingly suspending its disbelief at the unfolding spectacle, that the act of violently reframing the audience's platitudinous religious beliefs and prejudices takes place. For example, when the curtain is drawn and Faustus is revealed in his study, or when Barabas is shown in his counting house, the spatial image of the actor sitting inside a revealed onstage inner space amplifies the metaphorical conceit that we are about to be shown into a private psychological interior. Yet as soon as the actors in question begin reciting their mighty lines, the sense of limitless power that cannot be contained in any space whatsoever pours out across the theater's mimetic divide, creating a deeply unsettling stylistic and dramatic effect. Of course, such stylistic effects vary in their trajectory and shape; in Faustus's opening soliloquy the transgressive movement aspires upward, quickly spiraling out of control at the prospect of gaining "a deity" (*Doctor Faustus,* A-Text, 1.1.65), whereas the a priori infernal Barabas dazzles his audience with baser materials and excesses. Fingering his heap of gold coins, Barabas exclaims, "Fie, what a trouble 'tis to count this trash!" (*The Jew of Malta,* 1.1.7). For Barabas the excess of material wealth is mere trash because the very idea of excess has already transported his poetic imagination to think of the paradoxical impossibility of "infinite riches in a little room" (1.1.37). Audiences and readers, then as now, immediately note the blasphemy of this line, which mocks the Christian belief in the miracle of the Incarnation. This mockery, however, is finally incidental to the bathic humor of the Jew. Christian belief in the scriptural truths, on which institutional religion depends for its mythic authority, has no place in Barabas's counting house or, for that matter, in Marlowe's Malta. However, such ideas do frame the action in relation to the offstage consensual social reality in a profound way. In conjuring up the fabulous geographic wonders of "Indian mines" (1.1.19) in his opening soliloquy—"The wealthy Moor" (1.1.21) heaping "pearl like pebble-stones" (1.1.23) and the "Nilus' wandering banks" (1.1.43)—the silky opulence of Barabas's excessive rhetoric generates its own heretical tremor of blasphemy that cuts across the metatheatrical space to clash with the *obvious* blasphemy on which the audience seizes at the thematic level. It is this double stylistic effect, plotted through theatrical contrivance, that gives Barabas his sense of precarious danger and alien exclusivity, allowing him as well to step out of the social realities represented onstage and violently attempt to reorder them.

In this context James Knowles has analyzed what he terms "the aesthetics of the closet" in Marlovian drama, where the theatrical medium negotiates closeted secrets through the rhetorical juxtaposition of poetry on space. Such an aesthetic, argues Knowles, gives a place and a voice to the otherwise unspeakable social truths that Marlowe's audience would never dare discuss in public but apparently relished to see displayed, as though in secret, on a public theatrical stage. As Knowles points out, the art of rhetoric, widely pictured in the period "as an opening or revelation (in contrast to the closed fist of logic)" metaphorically lends itself to this transaction in that its "verbal productivity [embodies the drive toward] newly discovered meanings."[21] When Barabas therefore evolves in the course of his tragicomedy from victimized Jew to playacting revenger, the mimetic boundaries, which would delineate the onstage action as theatrical illusion and the offstage reality as its ideological frame, are radically destabilized. The various imagined Maltese spaces designated by the stage throughout the play—from the senate and Barabas's house to the marketplace, brothel, and nunnery—are all spaces out of which Barabas is continually shut. Instead, driven by an indefinable end, Barabas relentlessly perfects the means of his rhetorical power to redefine such spaces, often violently.

> I'll be revenged on this accursèd town,
> For by my means Calymath shall enter in.
> I'll help to slay their children and their wives,
> To fire the churches, pull their houses down,
> Take my goods too, and seize upon my lands.
> (*The Jew of Malta*, 5.1.62–66)

As with the opening speech, here also the tremor of blasphemy extends from the religious frame being mocked. The Barabas who speaks these lines has just performed a mock-resurrection in rising from the dead, bringing his biblical namesake into sharp ironic focus. This namesake is of course the condemned criminal Barabbas, whom the Jews chose to redeem from crucifixion instead of Christ, leading in the Gospel according to Matthew to the notorious verses responsible for centuries of dark anti-Semitism and blood libels. Crucially, however, there is a large gap in the play between how Barabas's victims conceive of him and how he conceives of himself when he executes his policy. Even to his own daughter Abigail (perhaps especially to her), Barabas is nothing more than a living embodiment of the theological caricature conjured by his biblical type. The rhetorical power that Marlowe lends him, however, makes it impossible for the audience watching this spectacle to contain Barabas under any racial-religious denomination or slur. Barabas is his own man despite a world that would marginalize, ostracize, and vilify him.

It is especially significant in this respect that early in the play Barabas takes care to separate himself from the submissive Jewish community of Malta, represented by the three nameless Jews whom Barabas, disdaining the offered model of the patient sufferer Job, considers to be "base slaves" (*The Jew of Malta*, 1.1.215), who are like a man "that in a field amidst his enemies, / Doth see his soldiers slain, himself disarmed, / And knows no means of his recovery" (1.1.204–6). For his part, as Barabas tells us in the ensuing soliloquy (anticipating that of the Guise in the later play), he was "born to better chance, / And framed of finer mould than common men, / That measure naught but by the present time" (1.2.219–21). Unlike his fellow Jews who bow down to their slavish fate and play the predetermined part plotted for them by the hypocritical Christians and Muslims, Barabas is a man of policy who "cast[s] with cunning for the time to come" (1.2.223). Indeed, as the play progresses, Barabas is gradually transformed by the poetic energy animating his ambition from a stereotypical embodiment of traditional Christian anti-Semitism into a protean, insatiable force of murderous revenge and zany theatrical caprice. It is only fitting, therefore, that the terminus of such relentless force moving forward is the execution of a cunning theatrical "policy" (5.5.24). Barabas enters above with carpenters and instructs them to build a "dainty gallery" (5.5.33), or a stage, complete with a balcony and a trap door, where he plans to deliver Malta and his own fortune from the Turks. The effect of having to imagine not just a play within a play but literally a stage within a stage forces us (as Julia Reinhard Lupton argues) to recognize that "artists, like Jews, can recreate, reinhabit, and remap the civil spaces left over by the incomplete transformations and uncanny survivals of religious forms in modernity."[22]

This idea is hard to reconcile, however, with the final catastrophe of the play, where the Jew, naively trusting in Ferneze to appreciate the sheer cunning of his plot, literally and figuratively forgets his place and is double-crossed by the earnest Christian. The artist-playwright-devil-Jew falls victim to his own extravagance; the trap is sprung and a curtain is once again drawn to discover Barabas in an inner space, this time boiling in a cauldron. The death is slow. As he boils, Barabas, "in the fury of [his] torments," strives "to end [his] life with resolution" (*The Jew of Malta*, 5.5.78–79) and confess to his crimes—not so that he might gain absolution for them but so that he might gain an eternal artist's credit for the ingenuity of their plotting. Barabas's final dying apostrophe to his tongue, the very instrument of his manipulative eloquence, is disquieting: "Tongue, curse thy fill and die!" (5.5.88). You can boil Barabas away, but to the last you cannot silence him. At such brutal moments Marlowe's unique blend of rhetorical dramatic poetry and emblematic drama, always flirting with religious allegory and typology, offers itself as a radical vehicle through which to rearrange, reappropriate, and finally reframe such materials so that their conceptual implications for human life can be redirected elsewhere.

Where, then, does Marlowe redirect the conceptual implications about human life that his drama otherwise empties of its platitudinous meanings? To answer this, it is important to note not only the metatheatrical instability of Marlovian drama but also the way in which Marlowe's villains are uncannily complicit in this dramatic process. Indeed, it could be said without controversy that all of Marlowe's historical or pseudohistorical protagonists have an acute sense of history and of their role as actors in a predetermined, carefully plotted script. The anxiety and restlessness that drives them is that of men being watched, evidently quite literally. This is to say that all of Marlowe's protagonists, not just the historical ones, have an acute sense of theater. The existential cliché of the *theatrum mundi*, made famous by Shakespeare's "all the world's a stage," is nevertheless conceptually important here. Shakespeare, especially in the earlier history plays, also gives us characters caught up in their own historical role as actors. Young Hal, Brutus, and Caesar are perhaps the most famous, but so is the earlier Richard II, the quintessential actor-king who goes on performing the role of the deposed monarch long after anyone around him cares to watch or listen. In his memorable soliloquy at the end of the play, in which the jailed Richard pretends to people the empty world of his prison with thoughts, Shakespeare has him remark despairingly: "Thoughts tending to ambition, they do plot / Unlikely wonders" (*Richard II*, 5.5.18–19).[23] The deposed Richard is more of a theatrical martyr than a Marlovian villain; in these lines and in the speech that follows he mocks his own flight of earlier solipsistic fancy and resigns himself in his own artful way to the unbearable fact that it is precisely Bolingbroke's ambition that has plotted what Richard considered the unlikely political wonder of deposing an anointed monarch. Theatrical solipsism then melts away, the murderers rush in, and cold reality fatally catches up with the player-king. In Marlowe's dramatic universe, however, thoughts tending to ambition often literally plot unlikely wonders—unlikely theatrical wonders—where for a brief period of stolen time (usually spanning upward of twenty scenes) the conqueror, the conjurer, the deviant king, the Machiavellian Jew, or the murderous Catholic duke will stop at nothing to be all they can be in a world that cannot otherwise contain their raw individual energy. When Marlovian overreachers offer us as a matter of theatrical policy infinite rhetorical riches "in a little room," the indifferent hellish world offstage that finally consumes them begins to lose its moral and theological coherence. Moreover, its grip on the implied audience's religious imagination begins, as a consequence, to loosen. The choral epilogue to *Doctor Faustus*, for example, tellingly addresses the audience with the following exhortation:

> Regard this hellish fall,
> Whose fiendful fortune may exhort the wise
> Only to wonder at unlawful things,
> Whose deepness doth entice such forward wits
> To practice more than heavenly power permits.
> (*Doctor Faustus*, A-Text, Epilogue, ll. 4–8)

For all the pseudomoralizing of Calvinist tyranny that governs the theological horror of Faustus's damnation, as well as the strange sight of devils carrying him away kicking and screaming to an offstage eternity of torment, there is always a sense in which Marlowe's theater gives its audience a limitless, even if never entirely guilt-free license to "wonder" at the unlikely and consequently blatantly unlawful. After all, the "wise" men and women to whom Faustus's epilogue appeals are not the puritanical zealots who reviled the theater as a source of moral inequity but arguably the sort of culturally informed, intellectually curious Londoners who were forced to enjoy theatrical entertainment as a form of guilty pleasure in an increasingly radicalized religious climate.

For the Guise in *The Massacre at Paris* everything is in this qualified sense perverse theatrical pleasure. When he plots to have Admiral de Coligny assassinated, he calls on the soldier who is to shoot the admiral by saying, "Come thou forth and play thy tragic part" (2.28). Subsequently, when he briefs Catherine de Medici on his plans for the massacre, he again alludes to the soldiers who will be perpetrating the atrocity as "actors" in a carefully plotted stage production, timed by musket fire and bell ringing, indicating the beginning and end of the action. He is, moreover, especially concerned about costume. He insists that his actors all wear distinct attire that will make them easy to recognize in the ensuing chaos.

> They that shall be actors in this massacre
> Shall wear white crosses on their burgonets,
> And tie white linen scarfs about their arms;
> He that wants these and is suspect of heresy,
> Shall die, be he king or emperor. Then I'll have
> A peal of ordinance shot from the tower,
> At which they all shall issue out and set the streets;
> And then, the watchword being given, a bell shall ring,
> Which when they hear, they shall begin to kill,
> And never cease until that bell shall cease;
> Then breathe a while.
> (*The Massacre at Paris*, 4.29–39)

This speech is full of metatheatrical ironies, not least of which is the mockery of Elizabethan sumptuary laws that actors regularly flouted for the sake of theatrical illusion in their performances. Especially chilling is the apparent collapse of the theatrical illusion when the expediency of theater—having all soldiers in one army dress the same so the audience knows who is who—becomes the expediency of mass murder.[24] Indeed, the ease with which the Guise links the theatrical transgression of social order on an *actual* stage with acts of extreme violence and religious heresy in the real world that is only *represented* on a stage is unnerving. It is hard to decide what is more horrifying: the realization that the onstage Guise and his coconspirators callously treat human life as theater, or the uncomfortable realization that once the play is over, the audience must leave the theatrical space of make-believe and reenter a world in which the Guise and his ethos cannot be dismissed as mere artistic fancy.

In *Why Does Tragedy Give Pleasure?* A. D. Nuttall applies Karl Popper's observation that in modern life our hypotheses "die in our stead" to the psychological effects of tragedy on theatergoers.[25] This, argues Nuttall, is exactly what tragic theater allows us to do as spectators: to see our hypotheses acted out and fall before us as part of a "death-game . . . in which the muscles of psychic response, fear and pity, are exercised and made ready, through a facing of the worst, which is not yet the real worst."[26] As a general rule, this formulation is helpful in thinking about the psychological cathartic effects of tragedy. What Nuttall does not take into account, however, are generically elusive plays like those written by Marlowe, in which hypotheses are shown to be more potent and more dangerous than the men who engender them. Or rather, it should be said that Nuttall senses the danger in such a possibility, when he continues in his argument and warns that "when hypothesis lapses into actuality one has indeed a corruption of tragedy, and the element of self-trial is replaced by simple cruelty."[27] This is especially true in *The Massacre*, in which the Guise, caught up in his own hypothetical fantasy of being a second Caesar, is so smitten by his own illusory sense of power that he blindly walks into the obvious plot laid for him by the recently crowned Henry III and his Protestant ally Navarre. In other words, theater and cunning plotting are shown here killing not just the hypothesis but also the man who engenders it.

> Third Murderer: Ay, my lord; the rest have ta'en their standings in the next room; therefore, good my lord, go not forth.
> Guise: Yet Caesar shall go forth.
> Let mean conceits and baser men fear death:
> Tut, they are peasants, I am duke of Guise;
> And princes with their looks engender fear.
> (*The Massacre at Paris*, 21.63–68)

To the last, and to his eternal credit as a mock artist, the Guise remains committed to the grand "conceit" he has become (as opposed to the "mean conceits" of lesser men). His dying words are wonderfully absurd politically but entirely serious and poignant theatrically: "Thus Caesar did go forth, and thus he died" (21.86). It is tempting to think that something of the Guise's histrionics lingered in Shakespeare's imagination when he contrived the inside theatrical joke in *Hamlet*, in which Polonius recounts his acting days by saying, "I did enact Julius Caesar. I was killed i' th' Capitol. Brutus killed me" (3.2.102–3).[28] Yet what in Shakespeare is a professional joke is in Marlowe a serious and disturbing metatheatrical proposition that turns the platitude that would view the world as a stage upside down. Instead of allowing his art to offer up the convenient analogy between life and theater, where "all the men and women [are] merely players,"[29] Marlowe's visceral poetic energy, cutting across the theatrical space and its mimetic boundaries, engenders the confusion that views the stage as the only viable account of reality and that which is offstage as the weaker ideological hypothesis. It is in this qualified but powerful sense that Marlovian poetic craft emerges as a new kind of pluralist mock religion and the theatrical stage on which such poetry competes with reality emerges as the secular spatial alternative to the churches and courts of Europe where absolute metaphysical or temporal power corrupts absolutely. It would seem, therefore, that there is at least some truth in the Baines Note, for Marlovian drama indeed can be said to be engaged everywhere in "writing" and framing a new and highly subversive religion—not for those who have lost faith in God but for those who have long ago lost any faith in humanity.

Notes

1. A typical expression of this view can be found in Emily C. Bartles, *Spectacles of Strangeness: Imperialism, Alienation, and Marlowe* (Philadelphia: Pennsylvania University Press, 1993). Bartles shows that Marlowe's plays offer "one of the most visible, most popular, and most radical voices of resistance to a dominant discursive trend, which was shaping ideas of self and state" (xv).

2. After the initial tendency in the nineteenth and early twentieth centuries to either revile or admire Marlowe for his undisputed godlessness, as it is exposed in the Baines Note and allegedly revealed in the plays, scholars such as G. K. Hunter ("The Theology of Marlowe's *The Jew of Malta*," *Journal of the Warburg and Courtauld Institutes* 27 [1964]: 211–40) and W. L. Godshalk (*The Marlovian World Picture* [Paris: Mouton, 1974]) began to question Marlowe's atheism on both fronts by arguing that outright atheism was not possible in the period and by arguing from the plays themselves that what modern readers construe as atheism is in fact perfectly orthodox Christian satire of an irreligious world of sin. With the advent of New Historicism the debate took a more detailed contextual turn, and we are now asked to understand Marlowe's atheist reputation in a wider cultural context as a symptom of the growing pressures and strains placed on orthodox Protestantism in Elizabethan society at the time. See especially Nicholas Davidson, "Christopher Marlowe and Atheism," in *Christopher Marlowe and English Renaissance Culture*, ed. Darryll Grantley and Peter Roberts (Aldershot, UK: Ashgate, 1996), 129–47; and David Riggs, "Marlowe's Quarrel with God," in *Marlowe, History, and Sexuality: New Critical Essays on Christopher Marlowe*, ed. Paul Whitefield White (New York: AMS Press, 1998), 15–37.

3. For the complex implications of this inherent paradox in our continuing fascination with the "atheist" Marlowe, see John Parker, *The Aesthetics of Antichrist: From Christian Drama to Christopher Marlowe* (Ithaca, NY: Cornell University Press, 2007). As Parker provocatively argues, what we construe today as Marlowe's outright secular atheism should be understood in fact as a far more complex aesthetic reaction to a rich tradition of Christian orthodoxy that always depended on inventive mimetic drama, fables, and playacting to

convey its otherworldly message: "The aesthetic of Christ and his doubles depends above all on the power of fallen material to represent the pure and immaterial, of history to signify the timeless, of human finitude to approximate the infinite as an asymptote approaches its impossible limit" (x).

4. "The Baines Note," as reproduced from the British Library manuscript in Frank Romany and Robert Lindsey, eds., *Christopher Marlowe: The Complete Plays* (London: Penguin, 2003), xxxiv–v. All quotations from the plays will also refer to this edition.

5. "Baines Note," xxxiv.

6. See Brian Cummings, *The Literary Culture of the Reformation: Grammar and Grace* (Oxford, UK: Oxford University Press, 2002): "By the end of the Tudor period, protestant culture appears to occupy two contradictory positions in relation to the literary act: it is literature's most enthusiastic friend and its most articulate enemy" (207).

7. "Baines Note," xxxiv.

8. Ben Jonson, *Ben Jonson: The Complete Poems*, ed. George Parfitt (London: Penguin, 1975), 264, l. 30.

9. Stephen Greenblatt, *Renaissance Self-Fashioning: From More to Shakespeare* (Chicago: University of Chicago Press, 1980), 209.

10. Although Greenblatt's paradigm is widely accepted, it is not unassailable. One significant voice of dissent is that of Thomas Cartelli, who rightly argues that "however compelling one may find [Greenblatt's] formulation, it casts Marlowe's protagonists in roles that have more to do with an abstract critical construction of resistance than with dramas that are materially realized in theatres where the 'social construction of identity' must necessarily yield to the more provisional identifications that are negotiated by playgoers." Thomas Cartelli, *Marlowe, Shakespeare, and the Economy of Theatrical Experience* (Philadelphia: Pennsylvania University Press, 1991), 162.

11. Harry Levin, *Christopher Marlowe: The Overreacher* (London: Faber, 1961), 76, 83, 86.

12. The critics listed produced various amounts of scholarship across a wide number of publications, but see especially Paul H. Kocher, *Christopher Marlowe: A Study of His Thought, Learning, and Character* (Chapel Hill: North Carolina University Press, 1946); Eugene M. Waith, *The Herculean Hero in Marlowe, Chapman, Shakespeare, and Dryden* (London: Chatto & Windus, 1962); J. B. Steane, *Christopher Marlowe: A Critical Study* (Cambridge, UK: Cambridge University Press, 1964); Judith Weil, *Christopher Marlowe: Merlin's Prophet* (Cambridge, UK: Cambridge University Press, 1977); and Clifford Leech, *Christopher Marlowe: Poet for the Stage* (New York: AMS Press, 1986).

13. Godshalk, *Marlovian World Picture*, 7–8.

14. For more on the theory underpinning this connection, see Noam Reisner, "The Paradox of Mimesis in Sidney's *Defence of Poesie* and Marlowe's *Doctor Faustus*," *Cambridge Quarterly* 39 (2010): 331–49.

15. Much of the meager scholarly attention *The Massacre of Paris* has attracted over the years has centered on the play's historical context and on Marlowe's manipulation of Protestant anti-Catholic pamphlets, which sought to capitalize on the hysteria stirred up in England following the St. Bartholomew's Day Massacre of 1572. For example, Julia Briggs ("Marlowe's *Massacre at Paris*: A Reconsideration," *Review of English Studies* 34 [1983]: 257–78) shows that the play achieves a remarkable degree of impartiality in its treatment of documented historical facts that would have deeply embarrassed the anti-Catholic Protestant consensus. See also Penny Roberts, "Marlowe's *The Massacre at Paris*: A Historical Perspective," *Renaissance Studies* 9 (1995): 430–41; and Rick Bowers, "*The Massacre at Paris*: Marlowe's Messy Consensus Narrative," in *Marlowe, History, and Sexuality: New Critical Essays on Christopher Marlowe*, ed. Paul Whitfield White (New York: AMS Press, 1998), 131–41.

16. Weil says, "Marlowe mocks his heroes in a remarkably subtle fashion. Their knavish speeches sleep so well in our ears because he has carefully obscured the folly of his speakers. Nevertheless, these speakers, with their mighty lines, are often the objects as well as the agents of his irony" (*Marlowe*, 2).

17. Levin, *Marlowe*, 105.

18. Much has been made of the word *policy* in Marlowe's drama in this context, especially in *The Jew of Malta*, where it recurs most frequently. For Howard Babb ("Policy in Marlowe's *The Jew of Malta*," *English Literary History* 24 [1957]: 85–94) the word anchors and binds together the *Jew*'s disparate dramatic acts, giving an otherwise uneven play its sense of unity. Bartles (*Spectacles of Strangeness*) sees in *policy* a nefarious political ethos that infects the Marlovian world and defines in the process the aliens at its center, whereas Cartelli significantly relates it to the implied Machiavellianism of Marlowe's stage craft, where the manipulation of audience response becomes "a virtual policy of playmaking" (*Marlowe*, 122).

19. See Sara Munson Deats and Lisa S. Starks, "'So Neatly Plotted, and So Well Perform'd': Villain as Playwright in Marlowe's *The Jew of Malta*," *Theatre Journal* 44 (1992): 375–89, esp. 380; Darryll Grantley, "'What Means This Shew?': Theatricalism, Camp, and Subversion in *Doctor Faustus* and *The Jew of Malta*," in *Christopher Marlowe and English Renaissance Culture*, ed. Darryll Grantley and Peter Roberts (Aldershot, UK: Ashgate, 1996), 224–38; and Arata Ide, "*The Jew of Malta* and the Diabolic Power of Theatrics in the 1580s," *Studies in English Literature, 1500–1900* 46 (2006): 257–79.

20. The essay that spearheaded this line of inquiry is Marjorie Garber, "'Infinite Riches in a Little Room': Closure and Enclosure in Marlowe," in *Two Renaissance Mythmakers: Christopher Marlowe and Ben Jonson*, ed. Alvin Kernan and Margaret R. Higonnet (Baltimore: Johns Hopkins University Press, 1977), 3–21. See also James Knowles, "'Infinite Riches in a Little Room': Marlowe and the Aesthetics of the Closet," in *Renaissance Configurations: Voices/Bodies/Spaces, 1580–1690*, ed. Gordon McMullan (Basingstoke, UK: Macmillan, 1998), 3–21; and Andrew Hiscock, "Enclosing 'Infinite Riches in a Little

Room': The Question of Cultural Marginality in Marlowe's *The Jew of Malta,*" *Forum for Modern Language Studies* 35 (1999): 1–22.

21. Knowles, "Infinite Riches," 17.

22. Julia Reinhard Lupton, "*The Jew of Malta,*" in *The Cambridge Companion to Christopher Marlowe,* ed. Patrick Cheney (Cambridge, UK: Cambridge University Press, 2004), 156.

23. William Shakespeare, *King Richard II,* Arden edition, ed. Peter Ure (London: Routledge, 1961).

24. See Clayton G. MacKenzie, "*The Massacre at Paris* and the Danse Macabre," *Papers on Language and Literature* 43 (2007): 311–34. MacKenzie makes an interesting case for viewing *The Massacre* as offering "visual and even psychological recreation on stage of a series of *danse macabre* vignettes" (314). According to MacKenzie, the ritualistic, macabre set pieces of mass slaughter enacted in the play create a sense of irony that allows for a typically medieval memento mori to overwhelm the partisan politics of Catholic-Huguenot aggression. As I argue, however, the emblematic iconicity of the stage imagery is unsettled by its metatheatrical instability. It is one thing for an audience to recognize remotely emblematic resonance and quite another to have the implied violence of the emblem's allegorical import spill across the mimetic divide of the theater to directly threaten the audience's sense of settled identity.

25. A. D. Nuttall, *Why Does Tragedy Give Pleasure?* (Oxford, UK: Clarendon Press, 1996). Nuttall is quoting Popper's essay "Of Clouds and Clocks," in Popper's *Objective Knowledge: An Evolutionary Approach* (Oxford, UK: Clarendon Press, 1970), 244.

26. Nuttall, *Tragedy,* 77.

27. Nuttall, *Tragedy,* 77.

28. William Shakespeare, *Hamlet,* Arden edition, ed. Harold Jenkins (London: Methuen, 1982).

29. William Shakespeare, *As You Like It,* Arden edition, ed. Agnes Latham (London: Methuen, 1975), 2.7.140.

13

SANFORD BUDICK

Shakespeare's Secular *Benediction*

The Language of Tragic Community in King Lear

In this essay on *King Lear* I am responding in part to the recent, widely held notion that, even in the face of skepticism, ethical values continually emerge in the narrative of a community. Among philosophers this idea has been made prominent by Stanley Cavell, Martha Nussbaum, and Richard Rorty, in the late writings of Jacques Derrida, and in the much earlier writings of Iris Murdoch.[1] I show that in *King Lear* a narrative of community and an ethical language are, in fact, made central by enlarging the focus of awareness from the tragic hero to a group of tragic protagonists.[2] My larger contentions are (1) that in *King Lear* the collective narrative from which ethical values emerge takes the form of a kind of tragedy in which humiliation and blessing are of central, transformative importance; and (2) that the efficacy of this form depends on structures of representation that are inherited from religious narrative, yet in *King Lear* these structures are secular, which is to say that they do not require religious belief to achieve what Cordelia terms "benediction" (4.6.55).[3]

To be more specific, the transformative form of this kind of tragedy is constituted by effectively endless repetition of the narrative unit that represents the protagonists' sufferings and, especially, their repeated humiliation. Humiliation of this order is the impact on the ego of giant affliction—the effect of being humbled without limit, crushed, and mortified. A narrative of such endlessly repeated humiliation finally works against narrative in that it tends to obliterate the time and place coordinates of narrative and even momentarily suspends consciousness in the protagonists who try to recount, or play out, the narrative. It is at the point of negation in this narrative process that the possibility of transformation and of blessing opens up. I refer to this process in *King Lear* as the zero narrative because of these negating features but also because Shakespeare coordinates this process with a transformative language of the "nothing." I show how the collective zero narrative and the language of the nothing enable the emergence, in self-transformation, of human moral capacity.[4] Kenneth Burke famously suggested that literature is indispensable "equipment for living."[5] I propose that in *King Lear* Shakespeare uses—and shows us how to use—a collective zero narrative and a language of the nothing as equipment for disclosing the human.[6] Perhaps more than any other work in the Western tradition except for *Oedipus at Colonus*, *King Lear* shows why at any moment, at any age, humanity is defined by the possibility of this individual rebirth in concert with others. In *King Lear* this rebirth of the human, within the tragic community, expresses itself in a secular benediction.

In my view the most telling fact about *King Lear* is that it concludes with a fulfillment of the design that first sets the tragedy in motion, namely, the division of the kingdom. It may be objected that it is not the design of dividing the kingdom but rather the so-called love test that catapults the protagonists into tragedy. The love test, however, is in my view only one expression of a larger impulsion, and a larger emergence, that this play represents. These are the impulsion toward and the emergence of a shared kingdom of moral being. From the beginning this impulsion is Cordelia's as much as it is Lear's. This is not to deny that Lear's initial desire for division of the kingdom is defective. Certainly the scheme that he has devised to divide the kingdom must produce flattery and inequality. Yet Lear will later show that he is also motivated by a need for a genuinely shared kingdom. This need will also be disclosed in Gloucester, Edgar, Kent, Albany, and the Fool.

One reason that *King Lear* forces us to seek a collective narrative is that its victim-protagonists are continually crushed together. Parallels and mirrorings of scenes of misfortune make this pressure of agglomeration clear throughout the play. This effect is represented paradigmatically in the collective suffering of the storm scene. A second reason that we attend to these characters as a group who play out a single story is the way in which they trade places across lines of social caste. This interknitting does not make them a herd but rather a community of remarkably freewilled individuals. Thus a nameless, formerly loyal serving man steps forth as the challenger to his ducal master, the Fool mordantly disciplines the King, Kent becomes a servant who keeps his own spontaneous counsel, and Edgar metamorphoses into a "beggarman" (4.1.29) whose resourcefulness sustains an outcast earl. In their shared story of affliction these and other protagonists huddle under the arc of a common humanity. We do not need to sign on to any one humanist essentialism to recognize that the driven rout of this tragedy does not struggle simply to stay alive. Rather, they agonize to achieve, in consort, an irreducible human expression—irreducible, at least, to them.

In the world of *King Lear* individuals grope toward moral being in terrifying aloneness, but they attain it by completing a circuit of moral reason and moral feeling with other individuals. The activity and meaning of this circuit are not immediately apparent. To comprehend it, we are forced to learn a new language that the protagonists of this tragedy speak collectively, which is to say, often without individual awareness of the collective meanings of that language. I demonstrate how *King Lear* represents this collective language. The two steps of my demonstration are (1) to show the narrative process, or zero narrative, that is represented by the tragic community and produces the conditions for freedom and moral feeling; and (2) to show the collective, transformative language of the nothing that is the counterpart of that narrative process. Together, this process and language enable the emergence of the human, that is (at least in this case), of freedom and moral feeling, in benediction.

The Zero Narrative

Gloucester describes Edgar as one "whom the heavens' plagues / Have humbled to all strokes" (4.1.59–60). Mutatis mutandis, the same description applies to Gloucester himself and to Lear, Cordelia, the Fool, and Kent. *King Lear* is a spectacle of high-speed humiliations. What interests me in this broad and rapid desolation is what is produced within the collectivity by the relentless impetus of the humiliations. The Fool warns Kent, who has hitched his fate to Lear's, "Let go thy hold when a great wheel runs down a hill" (2.4.65–66). Lear adopts the Fool's metaphor of the careening wheel and gives it an even more destructive, more energetic signification: "I am bound / Upon a wheel of fire" (4.6.43–44). This intensification of the metaphor of the wheel corresponds to Lear's experience of an energy of destruction that is raised to ever higher powers.

In like manner, Edgar's imagined worst case of humbling strokes is forced down to ever lower depths of worst. Beyond becoming fugitive and beggared, he must yet witness not only his father's blinded, bleeding eyes and his father's loss of any desire to live but also, when comfort seems at hand, the bursting of his father's heart, a calamity for which Edgar will blame himself. And in all of this, Edgar has not yet reached the climax of his afflictions. "The worst is not," he realizes, "So long as we can say 'This is the worst'" (4.1.27–28). A logic of tragic process issues from this realization. According to this logic, (1) imagining the true worst case is possible only in a stage *after* an unrelenting series of losses, that is, of humiliations of our prepossessions; and (2) imagining the true worst entails the surrender of our hold on our life itself. This worst would seem to leave no one, and no hope, standing. Yet this relinquishment can also be attended by a momentous recognition of a moral feeling that is completely separate from any thought of preserving our own lives. Contemplating each other, the humiliated protagonists of this play struggle to see what form this imagination of moral feeling can take.

To repeat: The tragic affirmation of *King Lear* depends on the proposition that the process of suffering an effectively endless series of humiliations of self-conceit, even and especially including the imaginative surrender of the individual's hold on his or her life, can produce moral feeling. Yet the truth of this proposition is by no means self-evident. Why could not the same process produce mere numbness or even evil? In this play we are shown that all the other major protagonists who, like Lear, suffer what Cordelia calls "the good man's distress" (4.3.18) are throughout headed not merely for a fall but for a fission of "huge sorrows" that will release "ingenious feeling." These are Gloucester's phrases in Act 4 (4.5.268–69). I understand the word *ingenious* to carry both of its possible meanings simultaneously, that is, sensitive as well as inventive.[7] Although this "ingenious feeling" is as yet beyond Gloucester's full comprehension, it already signifies for him a sensitivity to others' pain, a capacity to "see it feelingy" (4.5.143), as he says. And the further reach of this art of both seeing and feeling—both apprehending and feeling—is that it can actually be invented, found or discovered, in the self-conscious process of experiencing "fortune's blows." Very much in these terms, Edgar earlier describes himself to Gloucester as

> A most poor man, made tame to fortune's blows,
> Who by the art of known and feeling sorrows
> Am pregnant to good pity. Give me your hand;
> I'll lead you to some biding.
> (4.5.212–15)

In *King Lear* "ingenious feeling" and "good pity" even express themselves in a characteristic form or maxim, namely, the requirement of treating all human beings as though, a priori, they have equal claims, at least, on nature's means of subsistence. This maxim is articulated especially by Lear and Gloucester.

> Lear: Take physic, pomp,
> Expose thyself to feel what wretches feel,
> That thou mayst shake the superflux to them.
> (3.4.33–35)
>
> Gloucester: distribution should undo excess,
> And each man have enough.
> (4.1.65–66)

It is tempting to see in these verses Shakespeare's prescient vote for socialist or Marxist ideologies. But if we take Shakespeare seriously—indeed, especially if we happen to take these ideologies seriously—we should follow the process of deriving this moral feeling, this maxim, in the work done by his play. Otherwise, we have only the grand sound without the grand thing. Shortly after Lear's manifesto on shaking superflux to the poor, he cries, "Off, off, you lendings! Come, unbutton here" (3.4.97). This Lear has still not taken enough of the medicine against pomp that he prescribes. The art of sorrows in this play must be supplied with a fuller, more persuasive logic than Lear or Gloucester is capable of providing by himself.

To describe where this logic may exist within the play, I briefly step outside it. *King Lear* especially reproduces one recognizable pattern within the history of tragic literature, a pattern that is most memorably exemplified by the book of Job, by Aeschylus's *Prometheus Bound*, and by Sophocles' Oedipus plays, especially the second, *Oedipus at Colonus*. John Holloway, Ruth Nevo, and Rosalie Colie have shown, in Nevo's words, that *King Lear* "is a Shakespearean version of the Book of Job."[8] The relation of *King Lear* to Sophocles' Oedipus plays (available to Shakespeare in numerous Latin translations) has been considered more general. I believe that this relation is more specific than has been noticed, but that is a subject for another time. With regard to our present concerns, the pattern of humiliations and their climax shared by these works is most relevant. This pattern is undoubtedly a specific form of the general pattern of catharsis and recognition described by Aristotle in his analysis of the first of Sophocles' Oedipus plays. Two features of the more specialized pattern stand out.

First, the pattern is focused in a fused series of humiliations of self-conceit. For example, for Job the series is anchored in the confrontations with the comforters. The series of false comfortings blazons the series of misfortunes with which Job's tale opens. In *King Lear* the larger series is foregrounded in the successive numerical reductions of Lear's retinue, but this local series of reductions only betokens the merciless progressive reductions in Lear's and his followers' conditions of existence. Although many further constituents of the prime series are propagated in each tragedy, thus making the extent of each series effectively endless, what is crucial for the larger form is the sense of endlessness in the repetition and continuity of the series. In *King Lear* we see clearly that the individual protagonist's sense of this endlessness is created in collective augmentations: for example, the Fool's, Gloucester's, Kent's, or Cordelia's vicarious experiences of the suffering of Lear; or conversely, Lear's slowly emerging responsiveness to the sufferings of the Fool, Edgar, and Gloucester—and then of Cordelia. The so-called double plot of *King Lear*, focused on the running parallels between Lear's and Gloucester's fates, braids only one strand of this endlessness. In Shakespeare's representation of the series of humiliations, endlessness is thus not merely a function of the individual's extrapolations from his or her discrete experience. Rather, it is dependent on the individual's experience of others', of the community's, experience.

Second, the impact of the endless series somehow issues in recognition of something exalted, or sublime, in human nature. Yet the explanation of how this recognition is wrought is certainly not self-evident. In fact, the rudiments of an explanation of this paramount effect were provided only two centuries after Shakespeare composed *King Lear*. The characterization of this pattern as sublime, specifically in Job and in the Oedipus plays, was itself well established in the eighteenth century even before Kant's writings on the sublime. Yet Kant surpassed all earlier and later commentators by explaining the aesthetic-moral nexus within the tragic pattern that produces the sublime.

Harold Bloom has usefully drawn attention to the connection between "the sublime" and what he calls "the invention of the human" in *King Lear*, which he finds in Lear's "greatness" and "capacity for significant emotion." But Bloom does not attempt to explain systematically what this greatness of sublimity is or how it produces a human specificity. He apparently assumes that these things become self-evident in the experience of their impact. "I marvel," he says, "that anyone among us could fail to apprehend Lear's sublimity."[9] To be sure, Bloom has elsewhere written extensively about the sublime, but for him this is a Freudian, Oedipal sublime of ego defenses. Bloom even eschews the emergence of moral feeling that is basic to Kant's sublime. I am proposing that we can be quite circumstantial in describing the moral sublimity and the specification of the human in *King Lear*. We can do so if we attend to how Kant, the greatest theorist both of the sublime and of what might be inherently human, defined how the sublime works, especially with regard to tragic consciousness. We find that *King Lear* illuminates Kant's theory of the moral sublime as much as or even more than Kant's theory of the moral sublime illuminates *King Lear.* Yet both thinkers, both writers, are indispensable.

To reap the benefit of Kant's thought here, we must begin with tragedy to fill in the linkages between Kant's illuminations of the sublime and his grasp of tragic consciousness. I have elsewhere traced the ways in which Kant worked out his explanation of the sublime in his lifelong reflections on the sublime in Milton, not least in *Samson Agonistes.* In these Kantian reflections we see the close relation, if not even identity, between his idea of the endless progression of representations that produces sublime freedom and his idea of the sublime series of humiliations of self-conceit that produce the spontaneity of moral personality. Together these processes constitute his explanation of the aesthetic-moral nexus in the sublime. Not surprisingly, this explanation also complements his reflections on the aesthetic-moral significance of the book of Job.[10]

Aside from Kant's comment on Shakespeare's use of the Fool in *King Lear,* he left us no other remarks directly on the play—or none have survived or have so far been discovered.[11] Yet because in *King Lear* Shakespeare makes significant use of the book of Job and likely of the Oedipus plays as well and because Milton in *Samson Agonistes* makes strong use of the visitation structure of the book of Job and of the connections between blindness and redemption in *Oedipus at Colonus* and *King Lear,* it is not surprising that Kant's comments on tragic form and the sublime apply significantly to *King Lear.*

Kant's second *Critique* contains an explication of the condition that is constituted by an effectively "endless progression" of "humiliations" of "self-conceit" (*CPrR* 5: 73–77).[12] For purposes of this explication Kant summons up an archetypical tragic scene that is a distillation especially of Job, *Oedipus at Colonus,* and *Samson Agonistes.* To be sure, the force of Kant's logic for understanding what is occurring in this scene is not dependent on any empirical examples. On the contrary, the importance of the scene for Kant is that its constitutive exemplifications disclose a priori capacities of the human mind.

> When an upright man is in the greatest distress, which he could have avoided if he could only have disregarded duty [we think of Cordelia's "bond"], is he not sustained by the consciousness that he has maintained humanity in its proper dignity in his own person and honored it, that he has no cause to shame himself in his own eyes and to dread the inward view of self-examination? This consolation is not happiness, not even the smallest part of it. For no one would wish the occasion for it on himself, or perhaps even

> a life in such circumstances. But he lives and cannot bear to be unworthy of life in his own eyes. This inner tranquility is therefore merely negative with respect to everything that can make life pleasant; it is, namely, only warding off the danger of sinking in personal worth, after he has given up completely the worth of his condition. It is the effect of a respect for something quite different from life, something in comparison with which life with all its agreeableness has no worth at all. He still lives only from duty, not because he has the least taste for living. (*CPrR* 5: 88)

In passages such as this the power of Kant's moral thought is concentrated in its identification of the primacy and inescapability of the need to be human, that is, to have moral feeling. The relevance of Kant's explanations to Shakespeare's representation of what Cordelia calls the "good man's distress" requires no special pleading. This relevance is strongly felt even if interpretations inevitably differ about how much the continuing distress of any one such good individual could have been avoided (e.g., if Oedipus had not tenaciously sought his father's murderer, if Job had cursed God and died, if Samson had opted to leave prison with Dalila, if Cordelia had ignored the supremacy of her bond or duty). Kant's narrative of the good individual in extremis, at the point of becoming zero, contains more elements than are immediately apparent. D. G. James applied to *King Lear* Keats's remark that in *Paradise Lost* Milton had to "commit himself to the Extreme."[13] The condition of being in extremis is as indispensable to Shakespeare in *King Lear* as it is to Kant. This condition issues in a complete indifference to what Kant calls all "incentives" for continuing in life, so that such an individual is motivated only by an "incentive" for "something quite different from life" in itself. This Kantian something is "moral feeling" or a "respect" for (a "duty" to) the good. At that point of zero life incentive, consciousness of empirical narrative dissolves and is absorbed into an inward narrative or the a priori. Cordelia already speaks from the aftereffect of this inward narrative when *King Lear* opens. This aftereffect needs to be unfolded.

In neighboring passages in the second *Critique* and in closely related passages of the third *Critique*, Kant explains the process that brings the individual to the distinctively human condition of moral feeling. The final stage of this process is an inward representation of a progression of humiliations. The outward progression of humiliations initiates the "disclosure" of this inward experience of the sublime. Among other things the attainment of sublime experience is for Kant distinguished from a false show of the sublime by the fact that a given mind's representations in the progression toward a true sublime must represent those representations' partial inadequacy to represent (as, for example, in someone's recording of the experience of a heath that cannot be placed on any map). In other words, each such representation that the mind of the individual represents to itself is a representation of that mind's partial representational incapacity, so that a ground of humility is from the outset present in the structure of each of the representations. Together, that is, serially and in their cumulative impact, these representations create the sublime in the minds of the afflicted and self-afflicting protagonists.

We have arrived at the description of a climactic moment of the Kantian sublime, especially of what Kant calls "the mathematical sublime." This moment is also crucial in *King Lear*. In its empirical form experience of the endless progression of representations causes "a momentary check to the vital forces." In the empirical experience of the mathematical sublime this occurs because the mind cannot bring together (1) the imagination's projection of the infinite extensibility of the progression with (2) reason's requirement of a defined whole that would delimit the progression (*CJ* 5: 250). Precisely in that moment of loss of power, or blackout, the mind experiences a freedom from all encroaching pressures, needs, or incentives. The sublime progression of a series of humiliations thus brings about a perfect humility, a zero or nothingness of ego, and then a "discharge [of energy] all the more powerful" (*CJ* 5: 245) toward respect for moral obligation. Only in that moment of nothingness and freedom are the obstacles to spontaneous moral feeling removed. The Kantian species of nothing momentarily obliterates consciousness of everything worldly. As I suggested earlier, the experience of the Kantian nothing in the sublime of tragic form is a decisive deepening of the Aristotelian idea of catharsis. Despite Aristotle's use of ethical terms to classify types of tragic heroes, he does not offer any explanation of the causal relation between tragedy and the good. Kant's advance over Aristotle is in seeing and placing an a priori of moral being within tragic form.

It must be emphasized that the attainment of Kantian humility does not require the effacement of personality. On the contrary, as in the archetype of Christ that Kant cites, with perfect humility comes the consolidation and self-awareness of the only real kind of personality, namely, moral personality. This requires further explanation, but we can begin to see how this is the case by a first glance at Cordelia's personality. Many commentators have observed that Cordelia is from the beginning a figure of moral perfection.[14] The principal ground for such an observation, I take it, is that her character undergoes no development. She is at the end what she was at the beginning, both perfectly humble and perfectly good. Kant names "holiness" the internal goal toward which the experience of the "endless progress" of humiliations leads us (*CPrR* 5: 122 and *passim*). Shakespeare, as I have said, gives us reason to feel that Cordelia has from the beginning internalized that experience. Perhaps it is the inaccessibility, to us, of the experience that precedes this internalization which makes Cordelia seem part of a Christ-like mysterium. Among other things that we do not know, she has already foreseen, as she says, the series of humiliations of Lear, and of all those attached to him, that his test of love will let loose: "Time shall unfold what plighted [pleated] cunning hides" (1.1.274). Later the Fool will name the air of "prophecy" that hangs over this play (3.2.77 ff.). Cordelia is from the beginning both holy woman and prophet. For everyone else in *King Lear*, however, the unfolding of the zero narrative, as well as what succeeds it, will have to be gained as new knowledge.[15]

For Kant, and I believe for Shakespeare as well, moral feeling, respect for duty, is a precondition for feelings of uniquely human love. Bernard Williams has put forth a well-known criticism of Kant on this score. Williams cites Charles Fried's example of Kantian morality as the case of a man who can save only one person from a shipwreck and, after careful deliberation, decides that his duty allows him to save his wife. Williams's often quoted remark is that this Kantian husband has had "one thought too many."[16] If we think that this criticism is telling, then it tells on Shakespeare as well. Cordelia's statement "I love your majesty / According to my bond" (1.1. 87–88) may also be felt to require one thought too many. Yet Shakespeare's representation of Cordelia does not warrant that judgment, that is, not about the love that she exemplifies in its human specificity. When, after viewing Cordelia's response to Lear, France says, "Gods, gods! 'Tis strange, that from their cold'st neglect / My love should kindle to inflamed respect" (1.1.249–50), he has discovered the generative relation between passionately felt respect for an other's moral being and love for that other. His love has found its ground in respect. This may seem to run counter to our intuition of what love is, yet Shakespeare, like Kant, works to transform that intuition. That Cordelia loves according to her bond or duty is finally what makes her love different from that of her sisters. Who is to say whether or not those "pelican daughters" (3.4.70) experienced, at some time, the love of an animal for its feeder or its dam? Shakespeare is in search of the human feeling that is prior to and distinguishes human love. For Kant, in tandem, moral feeling that is derived in inward sublime experience is the only feeling that is a priori human; only that human feeling can open, continuously, into what is specifically human in human love.

Cordelia has not thought one thought too many. In fact, there was yet another thought, also prior to love, that she needed to think at the play's opening. This would have been a shared thought in a circuit of shared moral feeling: Cordelia *with* Lear—and with others—ministering to the heads and hearts of the divided kingdom according to the human bond. Kant also famously sees the need for a divided, shared kingdom of moral being, which he calls a "kingdom of ends" (*GMM* 4: 433–34).[17] In this shared kingdom each person must exercise his or her a priori moral judgment in colegislation. At very least this circuit of mutual awareness keeps alive the possibility of bridging self-awareness with awareness of humanity. Without this bridge, moral judgment (as in the categorical imperative) is impossible.[18] In the opening of *King Lear*, just at the moment of proceeding to divide the kingdom, Lear has for the time being blocked this bridging or sharing.

The Language of the Nothing

The language of the nothing is perhaps the greatest challenge to comprehension in *King Lear*. To a considerable extent, it begins to be made comprehensible through its relation to what I have called the zero narrative; that is, the aftermath of that radical narrative process begins to explain what it means to be in the condition of the nothing. Yet the power and complexity of Shakespeare's usage of the language of the nothing make clear that by itself even this is not a sufficient explanation. To open this explanation to further possibilities, I present, first, Shakespeare's way of broaching the language of the nothing with Cordelia and then, second, the disturbing cross-purposes with which he loads that language.

Shakespeare assigns an astonishing firmness, a hard certainty, to Cordelia's saying of "nothing." In an aside she had said, "What shall Cordelia speak? Love, and be silent" (1.1.57). But then, as though she has entered a different world, she does not remain silent. Instead, risking all, she supplies the one word that says her all, firmly. Shakespeare has left no room for imagining hesitation in her response.

> Lear: What can you say to draw
> A third more opulent than your sisters? Speak.
> Cordelia: Nothing, my lord.
> Lear: Nothing?
> Cordelia: Nothing.
> (1.1.80–84)

Lear is staggered especially by the firmness in her double enunciation of the word. Later in the scene he lashes out with a direct echo of both her pronouncement and her tone. He tells Burgundy that he will not give

Cordelia even the smallest dowry: "*Nothing*, I have sworn; *I am firm*" (1.1.240; emphases added). When Lear says, after Cordelia dies, "Her voice was ever soft, / Gentle, and low, an excellent thing in woman" (5.3.246–47), he is only in denial of the firmness that he himself tragically caused in that voice, which he also heard in Cordelia's declaration to Burgundy: "I shall not be his wife" (1.1.244). As the action of the play proceeds, dozens of repetitions of the word *nothing* and its cognates take their reinforcing or contrastive force from Cordelia's opening pronouncement. I suggest that, far from being disdainful of Lear's deepest human desires, Cordelia here provides him with the key term for the fulfillment of precisely the design that he is thwarting—that is, the division of the kingdom, the sharing of moral reason and feeling. In her opening utterance into the public world of this play she invents a language—for this community—in which moral feeling will eventually, finally, be able to emerge.

This language of the nothing is characterized by doubleness and transformability. Shakespeare compels us to assume that the Fool has heard reports of Cordelia's "nothing," because later in Act 1 the Fool addresses Lear with the stark alternative to Cordelia's saying nothing, that is, with Goneril's saying—or looking—"nothing." As the play's premier spokesperson for the depth of nonsense, we are not surprised that the Fool in effect highlights the doubled meanings that throughout this play accompany "nothing," "naught," and even "o":

> I had rather be any kind **o' thing** than a fool, and yet I would not be thee, nuncle; thou hast pared thy wit **o'** both sides and left **nothing** i' th' middle. . . . Now thou art an **O** [i.e., zero] without a figure. I am better than thou art now; I am a fool, **thou art nothing**. [*To Goneril*] Yes, forsooth, I will hold my tongue, so your face bids me, though you say **nothing**. (1.4.145–55)[19]

The Fool plays a lexical, visual, and even typographical game with *nothing* and the *o*. The game runs wide and deep in this tragedy. O's, rounds, circles, sockets, wheels are everywhere we look; they seem to be saying something to us or to be looking askance at us, squinting. We are like the apparently deranged Lear who says to Gloucester and his "bleeding rings" (5.3.180), "Dost thou squiny at me?" (4.5.132). We are gradually made to feel that we too are beginning to see things or to read desperately into them. As though in a phantasmagoria, we see varieties of these bleeding rings all around us. They come at us like fulfillments of a gigantic curse projected by the empty circle of Cordelia's "Nothing." Gloucester reports portentous black holes in the sky, "eclipses in the sun and moon" (1.2.91). Slowly, ceremoniously, ominous apertures—stocks—are carried out to ensnare Kent's feet (2.2.114–34). Lear, as we have noted, is twice pictured in the condition of being bound to deadly wheels (2.4.65–66; 4.6.43–44).

Perhaps the most vexing part of this language of the nothing are its smallest, least noticeable units, the "o" or "oh." In Shakespeare's orthography and phonology in *King Lear* the equation of "Oh" with zero is always an open possibility. Like all the other usages of "nothing" in *King Lear*, these "oh"s can cut two ways. "Thy sister's **naught**. **Oh** Regan," Lear will cry out to the other empty shell, another naught, who progressively drives him to humiliation (2.4.126). Shakespeare's word game here with the "Oh" that is tied on Regan is not concealed from the reader. Gloucester will later unwittingly confirm this specific instance of the game with "Oh" by calling Regan, too, "**naughty**," worthless, wicked (3.7.37). In the opposite direction, the "O" of Cordelia's "O look upon me, sir, / And hold your hand in benediction o'er me" (4.6.54–55) sounds, and plumbs, the nothing of humility, just as in her most directly Christ-like, most self-emptied utterance (echoing Luke 2:49) she says, "**O** dear father, / It is thy business that I go about" (4.3.23–24).

By punitively drawing Lear's attention to Goneril's saying "nothing," and its vast difference from Cordelia's, the Fool is the first to distinguish the two kinds of nothing on which the action of the entire play turns. Thus one kind of nothing is, or is associated with, the Cordelian condition of humility that Lear was incapable of seeing. This humility is born of effectively endless humiliations of self-conceit; it is the springboard of moral feeling and of the love that is specifically human. The other kind of nothing is, or is associated with, the terminal loss of self-worth. The deepest moral and ontological tension of *King Lear* is constituted from the indistinguishability, in themselves alone, of the condition of the nothing of perfect humility and the condition of the nothing of loss of self-worth. Both equally seem to entail negations of the self and of everything worldly or heavenly. Our perplexity about this apparent continuity, or lack of continuity, between the two kinds of nothing is deep and painful.

Here are some of the instances of the nothing that seem to defy an intelligibility that is based on its initial association with Cordelia:

> Gloucester [to Edmond]: What paper were you reading?
> Edmond [using Cordelia's first words spoken to Lear]: **Nothing**, my lord.
>
> Gloucester: Let's see. Come, if it be **nothing**, I shall not
>   need spectacles.
>   (1.2.30–35)

Just as surely as Gloucester will all too soon not need spectacles, Edmond's "nothing" is already as massive in its efficacy as Cordelia's will be, even if we continue to flail around in trying to understand what that deadly definiteness—of the nothing—can be.

> Edmond [to Edgar]: I have told you what I have seen and heard—but faintly, **nothing** like the image and horror of it.
> (1.2.146–48)

> Fool: Can you make no use of **nothing**, nuncle?
> Lear: Why, no, boy; **nothing** can be made out of nothing.
> (1.4.115–16)

> Kent [to Oswald]: [Thou] art **nothing** but the composition of a knave, beggar, coward, pander, and the son and heir of a mongrel bitch
> . . . Knowing **naught**, like dogs, but following.
> (2.2.18–19, 71)

> Kent: **Nothing** almost sees miracles
> But misery.
> (2.2.148–49)

> Edgar: Edgar I **nothing** am.
> (2.3.21)

> Lear: I will be the pattern of all patience.
> I will say **nothing**.
> (3.2.35–36)

> Lear (to Poor Tom about depraved daughters):
> Couldst thou save **nothing**?
> (3.4.60)

> **Nothing** could have subdued nature
> To such a lowness but his unkind daughters.
> (3.4.65–66)

> Edgar: Welcome then,
> Thou unsubstantial air that I embrace:
> The wretch that thou hast blown unto the worst
> Owes **nothing** to thy blasts.
> (4.1.6–9)

Edgar: In **nothing** am I changed
But in my garments.
(4.5.8–9)

Albany [to Goneril]: thou art in **nothing** less
Than I have here proclaimed thee.
(5.3.87–88)

We begin to discern alignments among Shakespeare's sharply diverging usages of the nothing by experiencing their transformative liminality. Thinking the nothing entails a clean sweep of the empirical. As such, it marks the boundary between experience of what is external and what is internal to consciousness. Having subtracted the empirical, the residue of the nothing is the mind's self-consciousness. Yet this nothing is not purely suspended or immobilized self-consciousness because it is propelled by the zero narrative toward a disclosure of the human. Kant too was centrally concerned with this power of the human mind to experience and to make use of what he called "cessation in nothingness (= 0 = *negatio*)." Only alternation "between reality and negation, or rather a transition from one to the other," he says, "makes every reality representable" (*CPR* A143, B182–83). Kant even ascribes a special power to the experience of such nothingness in the moral sublime. Through this experience the mind can gain an incomparable "extension" and "might" of the freedom that is a precondition for the achievement of personality (*CJ* 5: 269, 208–9).[20]

"*Personality*," Kant will write, is "freedom and independence from the mechanism of the whole of nature." In this condition of freedom, personality can exercise the "capacity of a being subject to . . . pure practical laws given by his [or her] own reason" (*CPrR* 5: 87). In this sense Goneril and Regan, and Edmond with all his rhetorical shows, do not have personality. They are wholly given over to the rapacious mechanisms of nature. Edmond's last-minute spark of regret only emphasizes how greatly he has forgone the possibility of fanning that spark into the human personality he might have been. He dies a nonentity, just on the verge of—but beside—the point of being human.[21]

It may seem that Kant's belief in the possibility of freedom from the mechanism of nature is optimistic to the point of naïveté and that Shakespeare's realism precludes such delusions. But we should recall D. G. James's remark linking *King Lear* and *The Tempest*: Although Shakespeare, says James, "saw evil . . . and suffering . . . he also saw a certain power in human nature to overcome the world and to make the world fade in our imaginations and leave not a rack behind."[22] This mental power to overcome the world discloses the spontaneity of personality.[23]

I am proposing that for Shakespeare in *King Lear* the relations of the experience of the nothing, freedom, and the achievement of moral personality—the emergence of the human—are much the same as they are for Kant. Yet Shakespeare perhaps shows us that the experience of the nothing and of transformation in that experience is for the individual never at the level of discursive articulation. In theatrical tragedy we experience its alternations between reality and negation in the represented quantum that freely chooses the human in company with the human. This is to suggest that in Shakespeare's representation of the community's speaking of the language of the nothing, he harnesses the magic of presence and disappearance in tragic theater. We experience this overwhelming uncanniness when Edgar says "Edgar I nothing am," thereby plunging into a cessation in nothingness, as does Lear when he says, in distraction, "**No,** I will be the pattern of all patience. / I will say **nothing**" (3.2.35–36). These utterances are in the first place generated by the waves of the zero narrative that sweep the minds of these protagonists toward momentary annihilations. These individuals speak and hear this language together.

Except perhaps for Cordelia and the Fool, Shakespeare denies his protagonists any direct awareness of the double possibilities of their speaking of the nothing. The awareness emerges collectively. With a collective perspective in mind, we can begin to understand that when Edgar says, "Edgar I nothing am" (2.3.21), he is unawares approaching Cordelia's holiness of the nothing. This human version of a *creatio ex nihilo* and of the divine self-naming, "I am that I am" (*ego sum qui sum*) (Exodus 3:14) precedes Descartes's cogito by two decades and indeed, from the point of view of moral reason, is far in advance of Descartes's relatively static picture. Even when Edgar says, "In nothing am I changed," we can begin to understand that he is actively changed in the nothing and that that change extends to far more than his garments (4.5.8 ff.). We can then see too that he very much "owes nothing"—owes, that is, the gains of the nothing that Cordelia has already exemplified—to the blasts and humiliations of fortune (4.1.1 ff.).

Shakespeare holds onto these equations with steel-trap calculation. Thus he incorporates the power of the "O" or the nothing into the great meeting between Lear and Gloucester in Act 4. Frank Kermode remarks that the poetry of this scene is "the boldest effort of imagination in Shakespeare" but that it "has no *narrative* value."[24] We can begin to resolve this apparent paradox by noting that this arrival in a moment of zero narrative is deepened with an emergence and teleology of the Cordelian nothing.

Gloucester's blind glimpse of this other "naught" projects the blueprint of the tragedy's dénouement and anagnorisis or recognition. At the climax of the scene Gloucester exclaims to Lear: "**O** ruined piece of nature! This great world / Shall so wear out to **naught**" (4.5.130–31). The chiasmus is forthright. The "O" and "naught" of perfect humility will emerge firmly, but only after the progressive degradations of the world into an absolute wearing out.

Just so, in Act 4 Cordelia will say:

O thou good Kent, how shall I live and work
To match thy goodness? My life will be too short,
And every measure fail me.
(4.6.1–3)

This moment is powerful not least because it brings to bear the force of the zero narrative and the language of the nothing. The failure of every measure expresses once again the condition of the nothing, the "O" without a figure in which the human can emerge and where Cordelia was located from the beginning, in solitude. Cordelia's and Lear's trading of "Nothing" at cross-purposes at the inception of the tragedy is finally transformed into a continuous circuit of humility in their great coordinated moments of benediction and forgiveness in Acts 4 and 5.

Cordelia [to Lear]: O look upon me, sir,
And hold your hand in benediction o'er me.
You must not kneel.
(4.6.54–56)

Lear [to Cordelia]: Come, let's away to prison. . . .
When thou dost ask me blessing, I'll kneel down
And ask of thee forgiveness.
(5.3.8–11)

My argument comes to this:

First, *King Lear* represents the most elemental of all specifically human cravings: the craving for an emergence of the capacity for moral feeling and the love that belongs to moral feeling. It is Shakespeare's greatness to envision and represent this reality. It is Kant's greatness to begin to explain it.

Second, the instrument of this emergence, or inward disclosure, is the tragic community's zero narrative and its transformational language of the nothing. In this radical narrative and radical language we can be transformed from the nothing of pure banality to the nothing of humility and moral feeling. Only our experience of the zero narrative determines whether we can move toward the nothing where moral personality can be disclosed. For Shakespeare as for Kant, there is a close kinship between religious experience and the sublime experience of an endless series of humiliations of self-conceit. Yet on the secular side of cognizing such experience, that which emerges, for both Kant and Shakespeare, is beyond empirical psychology or a calculus of gratification and pain. For Kant what emerges here is the mind's a priori moral feeling; for Shakespeare it is the bedrock of the human.[25]

Third, the capacity for moral feeling that is thus shown to emerge is by no means indifferent to the pain that life suffers. Yet moral feeling is focused on, and finally affirms, not simply life ("a dog, a horse, a rat" have that [5.3.280]), as Lear cries out, but rather "something quite different from life [in itself], something in comparison with which life," Kant says, "has no worth at all." Experienced as the mind's deepest feeling, this duty or bond to others' well-being is the ground of a *human* personality. This is the ground of human life to which we look, morally, whether or not we retain "the least taste for living." Love that is human begins there. Shakespeare teaches us to hear a transformed language of the nothing. In his play's final analysis "Nothing," which is to say the nothing of humility that discloses moral feeling, is that which can make something matter.

Shakespeare concretely represents the emergence of human benediction—benediction of the human by the human—in the instant of life's total humiliation. He does this when he allows Lear to fulfill Cordelia's plea: "O look upon me, sir, / And hold your hand in benediction o'er me" (4.6.54–55). That is, almost immediately after Albany, looking at Lear, exclaims, "O see, see!" (5.3.278), Lear fulfills Cordelia's plea in his last words: "Look on her! Look, her lips. / Look there, look there" (5.3.283–84). Although I do not find it recorded in the commentaries on *King Lear*, it must have been proposed, or at least thought, by many before me that the very first word that Cordelia speaks to Lear in this play, the word that risks and costs everything—"Nothing"—is the word that Lear is remembering, trying to resuscitate, with his last words. Not by Lear alone but by the saving remnant of this tragic community, only that first word of Cordelia, "Nothing," can be made out, on her lips—parted, rounded, motionless—a breathless word saying *nothing*: "Look, her lips."[26] (Here the Fool's words to Goneril come back to us, perhaps acting as well as prompt, or goad, to Lear at this moment: "Yes, forsooth, I will hold my tongue, so your face bids me, though you say **nothing**" [1.4.154–55].) Only an effectively endless series of humiliations of self-conceit can conceive or produce the "O." Only the "O" can open the moral feeling of benediction. This looking, with love, upon the human nothing and its condition of humility is not just Lear's and Cordelia's two-way street. Rather, it becomes a thoroughfare of benediction for the community, for humankind, in a categorical imperative that is spoken in the zero language. At the tragedy's conclusion, as at its inception, the necessity of a harmonious deployment of the kingdom's members, in pursuit of their collective ends, is articulated by Cordelia's "Nothing" and Cordelia's "O."

Notes

1. For an account of the general relevance of these views to Shakespeare, see Ian Ward, "Shakespeare and the Politics of Community," *Early Modern Literary Studies* 4.3 (January 1999): 2.1–45. A recent publication that responds to Cavell's thinking about community is Andrew Norris, ed., *The Claim to Community: Essays on Stanley Cavell and Political Philosophy* (Baltimore: Johns Hopkins University Press, 2006).

2. In this vein Dennis Brown, "King Lear: The Lost Leader—Group Disintegration, Transformation, and Suspended Reconsolidation," *Critical Survey* 13.3 (September 2001): 19–39, has proposed that the play anticipates many of the principles of "contemporary group-theory" (19). Brown's approach is highly suggestive, although it does not address the question that seems to me most important about the group, namely, how it locates and ratifies the ethical values that it chooses to sustain.

3. Citations from the play are to *The Tragedy of King Lear,* New Cambridge Shakespeare edition, ed. Jay L. Halio (Cambridge, UK: Cambridge University Press, 1992). Halio closely follows the First Folio.

4. At this moment of setting out it is worth recalling T. S. Eliot's remark about "the error of presenting the work of Shakespeare as a series of mystical [or philosophical] treatises in cryptogram, to be filed away once the cipher is read; poetry is poetry, and the surface is as marvelous as the core." Coming as it does in Eliot's introduction to G. Wilson Knight's *Wheel of Fire,* the remark actually says far more than Eliot consciously intended. I propose that the special power of the poetry of *King Lear* is in large part attributable to the fact that here the cipher—the zero or nothing that needs to be read and marveled at—is both surface and core. This openly inscribed, not encrypted, cipher is at the core and the surface of a meaning that is at once poetic and philosophical, aesthetic and ethical. See T. S. Eliot, Introduction to G. Wilson Knight, *The Wheel of Fire: Interpretations of Shakespearean Tragedy* (New York: Meridian Books, 1957), xx. Although Eliot here explicates the pitfalls of a reductive imposition of philosophical schemes on poetry, he does not find this kind of error in Knight's interpretations.

5. Kenneth Burke, "Literature as Equipment for Living," in his *Philosophy of Literary Form*, 3rd ed. (Berkeley: University of California Press, 1974), 293–304.

6. I must acknowledge at the outset that to some extent this interpersonal, plural emergence and rebirth will, in their very nature, remain beyond the reach of any single first-person perspective. Yet if we locate the theatrical power of Shakespeare's representations of his collective narrative and collective language, I believe this obstacle will be significantly surmounted.

7. Halio (*Tragedy of King Lear*) here cites C. T. Onions's *Shakespeare Glossary*, revised by Robert D. Eagleson (Oxford, UK: Clarendon Press, 1986) for the meaning of *sensitive*.

8. Ruth Nevo, *Tragic Form in Shakespeare* (Princeton, NJ: Princeton University Press, 1972), 261.

9. Harold Bloom, *Shakespeare: The Invention of the Human* (New York: Riverhead, 1998), 512–13.

10. See Sanford Budick, *Kant and Milton* (Cambridge, MA: Harvard University Press, 2010), especially chaps. 4 and 5.

11. For Kant's comment on the Fool in *King Lear*, see Otto Schlapp, *Kants Lehre vom Genie und die Entstehung der "Kritik der Urteilskraft"* (Göttingen: Vandenhoeck & Ruprecht, 1901), 246n.

12. Except for one instance (noted later), quotations from Kant are from the following translations: *Immanuel Kant's Critique of Pure Reason*, trans. Norman Kemp Smith (London: Macmillan, 1993), *Groundwork of the Metaphysics of Morals* and *Critique of Practical Reason*, in Immanuel Kant, *Practical Philosophy*, trans. Mary J. Gregor (Cambridge, UK: Cambridge University Press, 1996); and Immanuel Kant, *The Critique of Judgement*, trans. James Creed Meredith (Oxford, UK: Clarendon Press, 1973). References to the *Critique of Pure Reason* are given to the A and B texts. Volume and page number references for Kant's other works are those of *Kants Werke: Akademie-Textausgabe* (Berlin: de Gruyter, 1968), which Gregor and Meredith give in the margins of their translations and which appear in parentheses immediately after my citations. Version letter (A or B) or volume number and page numbers of the *Critique of Pure Reason*, *Groundwork of the Metaphysics of Morals*, the *Critique of Practical Reason*, and the *Critique of Judgment* are preceded by the abbreviations *CPR*, *GMM*, *CPrR*, and *CJ*, respectively.

13. D. G. James, *The Dream of Learning: An Essay on the Advancement of Learning Hamlet and King Lear* (Oxford, UK: Clarendon Press, 1951), 85.

14. James says that "in Cordelia and Edgar Shakespeare is contemplating figures of spiritual perfection" (*Dream of Learning*, 113). In my view, however, Cordelia is in a category by herself, because even Edgar is significantly changed in the course of the tragedy. As noted, he is, in his own words, both "made tame to fortune's blows" and self-conducted "by the art of known and feeling sorrows" (*King Lear*, 4.5.212–13).

15. Kant terms our following or experience of the series or progression a procedure of "succession" (*Nachfolge*; *CJ* 5: 283). (In this case I have used the

translation of *Critique of the Power of Judgment,* trans. Paul Guyer and Eric Matthews [Cambridge, UK: Cambridge University Press, 2000].) As we have begun to see, Kant argues that the empirical succession procedure makes us conscious of—discloses—an autonomous succession procedure that is formally identical. In the experience of the sublime a "transfer" takes place between the empirical and a priori succession procedures (*CJ* 5: 266–67, 352–53). The a priori succession procedure finally issues in the preeminent sublime effect, namely, inner freedom and moral feeling (*CJ* 5: 313, 318).

16. Bernard Williams, *Moral Luck* (Cambridge, UK: Cambridge University Press, 1981), 18.

17. It is fascinating that Arthur Sewell's well-known essay on Shakespeare, "Tragedy and the 'Kingdom of Ends,'" never once refers to Kant. Sewell's essay originally appeared in his *Character and Society in Shakespeare* (Oxford, UK: Oxford University Press, 1951), 91–121, and is reprinted in Leonard F. Dean, ed., *Shakespeare: Modern Essays in Criticism* (New York: Oxford University Press, 1961), 311–32.

18. Christine M. Korsgaard, *Creating the Kingdom of Ends* (Cambridge, UK: Cambridge University Press, 1996), recently remarked that for Kant "the motivating thought of morality is the thought that you can contribute to making the world a Kingdom of Ends" (29). Korsgaard's reasons for her statement are different from those I have given.

19. All emphases in bold in this essay have been added.

20. Kant: "Only by what a man does heedless of enjoyment, in complete freedom, and independently of what he can procure passively from the hand of nature, does be give to his existence, as the real existence of a person, an absolute worth" (*CJ* 5: 208–9).

21. It is remarkable that the narrative shared by the victim-protagonists of *King Lear* overrides the individuation of their psyches, emotional histories, or, as we now say, their psychologies. Beyond what I noted at the outset, in this play there is an even stronger determinant of our feeling that "unaccommodated man" (3.4.95–96) and almost "silent" woman (1.1.57), "bare-gnawn" (5.3.112) humanity, are being anatomized in search of a common denominator of the human. Maynard Mack, "Action and World in *King Lear*," in *Shakespeare's Middle Tragedies: A Collection of Critical Essays,* ed. David Young (Englewood Cliffs, NJ: Prentice Hall, 1993), has written of "the relatively slight attention given in *King Lear* to the psychological processes that ordinarily precede and determine human action. . . . Psychic antecedents have been so effectively shrunk down in this *primitivized* world that action seems to spring directly out of the bedrock of personality" (169; emphasis added). I would here add the term *elemental* to *primitivized.* A combination of such related terms is needed to describe this complex, pervasive feature of *King Lear.* This complexity is enriched by the fact that Shakespeare inherits this feature, near or far, from Aeschylus's *Prometheus Bound* and Sophocles' *Oedipus at Colonus.* For readers after Shakespeare's time the same feature is further deepened, as well

as illuminated, by the fact that Milton's *Samson Agonistes* in turn inherits it not only from *Prometheus Bound* and *Oedipus at Colonus* but also from *King Lear.* These four plays make a great line of elemental, or in fact *mental,* tragedies. And in all four, I would add, the kind of psychic bedrock that centrally interests the playwright is, indeed, personality; but it is only personality according to a demanding conception such as Kant later formulated in discursive terms to cover the extremity of the tragic condition. Personality in this self-subsisting sense is achieved at the point of breaking free from determination by the empirical world.

22. James, *Dream of Learning,* 126.

23. In such a community part of the bedrock of each personality is a shared, distinctly human stratum of freedom and of seeing it feelingly (4.5.143), which is to say combining feeling with seeing in rational feeling. Kant will say that the only feeling that is a priori rational in the human mind is "moral feeling" (*CPrR* 5: 73–75).

24. Frank Kermode, "Introduction to *King Lear,*" in *The Riverside Shakespeare,* ed. G. Blakemore Evans (Boston: Houghton Mifflin, 1974), 1252.

25. In the last two sentences I have levied on Kant's language in insisting on the difference made by the disclosures of such sublime experience—that which distinguishes them from anything that can be understood, or gained, from "empirical psychology": "This is exactly what makes an *a priori* principle apparent in their case, and lifts them out of the sphere of empirical psychology, in which otherwise they would remain buried amid the feelings of gratification and pain (only with the senseless epithet of *finer* feeling), so as to place them, and, thanks to them, to place the faculty of judgment itself, in the class of judgments of which the basis of an *a priori* principle is the distinguishing feature, and, thus distinguished, to introduce them into transcendental philosophy" (*CJ* 5: 266).

26. Perhaps we should add that in this moment of Lear's final peripeteia or reversal, the prophetic force of Cordelia's plea—"O look upon me, sir"—is fulfilled in palindrome-like form while he looks at her lips: Sir, look upon me O.

Contributors

Sanford Budick is Professor of English at the Hebrew University of Jerusalem and was the founding director of that university's Center for Literary Studies. He is the author of *Poetry of Civilization: Mythopoeic Displacement in the Verse of Milton, Dryden, Pope, and Johnson* (Yale University Press, 1974), *Dryden and the Abyss of Light: A Study of Religio Laici and The Hind and the Panther* (Yale University Press, 1985), *The Dividing Muse: Images of Sacred Disjunction in Milton's Poetry* (Yale University Press, 1985), *The Western Theory of Tradition: Terms and Paradigms of the Cultural Sublime* (Yale University Press, 2000), and *Kant and Milton* (Harvard University Press, 2010).

Noam Flinker is Associate Professor of English at the University of Haifa. He is the author of *The Song of Songs in English Renaissance Literature* (D. S. Brewer, 2000) and of many articles on English Renaissance literature and culture.

Lowell Gallagher is Associate Professor of English at UCLA, where he teaches courses in Renaissance and seventeenth-century British literature, theory and criticism, gender and sexuality studies, and the literary and political cultures of early modern English Catholicism. He is the author of *Medusa's Gaze: Casuistry and Conscience in the Renaissance* (Stanford University Press, 1991) and of articles and book chapters on a wide range of topics: Shakespeare, English Catholic devotional culture in the Renaissance, postmodern ethics and hermeneutic theory, and nineteenth-century opera.

Chanita Goodblatt is Associate Professor in English and Comparative Literature at Ben Gurion University of the Negev. She is the author of *John*

Donne and Christian Hebraism: Written with the Fingers of Man's Hand (Duquesne University Press, 2010) and co-editor of *Tradition, Heterodoxy, and Religious Culture: Judaism and Christianity in the Early Modern Period* (Ben-Gurion University Press, 2006) and of *Women Editing/Editing Women: Early Modern Women Writers and the New Textualism* (Cambridge Scholars Press, 2009). She has also published articles in the field of Cognitive Literary Studies, most recently a monograph essay titled "Conversations with I. A. Richards: The Renaissance in Cognitive Literary Studies" (*Poetics Today*, 2010).

Achsah Guibbory is Professor of English at Barnard College. She is the author of *The* Map *of Time: Seventeenth-Century English Literature and Ideas of Pattern in History* (University of Illinois Press, 1986), *Ceremony and Community from Herbert to Milton: Literature, Religion, and Cultural Conflict in Seventeenth-Century English Literature* (Cambridge University Press, 1998), and *Christian Identity, Jews, and Israel in 17th-Century England* (Oxford University Press, 2010).

Phebe Jensen is Professor of English at Utah State University, where she teaches courses in Shakespeare and other early modern literature. She is the author of *Religion and Revelry in Shakespeare's Festive World* (Cambridge University Press, 2008) and of articles and book chapters on early modern English literature and culture.

Arthur F. Marotti is Distinguished Professor of English Emeritus at Wayne State University. He is the author of *John Donne, Coterie Poet* (University of Wisconsin Press, 1986), *Manuscript, Print, and the English Renaissance Lyric* (Cornell University Press, 1995), and *Religious Ideology and Cultural Fantasy: Catholic and Anti-Catholic Discourses in Early Modern England* (University of Notre Dame Press, 2005). He has edited or co-edited numerous essay collections, most recently, with Ken Jackson, *Shakespeare and Religion: Early Modern and Postmodern Perspectives* (University of Notre Dame Press, 2011).

Yaakov Mascetti is Lecturer in the Department of Comparative Literature at Bar-Ilan University. He has published articles on Aemelia Lanyer, John Milton, Margaret Cavendish, and George Herbert. His research interests include metaphysical poetry, early modern conceptions of sight and cognition, the role of occultism in the rise of modernity, and definitions of femininity in early modern English literature.

Avraham Oz is Associate Professor of Theatre and Hebrew and Comparative Literature at the University of Haifa. His publications include *Shetar hi-hiddah* (The Riddle Bond: Studies in *The Merchant of Venice*) (Hakibbutz Hameuchad, 1990), *The Yoke of Love: Prophetic Riddles in "The Merchant of Venice"* (University of Delaware Press, 1995), and other works in Hebrew and English.

Anne Lake Prescott is Emerita Helen Goodhart Altschul Professor of English at Barnard College. She is the author of *Imagining Rabelais in the English Renaissance* (Yale University Press, 1978) and *French Poets and the English Renaissance: Studies in Fame and Transformation* (Yale University Press, 1998) as well as many articles and book chapters on early modern English and French literature and culture. She has edited, with H. Maclean, an edition of *Edmund Spenser's Poetry* (Norton, 1992).

Noam Reisner is Senior Lecturer in the Department of English and American Studies at Tel Aviv University. He is the author of *Milton and the Ineffable* (Oxford University Press, 2009) and *John Milton's Paradise Lost: A Reading Guide* (Edinburgh University Press, 2011) and of articles and book chapters on early modern English literature and culture.

Jeanne Shami is Professor of English at the University of Regina (Canada). She is the author of *John Donne and Conformity in Crisis in the Late Jacobean Pulpit* (D. S. Brewer, 2003); the editor of a collection of essays, *Renaissance Tropologies: The Cultural Imagination of Early Modern England* (Duquesne University Press, 2008), and of *John Donne's 1622 Gunpowder Plot Sermon: A Parallel-Text Edition* (Duquesne University Press, 1996); and a co-editor of *The Oxford Handbook of John Donne* (Oxford University Press, 2011).

Elliott M. Simon is Associate Professor in the Department of English Language and Literature at the University of Haifa. He is the author of *The Problem Play in British Drama, 1890–1914* (University of Salzburg, 1978) and *The Myth of Sisyphus: Renaissance Theories of the Myth of Human Perfectibility* (Fairleigh Dickinson University Press, 2007). He has published essays on Thomas More, Philip Sidney, and Francis Bacon.

Index

Note: Page numbers for illustrations are shown in italics. Plates 1 through 4 are located between pages 82 and 83.